# Eight Shafts: Beyond the Beginning

## Personal Approaches to Design

Edited by Laurie Knapp Autio

COMPLEX
WEAVERS

TigerPress, East Longmeadow, Massachusetts

Eight Shafts: Beyond the Beginning:
    Personal Approaches to Design
I. Textile Crafts I. Autio, Laurie Knapp
II. Title: Eight Shafts Beyond the Beginning: Personal approaches to design
First Edition
Published by Complex Weavers
    www.complex-weavers.org
Printed by TigerPress, East Longmeadow, MA, USA
    www.tigerpress.com

ISBN: 978-0-578-33036-5

This book is dedicated in loving memory to Wanda J. Shelp (January 3, 1944 - March 28, 2015) of Worland, Wyoming. As an author, teacher, editor, weaver, and leader, Wanda leaves a lasting imprint on the modern weaving community. She was active in her local guild, Western Weavers, and the larger weaving community, including Complex Weavers. Over the years she served as editor of the *CW Journal* (1994-2005) and CW President (2006-2008). Additionally, she led the CW Passementerie and Bateman Study Groups and actively participated in others, served on a variety of committees, and was always generous and helpful behind the scenes.

Her classic book, *Eight Shafts: A Place to Begin* (Shelp and Wostenberg, 1991), has helped many weavers make the transition from four shafts to more, and was the inspiration for this book. Wanda was also the author of many articles in the *CW Journal* and editor of several CW books (Eatough and Shelp, 2000; Shelp, 1998, 2012a, 2012b). She is missed.

# Contents

# Introduction

## Complex Weavers and the Contributors

Complex Weavers (CW) is an international organization of weavers who are interested in learning more about all aspects of their craft and sharing their journey. Members may share work though the *CW Journal*, our many study groups, a biennial conference, and *Complexity*, our biennial juried exhibit. An extensive library, which includes copies of all the study group notebooks in addition to books and periodicals, helps preserve knowledge and extend it to current and future generations of weavers. Membership is open to all; no number of shafts, written tests, letters of recommendation, or secret handshakes are required! The biographies of the participating weavers provide an intriguing snapshot of the current CW membership. I continue to be impressed by the contributors, their thoughts, their passion, their dedication to learning, and their varied paths and experience. Their words speak strongly to who we are as members of Complex Weavers.

**Diversity.** The 72 weavers in this book come from nine countries: Australia, Canada, France, Ireland, the Netherlands, New Zealand, Scotland, the United Kingdom, and the United States. Of those, 55 are from the United States (roughly similar to the percentage of US members in CW), hailing from 22 states, with Massachusetts and California topping the list with eight each. The participants have been weaving from three years to more than sixty, while raising small children and in retirement, in apartments and professional studios, as professional artists and avid hobbyists, on no shafts, to eight shafts, to computer dobbies, drawlooms, and Jacquard looms. Arising from equally diverse backgrounds, these weavers have trained as artists, accountants, scientists, teachers, engineers, and every occupation in between. With styles ranging from ultra-traditional, to countryside comfortable, to avant-garde, they weave to wear, for homes, exhibits, teaching, and the pure pursuit of knowledge. Some are quiet introverts preferring to work alone; others are exuberantly extroverted community people who love to share.

**Passion.** One of the first things I noticed when reading the biographies was the weavers' use of language to describe their relationship to weaving. Some made me smile, but all caused a nod of recognition of the CW weaving family. Words like *captivated, cherish, committed, serious, passionate, fascination, enamoured, love affair,* and *lust* stud the writing. They are *bitten by the bug, immersed, hooked, fueled by joy, mesmerized,* and *obsessed.* They admit to planning vacations around textile-related symposia, workshops, and gallery tours; speak of their *inherent tendencies toward complexity*; and of *finding new structures to be like catnip.* They *can't seem to help coming up with more ideas,* and, *when they began weaving, everything came together.*

**What if...?** Although the words they use vary quite a bit, interest in learning is a common theme throughout the weavers. Mentors, teachers, classes, publications, guilds, and study groups feature prominently. The weavers speak of *widening horizons, improving, exploring, researching, figuring out, stretching, experimenting, creating,* and *inventing.* They talk of *insatiable curiosity, dedication, design possibilities, breaking the grid, pushing boundaries, creative pursuit, in-depth studies, problem solving, discovery, challenge, scholarly needs,* and *how things relate.* There is *always more to learn, infinite ways to create pattern, intellectual challenges involved in designing, the pleasure of exploiting weave structures,* and *enjoyment of restrictions which force creativity - or equipment and techniques which place no limits on what can be done.* They enjoy *distilling the essence* and *relish the "ah-ha" moment.* Their designs may be a *microcosm for creating order,* be *motivated by a desire to solve technical aspects of engineering the interlacements,* or express an interest in *exploring the effects of color interaction.* One (Helen Sellin) asks, *Why weave more* [than a sample] *once you understand how it works? There are so many more things to learn and try!* Others seek knowledge by working in series.

In the end, two statements by Lesley Willcock and Cheri Shelp sum up the weavers, and, by extension, Complex Weavers:

*The more you learn about weaving, the more you realize there is to know.*

*Desire and love for a thing make all effort and work insignificant.*

## Book Origin and Purpose

In honor of Wanda Shelp, this book continues Complex Weavers' long publishing tradition. Early discussions between Cally Booker, Kathi Spangler, and Laurie Autio pinpointed design as the unique specialty members of CW could offer. Cally suggested that a focus on 8-shaft weaving would put the ideas within reach of more weavers. Thus, *Eight Shafts: Beyond the Beginning* was born. The title pays homage to *Eight Shafts: A Place to Begin,* co-authored by Wanda Shelp and Carolyn Wostenberg, an informative, structure-oriented book for weavers new to eight shafts. In contrast, *Beyond the Beginning* concentrates on individual approaches to creativity. It explores many of the elements and techniques of design through contributors' work.

Submission was open to all CW members to represent our membership's span and diversity. Participants did not need to be a master weaver, published author, award winner, or known teacher to participate. Since our members enjoy weaving on a variety of looms, we decided to add a second part on extended design techniques to allow almost all of our members to participate if desired.

The focus was to be on design and what takes the work "beyond the beginning" into something uniquely belonging to the weaver. Entries had to be original, unpublished, and woven since the weaver joined CW. We asked the participants to think about what they love about weaving and how that factor is expressed in their work.

When talking about design, the first question which always comes up is, "*What is original?*" It's a good question and hard to answer succinctly. "*I know it when I see it!*" is not much help to the less experienced weaver. Taking a published draft and weaving it as written in one or two colors of a single yarn is not terribly original, more of a place to begin. Similarly, changing the color or making other slight changes to a published handwoven piece is rarely original. To make the work your own, change several major aspects: create a new border, change a scarf to a bedspread, change the yarn completely, etc. Other ways to make a more personal statement on a common base draft include unique color and weave effects, hand manipulations, pairing with another draft; changing the structure, tie-up, treadling, or symmetry; using ikat or surface design effects; and playing with finishing.

Developing a personal voice through a consistent set of design choices takes originality a step further. An underlying sense of aesthetics (a.k.a. a personal design toolbox) may make the weaver of a group of pieces, even if radically different, instantly recognizable. Something about the combination of color choices, use of materials, the type of line curvature or thickness, scale, cultural references, detailing, symmetry, etc. keys us immediately that we know the weaver. While it may take years of experience to develop a personal voice or design style, *Eight Shafts: Beyond the Beginning* points out some of the tools and processes weavers can use to create original handwovens.

## Book Organization

Although there is quite a bit of weaving information, this is a book about design, not a recipe or pattern book. We separated the pieces by design elements or techniques as a way to look at how original pieces are created by different weavers. Study the articles, particularly the design and tips sections, to develop your own take on any idea. While not intended as a book for beginners, we extend a helping hand through expansion of some of the drafts to show more than usual about how they work, and have included a glossary, an index, and a reference section for further reading. An effort was made to preserve the individual voices of the weavers throughout, especially in the design sections. There are some inconsistencies in terminology, the result of integrating weavers who have learned in different regions across the world, from different reference materials and traditions, in different languages, and even at different times.

The tips are envisioned as a conversation between the weaver, the editor, and the reader. What technical pitfalls occurred or might occur in the weaving that we could help you avoid? What design concepts or techniques could you take away to use in a general sense in your own work? Most of the technical weaving tips came from the weavers. The design tool tips are a combination of the weaver's and the editor's observations. As such, and due to space considerations, they do not cover everything. Another person with a different background might find completely different points to make. Some of the tips are intentionally straightforward and accessible to anyone; others are more advanced and may require experience or research to implement gracefully.

Each chapter opens with a brief lesson to introduce the design topic at hand. Within any given chapter, the pieces generally increase in complexity or difficulty, with some exceptions made for layout considerations. Note that many pieces could fit into more than one chapter; check the index when looking for more examples.

*Eight Shafts: Beyond the Beginning* is divided into two parts. Part I primarily consists of 8-shaft work, with or without further manipulation. Pieces in Part II fall on any number of shafts which work with the given techniques. In order to keep with our 8-shaft theme, and to help the less experienced 8-shaft weaver to make the leap, an artificial constraint was placed on the Part II pieces. These pieces, whatever the design technique or number of shafts, had to be based in some way on one or more 8-shaft components or have 8-shaft base structures.

Part I is organized by design elements, with chapters on using straight lines, curved lines, stripes of structure (color stripes may occur in any chapter), and a miscellaneous chapter with a variety of approaches. A few of the pieces in the miscellaneous chapter were made on special equipment using eight shafts in a very different way (skillbragd), or off-loom with tablet weaving or ply-splitting from an 8-shaft draft. Chapters in Part II extend the design techniques by using 8-shaft drafts as profile drafts, using 8-shaft blocks or sections, 8-shaft layers of various kinds, interleaving 8-shaft drafts, networking on an initial of 8, 8-tie weaves, and graphic techniques with 8-shaft components (sometimes known as Photoshop techniques but not limited to that drafting method).

With thanks to the many hands and minds which made this book possible, and to my husband, Wes, for his patience and support,

*Laurie Knapp Autio, Editor*

COMPLEX WEAVERS

# Acknowledgements

It takes many people to put together a book of this type. We are foremost indebted to the 72 weavers who shared their work. The range of design insight and possibilities is a credit to these talented weavers. We are also extremely grateful to all who contributed in any way, and apologize to anyone we missed here.

The original proposal for a book to honor Wanda Shelp was made shortly after her death by Laurie Autio. Cally Booker (then president of CW), Laurie Autio (a past president of CW), and Kathi Spangler (then incoming president of CW) refined the topic and the method of presentation. Cally and Laurie developed an informational webpage with input from Linda Davis and John Mullarkey, and an intake form which was tested by Georgia Hadley, Elaine Palmer, and Penny Peters. Cally made periodic website updates. Leslie Killeen managed intake, passing materials to Laurie. Jurying of the entries was done by Laurie, Janney Simpson, and Linda Davis, each excusing themselves on their own pieces.

The initial book format was put together by Wendy Morris, with input from Laurie Autio, Zac Autio, and Linda Davis. It was laid out by Laurie with further input from Zac Autio, Judith Seelig, Sue Powers, Lynn Smetko, and the weavers. The front cover fabrics were woven by Patricia Martin (magenta) and Molly McLaughlin (yellow) and the back cover fabric by Lynn Smetko. Design and text input from Zac Autio, Lynn Smetko, Molly McLaughlin, Barbara Elkins, and Ruth McGregor were very helpful.

Zac Autio and Elaine Palmer helped set guidelines for photographs. Weavers sent their own photographs. Zac evaluated the photographs, and helped many of the weavers through the sometimes daunting task of improving their pictures. Elaine took or retook pictures for a number of weavers. Zac retouched almost all of the photos.

Drafts were prepared by Laurie Autio and proofed in detail by Sue Powers and the weavers. The draft of Wanda Shelp on the dedication page was created by Laurie in Photoshop from a picture from Wanda's daughter, Cheri Shelp. The other drafts were primarily created in Fiberworks, with editing in Photoshop.

The main editor for all of the text was Laurie Autio. Sue Powers proofed all the weavers' articles, with help from Lynn Smetko. Julie George put together the weaving information. The tips are a combination of suggestions provided by the weavers (almost all of the weaving technique and some of the design tips) and Laurie (primarily design tips). Comments from several weavers who saw significant early portions of the book, including Norma Smayda and Barbara Elkins, and Alice Schlein and Becky Ashenden on specific questions, were very helpful. All of the articles were then proofed by the weaver who submitted them. Sadly, Kay Faulkner and Erica de Ruiter passed away during this process. Penny Peters and Lynn Smetko proofed Kay's article, and Kati Reeder Meek proofed Erica's.

The introductory pages were written by Laurie, with helpful input from Lynn Smetko and Sue Powers, plus Sally Orgren (introduction), and Cheri Shelp and Carolyn Wostenberg (dedication). Some of this material appeared previously in articles and advertisements related to the book in the *CW Journal* and the *CW Newsletter*. Laurie wrote the chapter header pages, which were proofed by Sue Powers, Norma Smayda, Lynn Smetko, and Janney Simpson. The glossary was created by Harriet Roadman and Jette Vandermeiden, then edited and proofed by Laurie and Alice Schlein. References were compiled by Mary Underwood, with editing and proofing by Julie George, Trudy Otis, and Laurie. The weavers' bios were assembled and edited by Linda Davis, Leslie Killeen, and Laurie Autio. Laurie created the index. Final proofreading was done by Lynn Harper and Norma Smayda.

Every effort has been made to correct errors. Anything missed is the sole responsibility of the editor, and should be reported to CW for an errata list (to be available on the CW website).

*Below, Detail of shawl by Inge Dam in 8-shaft crepe and card weaving.*

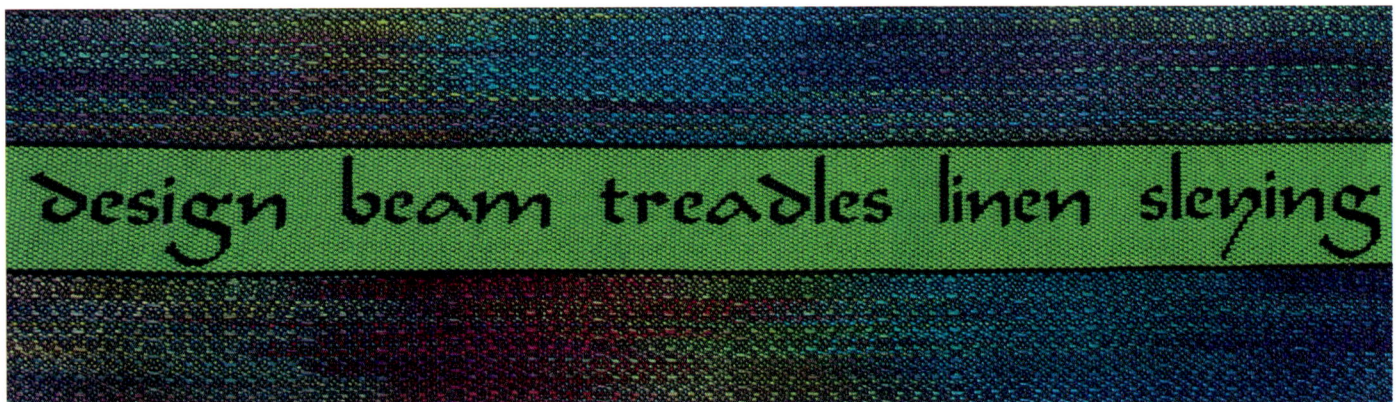

# Draft Conventions

The drafts submitted by the weavers came with a great variety of formats and conventions. Many of the drafts were reformatted for consistency. In general, the tie-down shafts in block weaves have been placed on the front shafts, and the tabby, if present, on the left-most treadles. Unless there was a good reason to spread out the threads, drafts were reconfigured to the lowest number of shafts required to weave them, even if they were woven on more shafts. Most drafts are presented with the fewest treadles needed to weave them. A few exceptions to the least treadles rule occur when it aids understanding of how the patterning works. Sometimes the shafts and/or treadles were rearranged to make the pattern control more obvious. Repeating sections are often shown as parts to be repeated as desired by the weaver.

Space, complexity, and educational goals for the book controlled the draft views used. In many cases, a simple threading draft (that is, a thread-by-thread or "normal" draft) in interlacement or filled square form worked well. Unless otherwise indicated, in structural (non-color) versions of these drafts, a black square indicates a warp thread on the surface and a white square indicates a weft thread on the surface. Sometimes, a more compact profile draft and key were needed. In these drafts, a black square in the drawdown indicates a block weaving pattern

and a white square indicates background or secondary pattern. In a few of these drafts a third color has been used to indicate half-tones or a third structural option. Profile tie-ups in deflected double weave use white squares to indicate blocks weaving weft floats, black to indicate blocks weaving warp floats, and gray for blocks weaving plain weave.

Double weave, warp-faced, or weft-faced cloth may be shown in special views so that they look more like the actual cloth. A number of the drafts were "expanded" (pulled apart) with blank space or colored lines added to separate blocks, sections, or threads with different functions (pattern versus tie-downs, for example). Skeleton drafts, particularly in tied weaves, were used to aid the reader's understanding of how structure relates to patterning and to reduce treadles. In Part II, the weavers were asked to use 8-shaft drafts as the basis of their draft in some way. To aid the reader, these 8-shaft components were usually depicted separately, and often could be woven as simpler fabric on their own. In a very few cases, some of the draft components were left out due to space considerations.

If any terms are unfamiliar or used in an unfamiliar way, please check the Glossary or References for more information.

# Photo Credits

*Except as indicated below, all photos were taken by the weaver.*

Alexander, Betty: Family member
Allison, Charlotte Lindsay: Kaleb Dale
Autio, Laurie Knapp: Elaine Palmer
Blackmon, Andrea: Kyle Vincentz Gula
Booker, Cally: Stuart Booker
Buchman, Ruth: Jeff Magridson/Artslides Digital Imaging
Carey, Sheila: Allan Carey
Complex Weavers Seminar 1988: Alexis Xenakis
Dam, Inge: Pete Paterson
Daslin, Naomie: Paul Kealy
de Ruiter, Erica: Timo Gieling (portrait), Mark Kinney of Association of Lifelong Learners Camera Club (weaving)
Devai, Edna: gregory case
Dickson, Debbie: Michael McKeon

Donald, Pat: Robert Stack
Donde, Karen: Karen Donde (weaving), Brian Gratwicke, Ph.D., Smithsonian Conservation Biology Institute (gecko)
Down, Jean: Steve Templeton
Driscoll, Eileen: Tim Fuss, Pixel Wave
Duxbury, Laurie: Stacey Evans
Faulkner, Kay: Kaz Madigan (portrait), Kay Faulkner (weaving)
Ford, Lucy: Joel Ford
Gingras, Marguerite: Lucie Gingras
Hadley, Georgia: Elaine Palmer
Hayman, Jan: Jon Hayman
Hodges, Susie: Sibila Savage
Kay, Bonnie: Eric Law: Color and Ink Studio Ltd.
Killeen, Leslie: Mary Kircher
MacMorris, Peg: Laurie Sand
Martin, Patricia: Elaine Palmer
McFarland, Teresa: John Brockway

McLaughlin, Molly: Brian McLaughlin
Meek, Kati Reeder: Mark Kinney of Association of Lifelong Learners Camera Club
Osten, Fran: Frank Siteman
Retzlaff, Geri: Larry Retzlaff
Sellin, Helen: Pichan (Sean) Kietsrichart
Shelp, Wanda: Cheri Shelp (base photo); Laurie Autio (draft)
Simpson, Janney: Marcus Simpson
Smayda, Norma: Elaine Palmer
Solbrig, Dorothy: Elaine Palmer
Strike, Kay: Kay Strike and Roxanne Zahller
Toole, Anie: Marc Andre Jesus, John Philippe Hernandiz, Marika Wheeler
van Duijnen, Alice: Rob Frijns
Wostenberg, Carolyn: Lyle Wostenberg
Zahller, Roxanne: Shannon Zahller

# Part I: Designing on 8 Shafts

# I.1  Straight Lines

Keep lines straight by using a constant
angle within a single line or line segment.

## Horizontal and Vertical Straight Lines

Horizontal Lines: Increase the thickness by repeating
in the treadling.

Vertical Lines: Increase the thickness by repeating
in the warp or by combining two or more adjacent
blocks. Increase the number of vertical lines by adding
non-adjacent blocks to the treadling.

*Left, 8-Shaft
Threading Draft
Example of using only
horizontal and vertical
lines to create a more
complex pattern.
Unlike the 6-block
profile draft (right)
for unit weaves, the
lines may need to be
interrupted to tie-down
long floats.*

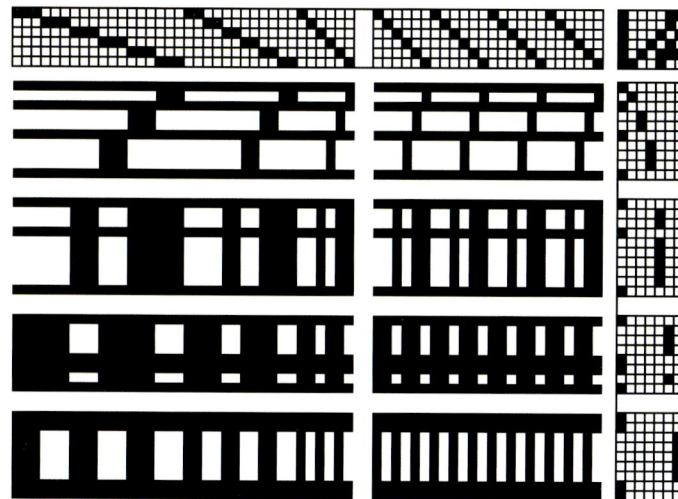

*Above, 6-Block Profile Draft for unit weaves
Treadle 1: Pattern in all blocks, ABCDEF
Treadle 2: Pattern in A
Treadle 3: Pattern in B
Treadle 4: Pattern in C
Treadle 5: Pattern in ABD
Treadle 6: Pattern in BCEF
Treadle 7: Pattern in BDF*

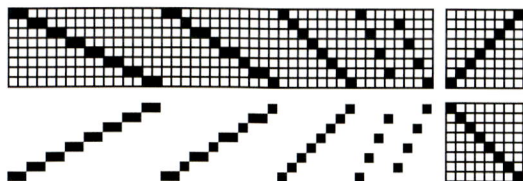

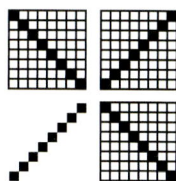

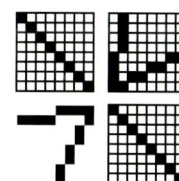

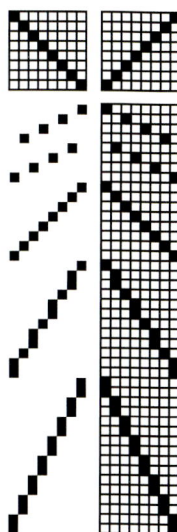

## Angled Straight Lines

Threading and/or Treadling: Change the
angle in the threading and/or treadling
by repeating or skipping some shafts or
treadles (*above left and left*).

Tie-up: Change the angle of the tie-up
pattern to change the angle of the line
(*three drafts above to right*).

Tie-up, Threading, and Treadling: The
final angle of the line in the drawdown
is a function of the angles of the tie-up,
threading, and treadling (*bottom right*).

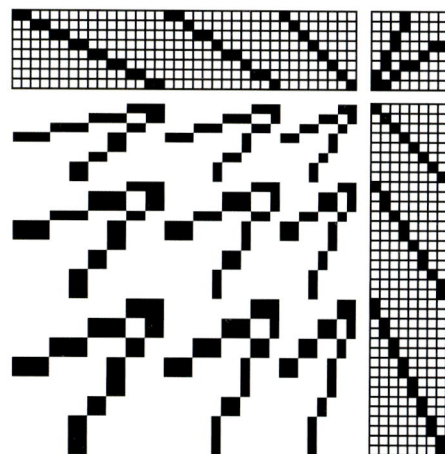

# Abstract Windows

## Naomie Daslin

### Wall Hanging in Double Weave (Plain Weave)

## Design Process

This project was inspired by the architectural beauty of windows in buildings that we pass everyday but often don't appreciate. Many years ago I fell in love with the Museo de Arte Contemporáneo de Castilla y León in Spain. One striking feature of this peculiar building is the façade of more than 3,000 colored glass windows. Combining ancient with modern, 'The Falconer,' a thirteenth century stained glass window in the local cathedral, has been pixelated in the manner of Roman mosaics to form the vibrant color patterning of the museum windows. I love the contemporary design and felt inspired to recreate the same concept in weaving with my own colors.

Technically, this piece was a challenge for me, but one I thoroughly enjoyed. The double weave windows echo the original window inspiration and the colors draw the viewer into the piece. The loom was too small to fit the pattern I had planned so I had to reduce the size of the fabric to fit the loom and think outside the box to adjust the design. The museum façade's line of shorter windows at ground level provided the solution of the narrow edge block. I love it, I simply love this piece and everything about it. I will certainly be making another piece similar to this again in the very near future and look forward to it.

## Weaving Information

Size: 70" x 24" plus 6" fringe on one end

Warp: Rug wool, about 300 ypp, blue, dark blue, yellow green, yellow, red orange, and magenta; 6 epi

Weft: Rug wool, about 300 ypp, various colors; 18 ppi

Source: Original draft

Weave Structure: Double weave (plain weave), 8 shafts

Finishing: Not washed. Handsewn hem on one end, the other secured with an invisible line of machine stitching above the fringe.

Take-up: Warp 5%

## Tips

• Add variety to a repeating draft through use of a non-repeating color sequence.

• Asymmetry lends a feeling of movement. Repeating the narrower blocks in the weft at intervals gives balance, rhythm, unity, and interest to the design. Without the repetition of the element in the weft, the single narrow warp block might have read as a mistake in the weaving.

• A design problem is an opportunity to think creatively.

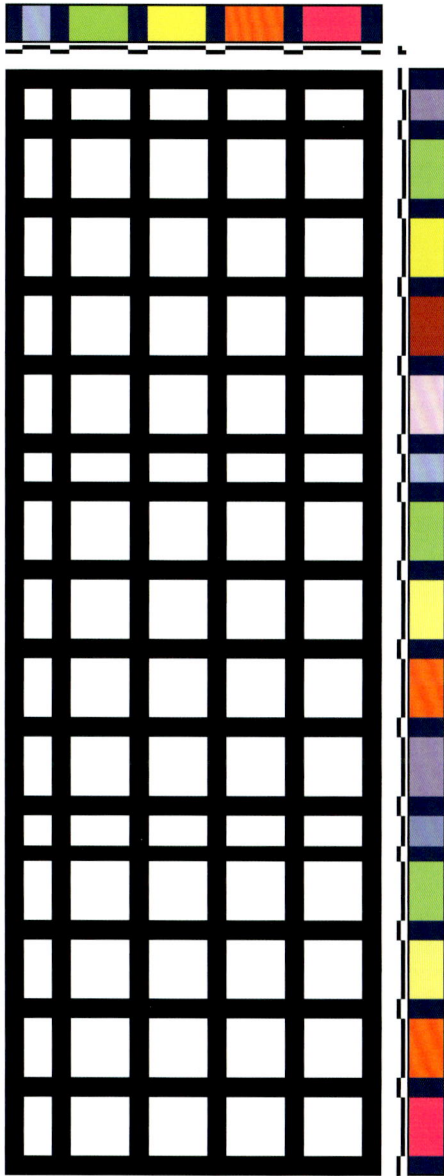

Profile Draft. Color placement in the blocks which form the "windows."

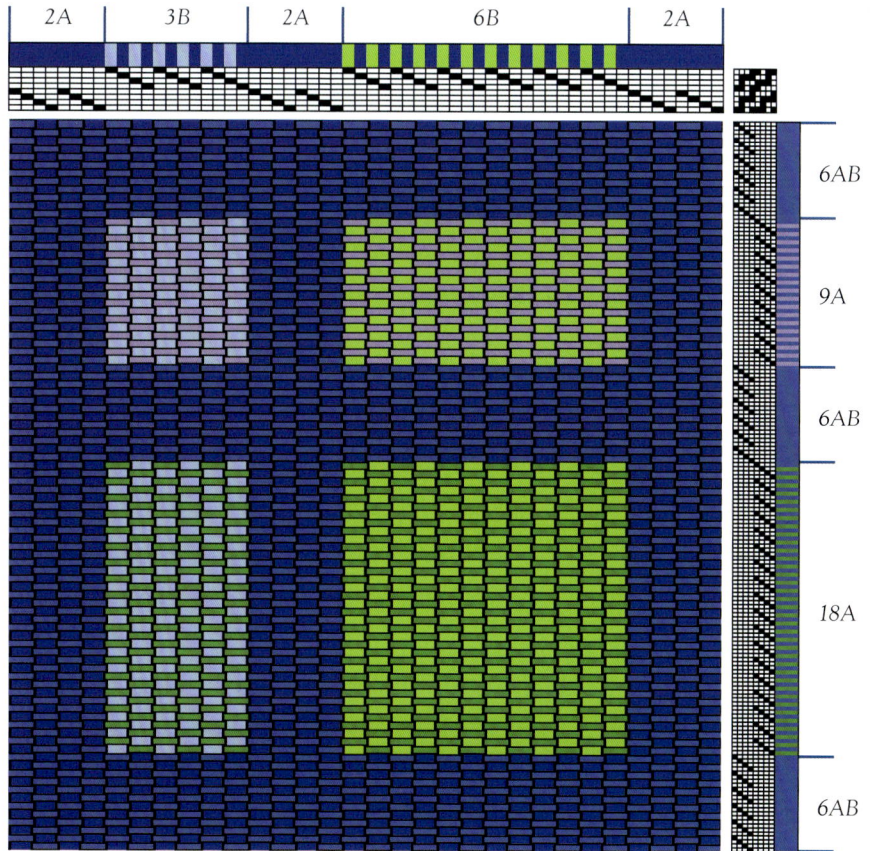

| 2A | 3B | 2A | 6B | 2A |
|---|---|---|---|---|

6AB

9A

6AB

18A

6AB

Threading Draft. A small section from the upper left hand corner of the profile draft is given as a guide to implementing the profile. The drawdown shows only the top layer of the double-woven cloth, with the colors reversing on the back.

# Air, Water, and Mist
## Ruth Buchman

Scarf in Double Weave (Plain Weave)

## Design Process

While working on double weave with my local study group, the Wednesday Weavers, I found a great deal of inspiration in Arn-Grischott (1999). Though I often work with color, I was drawn to some of the more graphic work in the book, such as the scarf on p. 126. One study group member, Eileen Goldman (also a CW member), was doing particularly inspiring graphic work on 12 shafts. I have only eight shafts, limiting me to two independent blocks of loom-controlled double weave. I was jealous of what she could accomplish with three blocks and decided to see if I could create the illusion of a third block on my loom. By flipping the dark/light threading order in areas of the warp, I was able to mimic the effect of a third block. I designed the horizontal striping on the loom while sampling.

I wove this with the selvedges open, hoping the cloth would be more fluid and have more drape than if the edges were closed. I believe this was successful. If I were to weave this piece again, I'd use two colors that blend well to make an identifiable third – say, blue and yellow, making green – in the hope that the "third block" would look even more different from the other two.

## Weaving Information

Size: 68" x 8" plus 5.25" fringe on each end

Warp: 10/2 bamboo, 4200 ypp, undyed and aquamarine; 48 epi

Weft: 10/2 bamboo, 4200 ypp, undyed and aquamarine; 48 ppi

Source: Original draft

Weave Structure: Double weave (plain weave), 8 shafts

Finishing: Hemstitched. Ends are twisted into fringe in solid colors below solid-colored cloth (two layers of fringe, one for each layer of cloth) and in mixed colors below mixed-colored cloth (single layer). Machine washed on gentle with warm water and Ivory for two minutes; machine dried on low until damp. Steam pressed on hot while damp but not until completely dry, then laid flat to dry.

Take-up and Shrinkage: Warp 15%, weft 19%

16

## Tips

• Weaving double weave with the selvedges open makes the cloth drape more fluid.

• Reversing order (XYXY to YXYX) in warps or wefts which alternate colors is interesting in many structures, adding an intriguing layer of complexity.

• Use simple symmetry to organize a complex design. A single mirror (reversal) in the center of the warp and one in the center of the weft adds balance to a lively design.

• Attention to color grouping and multiple layering in the fringe can add an elegant finishing touch.

*Key to Profile Draft. In the first two sections of the warp (marked A and B), the blue-white color sequence results in single-colored areas in the cloth. The third warp section (B') is threaded the same as B, but with the color order switched to white-blue. This change results in blocks which combine blue and white and creates the illusion of a third block. The drawdown shows only the top layer of the double-woven cloth, with the reverse coloring on the back.*

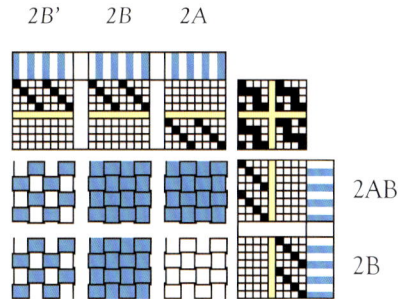

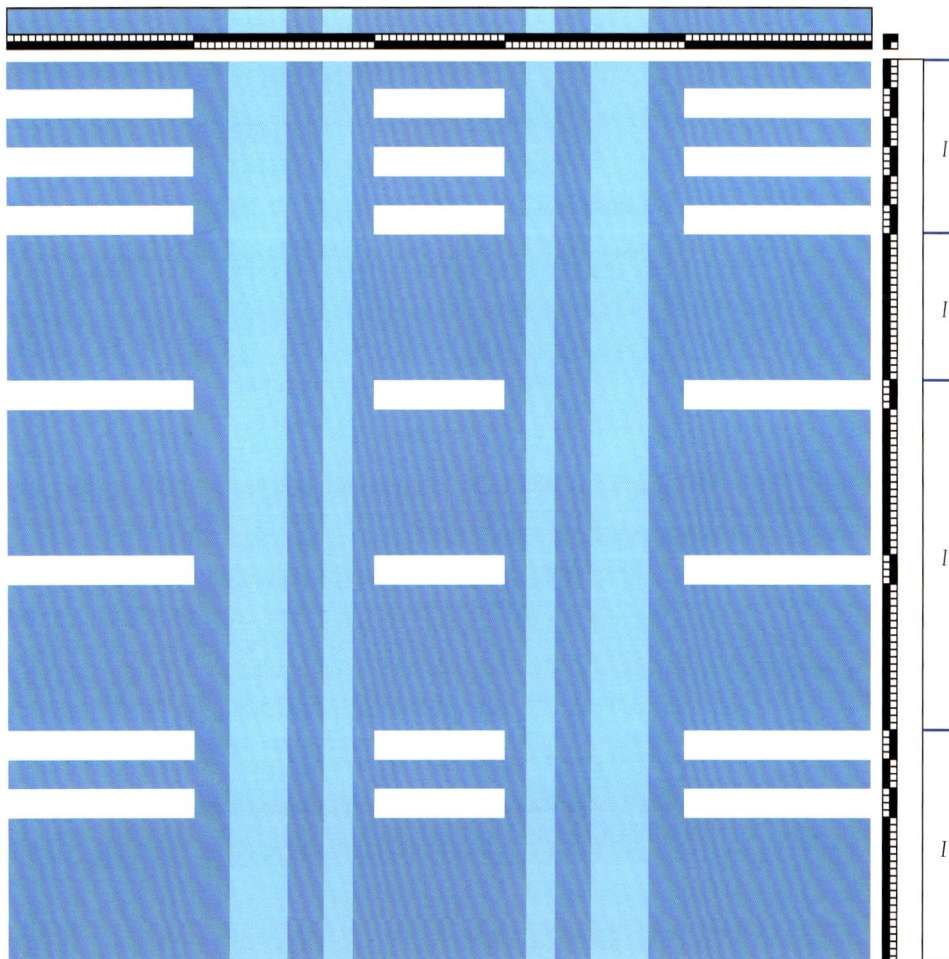

*Treadling Sequence*

*Repeat Treadling I four times.*

*Weave Treadling II.*

*Repeat Treadling III and IV as desired to make the body.*

*Weave Treadling III as balance.*

*Repeat Treadling I, reversed, four times.*

*Profile Draft. In the warp, blue marks the normal blue-white sequence and light blue marks the reversed white-blue sequence. In the weft, the sequence is always white-blue and is marked by white.*

# Doubly Deviant
## Lisa Devereux Hill

### Shawl in Double Weave Variant

### Design Process

This shawl is one of a series of experiments with a deflecting double weave variant I first saw on the website of Andreas Möller. His work intrigued me and I was very curious about the structure he used for his fool-the-eye scarves. After a few failed attempts to figure out what was going on, I hit on a standard, very familiar, double weave block draft with a tie-up twist. If you've woven block double weave you know that in a standard set-up one block weaves layer A on the surface and layer B underneath while the adjacent block weaves the reverse. That is, there are always two layers woven. In Möller's twist, one block weaves two layers while the adjacent block weaves one layer and the other layer floats. The float areas allow the surrounding plain weave blocks to expand and push into the float areas (an aspect familiar to me from my explorations of deflected double weave), deflecting and creating the illusion of discontinuous wefts. In his scarves, color placement enhances the illusion.

I became enamored with this fun variation. In my exploration I used multiple grays in the warp and weft and the deflection resulting from the unwoven layer to create a simulated gradient rather than the ovals which result in Möller's variant. An energized single-ply wool in warp and weft helps the movement and results in the shawl having a soft, springy texture. I feel like I have just begun a journey of exploration into the possibilities of this structure.

### Weaving Information

Size: 68" x 24" plus 5" fringe on each end

Warp: 1/10 wool/cashmere, 5600 ypp, black, charcoal, and dove grey; 36 epi

Weft: 1/10 wool/cashmere, 5600 ypp, black, charcoal, and dove grey; 33-34 ppi

Source: Experimentation based on a scarf on Andreas Möller's website

Weave Structure: Double weave variant, 8 shafts

Finishing: Fringes were twisted and bound. Hand washed in warm water with wool wash, rolled in towel, then hung to dry. Pressed on wool setting.

Take-up: Warp 18%, weft 20%

### Tips

• The weft must be cut and tucked back into the same shed at treadling block changes in order to maintain open selvedges.

• Wool helps stabilize longer floats.

• Help the threads move in any deflected area by using an unbalanced (a.k.a. energized, lively, overspun, active) yarn.

• When designing, consider how movement (deflection) of the warp and/or weft into an area with floats affects the perception of color by changing the density of threads per inch. A lower density makes colors less intense.

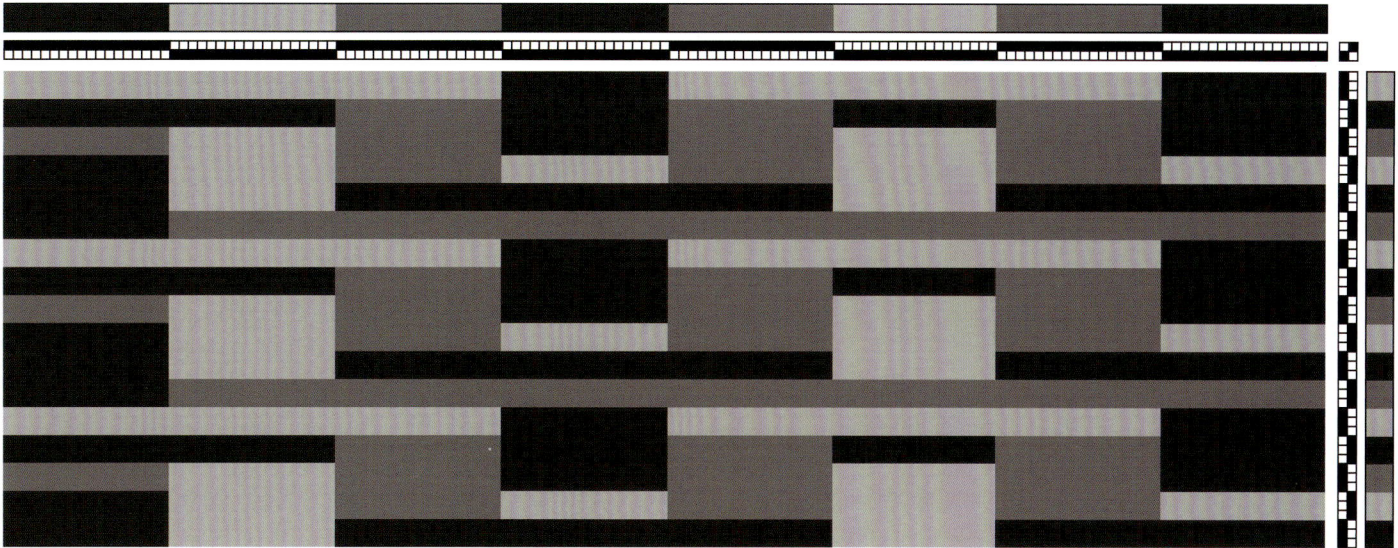

*Profile Draft. Color placement in warp and weft blocks.*

2B        2A

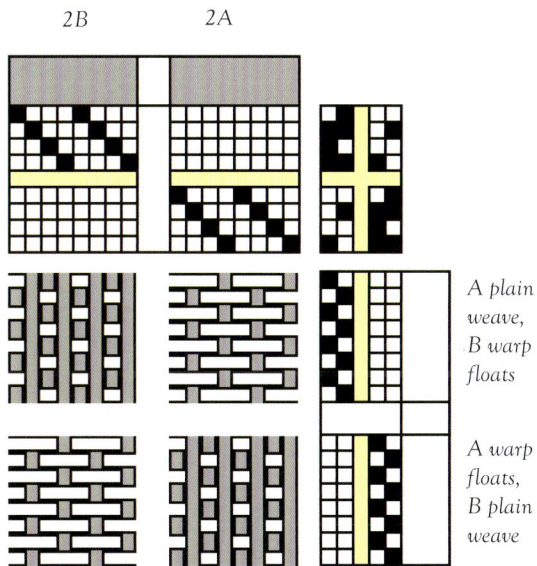

A plain
weave,
B warp
floats

A warp
floats,
B plain
weave

*Key to Profile Draft. When a block has plain
weave on the top, it has long floats on the back,
and vice versa. The drawdown shows only the top
layer of the double-woven cloth, with the reverse on
the back. The draft has been expanded to separate
the blocks in the threading, tie-up, and treadling.*

# Three Times Square
## Patricia Martin

### Wrap in Basket Weave, Twill, and Atwater-Bronson Lace

### Design Process

For the past few years the idea of playing with blocks in the tie-up has been an obsession. Recently, a discussion of honeycomb at my local guild study group spurred the idea for this wrap. I started with a classic 2-block threading with straight draw on four shafts for each block (Alderman, 2009). Rummaging through the process of block manipulation inspired me to start playing in a weaving program, working to modify the structures to create texture while keeping the square theme. I moved blocks of structure around in the tie-up until I found a couple of interesting patterns that I thought I might like to weave.

Going to my stash of pre-made, hand-painted warp chains I chose eight from the red family in a thick silk noil which was fun to paint and has a nice hand when woven. Finding the right weft was difficult. I wanted it to be flat and show off the weave structure. I needed something that was soft, thick and of the right color. I tried several different colorways from a light coral, to red, rust, metallic, and finally settled on the gray which was not flat. Like all grays, this gray has a blue cast sometimes and a red cast at other angles.

Weaving the piece was, as always, fun. I wove half of the wrap in the 2-block treadling in twill and basket weave and the other half in the 3-block treadling, adding Atwater-Bronson lace and a reversal of the twill direction. Seen side-by-side, the two sections have different textures. The two-structure section shows off the blocks cleanly while the three-structure section structure blurs the changes in the blocks with the third texture. The painted and textured warp then adds a scramble to the rigid lines of the blocks. Because it is flat, it may also be used as a table runner. Once the wrap was woven, I was out of warp but not out of ideas of how I can use this threading to create a variety of patterns by just changing the tie-ups and treadling.

### Weaving Information

Size: 49" x 16" with 0.5" fringe on each end

Warp: Silk, 1260 ypp, originally white, eight hand-painted warp chains in fuchsia, coral, red, and rust; 16 epi

Weft: Wool/acrylic yarn, 1260 ypp, charcoal; 16 ppi

Source: Original tie-up on a traditional threading

Weave Structures: Basket weave, twill, and Atwater-Bronson lace, 8 shafts

Finishing: Stitched 0.5" from edge with running stitch then extra threads removed to create a fringe. Machine washed on delicate with warm water, cool rinse. Hung to dry, then steam pressed on cotton/silk setting.

Take-up and Shrinkage: Warp and weft 10%

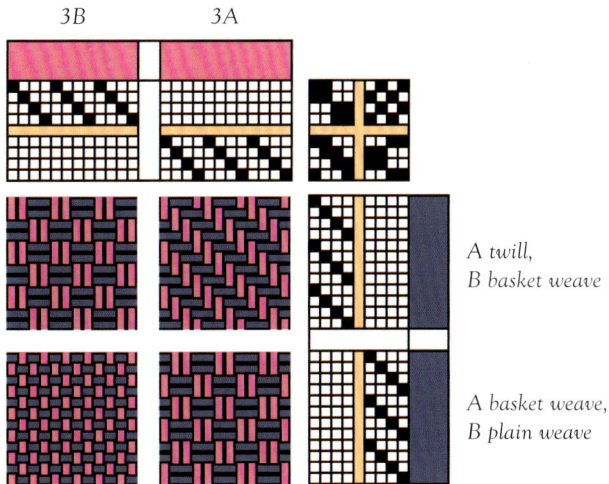

Threading Draft. The treadling for the first half of the wrap has one treadling block of 2/2 twill, two of basket weave, and one of plain weave. Three repeats of blocks are shown; repeat as desired.

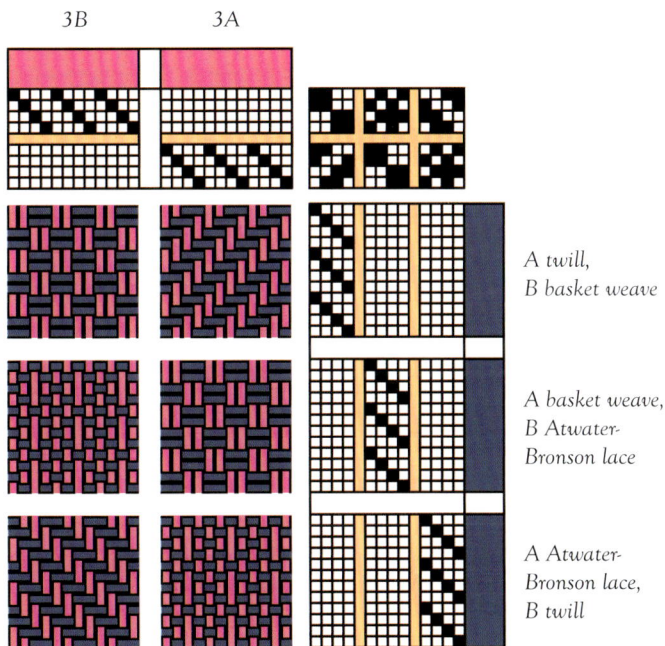

A twill,
B basket weave

A basket weave,
B plain weave

Threading Draft. The treadling for the second half of the wrap has three treadling blocks combining 2/2 twill in two directions, basket weave, and Atwater-Bronson lace. Repeat blocks as desired.

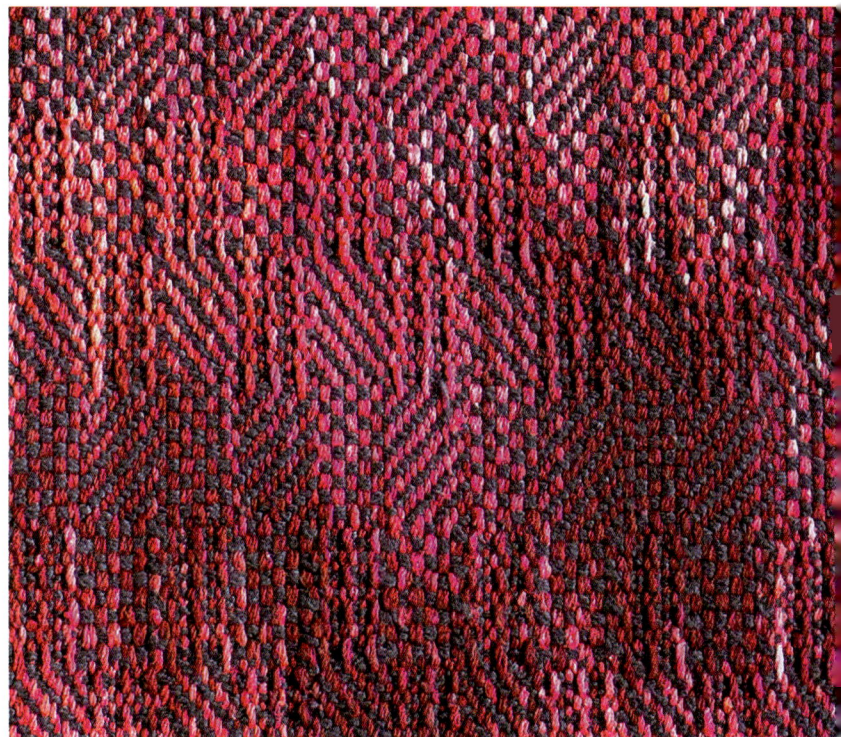

A twill,
B basket weave

A basket weave,
B Atwater-Bronson lace

A Atwater-Bronson lace,
B twill

## Tips

• Combining structures is a pleasure when you play in the tie-up. The design ideas can go on and on as you play in the treadling.

• Hand-painting the warp and/or weft in subtle variations and/or using yarn with textural interest adds variety and life to a small repeating pattern.

• Breaking the expectation that both halves of a piece must be the same can create a new dimension. Try it also in scarves, vests, and runners.

• While shown as a wrap, this piece works equally well as a runner. Cloth is cloth - don't be afraid to re-purpose as desired.

# For Douglas
## Brenda Gibson

### Scarf in Beiderwand

### Design Process

My starting point for this design was an exploration of a double two-tie unit weave threading with alternate dark/light coloration, guided by the classic publication by Barrett and Smith (1983). I threaded four units each of four blocks in straight progression and followed draft #5.11 which shows interesting color and weave effects where straight and broken twill are woven in different blocks on 10 shafts.

Each threading block of double two-tie requires two tie-down shafts and two pattern shafts. By always combining the B and D blocks in Barrett and Smith's draft, I created the simplified 3-block design (below), bringing it within the scope of 8-shaft weavers. This piece also departs from Barrett and Smith's example structures. I used a beiderwand variation which creates areas of double cloth and integrated single-layer cloth.

I love the shapes of the block combinations; they remind me of the wooden building blocks I played with as a child. I am also delighted with the two very distinct faces of the cloth. There are no long floats, making it very suitable for a scarf, and the double layer areas trap insulating air, increasing the warmth. Finally, the delicious wool/cashmere yarn I had just bought was ideal in terms of count and softness, giving a lovely hand and drape.

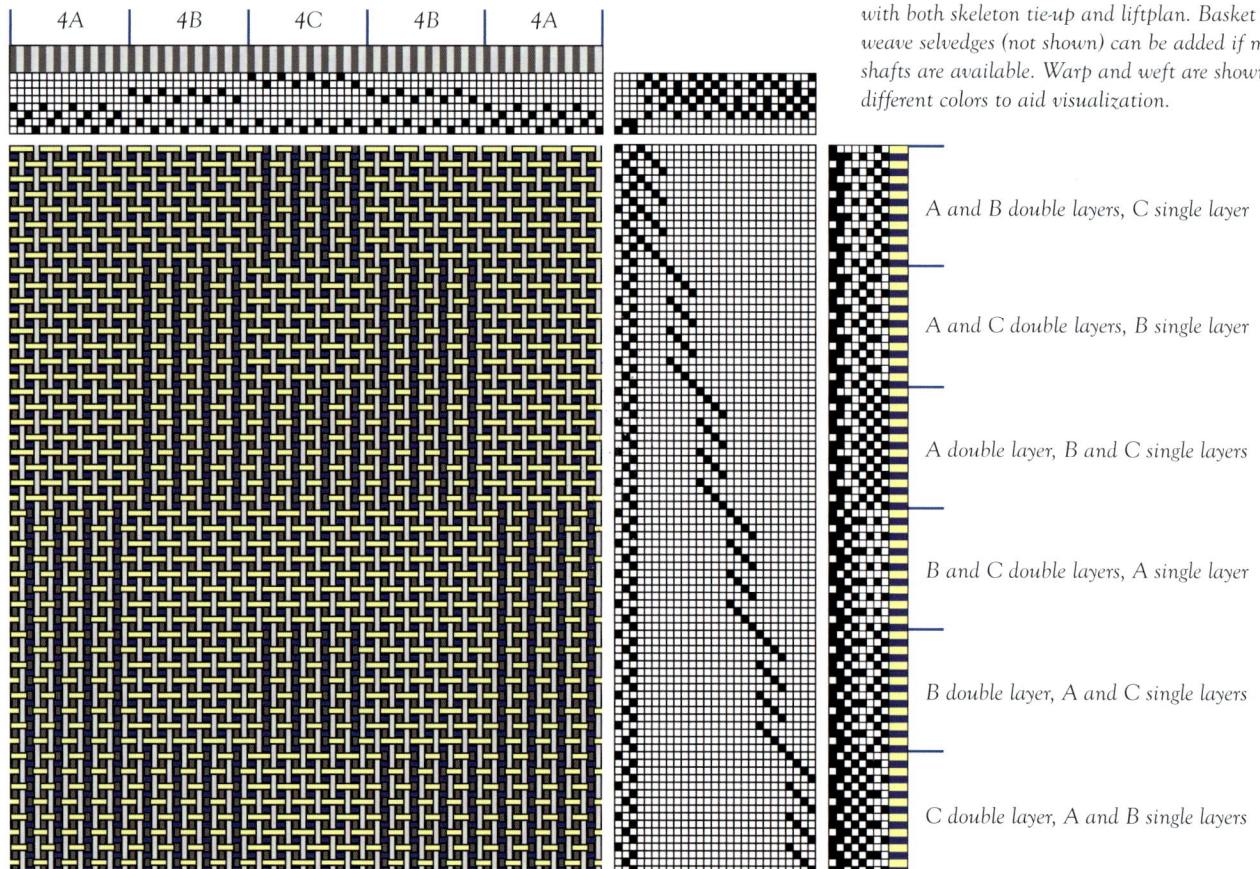

*Threading Draft. One repeat plus balance shown with both skeleton tie-up and liftplan. Basket weave selvedges (not shown) can be added if more shafts are available. Warp and weft are shown as different colors to aid visualization.*

A and B double layers, C single layer

A and C double layers, B single layer

A double layer, B and C single layers

B and C double layers, A single layer

B double layer, A and C single layers

C double layer, A and B single layers

## Weaving Information

Size: 66" x 9" plus 2.5" fringe on each end

Warp: 2/20 nm wool/cashmere (95/5%), 4960 ypp, navy and light blue; 30 epi

Weft: 2/20 nm wool/cashmere (95/5%), 4960 ypp, navy and light blue; 30 ppi

Source: Original draft

Weave Structures: Beiderwand (optional basket weave selvedges on additional shafts, not shown), 8 shafts

Finishing: Six picks plain weave in dark at each end of the scarf. Hemstitched, then 2-ply twisted fringe (one dark, one light ply) secured by overhand knots. Hand washed and lightly fulled in hot water with mild dishwashing liquid. Rinsed at the same temperature with fabric softener added to final rinse. Blotted in towel, air dried, and steam pressed.

Take-up and Shrinkage: Warp and weft 7%

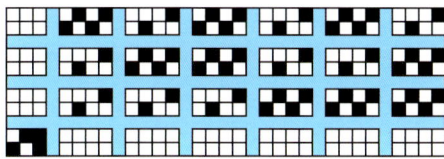

Pattern shaft tie-up for single-layer block

Pattern shaft tie-up for double-layer block

*Threading Draft Tie-up. The tie-up has been expanded to show how pattern is formed. A single integrated layer results when a pattern shaft box has four ties. Double layers result where only two ties are used. Compare to the profile tie-up.*

Balance | Repeat

Repeat

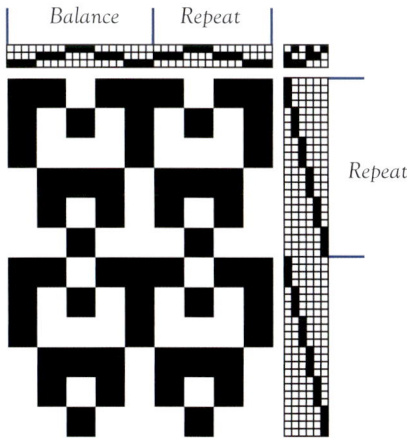

*Profile Draft. The treadling uses six combinations of the three warp blocks. Single layers are marked in white, double layers in black. Note that the second three profile treadles are a mirror image of the first three with single and double layers reversed.*

*Detail photo shows both front and back.*

## Tips

• If you have extra shafts, you can spread the threads on shafts 1 and 2 out over four shafts and add basket weave selvedges; these nuances are not shown in the draft. Using more shafts also may avoid the need to add more heddles to shafts 1 and 2 and would help if the warp is sticky.

• In preparation for the bi-color twisted fringe, the two colors were separated by a temporary pick at the start and end of the scarf.

• Always combining the same two (or more) blocks from a draft requiring more shafts can create interesting new patterns and lower the number of shafts required to the number available or increase the number of patterns possible.

• Playing with the tie-up can often lead to new structural possibilities.

• Try using more than the standard number of treadling blocks to create more complex patterns. It may require retieing treadles, or using a table or dobby loom.

• Reversing pattern and background across a mirror or other symmetry element is a useful tool to create interest and focus.

23

# Fun with Monk's Belt
## Geri Retzlaff

Runner in Monk's Belt

### Design Process

I have been wanting to try an original monk's belt project and this book seemed like a perfect opportunity. I checked out two books (Winderknecht, 1976, p. 40 and Dixon, 2007, pp. 96-101) from our Textile Center library to review the basics and learn how to expand this common four-shaft weave to eight shafts. Each block is given its own pair of shafts, allowing four blocks on eight shafts, rather than the two available on four shafts.

I had a lot of fun arranging and re-arranging the four available blocks and tried several designs before settling on this one. A pop of bright red weft brought the pattern to life, punctuating the blue pattern weft at every other reversal point. The profile draft could easily be used to make many other designs using additional treadles. I learned that it's hard to put monk's belt blocks on the selvages because the floats tend to draw in more and do not produce the best looking selvages. Floating selvedges help, and I have been exploring other ways to combat this problem. In the future, I plan to have more fun with this very old technique and explore different color arrangements. I hope others will be encouraged to try it!

### Weaving Information

Size: 37.25" x 13.75"

Warp: 8/2 unmercerized cotton, 3360 ypp, natural; 20 epi

Weft: 8/2 unmercerized cotton, 3360 ypp, natural (tabby); 5/2 mercerized cotton, 2100 ypp, blue jeans and brick (pattern); 30 ppi including tabby

Source: Original draft

Weave Structure: Monk's belt, 8 shafts

Other Weaving Information: Use floating selvedges (not shown).

Finishing: To reduce bulk in hem, 0.5" woven in sewing thread and 1.5" in 5/2 cotton. The sewing thread was turned to the inside of hem, pressed, and stitched. Machine washed warm with Method laundry detergent, medium spin, cool rinse. Hung to dry, then steam pressed on cotton setting.

Take-up and Shrinkage: Warp and weft 15%

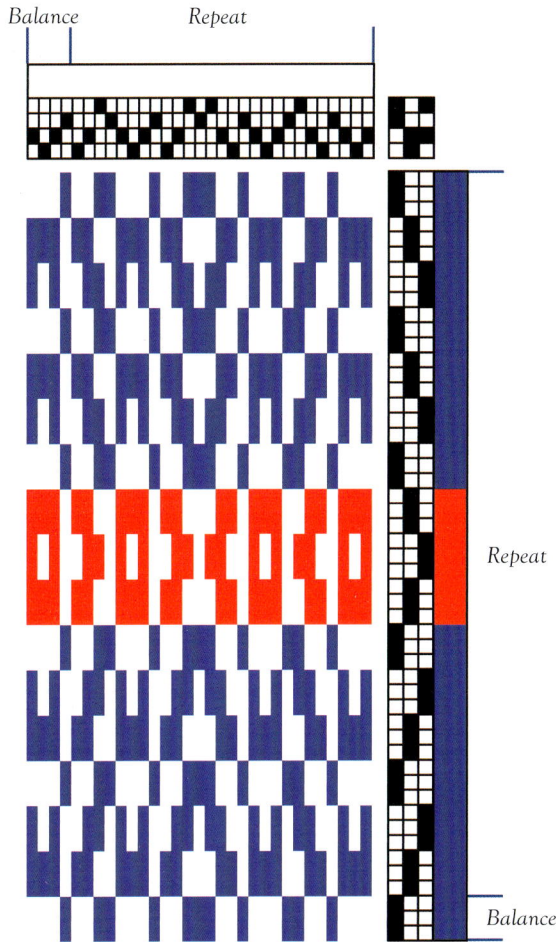

Balance    Repeat

Repeat

Balance

*Profile Draft. Color placement indicated. Three combinations of the four warp blocks are used.*

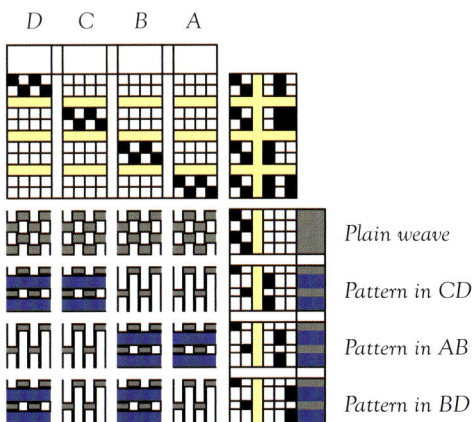

D    C    B    A

Plain weave

Pattern in CD

Pattern in AB

Pattern in BD

*Key to Profile Draft. Expanded to separate the 2-shaft, 4-thread blocks. When a block weaves pattern, neither of its shafts are raised; when it weaves background, both are raised.*

## Tips

• Placing a contrasting color at regular intervals provides rhythm and a dash of excitement.

• Using symmetry elements, such as reversal points, when placing a color change makes the changes feel logical and balanced, even when the overall pattern is complex.

• With four blocks available, there is an opportunity to combine blocks as desired, as long as the floats are not too long for the intended use.

• When floats at the selvedges are problematic, try using a floating selvedge, threading a small opposite block, or, if available, using extra shafts to control the selvedges separately.

# Kilim Dreaming

## Susan Porter

### Shawl in Point, Straight, and 2-Block Twills

## Design Process

I have always been drawn to Kilim rugs, and I live in the Southwest where many of the same shapes appear in weavings. Diamonds, zigzags (stylized snakes), and arrows or chevrons are common. Not being a tapestry weaver, I wanted to design a piece inspired by both Kilim rugs and Rio Grande style weaving that I could weave on my eight-shaft loom.

For several years I have played with combining different structures in one piece, so it felt natural for me to combine different twills. While working on another piece, I began trying to figure out ways to tie-up the turned twill draft I was working on to make chevrons, and then on blending those chevrons into other twills. Combining straight and point eight-shaft twills with two blocks of straight four-shaft threadings allowed the regular 1/1/1/1/1/3 twill tie-up to break into horizontal bands of plain weave and 1/3 twill chevrons in places threaded to blocks. Changes in threading were accentuated by changes in color. This shawl is the outcome of my exploration.

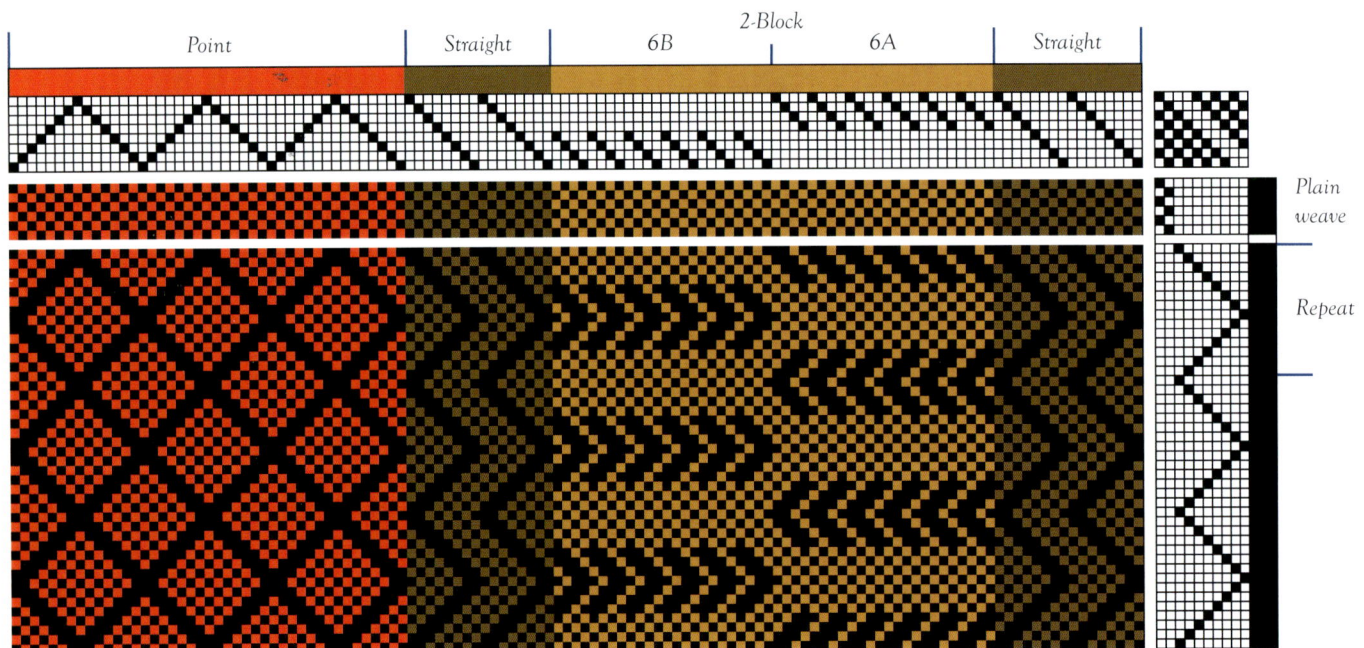

*Threading Draft. A portion of the draft showing color placement in the warp is given. A regular 1/1/1/1/1/3 twill tie-up is combined with point treadling. Expand or contract each warp section and order the sections as desired.*

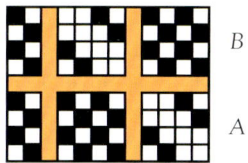

*Threading Draft Tie-up. Treadles 1 and 2 produce plain weave. The pattern area of the tie-up (treadles 3 though 10) is divided to emphasize the relationship to the 2-block twill area. When the 4-shaft A block weaves plain weave, the 4-shaft B block weaves a regular 1/3 weft-dominant twill (treadles 3 through 6) and vice versa (treadles 7 though 10).*

## Weaving Information

Size: 81" x 22" plus 3.5" fringe on each end

Warp: 8/2 spun rayon, 3360 ypp, brick, brown-gold, and dark brown; 24 epi

Weft: 2-ply baby alpaca, 3964 ypp, black; 26 ppi

Source: Original draft

Weave Structures: Point, straight, and 2-block twills, 8 shafts

Other Weaving Information: Floating selvedges used.

Finishing: Began and ended the piece with two picks plain weave and hemstitched over four ends. Hand washed in cool water with Eucalan Fine Fabric Wash, taking care not to agitate or wring. Water gently squeezed out, then rolled in a dry towel to remove the remaining excess water. Hung over a rod to dry. Steam pressed using a pressing cloth and moderate heat. Fringe trimmed to 3.5" on each end with a rotary cutter.

Take-up and Shrinkage: Warp 10%, weft 12%

## Tips

• Care must be taken with beat when weaving this draft. Using a clear plastic protractor makes it easy to check your beat with the strong diagonal lines of this twill

• Color may be used to unify or accentuate a pattern. Changing color at structure or pattern breaks emphasizes those changes, and value changes can make some patterns stand out more than others.

• When designing a threading, it may be possible to make interesting variations by using all the shafts in some areas and breaking into subsets in others. When you do this, see how the tie-up falls when broken. In this case, the regular tie-up chosen breaks nicely into two alternating simpler patterns. Move ties around until you get the effect you want in each area.

# ZZZZZ

## Debbie Dickson

### Throw in Advancing Wall of Troy Twill

### Design Process

The design started with the concept of repeating Zs. This led to the idea of a warm, cozy throw which you could fall asleep under (ZZZZZ), which influenced the selection of a merino wool/possum/silk blend yarn. This yarn blooms when washed, enhancing the warmth of the final throw.

Most of my weaving, including this piece, references the Fibonacci series in some way. There are three main color sections across the throw. The widths of the solid color sections are in the following proportions: 2, 2, 1, 2, 1, 2, 2. Between each solid section, the color grades. To help with the color transitions, I used Pascal's triangle (Froberg, 2012).

I started with an advancing Wall of Troy pattern (Inouye, 2000), then modified it and added reversals. To keep the design simple and uncluttered, small borders were added at each side but not to the ends. This helped balance the design. The border was initially slightly wider but during a final review of the pattern I made a decision to extend the main pattern and reduce the border. While this is obvious in the draft, it disappears in the throw. The final length of the throw was determined using the golden ratio (the width multiplied by 1.6) and finishing off the final pattern repeat once this length was met.

Because of the size and texture of the yarn used, the pattern is simpler and more subtle than if a smaller, smoother yarn were used where more repeats and transitions between advancing and reversing points are possible. However, the bold, noticeable stripes through both the straight lines in the middle section and the Vs at each side work well.

### Weaving Information

Size: 58" x 33" plus 2.5" fringe on each end

Warp: Merino/possum/silk (50/40/10%), 1290 ypp, black, red, and grey; 12 epi

Weft: Merino/possum/silk (50/40/10%), 1290 ypp, black; 12 ppi

Source: Modified from Inouye (2000)

Weave Structure: Advancing and reversing Wall of Troy twill, 8 shafts

Finishing: Hemstitched over three rows and three ends (including floating selvedge) except at the transition between the advancing and reversing twill where it was three then four ends per bundle. Twisted two fringe bundles and knotted at approximately 3" before washing. Removed the extra twist after knotting and trimmed to 1" from knots before washing, trimmed after washing to approximately 0.4". The throw was hand sewn into a donut shape (Lynde, 2015) before washing to ensure even fulling during wet finishing. Soaked for 15 minutes, then machine washed using Softly for approximately 3-4 minutes, spun on low speed. Blocked and laid flat to dry, then pressed over a wet linen towel.

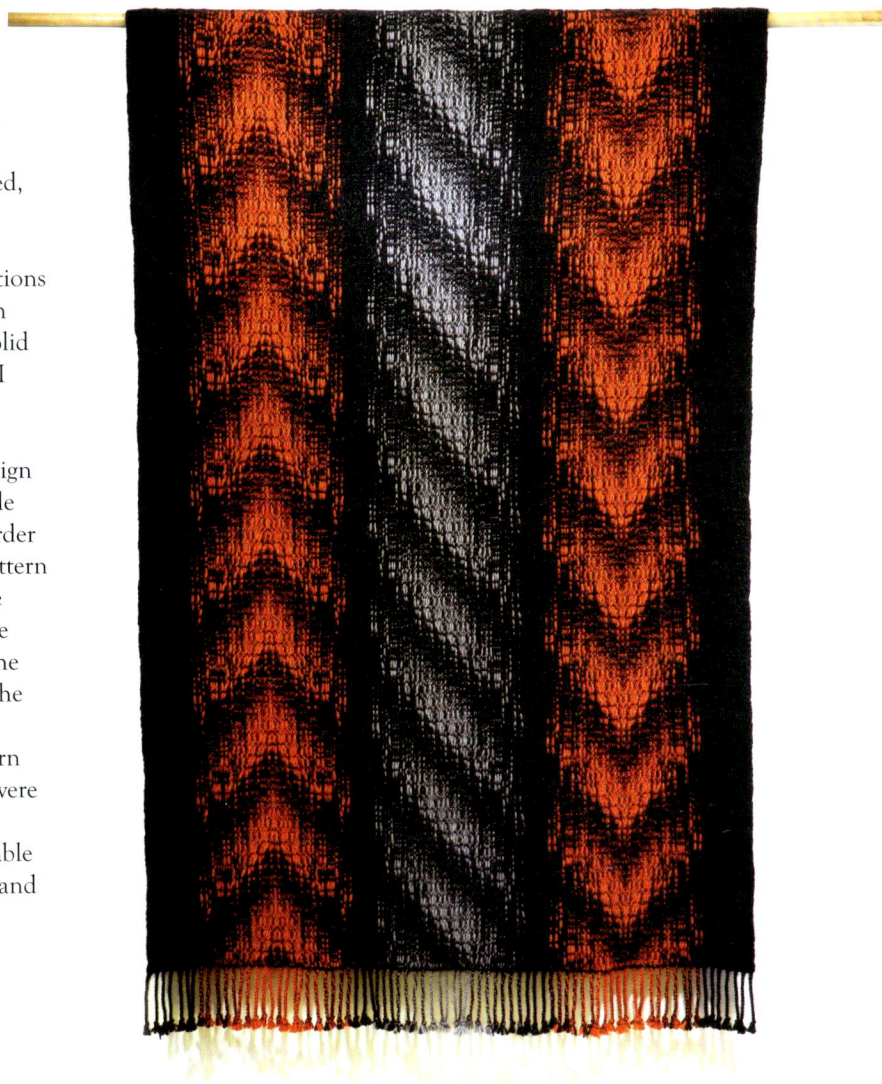

Take-up: Warp 18%, weft 14%

Right Side

Hemstitching

Repeat

Hemstitching

Left Side

Hemstitching

Repeat

Hemstitching

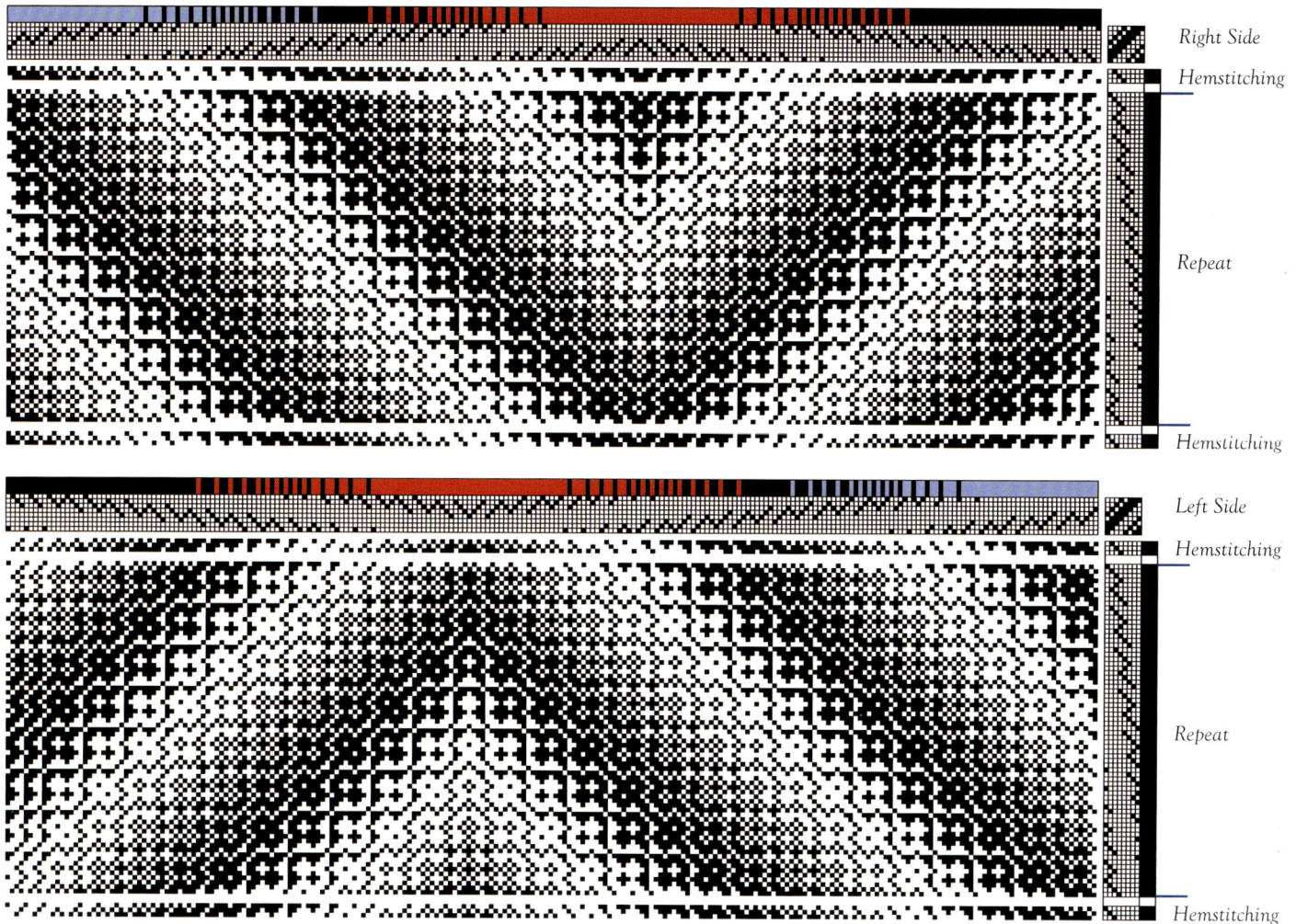

*Threading Draft. Split into two sections. The threading is an advancing Wall of Troy twill with reversals and the treadling is the same without reversals. A regular 3/1/1/3 twill tie-up is used. The first and last three picks are for hemstitching.*

## Tips

• Simple overall color groupings create a very bold, graphic feeling to a design.

• Grading color both softens a design and provides another layer of complexity.

• Having the pattern in the two red bands running in opposite directions and the center grey band something different and less directional, increases the interest over a simple mirror at the center of the warp.

• Shading caused by the interplay of the tie-up with warp and weft adds another dimension to the color interaction. In this draft, a single-color weft shades the warp coloring as the structure changes from warp to weft floats.

• Sometimes a pattern can be read in multiple ways. Here, some may see the ends of the Zs as red hearts, to wrap the user in love.

# The Septad
## Marta G. Williams

Handbound Books in Interleaved Broken Point Twills

## Design Process

It all started with the yarn (Gima 8.5, Ito) and its fascinating ribbon-like nature. Having no idea what I would do with it, I bought several skeins each of various colors. Sometime later, I was inspired by Marian Stubenitsky (2014) to try interleaving a point twill to create an intricate design through the interplay of warp and weft. Using PCW Fiberworks, I played with the threading, tie-up, and treadling and came up with a design of interlocking straight line diamond shapes that I liked. Then, the light bulb went off and I knew what I was going to use that Ito yarn for. The ribbon-like nature of the yarn would translate well into my interleaved design. And, the yarn texture would create a fabric well-suited to bookbinding. Of course, I had to buy more yarn!

The first warp was all one color, resulting in fairly simple diamonds. Starting with a sett of 15 epi for the blue and yellow cover fabric created a large diamond that was too large to create the interplay I was looking for. So, I changed to a sett of 30 epi for the rest of the covers. Different color wefts were used to create three different fabrics. To add more dimension, I then wove the same warp with two alternating colors. Initially using the same treadling, again different color wefts were used. To use up the two-color warp, I kept the tie-up and threading, but changed the treadling for an even more complex interplay of warp and weft.

## Weaving Information

Size: Seven books, each 1.5" square

Warp 1 (3 books): Cotton tape, 4200 ypp, mustard; 15 and 30 epi

Warp 2 (4 books): Cotton tape, 4200 ypp, mustard and cayenne red; 30 epi

Weft: Cotton tape, 4200 ypp, cayenne red, orient blue, cam green, and sand; 30 ppi

Source: Original draft

Weave Structure: Interleaved broken point twills, 8 shafts

Finishing: Not washed, steam pressed.

Mounting: Handwoven fabric was glued to 1.5" squares of cardboard with Jade 403 adhesive, 0.25" wrapped around edges. Coptic bookbinding technique was used to create the books, with interior signatures of off-white textured commercial paper and cardstock in various colors for the first and last signature. Embroidery floss in various colors was used for binding with a metal bead for the closures.

Take-up: Warp and weft less than 1%

## Tips

• Working in a series is a good way to explore several variables, such as color placement and choice or treadling variations. One idea leads to another, and the final group has an interesting, progressional cohesion.

• Explore different levels of scale and value contrast to create different effects with the same threading and treadling.

• When interleaving two drafts, consider whether you would like the two drafts to merge into one by using only one color in the warp and one in the weft, stay separate by alternating colors in warp and weft, or do something in between by alternating color in warp or weft, but not both.

• Interleaving a line offset with itself is a useful technique, with more complex results than a strictly parallel threading without an offset.

• Changing the angle at which a fabric is used changes its appearance, and is a good design tool to keep in mind. Note how placing the fabric on the bias in one of the books changes the pattern from diamonds to squares.

Component Drafts. In the first treadling (blue weft) the base component, with
orange warp, shows the different broken twills used in the warp and weft. The
second component, with yellow warp, is the same as the first but shifted by
18 threads in warp and weft. An extra pick is added to the top of the yellow
warp component and to the bottom of the orange warp component. In the
second treadling (purple weft), the components are tromp as writ.

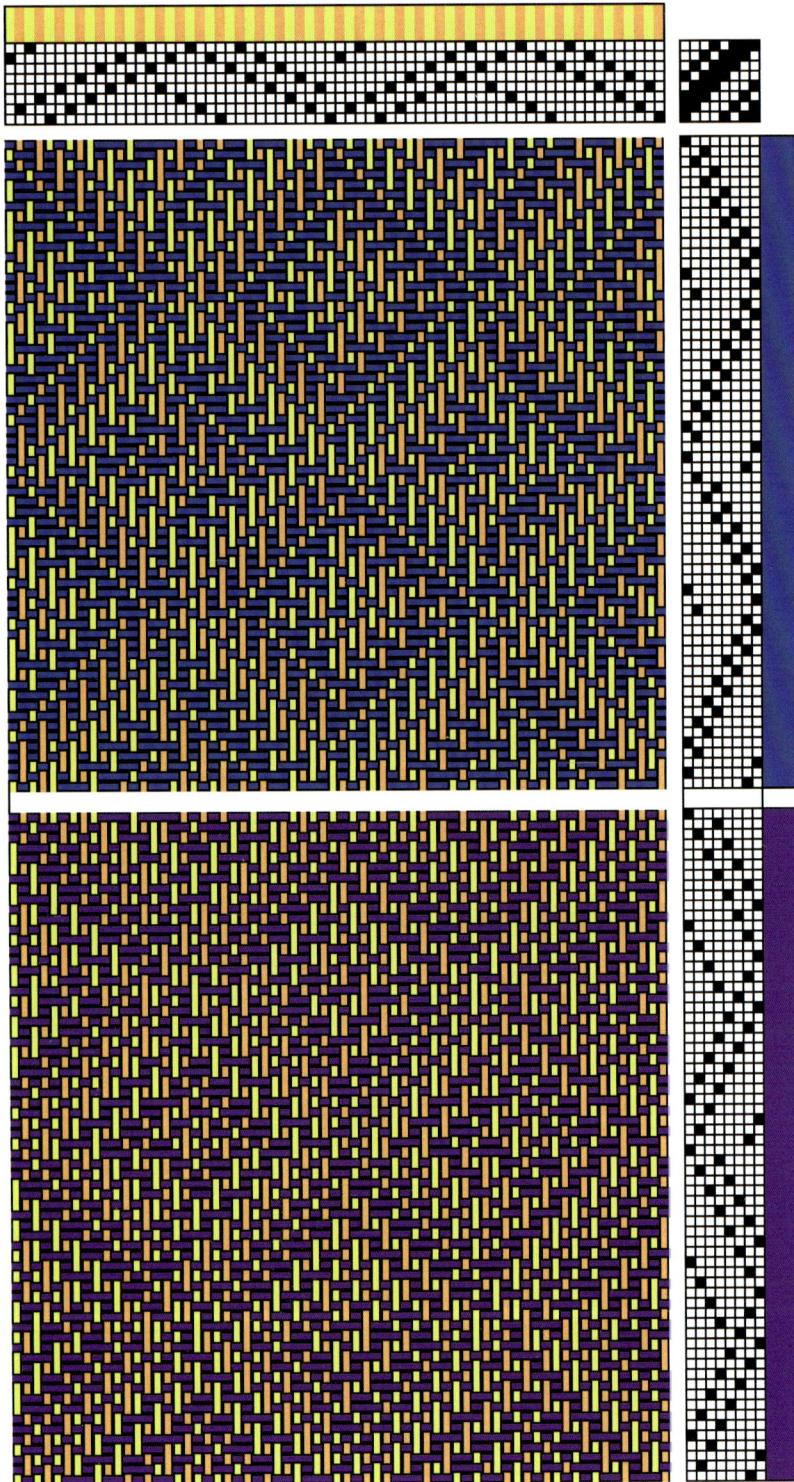

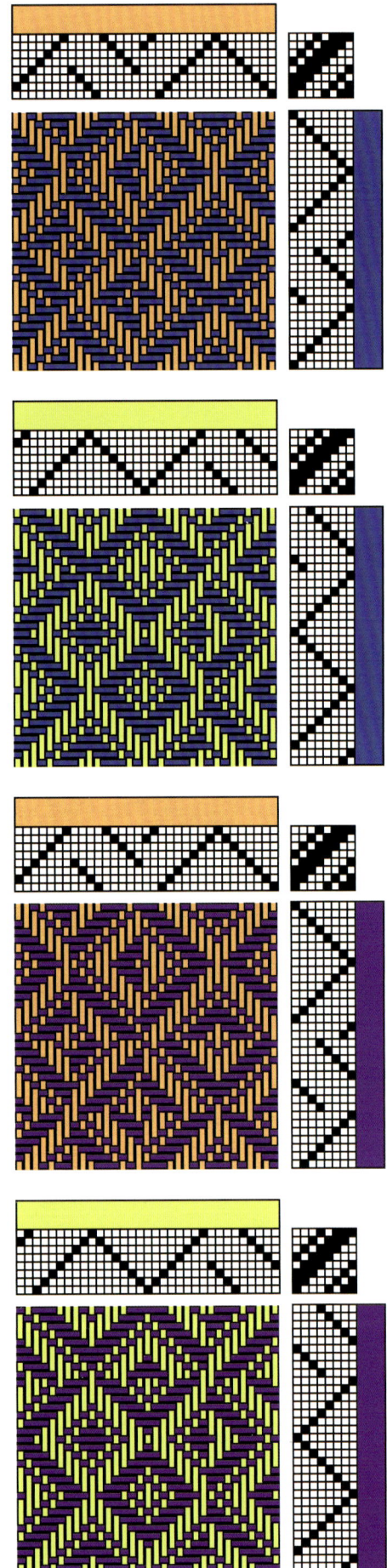

Threading Draft. Two treadlings are shown on the alternating warp-color version (single
color similar, not shown). A broken twill has been offset and interleaved in warp and weft,
using a regular 3/1/1/3 twill tie-up. The second treadling is tromp as writ.

# Faith
## Molly McLaughlin
### Wall Hanging in Extended Point Twill and Leno

## Design Process

My design process often involves creating a solution for how to combine concepts, visual images, and specific color palettes that have been collected from a variety of disparate sources, often unintentionally, and are sticking around in my mind. In the case of 'Faith,' I had been mulling over the problems of religious faith versus a secular world, at the same time as I was filling my house with the bright festive holiday colors that I associate with Hanukkah. For quite a while, I had also been wishing to design a piece that would showcase the beauty of unwoven warp fibers that often entice me to my loom. It occurred to me that the warp fibers were like faith in my life, offering support, structure and beauty. With concept and palette clear in my mind, I was able to start sketching out ideas for the piece. I tried several ideas for presenting the warp threads but large leno twists were by far the best solution. Once I had an image for the piece sketched out, I could begin weaving it.

The piece is comprised of a grid of nine windows which change color. The warp is threaded with the outer windows in shades of red/orange/yellow and the middle window in shades of blue. The piece is framed by one repeat on either side in dark purple warp threads. For the bottom and top rows of windows the weft changes from blue to red to blue across the three windows using the tapestry technique of hatching at the weft intersections between the windows. The middle windows have a continuous weft of purple running across. The leno twists are held in place by clear acrylic bars that are treated as weft and woven into the piece.

I had originally planned on calling the piece "Hanukkah Lights," but the very act of weaving it ended up supplying the title. Faith was the first large-scale piece that I wove in fine threads and I really enjoyed the result. Since then I have been encouraged to explore the challenge of designing other large-scale pieces in even finer threads.

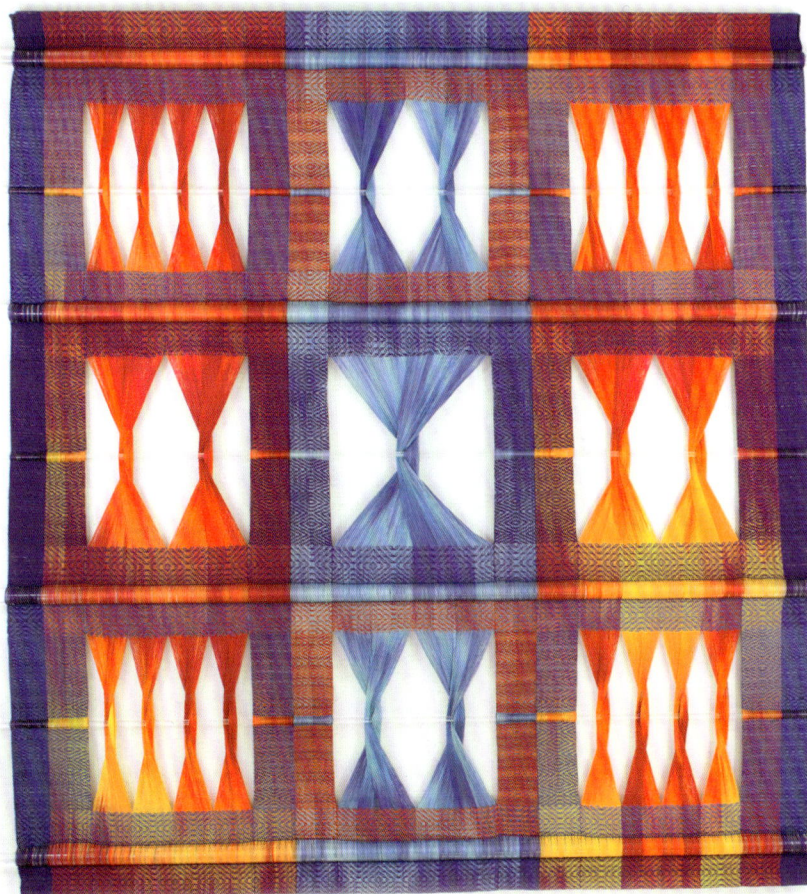

## Weaving Information

Size: 40" x 36"

Warp: 120/2 bombyx mori silk, 30,000 ypp, hand painted; 92 epi

Weft: 160/2 bombyx mori silk, 40,000 ypp, dip dyed; 100-110 ppi; 0.25" and 0.75" acrylic rods

Source: Original draft

Weave Structures: Extended point twill and leno, 8 shafts

Finishing: Ends hemstitched, folded under, spritzed with hot water, and pressed dry on hot.

Mounting: Top wrapped around an inch-wide flat ruler. Hanging attachments affixed to the back of the ruler.

Take-up: Warp 1%

## Tips

• In some circumstances you can skip a block. In this extended twill, both warp and weft blocks share shafts or treadles (1 and 2, 2 and 3, 3 and 4, etc.). One block is always skipped in the warp and weft (B, on shafts or treadles 2 and 3).

• Taking a regular draft and adding small variations adds interest. For example, here only the A block (on shafts 1 and 2 and treadles 1 and 2) has an odd number of threads, whether or not it is a turning point. The B block (on shafts 2 and 3 and treadles 2 and 3) is always skipped. The C block always has six threads rather than the four common to D through H. Repeating these variations in some regular fashion keeps them from looking like mistakes.

• An irregular twill tie-up, where the same pattern is not used on every treadle, results in consistent interruptions of the diagonal twill line. The interruptions punctuate the pattern, adding complexity.

• Constantly changing the tension in different sections of the warp for the leno requires creative and liberal use of fishing weights, careful patience, and "faith that everything will work out."

• Create cleaner color breaks by using multiple shuttles (up to eight here) and hatching, clasped weft, or other tapestry techniques.

• Molly suggests, "Plan on cultivating patience if you want to do hand-manipulated work on this scale!"

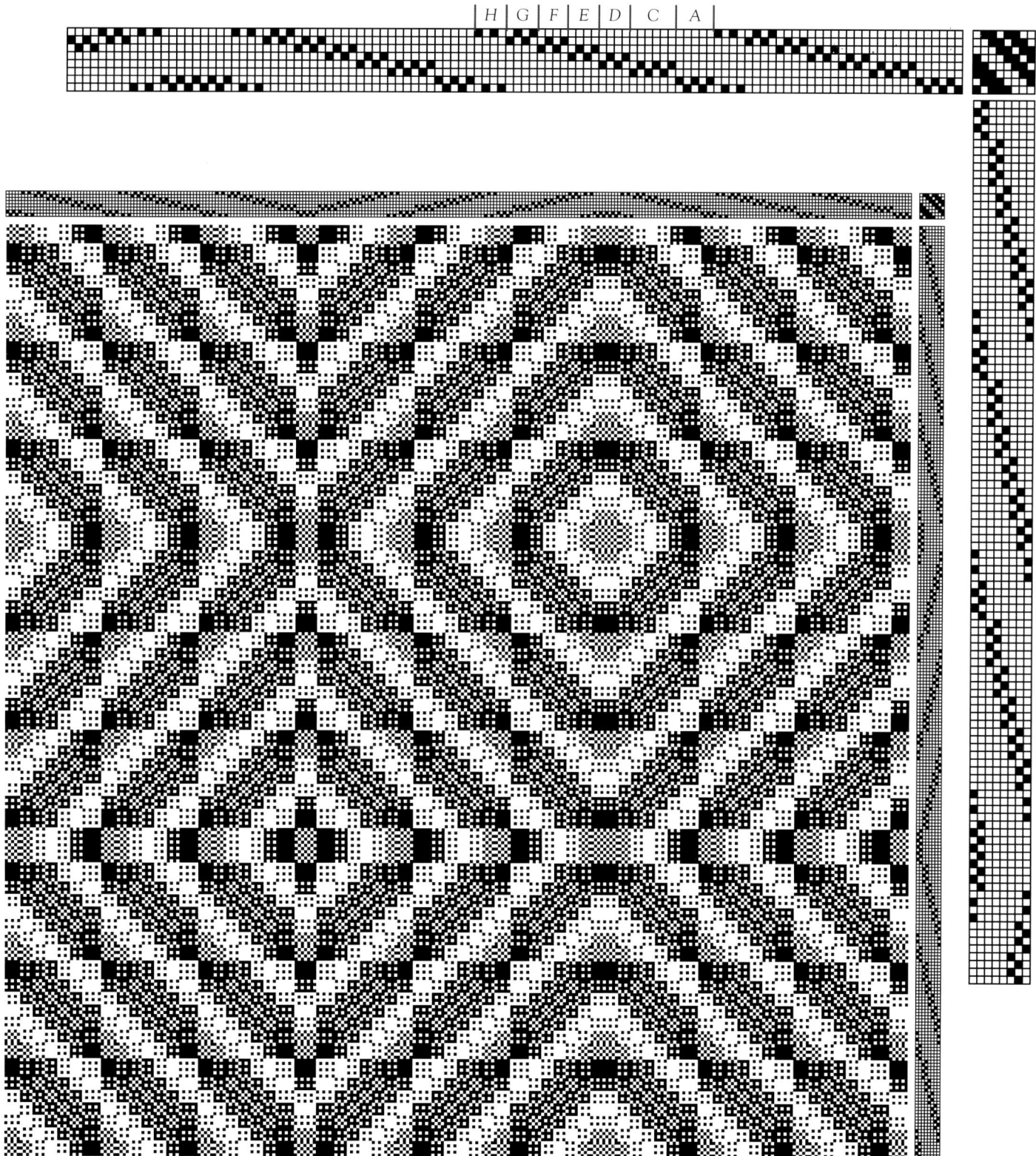

*Threading Draft. A portion of the draft is shown for the irregular extended twill base weave. The tie-up is an irregular twill tie-up, mirrored on one diagonal. There is no true tabby possible. An extra thread has been added to the A block at the right-hand selvedge. The tie-up and a portion of the threading and treadling are enlarged for visibility.*

# Reflecting Windows–Summer Evening

## Fran Osten

### Shawl in Turned Boulevard Weave

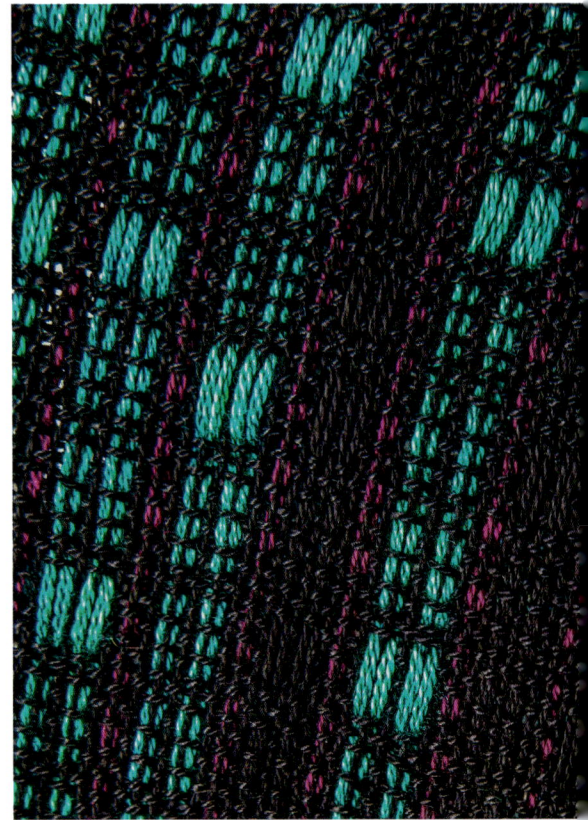

## Design Process

From the time I first thumbed through Strickler's book on 8-shaft weaving, I liked the example of Boulevard weave she included (Strickler, 1991; draft #607). At that time I knew nothing of Bateman's work (Harvey, 1982; Davis, 2017). I was still a "recipe" weaver when I tried a sample I now use as a bookmark. It never went further because I was unsure how to handle the differing strands of various colored pattern weft I was attempting to use. Much later, I decided to try turning the weave so it could be woven with a single shuttle. I used a hand-dyed warp, and the effect was glorious. Small sections could be framed as art pieces. Since that time I have woven several other pieces exploring this design and structure.

I learned a lot about the structure of boulevard by turning it and figuring out what changes needed to be made to the tie-up and why. Turning Strickler's draft yielded a six-shaft, one-shuttle draft, modified by eliminating repeats and simplifying the tie-up. The turned draft eliminated the need to stay within an odd/even progression of blocks in the threading so I could enhance the look of randomness I was seeking. Expanding to eight shafts enlarged the design possibilities by adding two more blocks and allowing more combinations of blocks. The threading block order was chosen to seem random to mimic the effect of Strickler's design. All threads on shaft 3 are red-purple, giving a border to each block. In the black stripes, the pattern threads are single threads; in color sections, the painted threads are doubled.

The weft progression was chosen on the loom to make sure that there were no more than four repeats of pattern in any block. In a further move to keep the random sense of the original, I designed the treadling sequence as I wove, choosing the treadling blocks spontaneously to take advantage of the color changes and to achieve the random look of city apartment windows reflecting the evening light – man-made design superimposed over and reflecting nature. Vertical black stripes were added to contrast and break the random over-all design, adding another layer and structure to the design. This process also gave me a window onto the possibilities for designing more formal pieces with boulevard, an effect almost opposite to the randomness I sought in this piece.

## Tips

• One could also use a heavier colored pattern thread rather than doubling the painted warp pattern threads. The effect would be somewhat different as the double thread spreads more to cover better and is more flexible than a heavier thread. In the case of the painted warp it also allows for two different colors to occur side-by-side.

• While most designs we see in Western weaving are highly symmetric, a random pattern can be particularly pleasing in a garment. Rather than creating focal points through mirrors and other symmetry elements, the eye is allowed or encouraged to travel smoothly over the whole piece.

• Punctuating each block with a "pop" of a single color (here, red-purple) adds rhythm to the random design.

• Using a single color as warp stripes and background, and as weft can calm a complex pattern and make painted pattern threads stand out without being overwhelming.

## Weaving Information

Size: 75.5" x 21" plus 1" fringe on each end

Warp: 8/2 Tencel, 3360 ypp, black, red-purple, hand dyed in blue/green/purple tones over natural; 26 epi (3-3-3-4 in 8-dent reed). The hand-dyed threads are doubled but in separate heddles.

Weft: 8/2 Tencel, 3360 ypp, black; 13 ppi

Source: Inspired by Strickler (1991, p. 180), draft #607

Weave Structure: Turned boulevard weave, 8 shafts

Finishing: Hemstitched over two picks and four ends. Fringe trimmed to 1". Hand washed in warm water using blue Dawn, rinsed and put in washer on spin cycle, then hung to dry. Pressed on rayon setting, lightly steamed.

Take-up and Shrinkage: Warp negligible, weft less than 1%

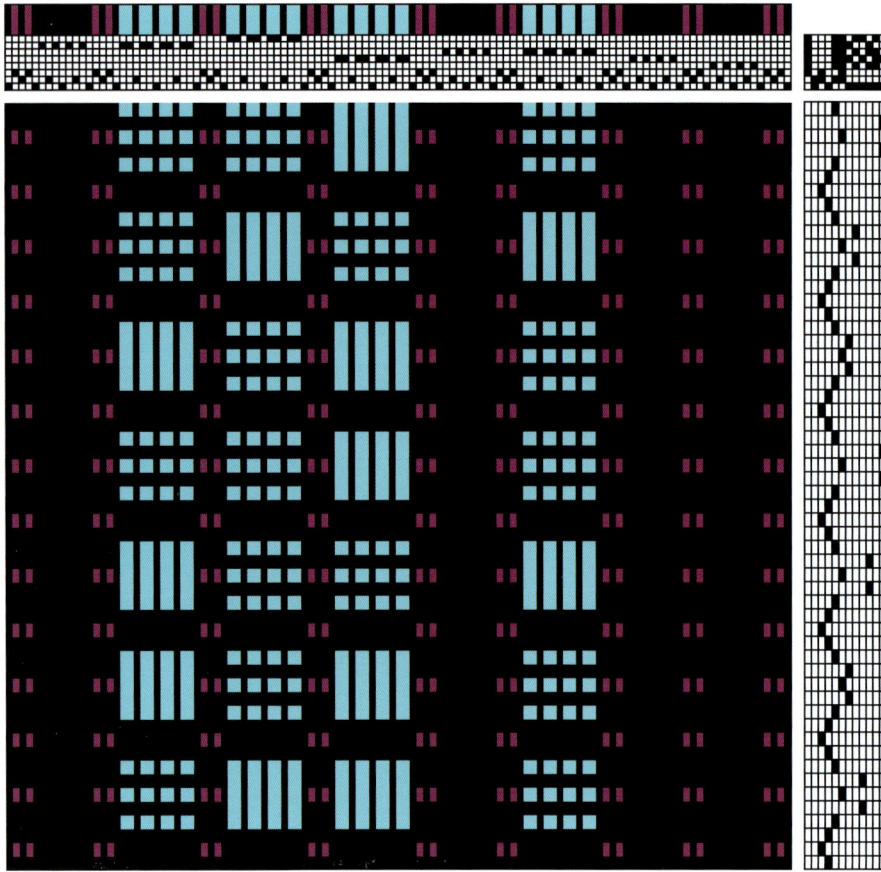

Profile Draft, above. Five blocks threaded and treadled randomly. The black blocks are thinner than the color blocks.

Threading Draft, left. A small portion of the draft shown as a color drawdown. Use floating selvedges (not shown).

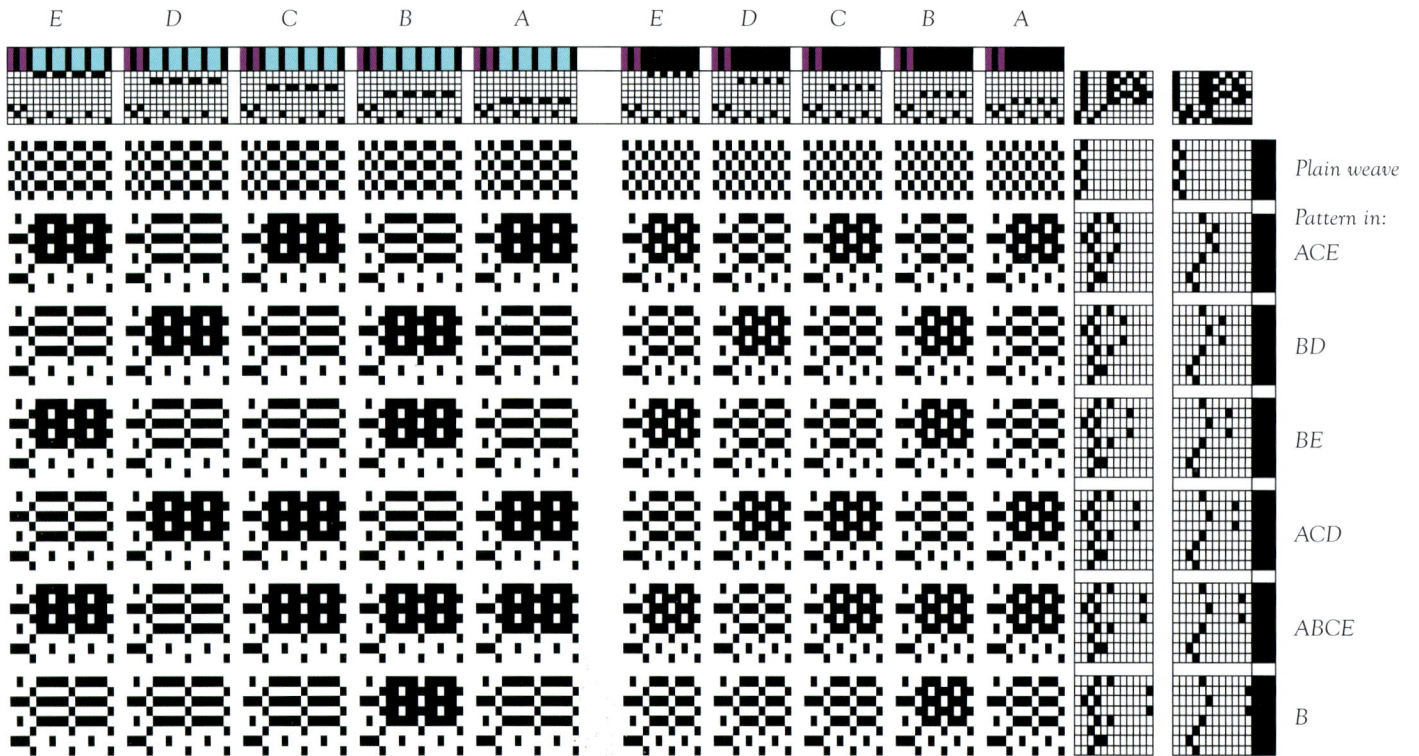

| E | D | C | B | A | E | D | C | B | A | | |
|---|---|---|---|---|---|---|---|---|---|---|---|
| | | | | | | | | | | Plain weave | |
| | | | | | | | | | | Pattern in: ACE | |
| | | | | | | | | | | BD | |
| | | | | | | | | | | BE | |
| | | | | | | | | | | ACD | |
| | | | | | | | | | | ABCE | |
| | | | | | | | | | | B | |

Key to Profile Draft. In the warp black threads are used singly while the painted warp ends (shown in turquoise) are doubled. Warp floats form the pattern. Both a skeleton and a simple treadling are shown.

# Strut Miss Lizzie

## Eileen Driscoll

### Coat in Summer and Winter

## Design Process

We formed a study group and committed to moving from idea to finished garment in nine months. Meeting monthly, we invited mentors and set deadlines. My ultimate goal was an opera coat from the 1920s with a motif that fit the time period. I searched Handweaving.net for inspiration and sampled several designs.

I finally chose #62725, a draft which used a tie-up from Zielinski (#61290, handweaving.net) with an 8-shaft "M and V" threading and treadling from the Divisional Drafting portion of handweaving.net (contributor unknown). Then, I modified the draft from eight shafts to six, and used that draft as a profile for a 6-block tied weave that fit my 8-shaft loom. I kept the "M and V" threading and treadling, and adapted the tie-up to look similar to the original, but on six blocks instead of eight. In my Complex Weavers Tied Weaves Study Group, Su Butler helped me determine the correct sett for my fabric. I am pleased with the drape of the fabric, perfect for a loose and flowing coat.

## Tips

• Chenille often works well with the small floats of tied weaves, such as summer and winter. It brings some of the texture and luster of velvet without the work of weaving true velvet.

• Using an "M and V" for the threading and treadling blocks instead of a simple point makes the design larger, as well as more complex and interesting.

• Reducing the number of shafts or blocks used to make a design can be done in many ways. In this one, the general shapes are retained but run over fewer shafts and/or blocks.

• Use careful choice of sewing details to support rather than overwhelm the handwoven fabric. The purple velvet collar and the aqua lining and piping contrast and set off the handwoven fabric. The lines of the piping form graceful curves which mimic the lines of the fabric drape.

## Weaving Information

Size: One size fits all

Warp: 8/2 Tencel, 3360 ypp, blue-purple, amethyst, and iris; 24 epi

Weft: 8/2 Tencel, 3360 ypp, blue-purple (tabby); rayon chenille, 1450 ypp, lemon-grass (pattern); 24 ppi

Source: Modified from Zielinski (handweaving.net, #62725)

Weave Structure: Summer and winter in brick (alternating) style, 8 shafts

Finishing: Machine washed hot on delicate for six minutes with Synthrapol, rinsed warm, then dried on delicate until just dry. Steam pressed on rayon setting.

Take-up and Shrinkage: N/A

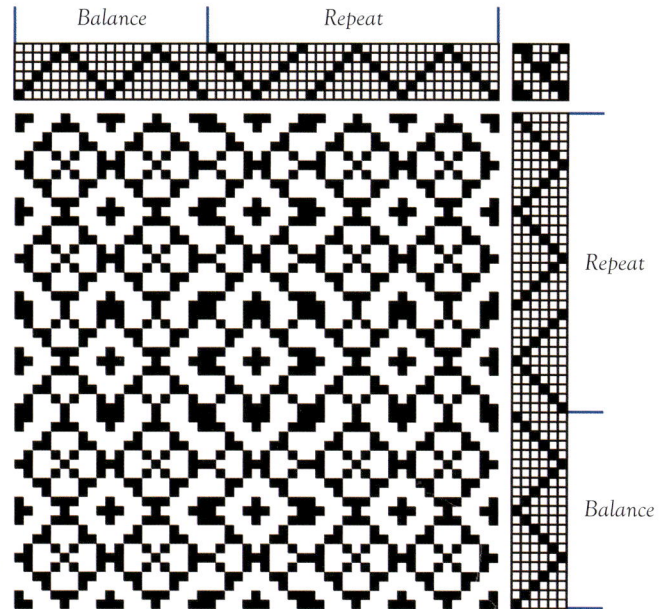

*Profile Draft. Warp and weft have both simple and enlarged points (Ms and Vs).*

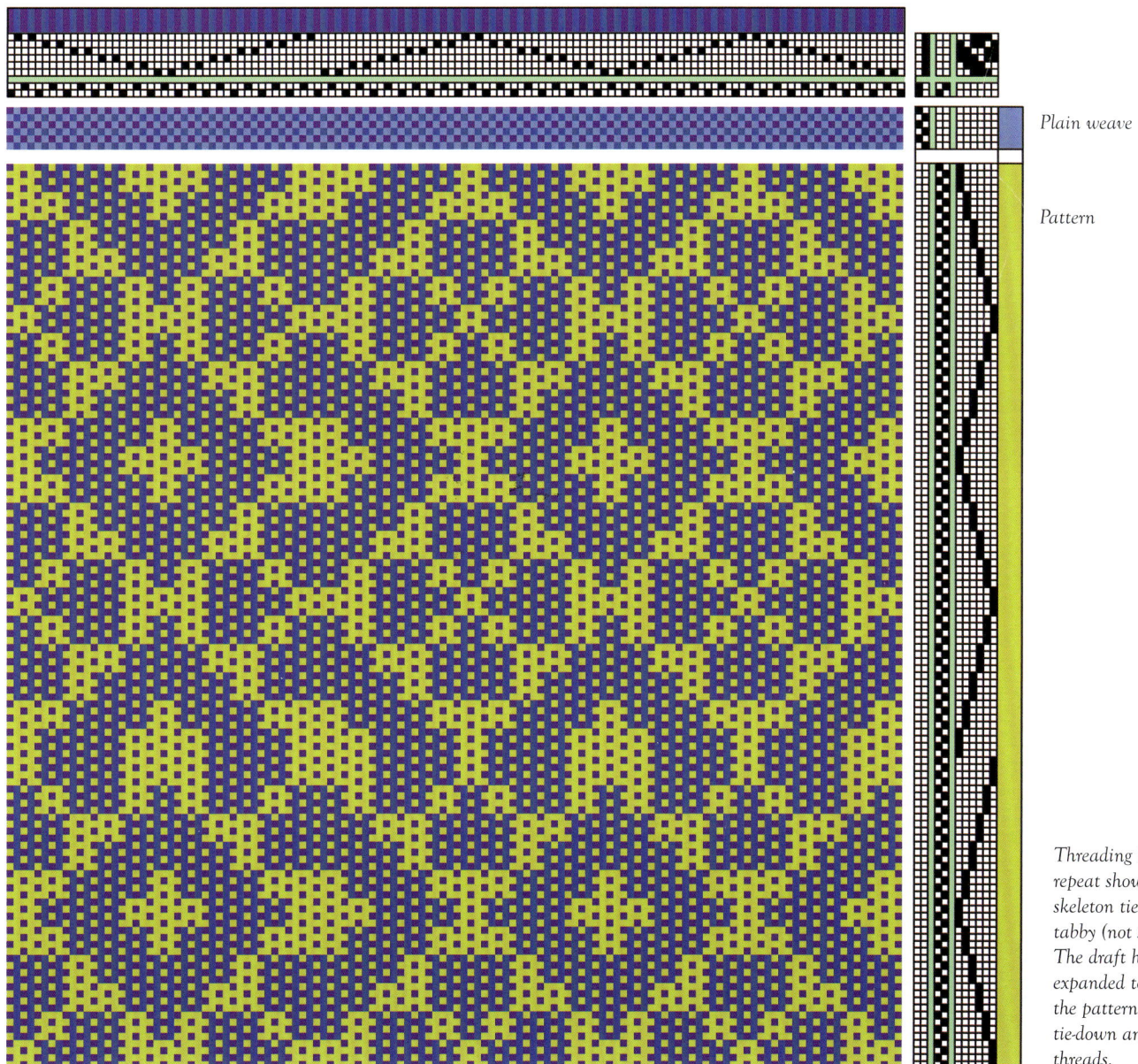

*Threading Draft. One repeat shown with a skeleton tie-up. Use tabby (not shown). The draft has been expanded to divide the pattern from the tie-down and tabby threads.*

Plain weave

Pattern

# Natural Geometry
## Teresa McFarland

### Scarf in Deflected Double Weave

#### Design Process

In the spring of 2015 I studied deflected double weave with Janice Sullivan at City College in San Francisco, and with a study group in the Loom and Shuttle guild of San Francisco. I became a little obsessed with the structure, and spent the whole summer weaving pieces with all sorts of motifs in all weights of yarn, from 3/2 cotton to 20/2 tencel. I wanted to discover the largest and smallest motifs possible, and used them in a wall hanging and in scarves. Then, I moved on to study other patterns and structures.

I often thought about weaving one more very fine deflected double weave scarf using some yarns I had dyed in indigo and usnea lichen. This scarf is the result. It's typical of my weaving in that it uses a very fine weight of yarn, is highly structured, and is slightly asymmetrical. The motifs grow in size from the edges toward the center of the scarf, lending an op art effect. In order to maintain the blue selvedges, I did not weave the straw-colored weft from edge to edge.

## Weaving Information

Size: 62.5" x 6.5" plus 4" fringe on each end

Warp: 20/2 Tencel, 8400 ypp, hand dyed with indigo and usnea lichen; 48 epi

Weft: 20/2 Tencel, 8400 ypp, hand dyed with indigo; 24/2 Tencel/alpaca/nylon (45/45/10%), 6800 ypp, hand dyed with usnea lichen; 36 ppi

Source: Original draft

Weave Structure: Deflected double weave, 8 shafts

Finishing: Began and ended with plain weave. Hemstitched over six picks and ends, then made twisted fringe of two bundles with overhand knots. Washed by hand in warm water with Dawn for 15 minutes, rinsed, then hung to dry until damp. Pressed on medium.

Take-up and Shrinkage: Warp 15%, weft 18%

## Tips

• Beginning and ending with a little integrated weave provides a stepping stone from the fringe to the pattern. It also gives a firmer edge to ply the fringe against.

• Not taking all threads from edge to edge is an unusual trick which can be very effective. If you try it, be sure your longer edge floats are stable. If not, you may get a similar effect by carrying extra shuttles up the edges to replace missing picks, or by using a stabilizing finger-manipulated weave such as leno or Brook's bouquet in those areas. If more shafts are available, the edges could be put on a separate set of shafts with a different, closer interlacement such as plain weave, or even doup leno.

• When using asymmetry, it needs to be asymmetrical enough (as here) to look like an enhancement rather than a mistake.

Balance    Repeat          Border (reverse to end)

Border (reverse to end)

Repeat

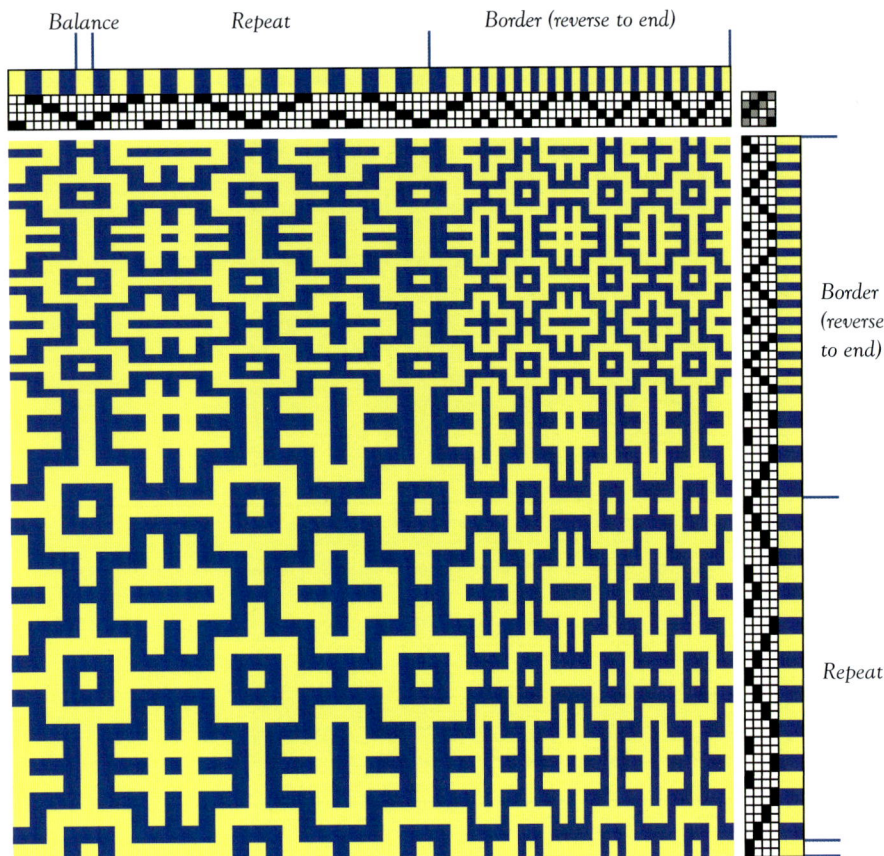

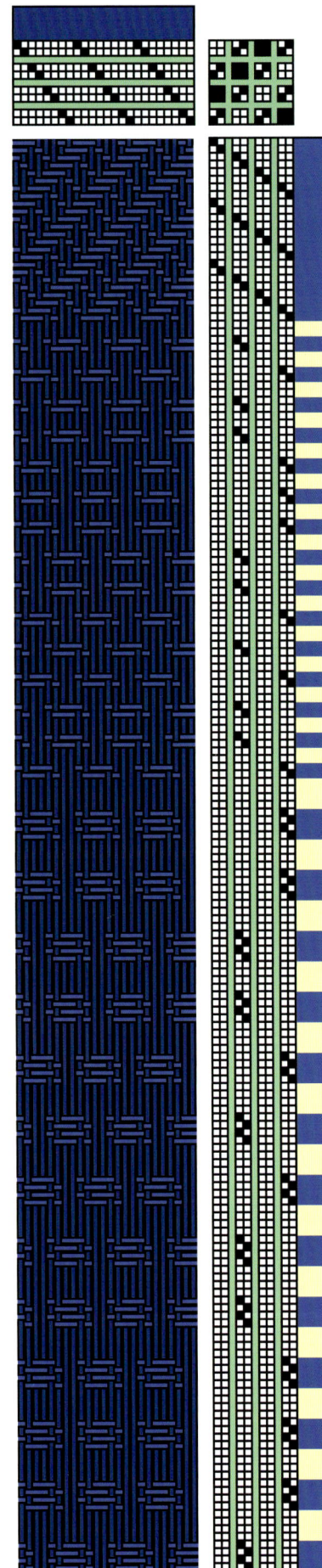

*Profile Draft. Body of piece. In the tie-up white indicates a block weaving weft floats, black indicates warp floats, and gray indicates plain weave. The blocks follow an irregular point pattern, expanding and contracting the points.*

D    C    B    A

Plain weave in AC, warp floats in B, weft floats in D

Plain weave in BD, warp floats in C, weft floats in A

Plain weave in AC, warp floats in D, weft floats in B

Plain weave in BD, warp floats in A, weft floats in C

*Key to Profile Draft. Expanded to separate the 2-shaft blocks. A block weaving weft floats has no ties, a block weaving warp floats has four ties, and a block weaving plain weave has two ties on the diagonal.*

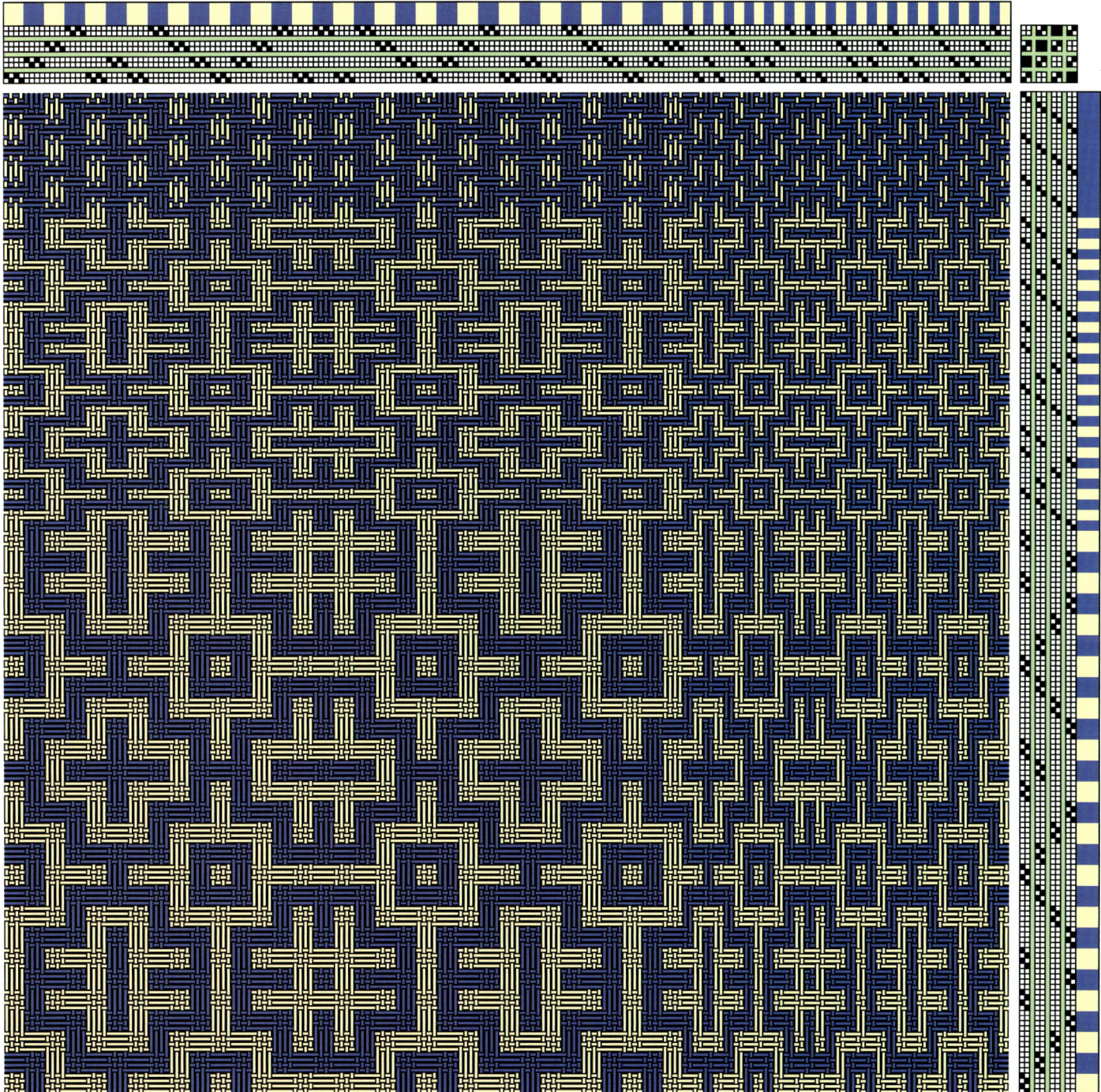

*Threading draft. Portion of draft showing top border and part of the body of the piece. The draft was expanded to separate the blocks.*

# Snowflakes on the Pine

## Gay Orpen McGeary

### Coverlet Hanging in Star Work (Odd Tied)

## Design Process

The 19th-century coverlet weavers who immigrated to the US from Germany adapted their multi-shaft point twill star patterns, used for weaving linen, to the star work weave to enhance their coverlets. Odd tied star work (McGeary, 1979; 2006; Gordon, 1995) is also called multi-shaft float work historically. Often referred to as uneven tied overshot in modern reference books (e.g., Keasbey, 1993; van der Hoogt, 1993), it is not actually overshot.

Each shaft in the twill pattern was enlarged to a block with at least two threads, creating larger, more decorative patterns for the early bedcoverings. With two shafts for tie-downs and 14 to 20 shafts for pattern, these star work patterns required 16 to 22 shafts. A second tradition of double weave coverlets also required 16 to 24 shafts for their 4- to 6-block patterns. By adapting the double weave block designs to star work the contemporary weaver can realize the beauty of the block designs in a different interlacement. With these concepts in mind, I have been designing a series of star work patterns on eight shafts or fewer with the flavor of the double weave designs.

For this coverlet, I chose the Virginia Beauty pattern often used for double weave and summer and winter coverlets. I redesigned the pattern for the star work weave keeping in mind the constraints of the multi-shaft float work weave. Tree motifs, a variation of the main pattern, were designed to frame the center field of the coverlet.

Fringe is an important design element for my coverlets. It surrounds my throw-size coverlets on three sides. For this coverlet, I decreased the size of a 19th-century tied fringe woven in plain weave to be applied to the finished piece. Finally, I added 1.5" hems at the top and the bottom of my coverlet so it could also be used as a wall hanging, which is my preferred treatment. I want to see the total effect of the yarn, pattern, weave structure, and fringe.

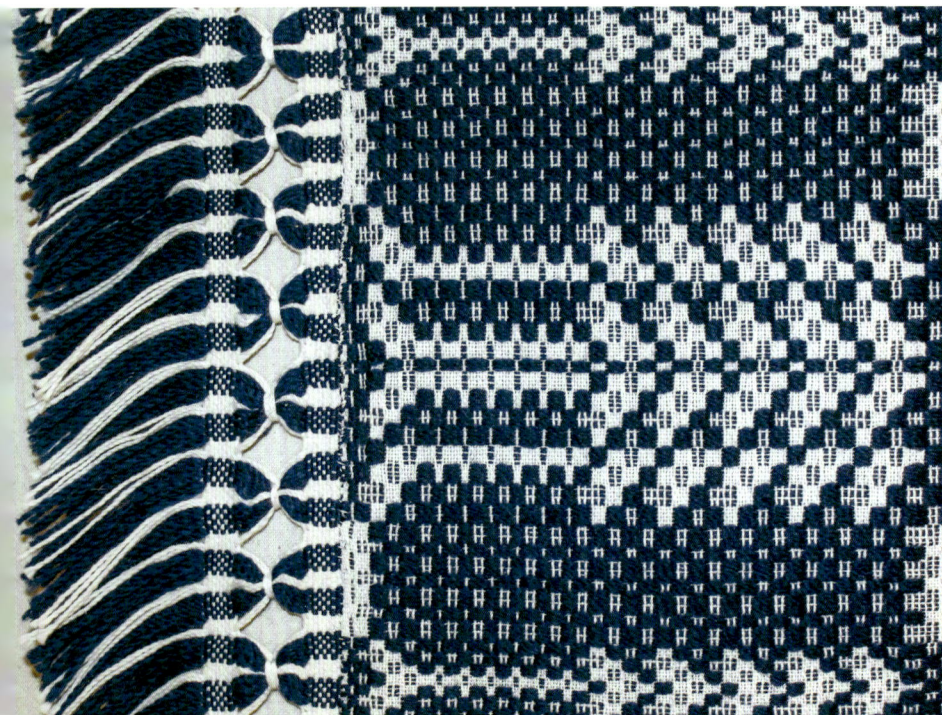

## Weaving Information

Size: 53.5" x 41" including added fringe of 4.5" on three sides

Warp: 10/2 unmercerized cotton, 4200 ypp, natural; 20 epi

Weft: 20/2 unmercerized cotton, 8400 ypp, natural (tabby); 8/2 wool, 2240 ypp, navy (pattern); 40 ppi including tabby

Source: Inspired by Virginia Beauty pattern historical double woven coverlet, found in research done by the weaver

Weave Structures: Coverlet, Odd tied star work, 8 shafts; applied fringe, plain weave with finger manipulations to tie bundles, 2 shafts

Finishing: Fringe woven separately and sewn onto coverlet with 20/2 cotton, gathering around corners. Placed in warm water and moved in the water for a couple of minutes. Laid flat to dry. Pressed and hems flattened with wooden mallet. Fringe trimmed to 4.5" after finishing.

Mounting: 1.5" sleeves are sewn to the top and bottom for hanging.

Take-up and Shrinkage: Warp and weft 10%

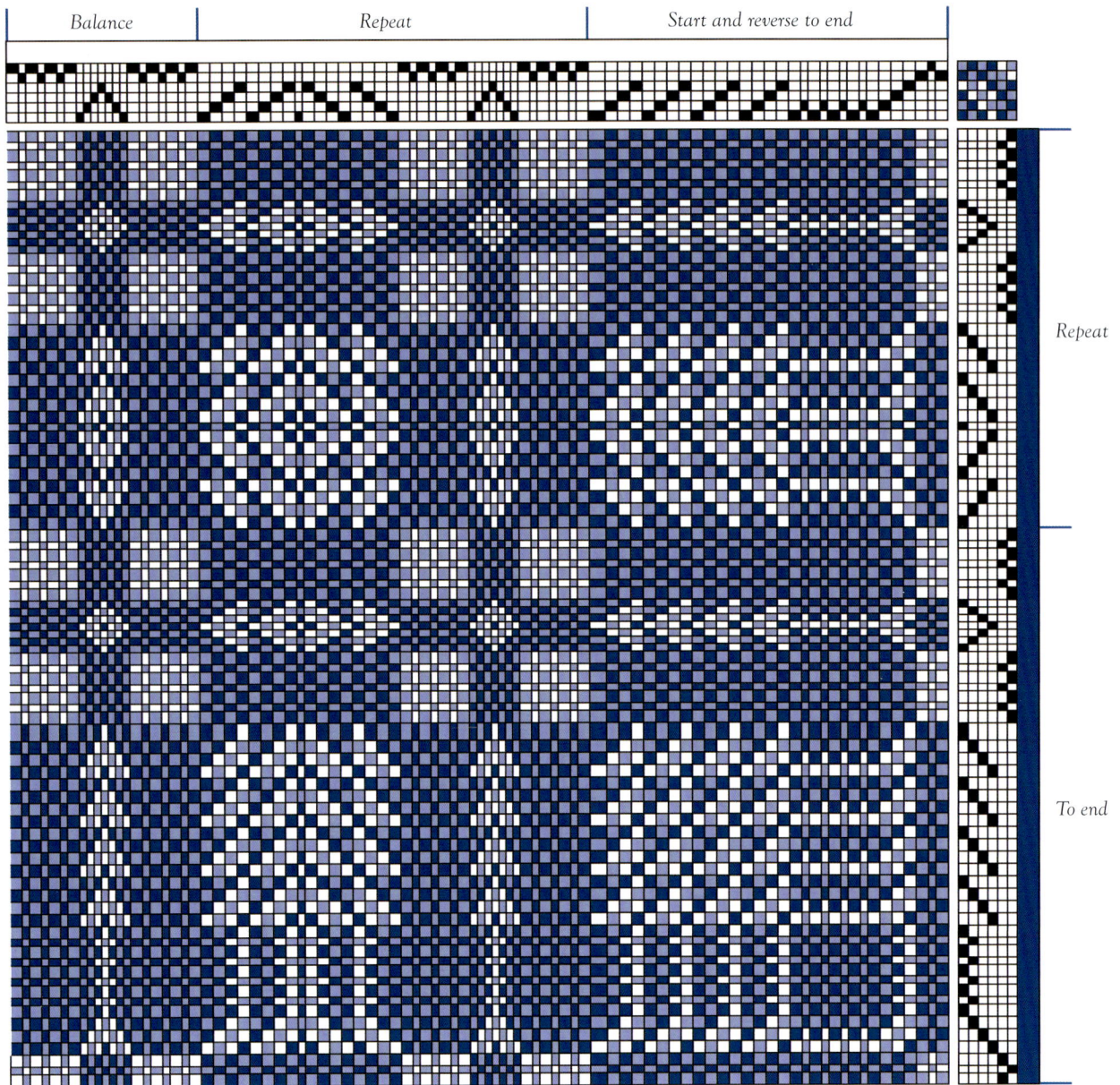

Repeat

To end

*Profile Draft. Lower right portion. The block size (3-, 5-, or 7-thread) is indicated by the relative widths of the blocks.*

*Full pattern (weft float) blocks are shown in dark blue, half-tones in light blue, and background, which forms the figures, in white.*

F E D C B A

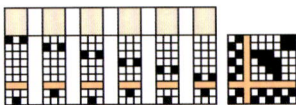

Pattern ACE, half-tones BF, background D

Pattern BF, half-tones ADE, background C

Pattern AE, half-tones CF, background BD

Pattern DF, half-tones BE, background AC

Pattern AC, half-tones BDE, background F

Pattern BD, half-tones ACF, background E

**Key to Profile Draft.** The key is based on 3-thread blocks. Adjust to larger blocks as needed and use tabby (not shown). Note that the figures are formed from the background blocks. The draft has been expanded to divide the pattern threads from the tie-down and tabby threads.

7     5     3

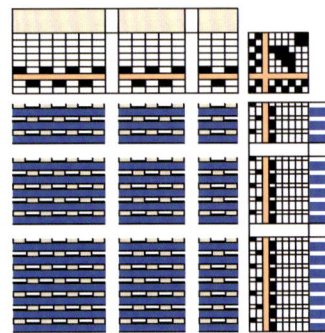

3

5

7

**Key to Block Size.** Blocks vary between three, five, and seven threads in the warp. In this draft, the A block is shown at all three sizes, with pattern plus tabby for each block size. The number of pattern threads in the weft equals the number of warp threads in the block.

48

## Tips

• When you find a pattern you like which requires more shafts than you have available, consider other structures. If the original blocks take three or more shafts per block, often you can reduce that to one pattern shaft and one to three tie-down shafts per block, with the tie-downs shared between blocks. Careful analysis will allow you to see if some features of the original can be preserved in the new structure. In this case, moving from one structure to another used similarly within the same tradition works well.

• Similarly, if you have more shafts available, consider changing to a structure which increases the number of shafts required if that complements your design direction.

• The float areas may be used as background rather than pattern.

• With care about float length, the blocks can vary in size.

• Other 19th-century fringe techniques can also enhance the weaving. These decorative fringes are woven separately with hand manipulation.

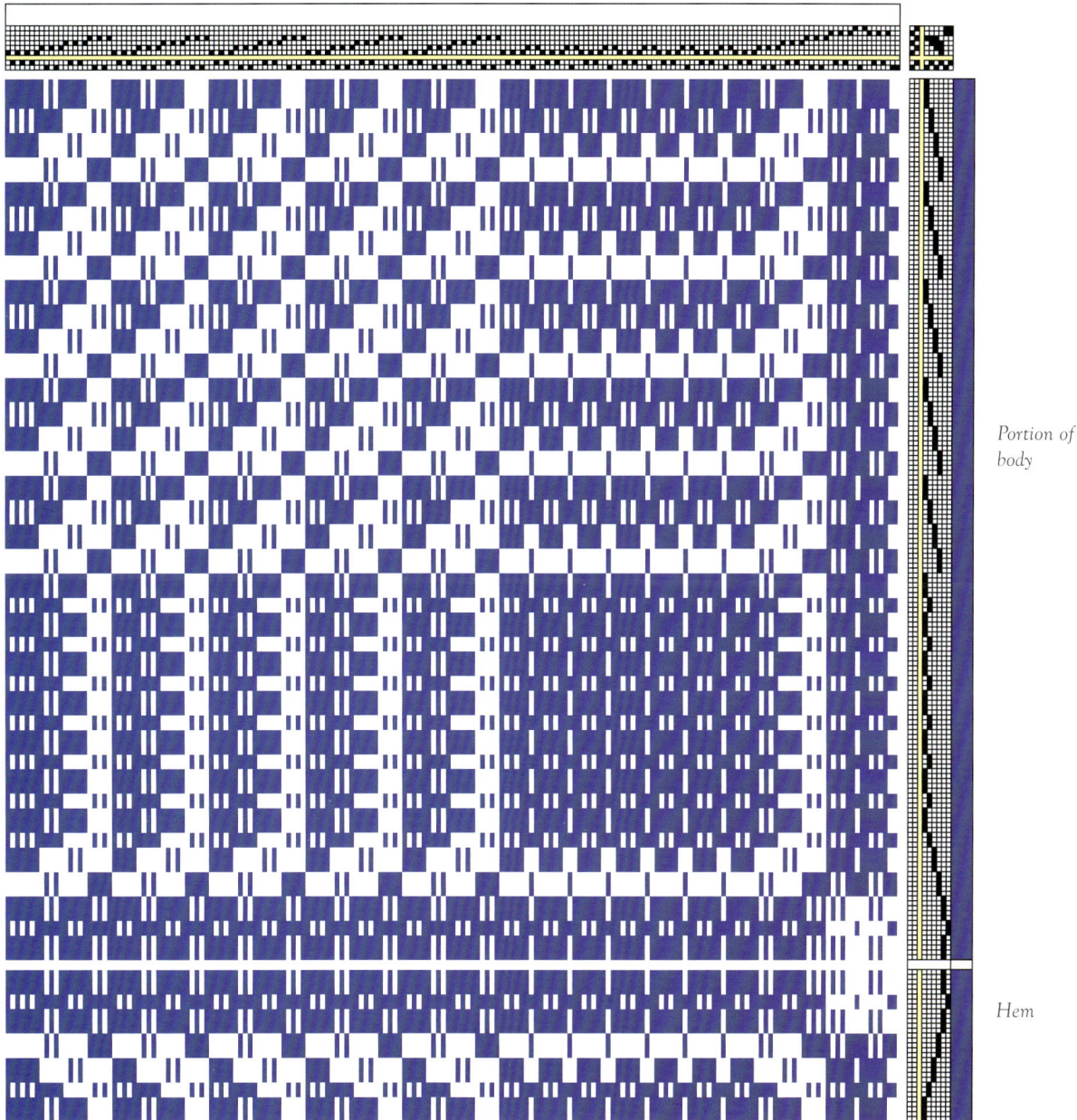

*Portion of body*

*Hem*

*Threading Draft. Lower right portion of draft with hem. Use tabby (not shown). The final threads at the selvedges are doubled. The draft has been expanded to divide the pattern threads from the tie-down and tabby threads.*

# Night Out
## Leslie Killeen

Vest in Point and Networked Twills

### Design Process

A 2012 Cross Country Weavers sample which featured black and white plus one color was the starting point for this fabric. I started drafting in Fiberworks PCW, working first in black and white. Failing to find commercially available colors to match a chosen graphic, I decided to use black and tan with very narrow stripes of stash colors, orange, blue, and green. The color placement was done in the draw program, using the light and dark areas as a guide. A single weft color, black, completed the piece. This fabric was awarded the Complex Weavers Award at the 2016 Complex Weavers exhibit, Complexity. Wendy Morris, one of the jurors, wrote in a WeaveTech entry (used with permission): "It would be easy to assume at first sight that this was a multi-block design woven on 24 or more shafts but in fact it was the result of extremely well planned and worked through threading and treadling variations incorporating aspects of color-and-weave, and it was woven on only eight shafts."

The threading is a straight draw with several reversals. The threading and color placement does not repeat across the piece of 659 warp ends (Killeen, 2014). The tie-up, worked in quadrants, has a plain weave area, two 3/1 twill areas, and a 1/3 twill area. The treadling includes sections of straight draw and networked areas, with a repeat of 620 picks. While a computer-aided loom for weaving is not necessary, it is doubtful that this design would have been produced without a drafting program.

My fabrics often find their way into clothing, usually vests. Recently, as is the case here, I have added color-coordinated handmade wet-felted pieces to complement the woven fabric. Commercial fabric is used to line and trim the vests with beads and buttons for surface design interest.

### Weaving Information

Size: Adjustable

Warp: 10/2 mercerized cotton, 4200 ypp, black, tan, orange, blue, and green; 30 epi

Weft: 10/2 mercerized cotton, 4200 ypp, black; 21 ppi

Source: Original draft

Weave Structure: Straight twill with reversals in the threading and a networked twill treadling, 8 shafts

Finishing: Hand washed in warm water with Orvus Paste, rinsed in cool water, and spun in washing machine. Hung to dry and pressed while still damp.

Sewing: Original vest pattern combined with hand wet-felted pieces. Beads and buttons were added.

Take-up and Shrinkage: Warp and weft, 4%

*Threading Draft. Partial draft (full treadling repeat with about a third of warp) showing complex interplay of color and structure. The warp consists of long runs of straight draw, reversing occasionally, and the weft has been networked on a straight initial of four. The weft is shown as dark gray rather than black to differentiate it from the warp.*

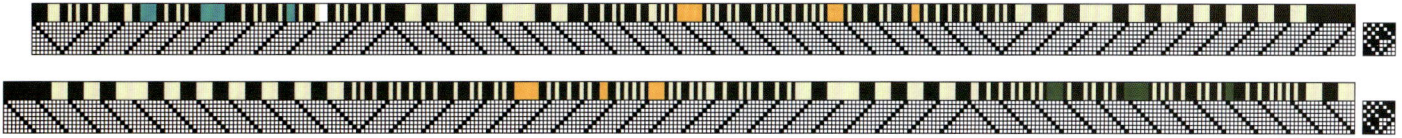

*Complete Threading. Color placement is indicated.*

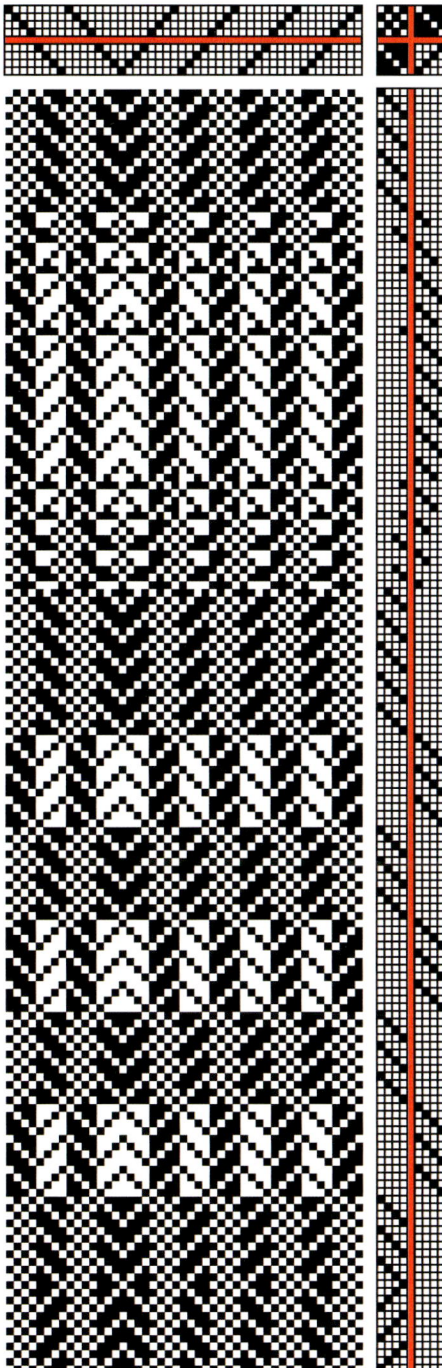

*Reversal point*

*Threading Draft. Expanded section to show structure without the color changes. The tie-up can be broken into a block tie-up with quadrants of plain weave (upper left), 3/1 (lower left and upper right), and 1/3 (lower right) twills. The networked treadling falls strongly into the left or right half. A lesser number of runs cross both, leading to visual grading in those areas.*

## Tips

• A drafting program can help you explore many options very quickly, often leading to a different and more intriguing endpoint.

• Subtle changes in color placement can have big effects. Here, the colored stripes are nestled into areas where the black and tan stripes are narrower (one to three threads vs. four to eight threads). These areas also have more black in them than in the wider stripe bands, making the colored stripes stand out more.

• Using stripes of black in the warp with a black weft creates a way to partition the design visually into many different sections, creates rhythm, and provides places to rest the eye.

# For My Brother
## Andrea Blackmon

### Scarf in Interleaved Irregular Twill

### Design Process

This project was close to two years in the making. I took a class in double weave with Jennifer Moore, who mentioned she was inspired by sacred geometry and other math concepts. I started researching sacred geometry, symmetry, math, and so on. In my research, I came across some articles on the web written by Ralph Griswold. In "*Designing with Power Sequences*" (Griswold, 2003), he developed several drafts based on these sequences. I didn't understand his process, but thought some of the drafts looked interesting.

I set that aside as a study group I belong to decided to go through *Weaving with Echo and Iris* (Stubenitsky, 2014). I began to explore iridescence and liked the challenge of using four parallel (echoed) lines. I made a couple of drafts based on Marian Stubenitsky's technique and enjoyed the process. Then, I remembered the power sequences and decided to try one of them. I extended the pattern by doubling each thread and made a threading with four parallel (echoed) lines. It didn't occur to me that I would get "stripes" from the breaks in the line of the threading because of the addition of the parallel lines. It was a pleasant surprise.

I typically work in 10/2 cotton or 10/2 Tencel. About a year ago, I bought some rayon embroidery thread with the plan of using it in my weaving one day. This seemed like a good time. The rayon gave the scarf a nice hand; it is soft and has a nice drape. I will definitely be doing more of this technique.

### Weaving Information

Size: 77" x 11.75" plus 3" fringe on each end

Warp: 10/2 mercerized cotton, 4200 ypp, antique, quarry, forest green, and lipstick; 32 epi

Weft: #40 rayon embroidery thread, 13,000 ypp, dark blue; 62 ppi

Source: Modified from Griswold (2003)

Weave Structure: Interleaved (echoed) irregular twill threading with advancing and reversing Wall of Troy treadling, 8 shafts

Finishing: Machine washed, delicate cycle, eight minutes. Hung to dry, steam pressed.

Take-up and Shrinkage: Weft 3%

## Tips

• Doubling (tripling, etc.) the threads on the base components expands the size of the motifs to fill the desired area without repeating the design and makes the complex pattern easier to read.

• Non-sequential areas ("skips") in the design line can be used to create an ikat effect in parallel or echoed threadings or treadlings.

• Taking two unrelated concepts and combining them often leads to fertile areas for original design.

• If you enjoy mathematics and are intrigued by the idea of integrating it into your own designs, you may enjoy the full series of Ralph Griswold's articles, available on handweaving.net. These articles are straightforward discussions of single, perhaps less familiar, mathematical concepts (often expanded from Wolfram, 2002), with design examples.

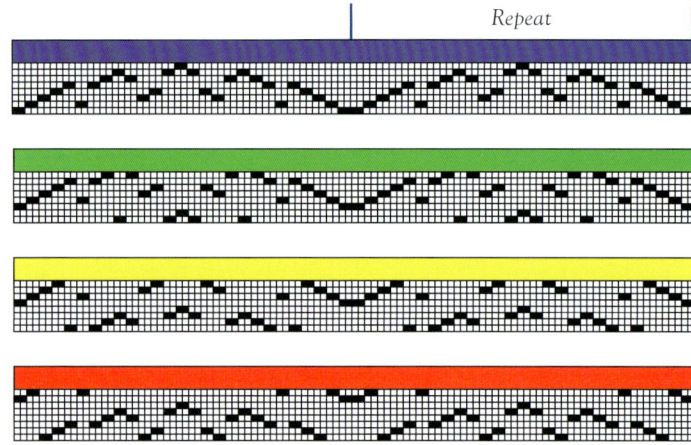

Repeat

Components. The four threading
lines are the same with an interval
of two shafts between them. They are
threaded in the sequence blue, green,
yellow, red.

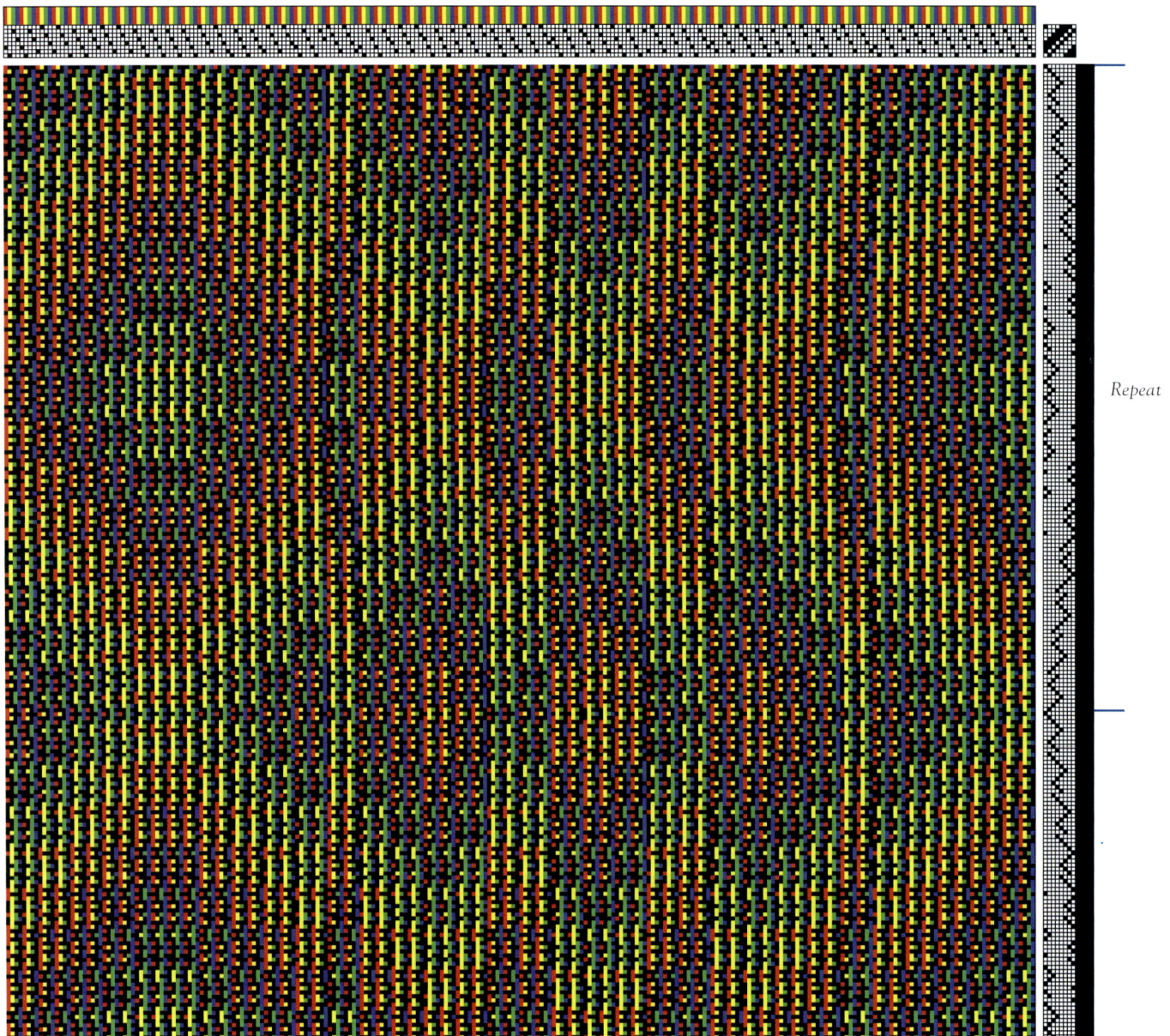

Repeat

Threading Draft. Partial drawdown of interleaved broken twill threadings. The treadling is
an advancing Wall of Troy twill with reversals. A regular 3/3/1/1 twill tie-up is used.

# I.2 Curved Lines

To make a curved line, change the angle rather than keeping it constant.

## Some Ways to Change the Angle

Alter the thread thickness or block size.
*Top left, 8-shaft 2/2/1/1/1/1 undulating twill.*

Alter the number of times the thread or block repeats.
*Top right, 8-shaft 2/1/1/1/1/2 undulating twill.*

Alter the curvature in the tie-up.
*Center left, 6-block profile draft of circles.*

## Continuity

Create flowing lines (*top two drafts*) by proceeding without jumps in warp and weft, with or without bobbles or reversals.

Create circles, ovals, and other closed figures by starting and ending at the same point (*center two profile drafts of circles*).

Even if a line is continuous, abrupt changes in curvature can give a discontinuous or folded feeling to the curve.

## Discontinuity

Create discontinuities by jumps in the threading, treadling and/or tie-up.

*Lower left, Warp and weft discontinuities with a regular 4/1/1/2 tie-up (use tabby, not shown).*

*Lower right, The fancy twill tie-up creates a continuous line in the weft float curves and a discontinuous line in the warp float curves (use tabby, not shown).*

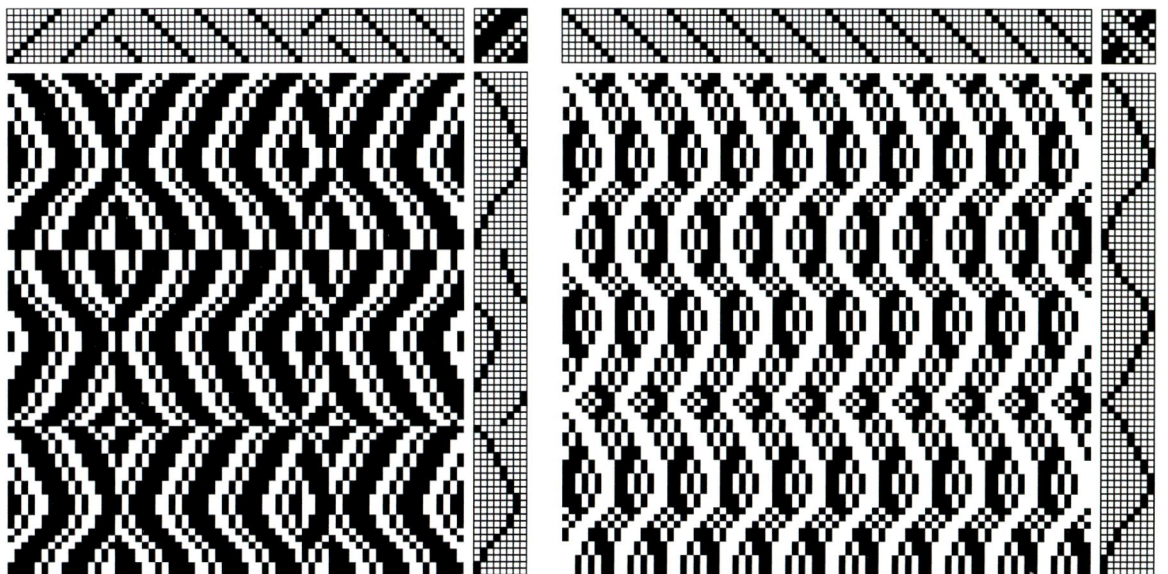

57

# Bubbles

## Lucy Ford

### Handbag in Diversified Plain Weave Variant

## Design Process

I bought a chair that has a cutout and angular back. However, the seat fabric was boring. I started thinking about curves and circles as a nice contrast to the straight lines of the chair.

I knew I needed a cloth with the shortest floats possible. After some research, I settled on diversified plain weave, with circles. Then, I sat down and created a draft using Fiberworks. The colors were selected to unify the putty gray and blue of the room, with a touch of a completely different color, pink, as an accent. The cloth used in this project was the sample. It turned out to not be a good cloth for upholstery because the wool was too stretchy, but the samples make a sweet evening bag!

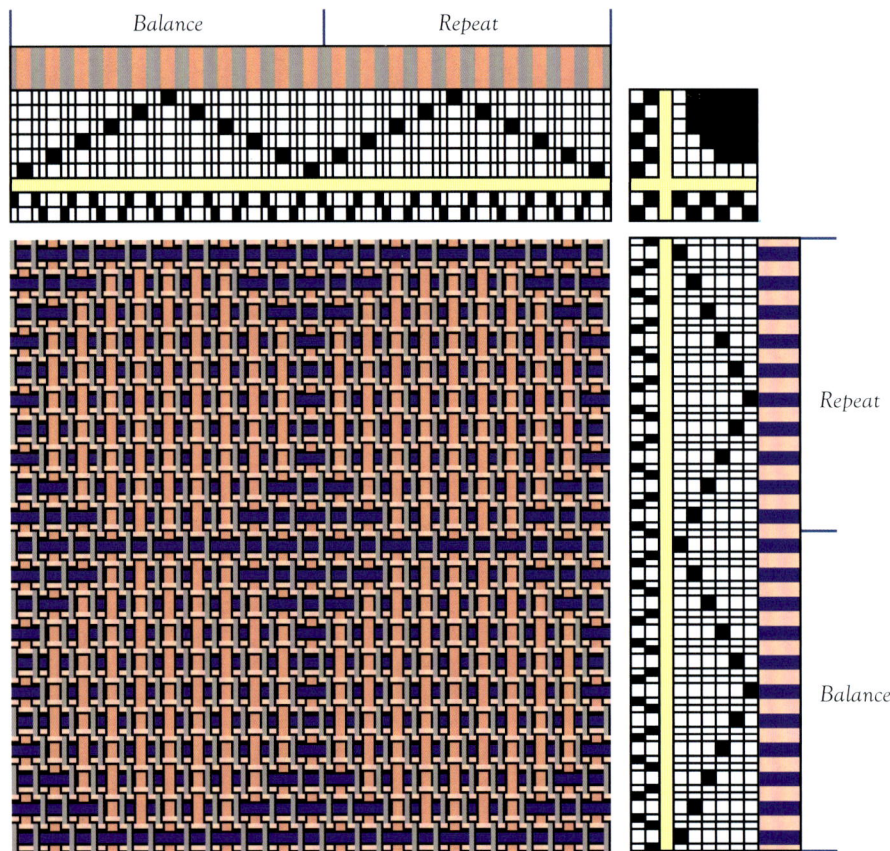

*Threading Draft. In a standard diversified plain weave, the tie-down shaft on a pattern treadle is the opposite of the tie-down on the tabby shots surrounding it. In this variant, the tie-down shaft on a pattern treadle is the same as its adjacent tabbies. Draft colors do not match the piece so that structure may be seen more clearly. The draft has been expanded to separate the pattern from the tie-down and tabby threads.*

## Weaving Information

Size: 7.25" x 6.25" plus cord handle

Warp: 20/2 mercerized cotton, 8400 ypp, gray (tie-downs); 3/5.7 tapestry wool, 1064 ypp, soft pink (pattern); 45 epi

Weft: 20/2 mercerized cotton, 8400 ypp, pink (tabby); 3/5.7 tapestry wool, 1064 ypp, gray and blue (pattern); 48 ppi total

Source: Original draft

Weave Structure: Diversified plain weave variant, 8 shafts

Finishing: Washed on wool cycle in machine, laid flat to dry. Hard pressed on wool/steam setting.

Sewing: No pattern was used. Edges were serged. Panels were pieced onto commercial cotton duck, and then hand-dyed commercial cotton was used for the lining. Side seams were machine stitched. The lining was then hand sewn into the bag.

Take-up and Shrinkage: Warp 15%, weft 10%

## Tips

• Perfect circles like these depend on good design and an exact beat. With a small number of blocks (three to ten), circle drafts generally have a flat or flattened top and sides, and unequal steps on the corners to change the curvature. Changing the beat, or adding or subtracting blocks from the top (warp) or sides (weft) can create ovals.

• Try drawing your circle on graph paper or with a drawing program on a grid that relates to the number of blocks available. Use finer grid paper with the same size circle for more blocks, or a coarser grid for fewer blocks.

• Pick accessories to complement your piece. Here, the diamond-shaped button picks up the diamond in the negative design space.

• Although we tend to stick to very strict rules about tabby sequences and which tie-down(s) to use with a given block, playing with these variables can yield interesting, viable results. Here, the tabbies are swapped from the usual pairing in diversified plain weave, resulting in a less common, softer variant. Always sample and finish to be sure that your innovation works.

• When a fabric does not work for its intended job, it may be very well suited to a different use. Step back from your initial assumptions and goals, have a time-out with your favorite beverage, and think about it from other angles rather than heading straight for the scissors.

# Summer Garden
## Dorothy Solbrig

### Runner in Deflected Double Weave

### Design Process

This project began as a set of placemats for a retirement/house remodeling present for my brother. His wife wanted green and pastels and I was looking to learn more about deflected double weave. I studied the structure (van der Hoogt, 2007) to learn how to predict the way blocks will shape themselves after deflection. Then, I developed the color profile I used here as a design tool. The profile drawdown doesn't translate completely to the threading drawdown. It is useful in designing, but you still have to understand when a block will be constrained in deflection by blocks from the other layer. It also does not show the color mixing within a layer, which is an important part of my design.

I wove a set of placemats, each one different. I began with a basic tromp as writ treadling, varying the order of the weft colors, but after two placemats I decided to use other treadlings. After a lot of time at the computer trying different treadling profiles, I chose some and wove six more. There was enough warp left for a runner for myself, so I augmented one of the placemat patterns.

I like playing with color variations, so I found some closely related colors to weave in combinations. I bought four colors of 10/2 cotton. The yellow was much stronger than the other colors, so I used it separately as an accent, and worked the combinations with the other colors. Blocks A and C are thin threads, with four threads per block; Blocks B and D are thick threads, with two per block. The order of the structural blocks (ABCDCDCB) is straightforward; the order of the colors of the thin cotton threads is more complex, aiming to give all possible color combinations of three colors in the various "flowers" (single structural repeat).

Within each repeat, the A block is yellow; the first and third C blocks are the same color, either pink, peach, or apricot; and the second C block is one of those three colors but not necessarily the same as the other C blocks. In the treadling, the basic repeat is ABCDCDCB, as in the threading, but groups of three or five flower repeats are separated by treadling blocks DCBABABCDA. Within the group of five flower repeats, the color pattern in the C blocks is similar to that in the threading, with colors rotating to give all possible combinations through the runner. Within the group of three repeats, all C blocks in a flower are the same color, the three flowers having different colors, and the order changing throughout the runner.

The color arrangement clearly works much better on the front side, but the reverse side is also interesting. I like the different patterns of the two layers. I had made a point of using the same amount of each of the 10/2 colors, so I was a little surprised at how yellow the reverse is compared to the front.

### Tips

• In deflected double weave, the two warps (thick and thin) have distinct selvedges. Here, the thick green threads are on the outside of both edges, and the thinner 10/2 cotton has a different selvedge which is sometimes above and sometimes below the green. When the layers change, the color of the 10/2 also changes. The old weft color can be carried along as needed by pushing the 10/2 shuttle through the warp just inside the two outer thick threads to the other side (upper or lower) of the warp.

• Complex color rotations and patterns are ways of making a few colors appear like many more. When the values are similar, as in this case, the effect is subtle and painterly.

• Circles and curves may not be apparent in the draft. Structures which deflect, such as deflected double weave, lace weaves, Ms and Os, and honeycomb, often do not look like their threading or profile drafts. To get a better understanding of the relationship of the look of the final cloth to the draft, weave and wet finish many samples, study other people's examples, and look at photos of the woven structure in each case with its threading draft.

*Profile Draft Threading. Full profile threading with block colors indicated.*

## Weaving Information

Size: 39" x 10.5" plus 4" fringe on each end

Warp: Block Island Blend, rayon/cotton/hemp (30/35/35%), 1400 ypp, green; 10/2 perle cotton, 4200 ypp, pink, peach, apricot, and yellow; 16 and 32 ppi (24 ppi overall)

Weft: Block Island Blend, rayon/cotton/hemp (30/35/35%), 1400 ypp, green; 10/2 perle cotton, 4200 ypp, pink, peach, apricot, and yellow; 16 and 32 ppi (24 ppi overall)

Source: Original draft

Weave Structure: Deflected double weave, 8 shafts

Finishing: Twisted 2-ply fringe with overhand knots combining thick and thin threads. Machine washed in warm/hot water with detergent and dye catcher, machine dried until damp, then pressed.

Take-up and Shrinkage: Warp 9%, weft 10%

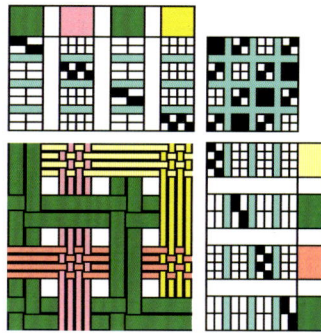

*D   C   B   A*

Plain weave in AC, warp floats in D, weft floats in B

Plain weave in BD, warp floats in A, weft floats in C

Plain weave in AC, warp floats in B, weft floats in D

Plain weave in BD, warp floats in C, weft floats in A

*Key to Profile Draft. Expanded to separate the 2-shaft blocks. The green blocks are always two thick threads in warp and weft, while the other colors are always four thinner threads per block. In the tie-up, a block weaving weft floats has no ties (right, #1), a block weaving plain weave has two ties on the diagonal (right, #2), and a block weaving warp floats has four ties (right, #3).*

*1      2      3*

*Block tie-up options.*

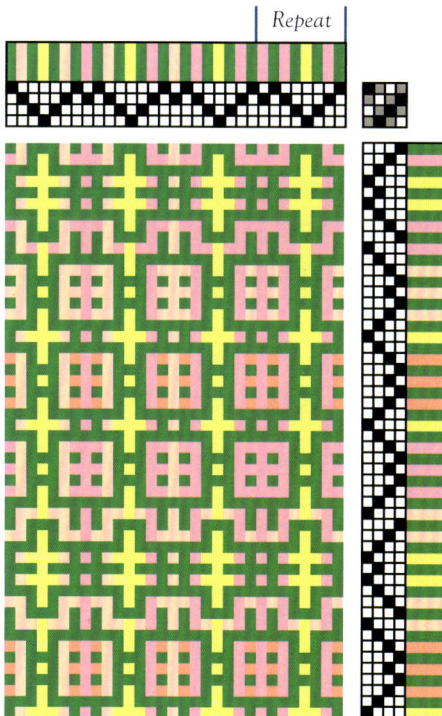

*Repeat*

*Profile Draft. Partial draft with block color indicated. The blocks in the warp follow an M-type point pattern, while the blocks in the weft follow an Ms and Ws-type point pattern (1W, 3M, 1W, 5M). In the tie-up, white indicates a block weaving weft floats, black indicates warp floats, and gray indicates plain weave. Note the change in the woven look after deflection.*

Threading Draft.
Portion of threading draft shown. Although the pattern looks very square, when woven and finished the squares become circles. This is an example of how the draft may be only an incomplete suggestion of the fabric.

# String of Ovals

## Eva Stossel

### Yardage in 4-Color Integrated Double Weave

## Design Process

I was inspired by the four-color double weave samples woven by my fellow members of the Complex Weavers Fine Threads Study Group, and so I studied the chapter on this topic in Stubenitsky's book (2014) with great interest. Among the various design methods described in the book, I chose the one used for designing plain weave layers that are integrated rather than being separate. Then, I used a tie-up for 8 shafts and 16 treadles that produces four-color blends that are the same on both sides but in different areas. Using weaving software, the draft was generated from my threading and treadling design lines. After making a few minor changes I thought the final pattern was rather pleasing.

My design process included extensive sampling by trying different types, sizes, and colors of yarn. The finished cloth turned out to be sturdy with a slightly heavy hand, and the longest floats are three threads. I plan on using the yardage to make a cushion for an indoor bench.

## Weaving Information

Size: 108" x 22"

Warp: 10/2 perle cotton, 4200 ypp, royal blue and melon orange; 36 epi

Weft: 10/2 perle cotton, 4200 ypp, lipstick red and scarab green; 32 ppi

Source: Original draft

Weave Structure: 4-color integrated double weave (echoed interleaved networked twills), 8 shafts

Finishing: Washed in lukewarm water and mild detergent on gentle cycle in washing machine. Hung on rack to dry until barely damp, then steam pressed on medium.

Take-up and Shrinkage: Warp 6%, weft 5%

## Tips

• Networking the design line in warp and weft on an initial of 2 in each component allows for smooth curves without long floats.

• The two regular twill tie-ups, 1/1/1/1/2/2 and 2/1/1/1/1/2, have no points with more than two sequential shafts raised or lowered. Combined with the initial of 2, no float in the final draft will be longer than three threads.

• Shifting the two lines by four shafts works well with the two regular twill tie-ups chosen. Other intervals (shifts) are possible and will give different, interesting results.

• Using two tie-ups, which are similar but related by inversion, switches the position of the warp and weft floats in the figures on the plain weave background for each component allowing for clear color separation.

• Color choice plays a particularly important role in interleaved drafts of this type. Changes in value as well as hue determine how strongly the pattern reads and whether the colors combine in a pleasing manner.

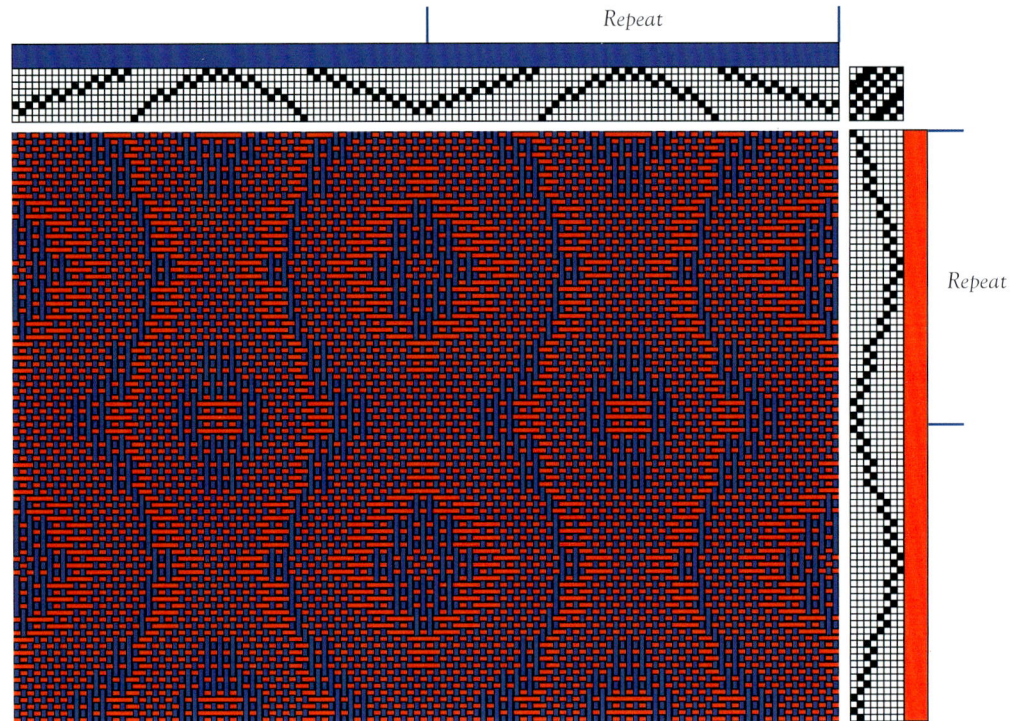

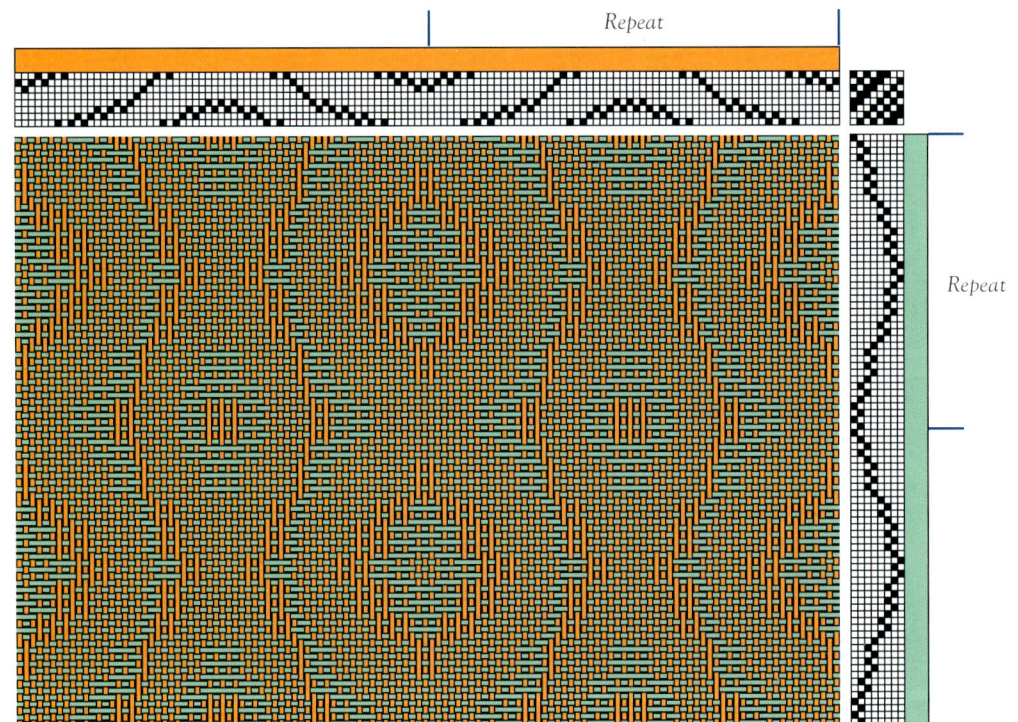

*Component Drafts. The base draft (with blue warp) has a curved point treadling and an enlarged curved point threading, both networked on an initial of 2. The orange component is the same, but shifted by 4 shafts. The regular twill tie-ups, 1/1/1/1/2/2 (blue warp) and 2/1/1/1/1/2 (orange warp) are related by inversion.*

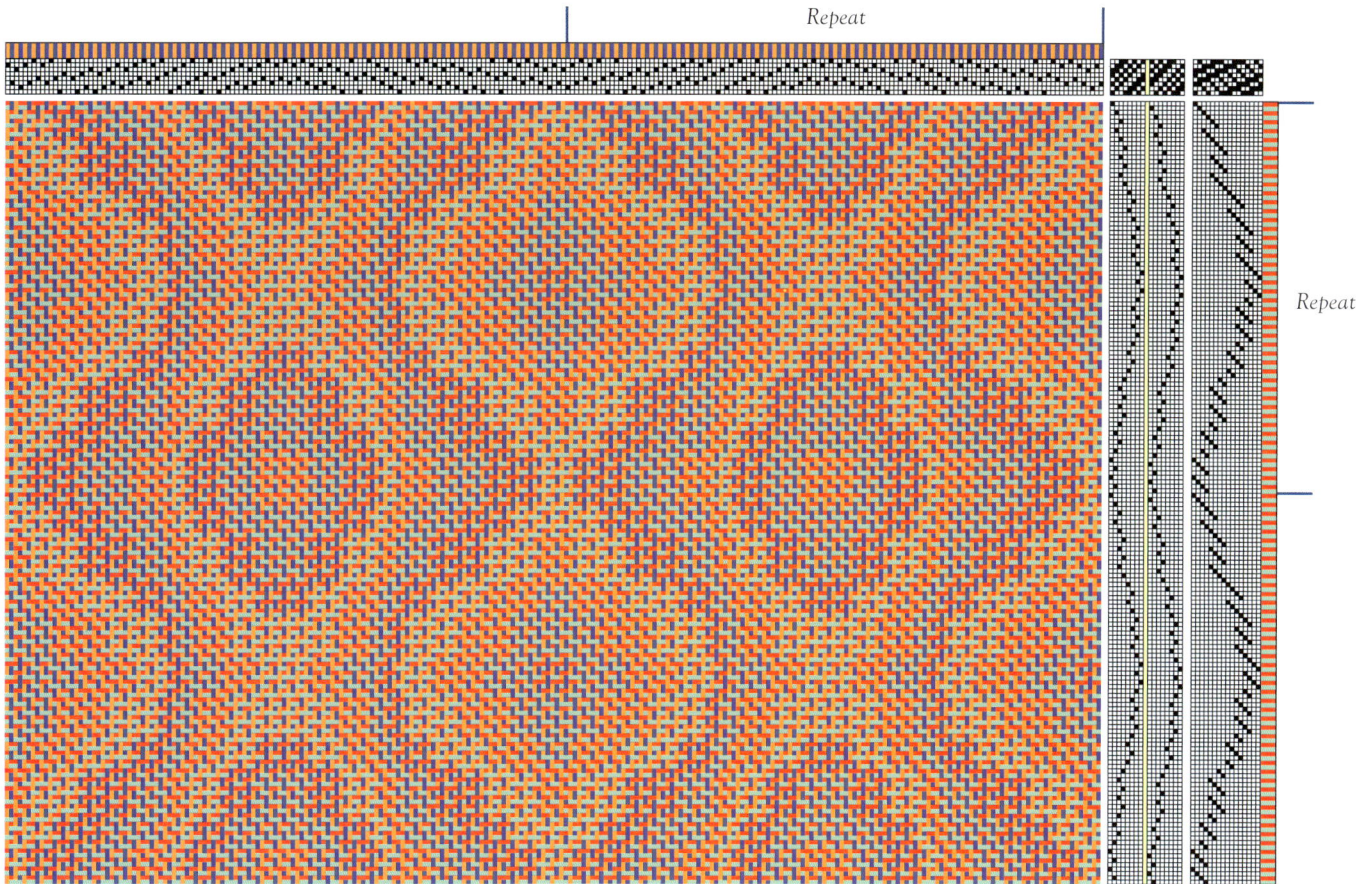

*Threading Draft. The networked component drafts have been interleaved in the warp and weft. In the left treadling the components are separated out, and in the right treadling they are shown in order on one tie-up. When the drafts are combined, the networked treadling initial of 2 becomes an initial of 4.*

# Wedding Rings and Snake in the Grass
## Laurie Duxbury

Scarves in Turned Taqueté

### Design Process

This piece grew out of explorations I started in the Complex Weavers' Tied Weaves Study Group. In 2016 I decided to learn about turned taqueté after seeing quite a few pieces woven in this structure. I dug in and studied as much as I could find. At the same time, I was weaving scarves for our local studio tour show using hand-painted tencel warps. I realized at some point that turned taqueté was a perfect weave structure to show off the movement of the painted warps.

When I came across Bonnie Inouye's article about using overshot patterns as inspiration for turned taqueté designs, the light went on. Overshot is my first love. Using Bonnie's method of converting overshot to turned taqueté meant I could combine the visual drama of overshot with the wonderful hand of tencel and avoid the bulkiness that often comes with supplementary weft pieces.

Inspired by the "Mary Ann Ostrander" overshot pattern (Davison, 1944), I reduced the 4-shaft overshot drawdown to a profile draft. Following the directions given in Inouye (2014), the profile was expanded to eight shafts. Then, using Fiberworks weaving software, I redrew the draft using a network with an initial of 2. I measured a second warp of commercially dyed yarn of equal length and number of warp ends to the pre-wound painted warp. The loom was warped alternating one end from the painted warp with one end from the solid warp across the width of the warp. The first scarf was treadled tromp as writ with the threading from the first component, and the second scarf with a simple point, both with tabby. I am happy with my results and converting traditional overshot into turned taqueté has become kind of an obsession.

### Weaving Information

Size: 72" x 8.25" plus 5" fringe on each end (both)

Warp: 8/2 Tencel, 3360 ypp, mermaid (hand painted and pre-wound by Kathrin Weber of Blazing Shuttles) and azure; 36 epi

Weft: 16/2 bamboo, 6720 ypp, magenta (Snake in the Grass) or azure (Wedding Rings); 30 ppi

Source: Original drafts

Weave Structure: Turned taqueté, 8 shafts

Finishing: Hemstitched on the loom in 12-end bundles. Two bundles were twisted and plied, then secured with overhand knots. Hand washed in warm water with Dawn for three minutes and hung on drying rack to dry. Steam pressed on a cotton setting.

Take-up and Shrinkage: Warp 10%, weft 21%

## Tips

- Alternating a painted or variegated yarn with a plain one showcases the more complex one.

- Traditional 4-shaft overshot patterns are a rich source of designs which can be used with many structures to quite different effect. Converting to a profile allows you to change structure and number of shafts easily.

- Picking a portion of the threading (here, a simple point) is a good way to make another treadling option.

- You do not need to have curves in both warp and weft to have curves in the drawdown.

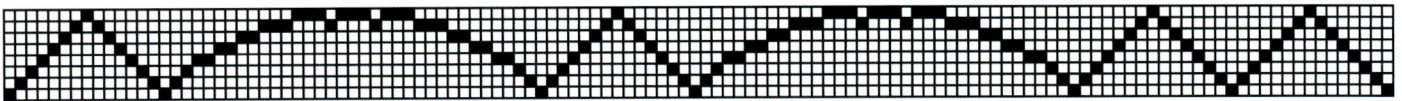

*Design Line. Starting point for the threading, with points and curves.*

*Component Drafts. Threading networked on an initial of 2 with the green threading offset from the purple by four shafts. The regular 4/4 twill tie-up combined with the 4-shaft shift make the resulting drawdowns on opposites. The purple threading above represents the painted warp, and the green, the plain warp.*

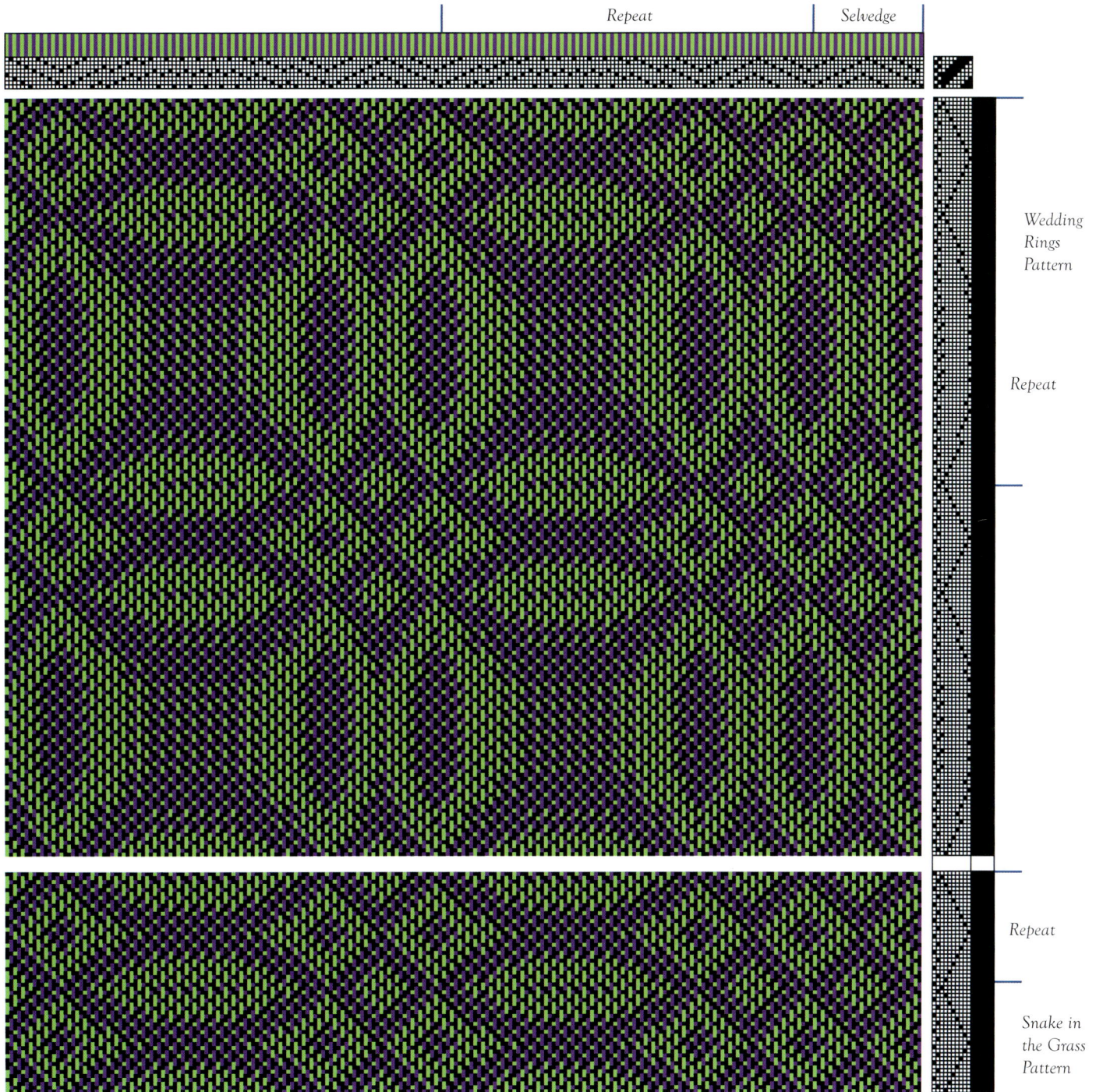

*Repeat* | *Selvedge*

*Wedding Rings Pattern*

*Repeat*

*Repeat*

*Snake in the Grass Pattern*

*Threading Draft. The two threadings are interleaved and woven with a 4/4 regular twill tie-up. Combining the drafts on opposites results in clear separation of the colors. The first scarf uses the blue component threading as the treadling, and the second, a simple point treadling. For both designs, use the same yarn for tabby as the pattern (shown in black for contrast in the draft).*

# Memories of My Mother

## Jean Down

### Shawl in Overshot as Twill

## Design Process

The inspiration for my shawl is the rose motif, a traditional overshot design found in coverlets (Burnham and Burnham, 1972, p. 263). This pattern originates in a coverlet found in Waterloo County, Ontario, Canada, where my mother was raised on a family farm with deep Scottish roots. I chose the rose motif to capture a memory of my mother who loved roses, and then altered the tie-up to create a pleasing modern-looking design. Unexpectedly, a lavender-like image emerged in the new motif, which reinforced more memories of my mother.

An overshot workshop with Bonnie Inouye in 2011 opened my eyes to the design possibilities in overshot designs using non-traditional materials. Fine silk allowed me to create a drapy cloth suitable for a shawl. A 60/2 silk warp was woven with a 30/2 silk tabby and 12/2 silk pattern floats. The warp and tabby weft were dyed in shades of pink and purple to complement the commercially dyed pattern silk in shades of blues, purples, and greens. When I weave my next overshot shawl, I will use 20/2 silk floats to make the cloth even more flowing.

## Weaving Information

Size: 86.5" x 23.5" plus 4.5" fringe on each end

Warp: 60/2 silk, 14,880 ypp, natural hand-dyed pink/coral; 44 epi

Weft: 30/2 silk, 7850 ypp, natural hand-dyed purple/pink (tabby); 12/2 silk, 2800 ypp, blue (pattern); 38 ppi

Source: Original draft

Weave Structure: Overshot woven as twill with tabby, 8 shafts

Finishing: 2-ply hand-twisted fringes of four strands per ply, hand knotted. Hand washed in warm water with Tide and spun in a washing machine. Laid flat to dry and steam pressed.

Take-up and Shrinkage: Warp and weft less than 10%

## Tips

• Changing materials and scale on traditional coverlet weaves expands the number of end uses for these lovely patterns.

• Using a published or traditional draft as a starting point is a good way to create new designs. Small, incremental changes to the tie-up may result in large changes to the drawdown without changing the threading and treadling.

• The elongated motifs in this piece fall in a very flattering way when worn. Not every design needs to be square. If you choose to weave a design that is not square either through beat or design, make sure it is consistent, works well with the intended use, and is far enough off square to read as deliberate, as this piece does.

• Adjust your draft to get the result you want. Removing or adding some pairs of threads in the treadling rather than using tromp as writ can help control the length of the pattern.

Threading Draft. Extended twill, also known as overshot woven as twill, woven with tabby (not shown) on a regular 2/3/2/1 twill tie-up. The pattern treadling is a shortened version of the threading with some pairs of threads removed. The selvedges are simple points while the body consists of longer curves. Plain weave and pattern treadles have been separated in the tie-up and treadling.

# Waves II
## Susan Wilson

### Scarf in Crackle Variant

### Design Process

Crackle is such a versatile weave, especially when weaving it as polychrome (Wilson, 2011). For this project I wanted to move a 4-shaft polychrome technique that Nancy Lyon (1987) called "broken twill polychrome" to 8-shaft 8-block crackle. Nancy's four blocks are treadled 1243, 2314, 3421, and 4132, (the numbers referring to the pattern treadles on a 4-shaft loom with a 2/2 twill tie-up, numbered left to right).

After experimentation on the computer and at the loom, I found that simply extending Nancy's little four-pick treadling sequences over the eight shafts worked best for controlling float length: 1243, 2354, 3465, 4576, 5687, 6718, 7821, 8132. I used a 2/2/1/1/1/1 regular twill tie-up. The bold curved design line from my profile draft floats on a plain weave background. When treadled with magenta weft first followed with turquoise, the design line is outlined by magenta, with turquoise in the center. If the weft color order were reversed, magenta would be in the center with turquoise outlines.

My sampling revealed another effective polychrome with the same treadling but using a 2/1/1/2/1/1 twill tie-up (not shown). The two weft colors made separate design lines, with soft blended edges and just a small amount of plain weave separating the two different colored lines.

### Tips

- Continuous flowing lines impart a feeling of smooth movement.

- Change the curvature by changing the number of repeated blocks in warp and/or weft.

- Elongate the height of the pattern by repeating the weft blocks more than twice; shorten it by using them singly.

- Interleaving two treadling lines which are not the same can result in more complex, nuanced patterning.

- Crackle is a weave with many possibilities. Using an interleaved, unusual treadling on any weave structure can open new corridors. Earlier 4-shaft weavers developed reams of unusual treadlings which are rarely used today. Look for older publications which contain many references to unusual treadlings on four shafts. With ingenuity, these techniques can be expanded to more than four shafts. The usual difficulty using these variants with an 8-shaft treadle loom is that they may require more sheds than the number of available treadles.

### Weaving Information

Size: 56.5" x 6.5" plus 4" fringe on each end

Warp: 60/2 silk, 14,500 ypp, dark blue; 36 epi

Weft: 16/2 soy silk, 6400 ypp, dark magenta and turquoise; 36 ppi

Source: Original draft

Weave Structure: Crackle woven as broken twill polychrome, 8 shafts

Finishing: Wove three picks of plain weave with warp yarn at each end. Hemstitched on loom over three picks and ends. Three hemstitched bundles were plied together and secured with overhand knots. Washed and rinsed by hand in warm water. Hung to dry and steam pressed.

Take-up and Shrinkage: Warp and weft less than 1%

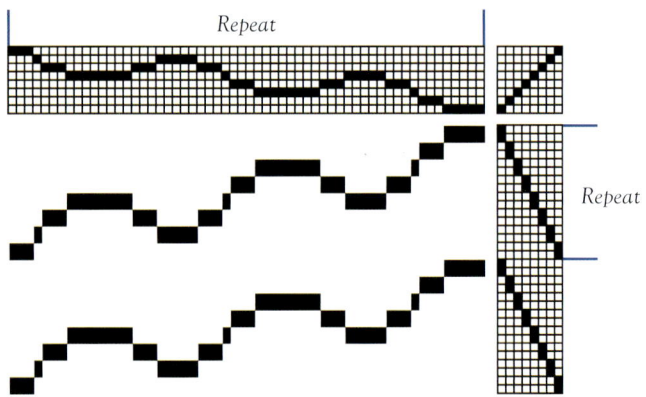

Profile Draft. Eight blocks form flowing curves in warp with simple straight treadling.

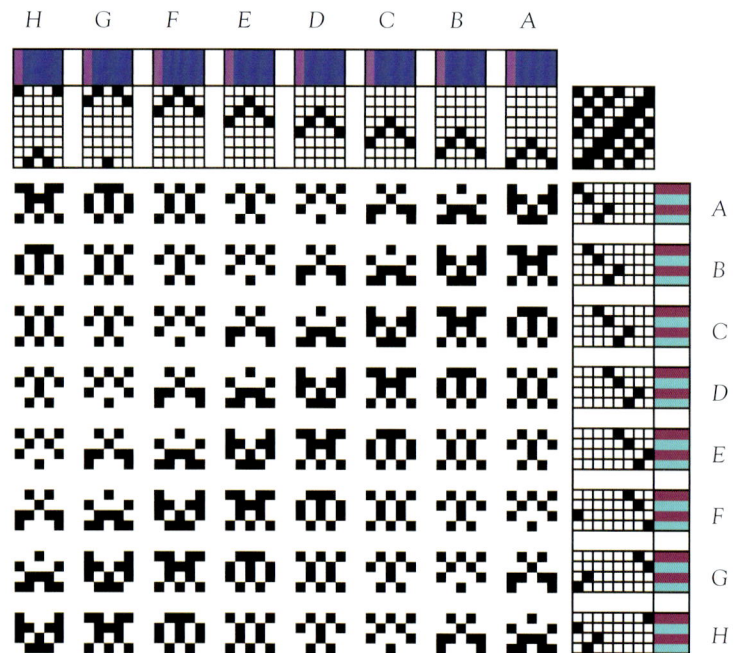

Key to Profile Draft. Crackle is an irregular block weave, requiring an extra thread in the warp when changing to an adjacent block. The incidental threads in the warp are indicated in purple for clarity.

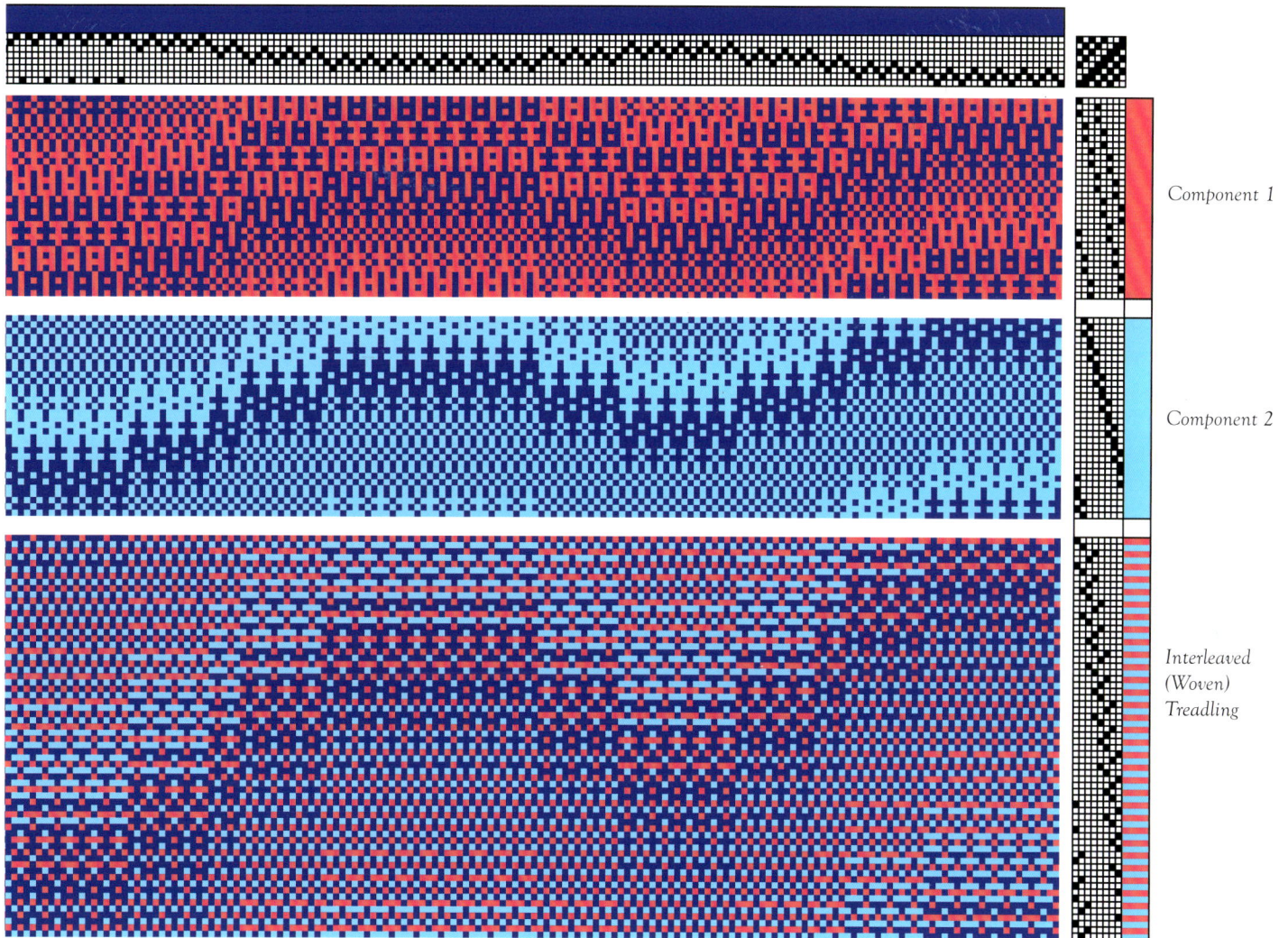

*Threading Draft and Treadling Components. The alternating colors of the unusual 4-thread broken treadling sample different parts of the regular 2/2/1/1/1/1 twill tie-up for a series of color interactions. The red weft treadling (component 1) has a set parallel skip of three treadles (1 then 4, 2 then 5, etc.) resulting in softly grading color bands. The aqua treadling (component 2) is more linear (2 then 3, 3 then 4, etc.) and has more sharply defined color banding. Interleaving the two results in a subtle, complex interplay. Portion of threading shown, with one full repeat of each treadling. Use floating selvedge (not shown). Note that each four-thread sequence in the woven treadling is repeated twice (repeat as desired).*

*Component 1*

*Component 2*

*Interleaved (Woven) Treadling*

# Swirls
## Sheila Carey

### Scarf in Deflected Double Weave

### Design Process

I was inspired by an article by Marguerite Gingras (2001) and wanted to try deflected double weave in some sort of advancing twill order. Looking though old Weaver's magazines, I found an article by Madelyn van der Hoogt (1999), which gave me the information needed to create a design. The colors were chosen partly by what was available and partly because red is my favourite color. I made the scarf and then bought a red coat to wear with it!

I had hoped that the wool would shrink more than the silk, causing the silk to pucker (Fry, 2002, project 20, p. 56). Instead, the wool I used did not full a lot, and pressing gave a smooth, soft hand to the scarf.

In hindsight, I find the treadling I used rather busy and would do another with just one repeat of the "diamond" pattern at one end with half repeats for the rest of the scarf. I also like the designs that I get when treadling just three of the four blocks. These are quite different, with no curves in sight.

I learned a lot about handling my shuttles in order to have good selvedges when weaving deflected double weave. Some day I would like to try this design with two yarns in complementary colors, or using a shiny and a dull yarn in different values of the same shade.

### Weaving Information

Size: 56" x 7.5" plus 1" fringe on each end

Warp: 20/2 silk, 4900 ypp, natural; 2/20 worsted wool, 5600 ypp, red; 30 epi

Weft: 20/2 silk, 4900 ypp, natural; 2/20 worsted wool, 5600 ypp, red; 30 ppi

Source: Original draft

Weave Structure: Deflected double weave, 8 shafts

Finishing: Ends hemstitched with the wool. Fringe cut to 1" with no further finishing. Machine washed in top loading machine in warm water with Ivory dish soap. Agitated for approximately ten minutes to full, rinsed in warm water. A dye magnet was used to prevent bleeding of color. Laid flat on a net sweater dryer until damp, and hard pressed.

Take-up and Shrinkage: Warp 14%, weft 12%

### Tips

• When working with two yarns with different elasticity (stretch), wind the two threads together on a warping mill or board to maintain the same tension on each rather than winding two separate warps and combining them at the loom.

• When weaving deflected double weave, wrap the weft ends around each other at the edge in the correct order to keep the edge joined. The order will change depending on which block is on top at the selvedge, so experimentation may be necessary.

• Designs do not need to repeat in both directions and are often more dynamic when they don't. Check the effect of a design which repeats only in the warp versus only in the weft to see which might suit the end product best.

• Repeating a design which is asymmetric in one or both directions adds rhythm.

• Selecting a portion of the design to extend one side and use on the ends can provide balance and is a useful design tool.

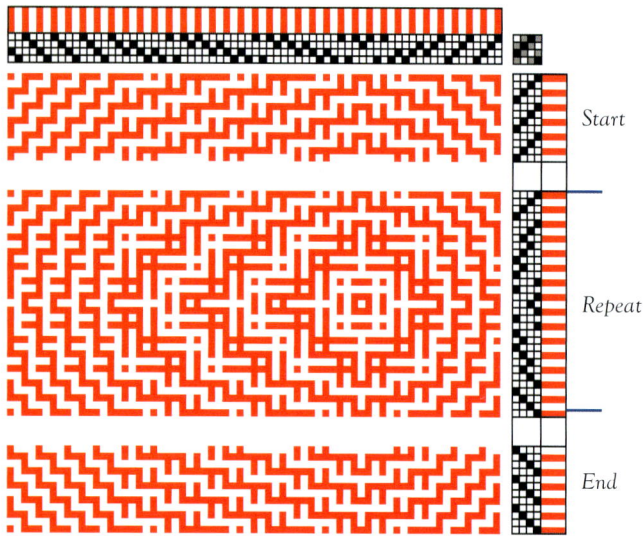

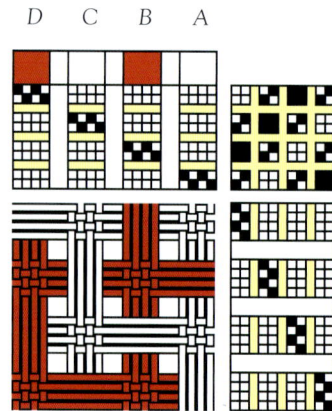

*Profile Draft. The blocks follow a long asymmetric curve with one point. In the tie-up, white indicates a block weaving weft floats, black indicates warp floats, and gray indicates plain weave.*

*Start*

*Repeat*

*End*

D  C  B  A

*Key to Profile Draft. Expanded to separate the 2-shaft blocks. In the tie-up, a block weaving weft floats has no ties, a block weaving warp floats has four ties, and a block weaving plain weave has two ties on the diagonal.*

*Plain weave in AC, warp floats in B, weft floats in D*

*Plain weave in BD, warp floats in C, weft floats in A*

*Plain weave in AC, warp floats in D, weft floats in B*

*Plain weave in BD, warp floats in A, weft floats in C*

*Threading Draft. Portion of the drawdown shown. When the fabric is finished, the curves of this deflected double weave become more pronounced.*

# Tribal Dance
## Bonnie Inouye

### Scarf in Echoed Threading with Point Treadling Variation

## Design Process

I enjoy weaving flowing curves. For this scarf, I started with a profile draft for a threading with an "S" curve using eight shafts. I made the base threading sequence alternate odd and even-numbered shafts by converting it to a network on an initial of 2. The result is the threading for warp A, the red wool, with 50 ends per repeat. A diagonal progression in the treadling will show the design of the curve, so I tested my profile threading with a long, straight diagonal line and then with variations.

My warp has three parallel (echoed) lines of threading, one line for each color. Sometimes known as "echo weave," this method is not a proper structure as it can lead to many different interlacements. I tested the intervals with several drafts using Fiberworks, inserting dark blue as the second line and purple as the third threading line. These three threading lines start on shafts 1 (red warp), 5 (dark blue), and 3 (purple). I had planned to use navy but found that I was running low. So, I added a dark blue wool of about the same size and alternated a few strands to ease the transition. Other options were also nice but this arrangement of the colors also works well with four-color double weave and turned taqueté (Inouye, 2014). I have woven samples of these and like them, too.

The regular 3/1/1/3 diagonal tie-up works well with the treadling sequence, where two points advance together. I have been working with advancing point sequences since 1993, often including two or three points before advancing (Inouye, 2000). The treadling is long enough for graceful curves but not too difficult to remember. The points show clearly in parts of the cloth so I can find my place if needed. In the scarf, I reversed the sequence several times, testing the overall design with weaving software. There is some iridescence to the fabric.

## Tips

• Create drafts to test various intervals between the lines in the threading and weave samples. An uneven spacing may prove interesting.

• A relatively close sett allows the warp colors to show in the scarf.

• Networking a design line on an initial of 2 creates an odd-even sequence, suitable to many interlacements (Schlein, 1994). It can be done by hand on graph paper, or, more quickly, using one of several different weaving programs.

• The double weave hems require an extra four treadles, shown separated from the pattern treadles in the draft. If your loom does not have 12 treadles, you can re-tie for the hems, or eliminate them and make fringes or use another end treatment.

## Weaving Information

Size: 75" x 8.5"

Warp: 2/28 wool, 6880 ypp, red; wool/rayon (65/35%), purple; wool/silk (50/50%), dark blue; wool, navy (all similar weights); 30 epi

Weft: Three strands wound together; 120/2 silk, 29,760 ypp, grass green; 60/2 silk, 14,880 ypp, medium blue; 50/3 cotton, 14,000 ypp, turquoise; 28 ppi

Source: Original draft

Weave Structures: Echoed threading with advancing paired point treadling and double weave hems, 8 shafts

Finishing: Two separate layers at the ends of the scarf are secured with machine stitching (zigzag or serger) and then turned inward and hand stitched together. Hand washed in warm water, rinsed. Briefly steam pressed while damp, then dried outside on clothes line.

Take-up and Shrinkage: Warp 4%, weft 15%

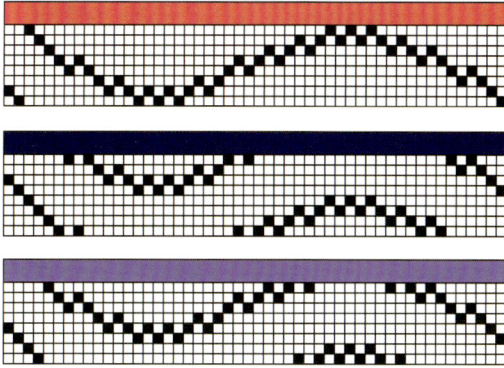

Component Threadings. The three threading lines are shown separated out by color. To start, a sine-wave-type curve was networked on an initial of 2. Each curve is the same but shifted from the red base, by four (blue) or two (purple) shafts.

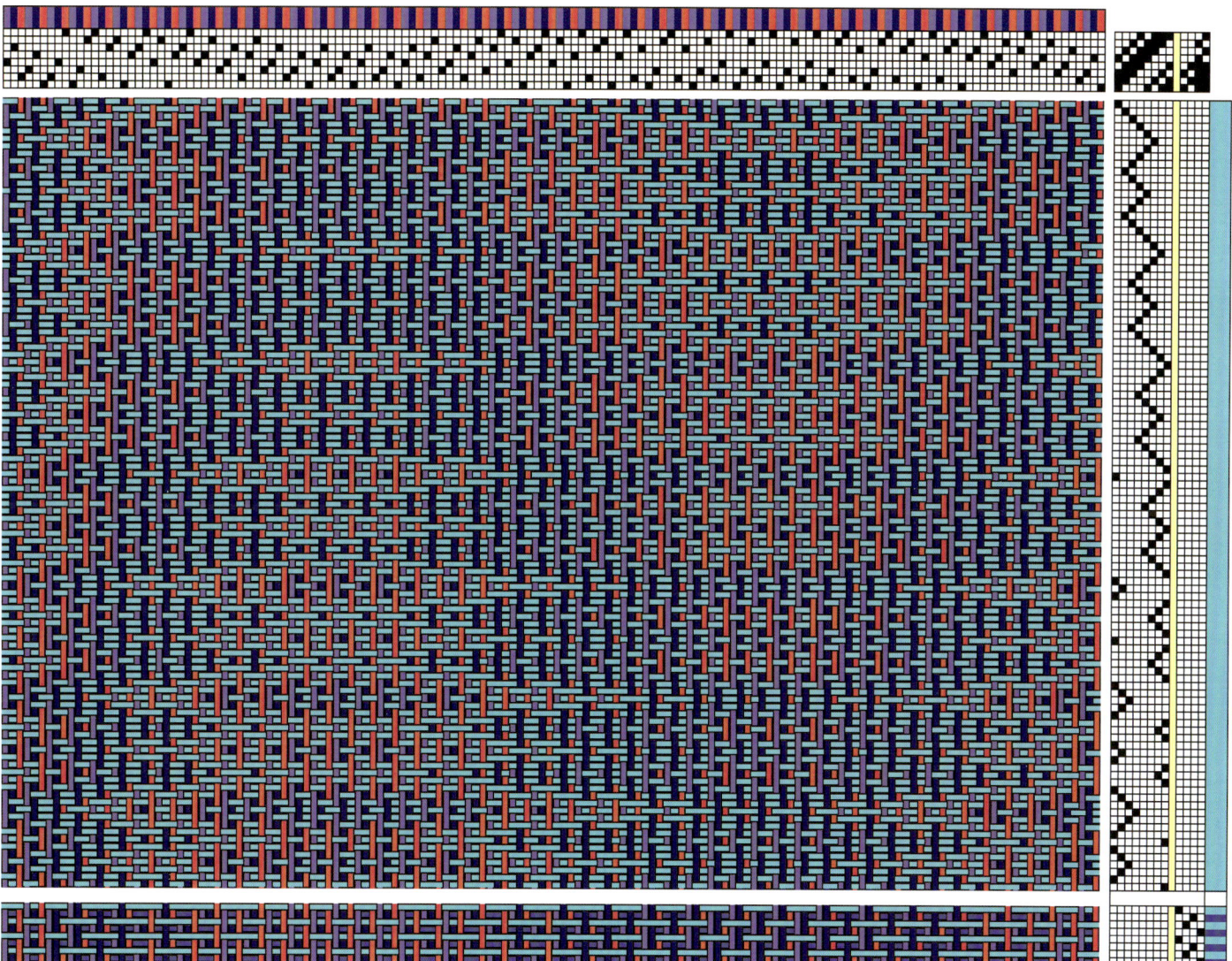

Threading Draft. The three threadings are combined and woven with a single treadling of advancing paired unequal points on a regular 3/1/1/3 diagonal tie-up. If desired, reverse the treadling of the body (first treadling) at the end of any point rather than repeating. The optional hems (second treadling and tie-up) are double weave.

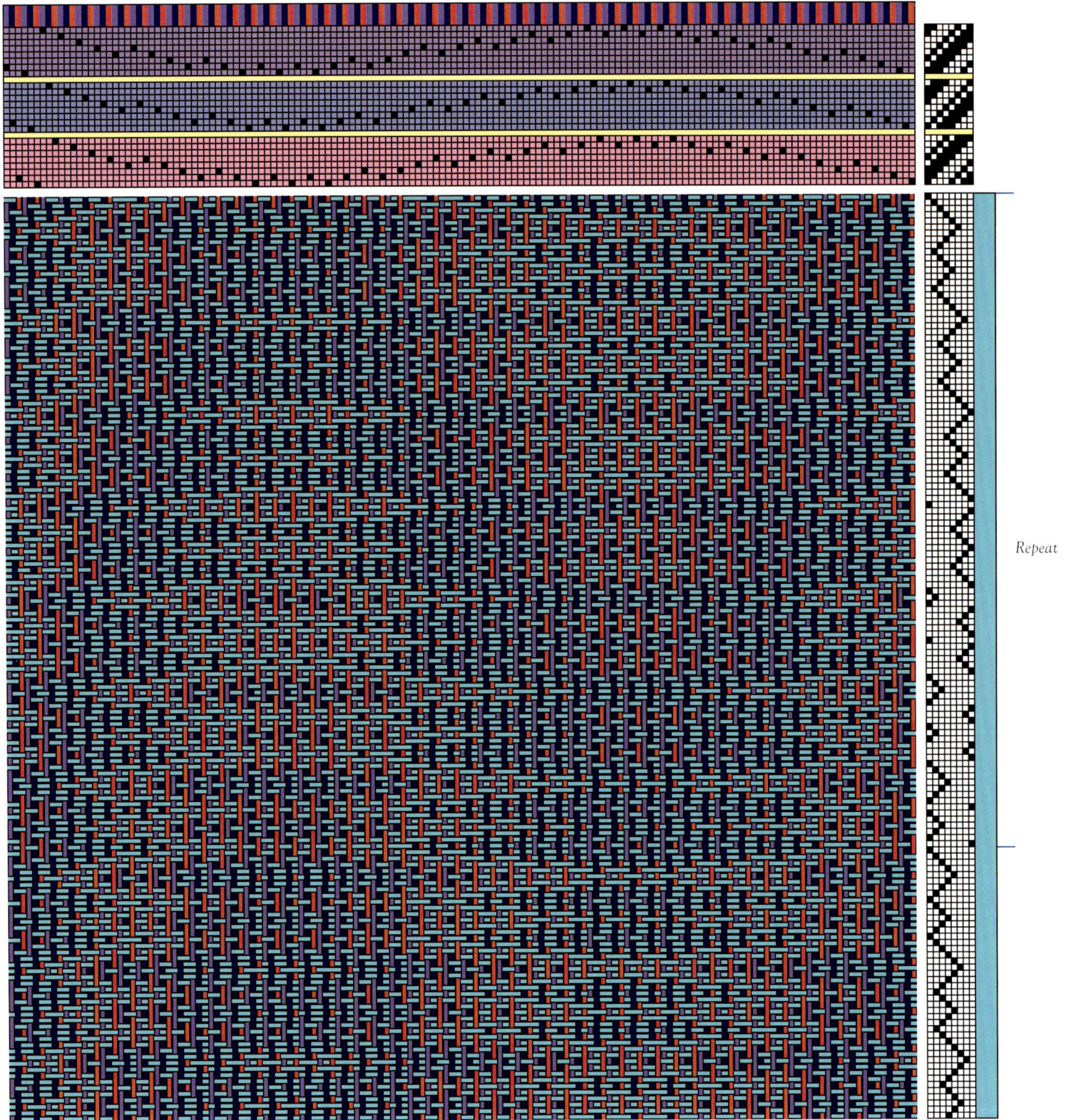

*Repeat*

*Alternate Threading Draft. This 24-shaft draft will produce exactly the same drawdown as the 8-shaft draft. Each color has been separated out onto its own set of shafts (red on 1 to 8, navy on 9 to 16, and purple on 17 to 24; separated by yellow lines). The individual design lines all have the same threading within their set of eight shafts. Rather than shift the lines to different shafts in the same group of shafts, the regular 3/1/1/3 tie-up shifts with each set of eight shafts. The repeat is marked on the side.*

*If you have the extra shafts, the advantage to using this draft is that the tie-up can be easily changed to create different intervals or to use different tie-ups entirely for the three lines without changing the threading. For example, one might also weave turned taqueté or double weave on this threading with appropriate changes to sett, tie-up, and treadling.*

# I.3  Stripes of Structure

Stripes of different structures can be as effective as color or texture stripes. A change in the dominance of the warp or weft may create the appearance of color change in a single color warp with a different color single weft. Additionally, changing the interlacement may change the texture, adding dimension through different float patterns. Of course, structural stripes may be combined with color or texture changes in yarn stripes for additional effects.

Loom set-up for vertical stripes may use separate groups of shafts for each structure, or different patterns with a single set of shafts. Horizontal stripes may be made in the weft by using two or more treadlings. Angled stripes at any slope can be made in the tie-up, often with a straight threading and treadling, to allow movement at any angle. An advantage of angled stripes is the elimination of tension differences arising from different interlacements.

*Top right, Plain weave, huck, and goose eye twill shown in liftplan form. The diamond huck pattern will form holes in the pattern areas after finishing. The draft has been expanded to separate the twill, huck pattern, and plain weave shafts and treadles.*

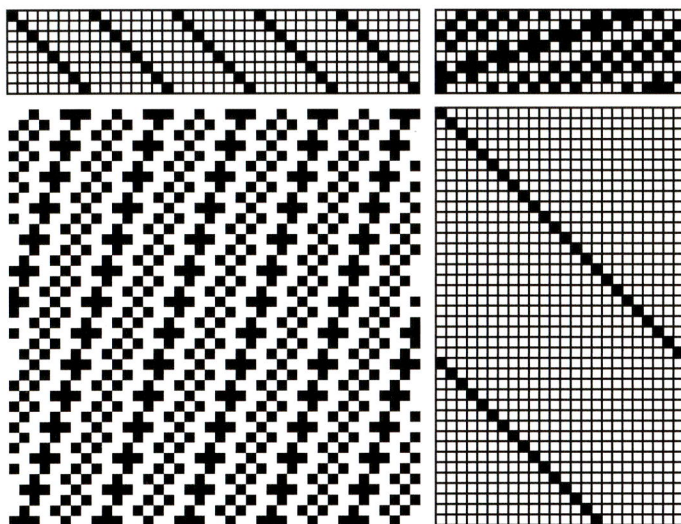

*Above, Angled stripes of plain weave alternate with stripes of a small warp-float figure on a weft-float background.*

*Right, Horizontal (weft-wise) stripes of weft-dominant and warp-dominant twills. The draft has been expanded to separate the two stripe treadlings.*

# Helen's Rescue from Troy
## Erica de Ruiter

### Runner in Twill and Double Weave (Plain Weave)

## Design Process

My starting point was a question from a weaver who admired the Andean textiles edged with colorful, tubular, crossed-warp diamond-patterned bands. She wondered whether it was possible to weave patterned tubular loom-controlled edge bands simultaneously with the piece. Sampling showed that it is possible to create something similar, using an extra four, six, or more shafts beyond what is necessary for the base textile. I shared some of these samples in de Ruiter et al. (2016).

I chose to restrict my larger project to eight shafts: four for the twill body and four for the double weave tubular edges. With only four shafts available for the tubes, they were limited to plain weave, which I sett to be balanced. With more shafts available, the tubes can be patterned in various ways.

The choice of a Wall of Troy twill for the body led, of course, to the name of the piece. Choosing rust and teal as the colors led to a big surprise - the iridescence in the weave. The tubes here are teal on one side and rust on the reverse. In the meantime, for health reasons I had to sell my big loom, so Kati Reeder Meek offered to assist with the weaving and finishing. This piece gives me lots of ideas for further study!

## Tips

• If you prefer to hem, using a half-basket weave for the hems (shown on draft) rather than plain weave will give a draw-in more similar to the twill.

• The tubular selvedges can be made as wide as you like, and could enclose some stuffer warps to make them round or puffed out.

• There is nothing which restricts the tubular areas to the selvedges. Consider including them in the interior of the piece if it is compatible with the desired final hand and usage.

• Exploring textiles from backgrounds other than your own can lead to some interesting cross-fertilization of ideas and innovations.

## Weaving Information

Size: 22" x 10.25" plus 0.5" fringe on each end

Warp: 10/2 cotton, 4200 ypp, rusts and teal; body, 24 epi; selvedges, 48 epi

Weft: 10/2 cotton, 4200 ypp, teal; 24 ppi

Source: Original combination of traditional drafts.

Weave Structures: Body, Wall of Troy twill; selvedges, tubular double weave (plain weave); 8 shafts

Finishing: Hemstitched over six ends. Soaked overnight, then hand washed in warm water. Mangled and steam pressed.

Take-up and Shrinkage: Warp and weft 2%

Selvedge   Balance |                                  | Repeat | Balance |   Selvedge

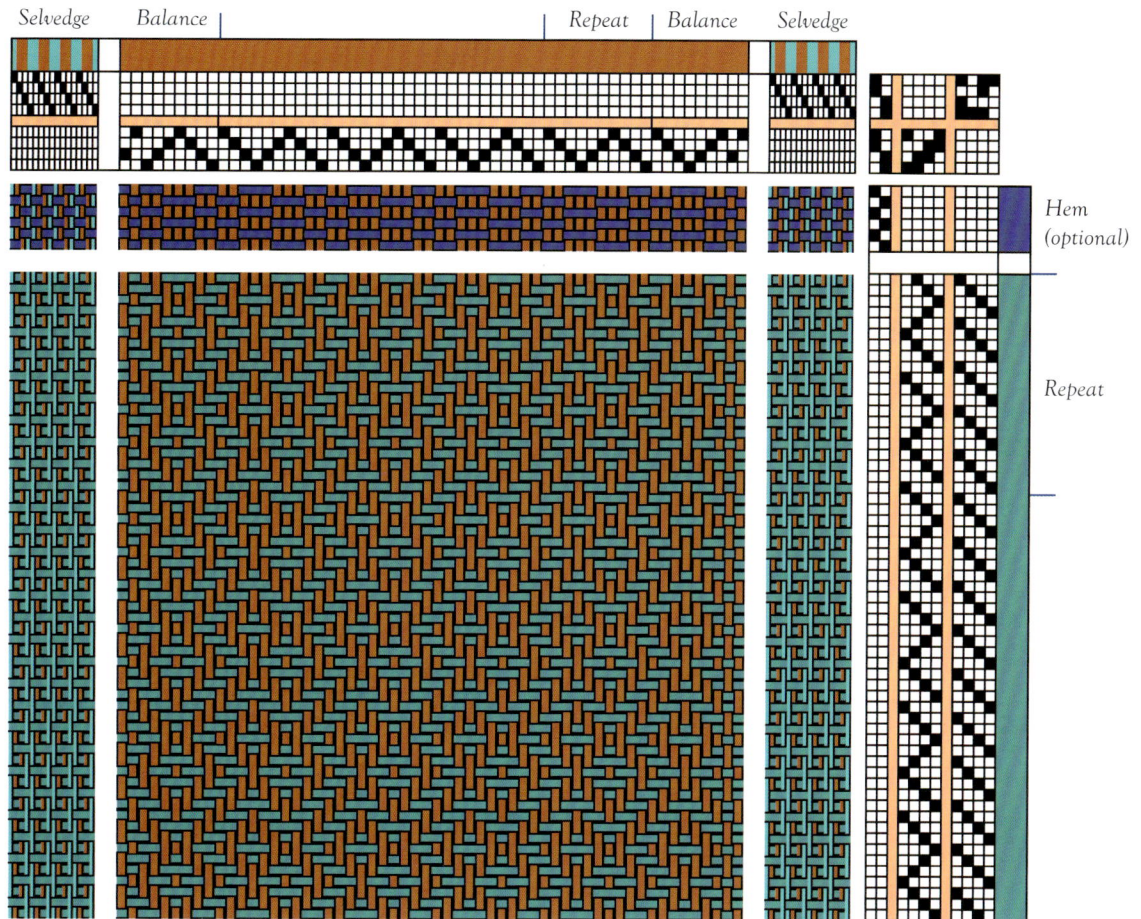

Hem
(optional)

Repeat

Threading Draft. The twill body and tubular selvedges are each on their own
four shafts. The body is a Wall of Troy twill with a regular 2/2 twill tie-up.
The selvedges are tubular double weave (plain weave) with teal on the surface
on one side, and rust on the other. The teal of the tubular warp selvedges is
shown slightly lighter to make it easier to see the structure. The optional hems
are half-basket weave. A skeleton tie-up allows the draft to be woven with 10
treadles rather than 20. The draft is expanded to separate the parts.

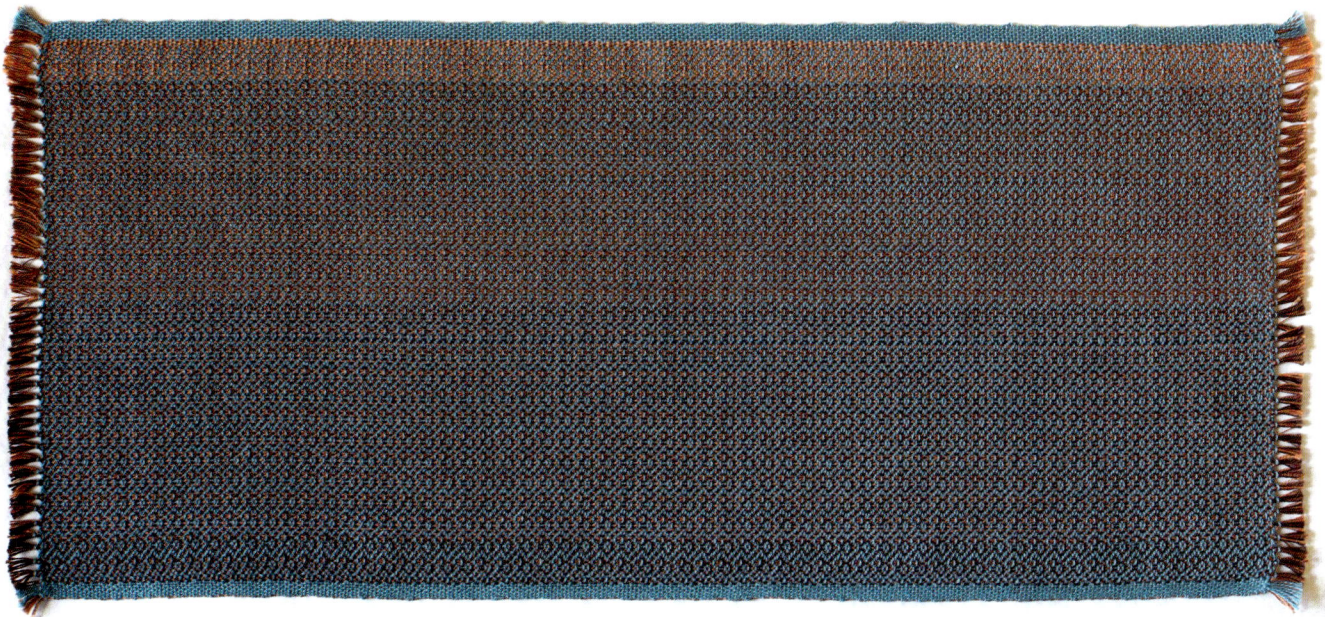

# Night Storm
## Patricia Donald

### Runner in Dimity Twills and Half-Basket Weave

## Design Process

I have been collecting weaving drafts that contain dimity patterns and exploring the different ways dimity stripes can be produced for over a decade. My fascination with dimity started with an interest in counterpanes, many of which contained a dimity element. Petticoats, vests, bed coverings, as well as window shades used dimity. One of the fun elements of dimity is that once the loom is warped, the weaving is easy and goes fairly rapidly. The ease of the weaving is probably why the fabric has been popular and easily produced commercially since the 1500s.

I have recently been interested in dimity which has patterns in the stripes. This became the inspiration for my piece. The dimity effect can be achieved through a variety of different techniques including the 1/5 twill with tabby used here. Beyond the patterned stripes, I added another dimity element, a thicker thread used to create a raised stripe to further add to the dimity theme. The red threads stand out not only in color, but also in grist (10/2 vs. 20/2 cotton). Then, I added half-basket weave between the stripes to set them off. In other pieces involving dimity I have used plain weave or honeycomb as is typical of counterpanes. The warp is reversed (mirrored) at the center, with the thin red stripes occurring near the selvedges and at the center.

The color interaction turned out to be a surprise to me. I originally planned the samples with the green in the warp also used as the weft color. That was fine and safe. However, I had picked up a bobbin of blue to put in the header for the samples and kept being drawn back to the interaction of the blue with the yellow, and the green with the red accents. I decided that the blue weft gave a depth to the piece that was lacking with the green weft and wove the final piece using blue weft. I'm glad I did. This surprise makes me think about other color interactions that I miss when I weave with the safe combinations.

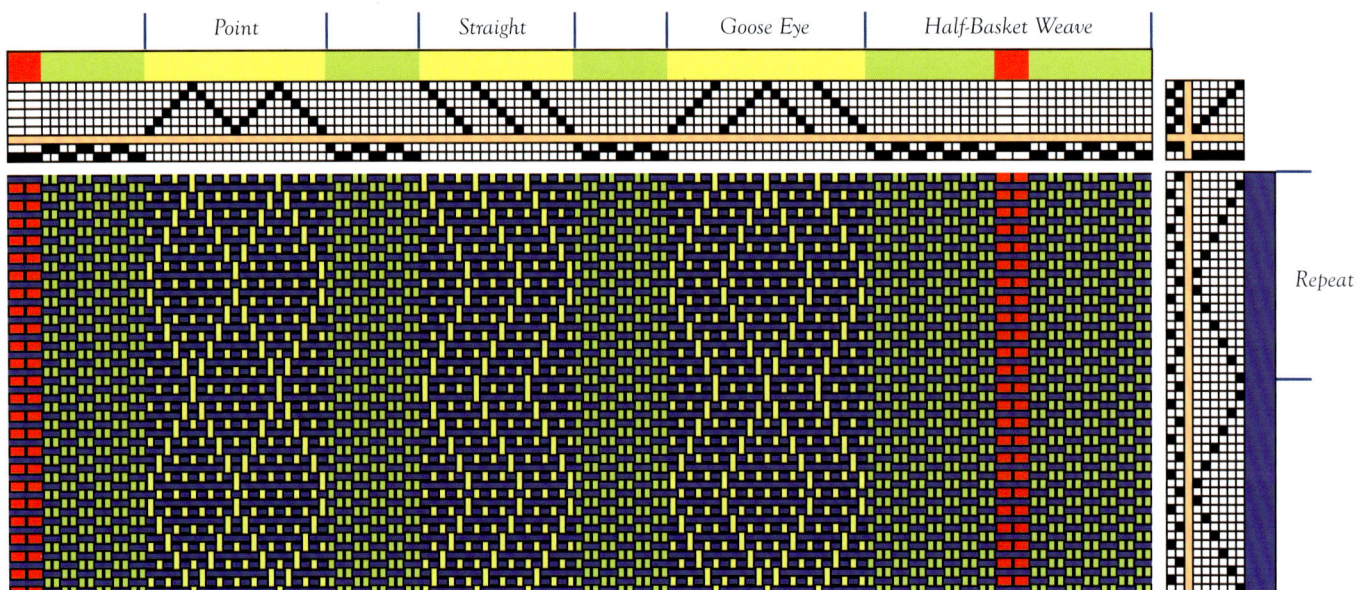

*Threading Draft. Half-basket weave stripes fall on shafts 1 and 2 (green and red), separating stripes of point, straight, and goose eye twills on shafts 3 to 8 in the warp. Treadling is a point twill with a non-tabby binder (shown), on a regular 1/5 twill tie-up. The doubling of the points in the pattern weft preserves symmetry in the binding picks. Treadles 1 and 2 function as tabby binding picks in the twill areas and half-basket weave in the rest. Adjust stripe widths as desired. The draft is expanded to separate the parts.*

## Weaving Information

Size: 76" x 8"

Warp: 20/2 mercerized cotton, 8400 ypp, champagne and willow green; 10/2 mercerized cotton, 4200 ypp, lipstick; 40 epi

Weft: 10/2 unmercerized cotton, 4200 ypp, medium blue; 40 ppi

Source: Original draft using parts of Joseph France twill drafts (1814, #43, 49, and 56; Butterworth, 1801)

Weave Structures: Patterned dimity (goose eye, straight, and point twills) and half-basket weave, 8 shafts

Finishing: Hand washed in warm water with Dawn for 15 minutes, rinsed in warm water, and dried on medium heat. Starched and steam pressed.

Take-up and Shrinkage: Warp and weft 10%

## Tips

• When combining structures, partitioning them onto their own sets of shafts is a good way to keep track of different patterns and/or structures. On eight shafts you can partition the shafts in many ways: 2 and 6 (used here); 3 and 5; 4 and 4; 2, 2, and 4; 2, 3, and 3; and 2, 2, 2, and 2.

• Try substituting your own different twill-type threading into the patterned dimity stripes.

• The patterned areas were kept about the same width here. The thinner half-basket weave stripes separating them are also all the same width, balanced by wider versions in the center and at the selvedges. They combine to provide rhythm and focus, reinforced by the thin red lines. If you change the stripe proportions, you will need to re-balance.

• The half-basket weave has a take-up more similar to the twill with tabby dimity stripes than simple plain weave stripes would have. It provides a calm background for the patterned stripes. Other interlacements could provide a similar effect.

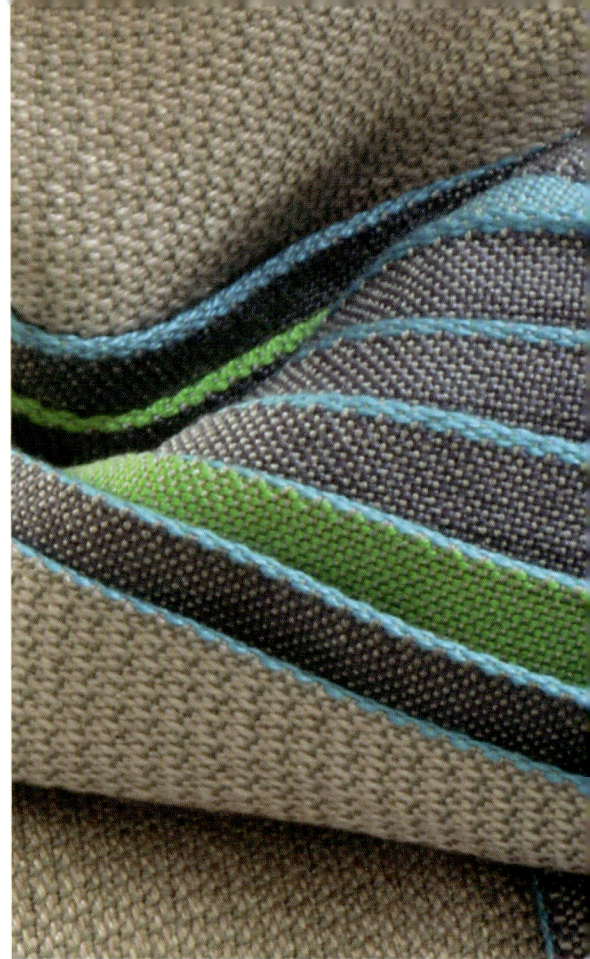

# Pleats Please Me
## Wendy Morris
### Scarf and Clutch Purse in Twill, Crepe, and Plain Weave

## Design Process

For many years I have admired the sharply pleated scarves and neck pieces created by the UK weaver Ann Richards – who doesn't? But her technique involves using a high-twist yarn to cause the cloth to fold at the pleats, coupled with a firm yarn to act as struts to prevent the cloth collapsing in the wrong places, and the result can be a little harsh to wear next to the skin. I wanted to see if I could create something softer with a gentler drape, using only normal yarns.

If the pleat walls are of equal width, the result is accordion pleats – just as attractive as these flat pleats, but the result can be a little bulky as a scarf, and you need quite a wide loom if you are going to achieve a respectably wide scarf and not a skinny neckpiece. A panel of flat pleats, flanked by non-pleating panels of whatever width you want, solves both those problems.

I still have a lot to play with!

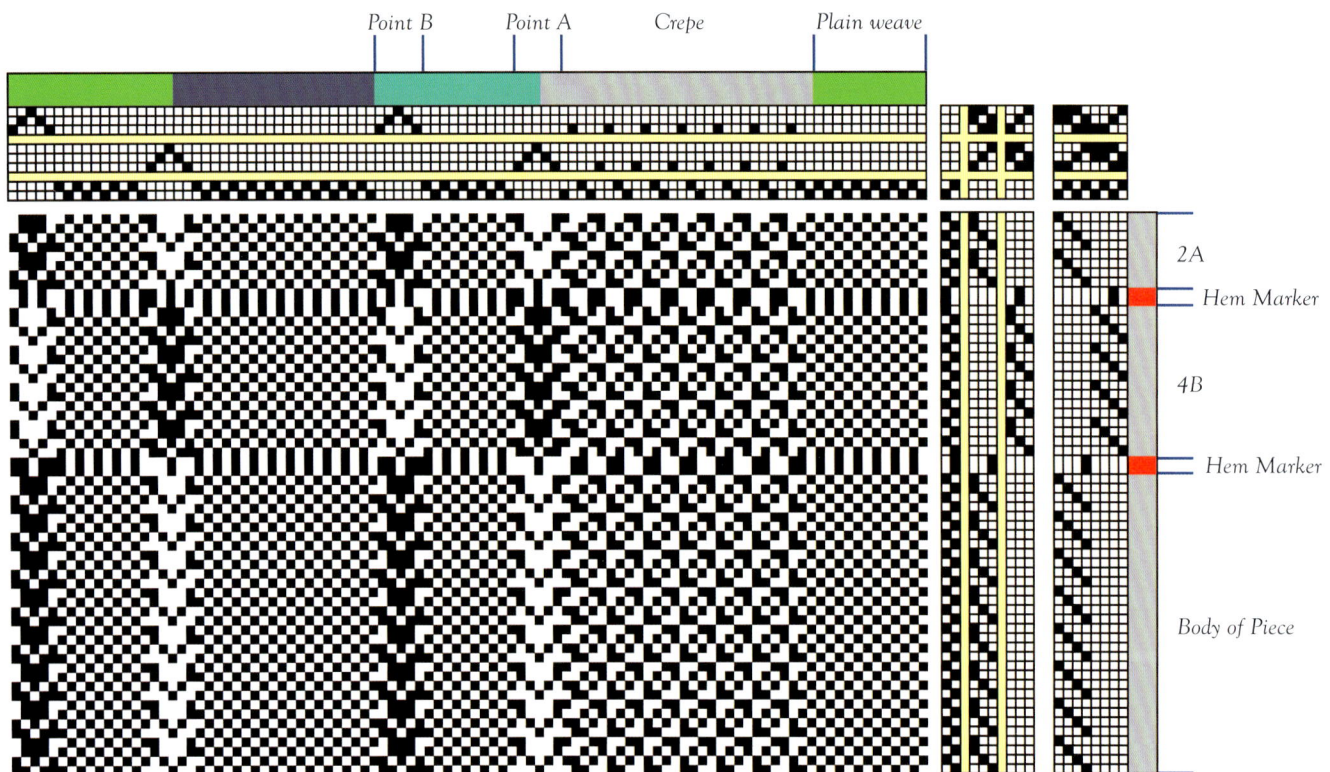

*Threading Draft. Warp stripes of plain weave alternate with 3-shaft points which form the knife edge of the pleats. The points are woven on a turned regular 1/2 and 2/1 twill block tie-up. The border stripes are of 4-shaft (1, 2, 3, and 6) crepe. Color stripes generally follow structure except where they split the "A" points. Adjust stripe color and the width of the plain weave stripes as desired. The draft was expanded to separate the parts, and both a skeleton and simpler treadling are given.*

## Weaving Information

Size: Scarf, pleated, 69" x 7.5" (unpleated, 69" x 12"); clutch, 3.5" x 6.5" x 2"

Warp: 30/2 spun silk, 7440 ypp, silver and cyan; side panels, 40 epi; pleat walls, 33 epi; pleat crests, 50 epi

Weft: 60/2 spun silk, 14,880 ypp, bright lime, deep sea, gunmetal, and blue-gray; 44 ppi

Source: Original draft

Weave Structures: 2/1 and 1/2 point twill blocks, crepe, and plain weave, 8 shafts

Finishing: Scarf, fine machine stitched to secure hem. Red spacer picks were removed and hem folded where pleats change direction, then hand stitched. Washed by hand in warm water for three or four minutes, rinsed cool, blotted, and laid flat. Pleats were encouraged to form by pulling firmly in sections along the length then air-dried. Flat side panels were hard pressed on medium; no pressing of pleat section.

Sewing: Clutch purse fabric backed with stretch fusible interfacing. Minaudière kit made up according to instructions.

Take-up and Shrinkage: Warp 5%, weft 14% without pleating (50% including pleating)

## Tips

• Both flat and accordion pleats can be used in other ways, such as godets or inserts in clothing, as sleeves or cuffs, in bags, or even in millinery.

• The apparent sharpness of the pleats can be accentuated by using a contrasting accent thread along the length of the pleat crest.

• Just one or two picks of a thicker novelty weft yarn near the ends is enough to make a scarf flare out at the ends.

• The sett and the choice of reed are crucial for self-pleating cloth using this technique. The pleat crests have to be crammed, preferably in a single dent, and the pleat walls must be sett for a firm plain weave.

• With self-pleating cloth like this, the pleats want to start forming on the loom, leading to inevitable draw-in. Avoid a warp yarn prone to fraying at the selvedges.

• The draft starts with two changes of pleat direction to allow for a folded hem. At each change of pleat direction a thick red marker pick in a slick yarn was laid in, which when removed during finishing allows the cloth to fold naturally for the hem at those points.

# Sigrid's Weave

## Norma Smayda

### Wall Hanging in Monk's Belt and Rosepath

## Design Process

This blended draft of traditional monk's belt and rosepath patterns by Palmgren (1939) has an unusual threading and tie-up, and no treadling was given. I ended the threading draft by adding a balance, and created my own treadling for rosepath and monk's belt motifs. The threading repeat has 40 ends, repeated as desired. It may be threaded with colored warp ends in threads number 1-14, threading randomly to coincide with the small monk's belt blocks, and natural for threads 15 - 40, as I did; or, the entire warp may be natural cottolin 22/2, as shown in draft.

The two patterns can be woven independently of each other (see drawdown), as was shown in Palmgren's book. More interesting, although not traditional, is to combine the treadling sequence in other ways. I made many decisions at the loom, using a mirror to aid in designing. For example, you might first weave a section of traditional monk's belt, then separate it with tabby before weaving rosepath. Play with the two monk's belt treadles, creating other designs. Do the same for rosepath. Weave a monk's belt block in the middle of a rosepath pattern. Change the pattern colors to suit your design. Intermingle the two monk's belt blocks with some of the rosepath treadles.

The two monk's belt blocks do not coincide with the rosepath motif, creating an asymmetric design. Flowing lines can be developed with rosepath, then interrupted by a monk's belt block. Inserting small blocks in a complementary color or in a color of different value will add interest.

Use the photograph of Sigrid's Weave wall hanging as inspiration, then create your own designs. Don't forget the mirror!

## Weaving Information

Size: 27" x 18"

Warp: 22/2 cottolin, 3200 ypp, natural, gold, brown, and light blue; 20 epi

Weft: 22/2 cottolin, 3200 ypp, natural (tabby); linen, 8/1, 10/1, 16/2, 20/2, assorted colors (pattern); 40 ppi including tabby

Source: Modified from Palmgren (1939)

Weave Structures: Monk's belt and rosepath, 8 shafts

Finishing: Not washed in order to keep linen fibers crisp. Hard pressed with steam on high heat.

Take-up: Warp 9%, weft 7%

## Tips

• It is not necessary to plan out the entire treadling sequence in advance. Improvising at the loom can lead to creativity through spontaneous choices of color, grist, and patterning.

• To use a mirror in designing, take an unframed pocket mirror (or L-shaped mirror used by textile designers) to help with elongation of motifs. For treadling, hold it at the fell to see if you want to weave a mirror image; if so, weave the pattern in reverse. Move the mirror back and forth over the woven cloth, near the fell, for other design ideas. This approach also helps with proportion and color placement.

• Blended drafts (van der Hoogt, 1993; pp. 114-115), though uncommon and less easy to thread, present many intriguing possibilities. Either of the two original blended patterns may be woven as weft-wise stripes in their original configuration. It gets even more interesting when you pick and choose from the two and start combining them intimately to form something new.

• Extend the idea by blending more than two drafts to create even more design possibilities.

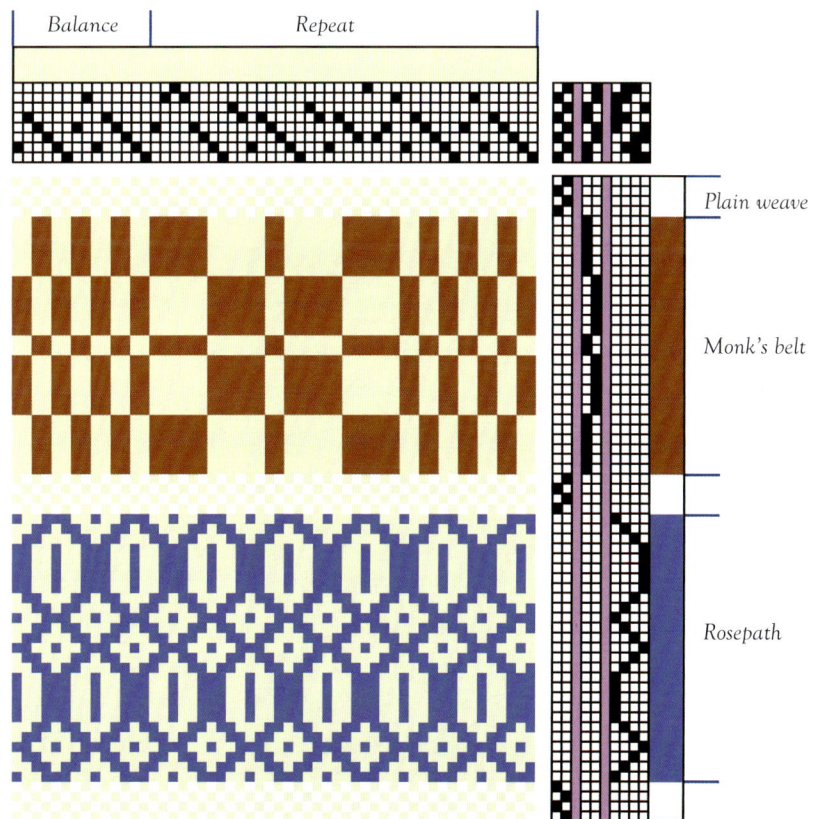

*Threading Draft. The blended draft allows plain weave, monk's belt, and rosepath twill to be woven as weft stripes. The weaver has played at the loom with color and variations on the treadlings to produce complex stripings of the structures. Tabby is used in the pattern sections but not shown. The draft was expanded to separate the parts.*

91

# Upon My Shoulders

## Janney Simpson

Scarf in Deflected Double Weave and
Double Weave (Plain Weave)

## Design Process

After weaving several scarves in deflected double weave and experimenting with different threading and treadling sequences, I became intrigued with creating layers, pockets, and connections (Simpson, 2016). The idea of a "cowl" that could be slipped over one's head was a result of this exploration.

This scarf has two areas of deflected double weave at the shoulders. At each end and in the neck area the scarf is woven with traditional double weave to create two layers of cloth. The open neck area forms a cowl. The top layer for the cowl area is reversed from the top layers seen on each end of the scarf.

The scarf is fun to weave and wear. I was challenged by the integration and separation of the layers, keeping things symmetrical, and making it the right dimensions so that it draped well when worn. The choice of fibers is endless and pattern possibilities are infinite. I hope this is the beginning of more creations in this style.

## Weaving Information

Size: 72" x 10" plus 6" fringe on each end

Warp: 2/18 wool/silk (50/50%), 5040 ypp, sable, suede, and copper (two dye lots); 12/2 bamboo, 6300 ypp, acorn; 30 epi

Weft: 2/18 wool/silk (50/50%), 5040 ypp, suede; 12/2 bamboo, 6300 ypp, acorn; 16 ppi, wool/silk; 20 ppi, bamboo

Source: Original draft

Weave Structures: Deflected double weave and double weave (plain weave), 8 shafts

Other Weaving Information: This scarf is created by weaving 22" of double weave at each end in two unconnected layers with the bamboo on top. At each shoulder, there is a patterned area of deflected double weave. Between the shoulders, there is an area of 20" of separated double weave with the wool-silk on top to form the cowl. Throughout the scarf, eight picks of wool-silk alternate with ten picks of bamboo. Picks are treadled in pairs either four times or five times (that is, 8 or 10 picks of one fiber before switching to the other). The bamboo weaves just to the edges of the first and last bamboo blocks, not to the edge of the wool-silk outer blocks.

Finishing: There are two layers of two-ply fringe. The wool/silk fringe used two and three strands per ply, and the bamboo fringe used five strands per ply. Hand washed in warm water with detergent, rinsed warm. Laid on towels to dry and pressed with a damp cloth on top.

Take-up and Shrinkage: Warp and weft 10%

## Tips

• Use a relatively light beat to achieve a light and airy drape to the handwoven fabric.

• Not connecting the two layers at the edges of the deflected double weave creates an elegant and more supple flanged finish. When you start each fiber block, be careful not to cross the two shuttles so that the two layers are free on the edges.

• After washing, the bamboo layer will be longer than the wool-silk layer because the fibers have different shrinkage. This is an interesting design element to exploit.

• Weaving a warp set up for deflected double weave as two separate double woven layers creates a soft, open plain weave, where the spaces become decorative elements. Treadling the picks in groups of eight or ten before switching layers keeps the weft spaced similarly to the warp.

• A skeleton tie-up (developed by Angela Schneider) is strongly recommended. It is advantageous when combining these structures to eliminate crawling under the loom to re-tie treadles between separated layers and deflected double weave sections.

• Note that a single layer of plain weave is also possible for filler and/or binders.

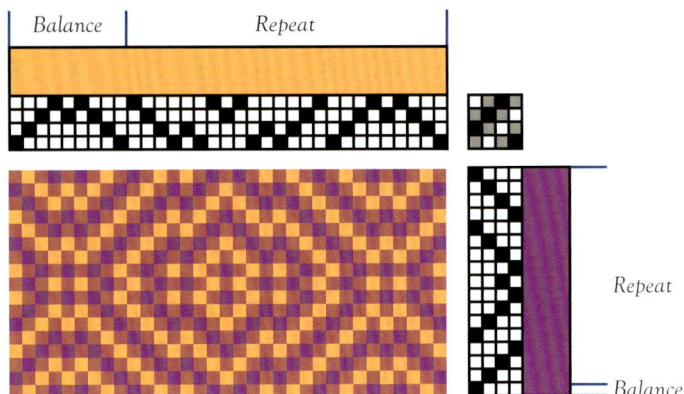

Profile Draft (above). In the tie-up, white indicates a block weaving weft floats, black indicates warp floats, and gray indicates plain weave. The blocks follow an Ms and Ws pattern. In the drawdown, orange indicates warp floats, purple indicates weft floats, and the intermediate tones are plain weave.

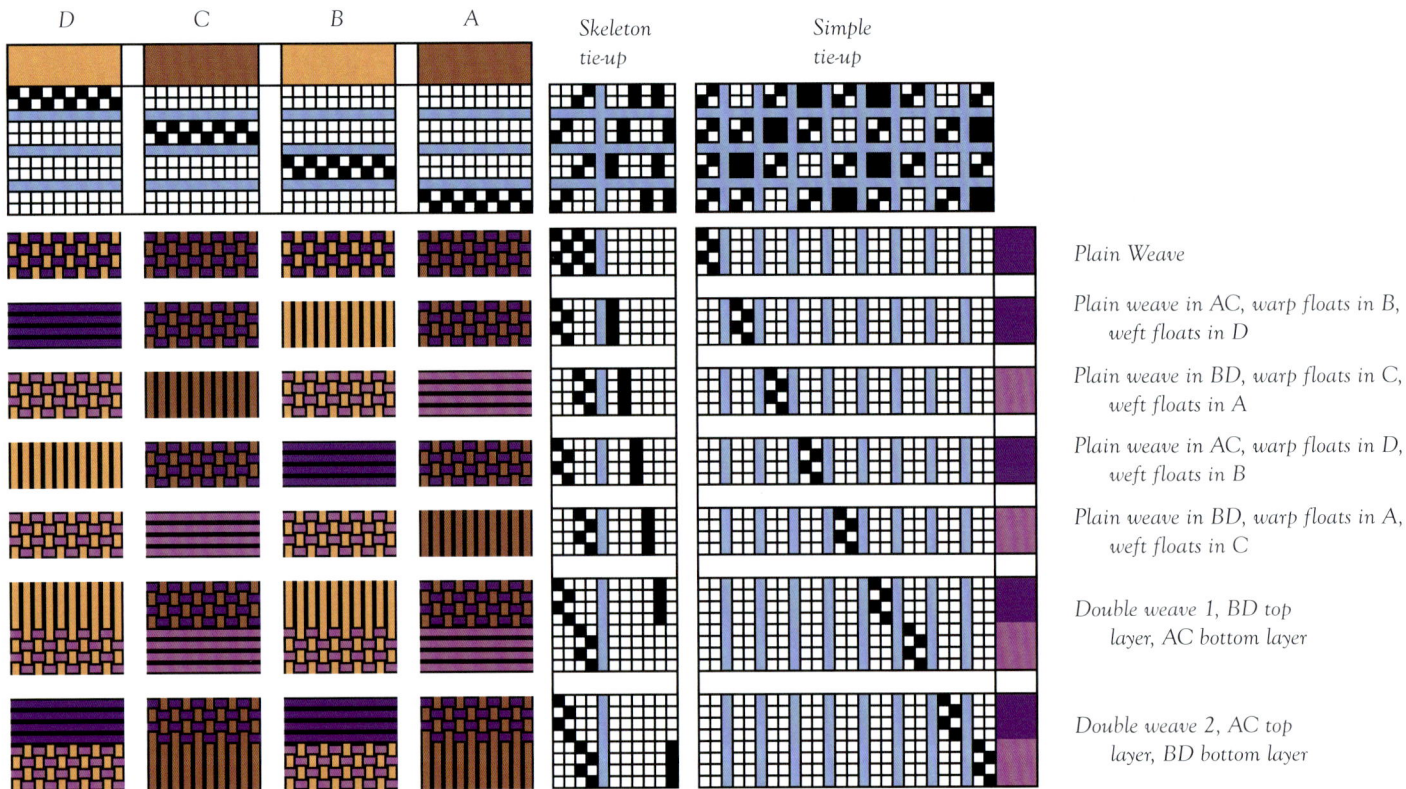

Plain Weave

Plain weave in AC, warp floats in B, weft floats in D

Plain weave in BD, warp floats in C, weft floats in A

Plain weave in AC, warp floats in D, weft floats in B

Plain weave in BD, warp floats in A, weft floats in C

Double weave 1, BD top layer, AC bottom layer

Double weave 2, AC top layer, BD bottom layer

Key to Profile Draft (above). A skeleton tie-up with ten treadles for ease of weaving and a simple tie-up with 18 treadles are shown. In the larger simple tie-up, a block weaving weft floats has no ties, a block weaving warp floats has four ties, and a block weaving plain weave has two ties on the diagonal. The second through the fifth treadlings are used in the deflected double weave bands. Repeat the pairs as needed to square the blocks. The last two treadlings weave two unattached double weave layers in unevenly spaced plain weave. To space the plain weave, repeat the first two treadles four times, then the second two treadles five times. The draft was expanded to separate the 2-shaft blocks. Colors are altered to improve visualization of the structure.

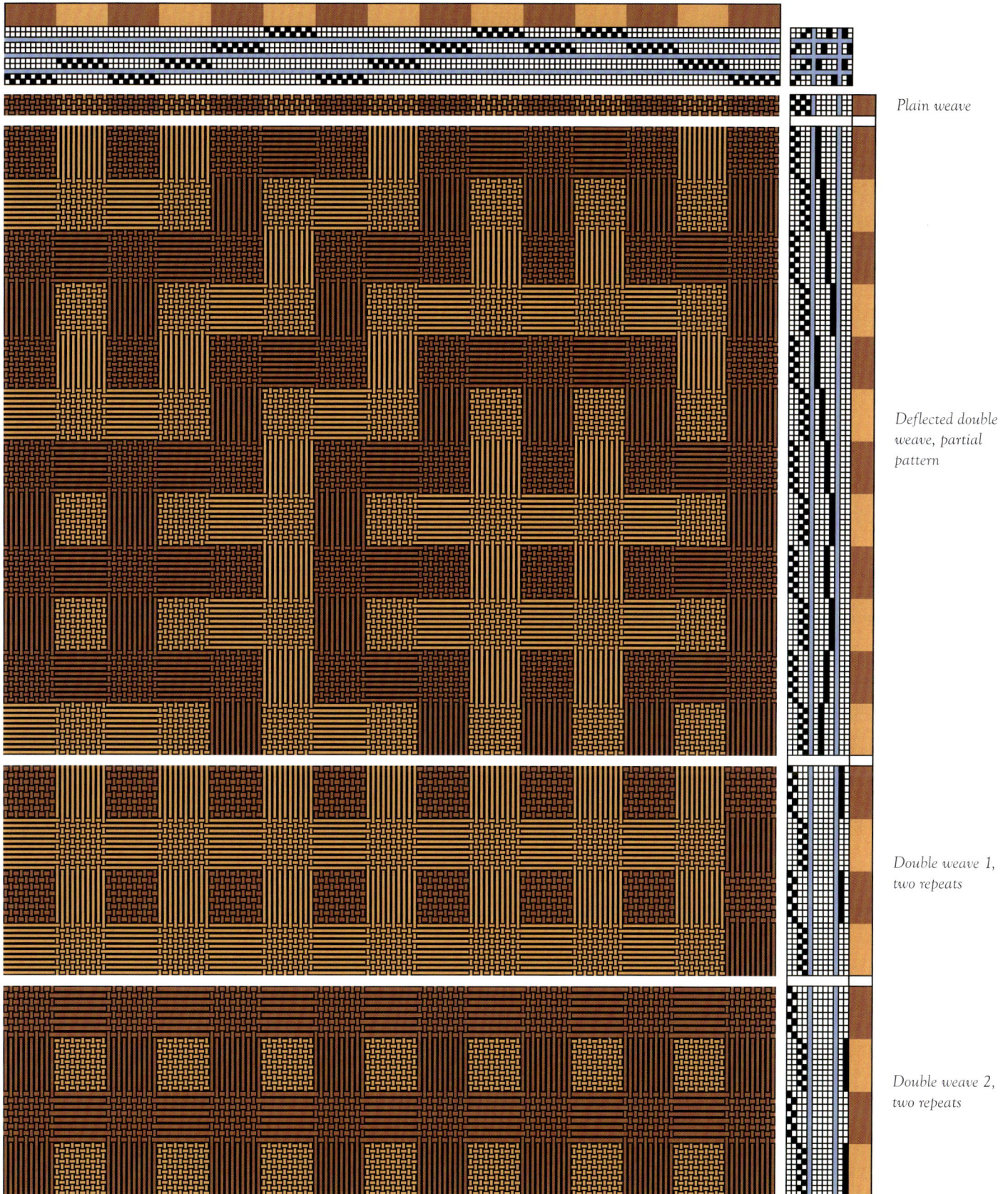

Plain weave

Deflected double weave, partial pattern

Double weave 1, two repeats

Double weave 2, two repeats

Threading Draft. The actual colors have been simplified to aid visualization of the structures, with darker brown as the wool-silk and light copper as the bamboo. At the selvedges, the bamboo only weaves to the last bamboo block. Adjust the repeats of the double weave and deflected double weave stripes as desired. The draft has a skeleton tie-up and was expanded to separate the 2-shaft threading blocks and the parts of the treadling. Finishing causes the final cloth to look very different as the threads shift.

# Gecko

## Karen Donde

### Yardage in Broken Twill Blocks

## Design Process

Looking through samples for potential skirt fabric, I found a simple, beautiful one that resulted from experimenting with tie-ups and treadlings on a favorite threading - a turned Beiderwand draft. The samples used a neutral ground warp and a supplementary pattern warp in multiple colors of 10/2 cotton, threaded one-to-one across the width. It was woven in straight twill on the two tabby treadles and the first treadle of the block tie-up, with a tweedy wool crepe I had bought from Silk City Fibers years before.

This sample was the perfect texture and hand, but I wanted to add a subtle stripe. I revisited the original draft and decided I could get a comparable textile with simple twill blocks using a similar combination of warp yarns and the same weft yarn. Twill blocks also afforded the option of creating a tie-up that would produce a structural stripe, either in warp or weft. I chose evenly spaced weft stripes that alternated between a broken twill and three-treadle straight skip twill, referring to the original draft.

For color inspiration, I started with a variegated 10/2 Tencel in shades of green, brown and turquoise. I selected a soft green and yellow for the neutral ground and pulled colors from my stash to match those in the Tencel. I couldn't find the right turquoise, so I dyed the yarn myself. It came out more blue than turquoise, but proved a nice contrast in combination with the other colors and the Tencel.

I wound two ends together for the warp for the odd shafts in a 2x2 cross, and three ends together for the even shafts warp in 3x3 cross. Eleven accent ends were randomly wound into the "even" warp every 2-3 inches. I threaded by alternating between the two warps, one-to-one, choosing one yarn from each randomly. While the structural repeat is 32 ends, the color repeat is variable because of the random selection of yarns. The color order in this draft is only a suggestion of how this looks. While winding the warp, I heard a soft noise in my studio. I walked around my desk to investigate and found a gecko had come to visit, and his coloring matched my warp perfectly. Hence the name of the yardage.

## Tips

• When working with a stretchy weft that is prone to twisting, like this tight crepe twist, be careful to wind your pirns or bobbins very tightly and evenly. Be prepared to manage the extra twist and kinking while weaving. The weft can curl and get caught in an end-feed shuttle tensioning slot, pulling on selvedges. Some shuttles may work better than others.

• This warp has a complex color order, chosen somewhat randomly while threading, alternating between two options. For similar warps, try winding warps for the odd shafts and even shafts separately. In this piece there is no differential take-up so they can be wound on the same beam using two crosses or put on separate beams.

• Keeping the ends grouped in the cross makes for faster winding and easier random selection from each warp. Here, a thread was randomly selected from the 2x2 cross in the odd shaft warp. Then, a thread was randomly selected from the 3x3 cross of the even shaft warp, picking one of the three different yarns or the accent yarn when it occurred.

## Weaving Information

Size: 150" x 27"

Warp: Organic cotton (about 16/2), 7000 ypp, lime; bamboo 12, 6300 ypp, golden wheat; 10/2 mercerized cotton, 4200 ypp, mead; 10/2 Tencel, 4200 ypp, variegated (dyed by Just Our Yarn); 10/2 organic cotton, 4200 ypp, hand-dyed blue heather; 10/2 bamboo, 4200 ypp, yellow green; 40 epi

Weft: Wool merino/viscose crepe (80/20%), 2250 ypp, Inca gold; 17 ppi

Source: Original draft

Weave Structure: Broken twill blocks, 8 shafts

Finishing: Machine washed cold on quick wash cycle (27 minutes) with 1 tablespoon Tide, a drop of Synthrapol, and color catcher sheet. Hung to dry, supporting yardage over two rods. Hard pressed on cotton setting with steam.

Take-up and Shrinkage: Warp 15%, weft 9%

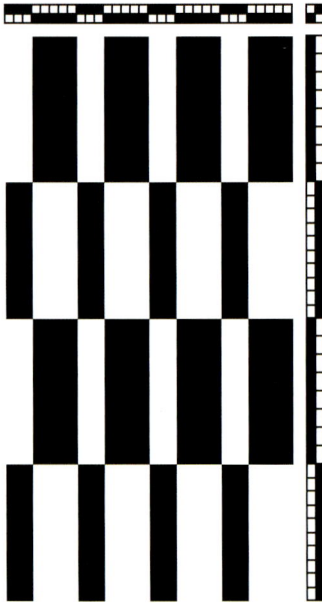

*Profile Draft. Broken 2-block stripes in warp and weft.*

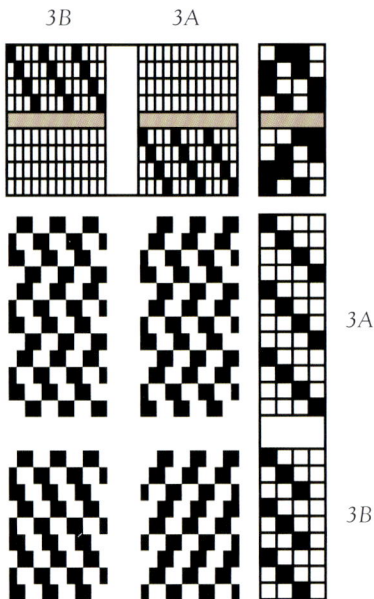

*Key to Profile Draft. This draft requires four treadles, all of which are used for the first treadling, and only three for the second. The tie-up is a broken regular 2/2 twill for both 4-shaft blocks. The two treadlings produce different broken twills. In the A treadling the twill line goes two in a row, skip one, back two. In the B treadling, the twill line goes three in a row, skip one. Additionally, the twills in the two threading blocks are offset by one pick in both treadlings. In the second treadling, the twill lines of the A and B threading blocks run in opposite directions. The draft is expanded to separate the parts.*

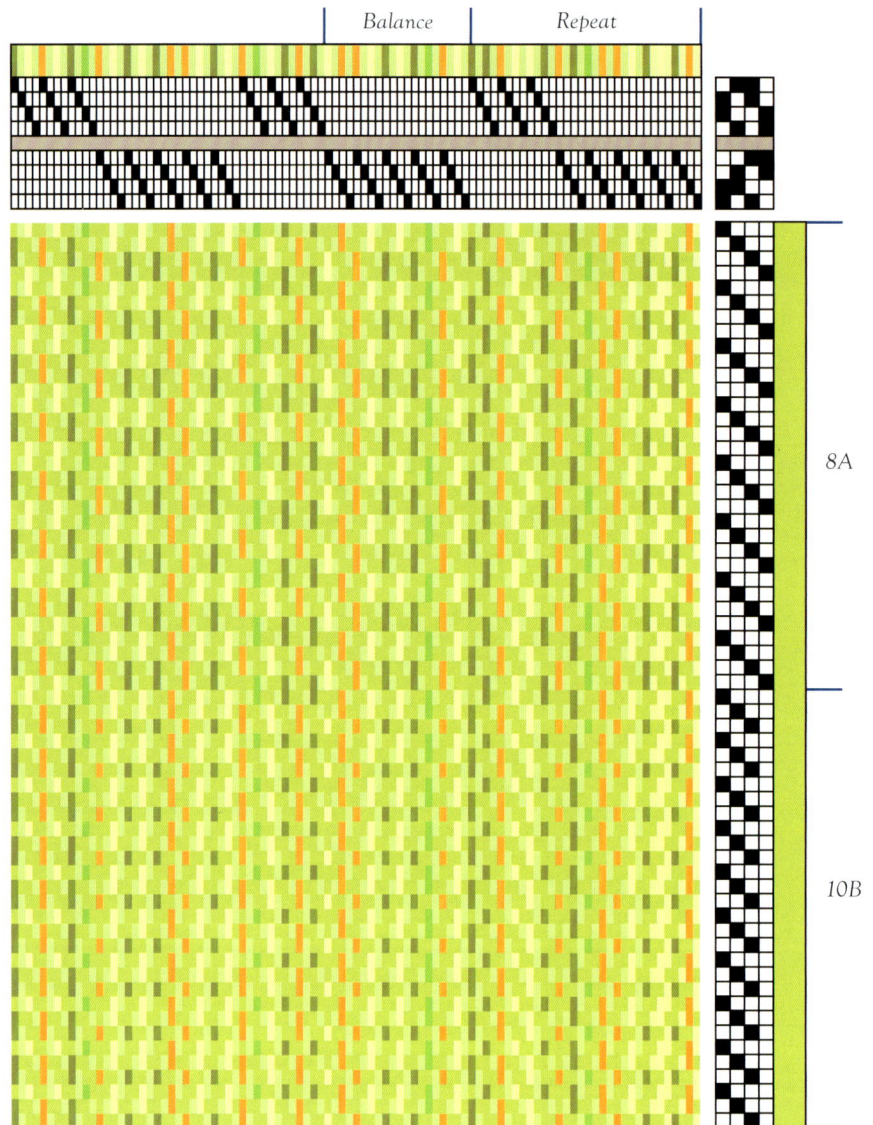

*Threading Draft. In this simplified coloring, every other warp thread is light green. In the first treadling, all of the other warp threads fall on 2-thread floats. In the second treadling, the longer warp floats fall on half of the green and half of the other color warp threads. The effect is a lower key, more overall pattern. Adjust stripe widths and color placement as desired. Use floating selvedges (not shown). While this draft could be turned and woven on four shafts, it would require many shuttles and a different approach to color choice. The draft is expanded to separate the parts.*

# I.4 Figures and More

This chapter contains a variety of designs and techniques which did not fit neatly into the preceding chapters. Figures, double weave techniques, and crepe weaves were woven on standard 8-shaft looms, and skillbragd on a modified 8-shaft loom. Additionally, one piece adds card weaving to an 8-shaft piece while weaving on loom. Two pieces are made completely off-loom, one in card weaving and one in ply-splitting. Both use an 8-shaft draft as a starting point, pointing up the idea that design is design and can be applied to many other techniques.

## Woven Figures

Combine curved and straight-line segments with visually different aspects of the cloth to create recognizable figures or words. Changes in warp- and/or weft-emphasis, or combining different interlacement patterns may also be used to add details.

*Left, profile draft. Simple geometric flower on 6-blocks. The small diamond in the center is made of straight lines; all of the other lines curve by varying the repeats in the threading and treadling blocks to form the petals.*

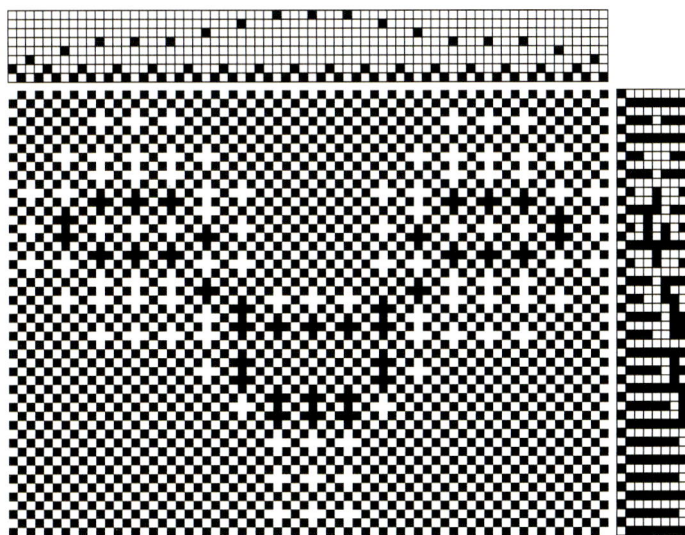

*Above, Threading draft. Laughing alien, taking advantage of the special features of turned Atwater-Bronson lace in 4-thread blocks.*

## Crepe Weaves

Crepe weaves produce small, allover patterns which are often chosen to act as an unobtrusive background without the strong diagonals (or drape) of twills. The patterns are designed to look randomized, though there is often a 90° rotation in their construction (Oelsner, 1952; Schlein, 2012). Crepe weave can function as the quiet surroundings of a more dramatic feature (e.g., tablet or other bands, warp painting, finger manipulation, the cut of a garment) which dominates the work.

## Double Weave

In addition to all of the design possibilities found in other chapters, double weave has the ability to weave tubes, double-width cloth with the fold on either side, and two separate layers of cloth. This capability can be exploited in itself as a design feature.

## Skillbragd

Skillbragd, also known as Smålandsväv or treadled opphämta, can be woven on a drawloom or a specially modified shaft loom. Each warp end is threaded through a regular heddle on one of the plain weave shafts placed in the back of the loom, then as a group through long-eyed heddles on zero to all of the pattern shafts in the front. This arrangement allows each end to be used in more combinations than would be possible on a standard shaft loom. Weft-float pattern picks alternate with tabby ground. A schematic (partial) threading is shown below.

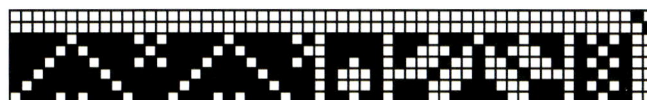

## Off-Loom Techniques

Card (tablet) weaving may be done on or off loom. In many card weavings, the cards have four holes, accommodating four warp threads per card, but other numbers are possible. Turning the cards raises some threads and lowers others, thus changing the shed. The color arrangement through the cards and the turning direction of the cards for each pick create the pattern. The structure of the woven band can be plain weave, warp twining, double-faced weaving, or even hopsack.

Ply-splitting is also accomplished off-loom. Cords with two or more plies are created, usually in contrasting colors to allow patterning effects. Cords are passed through each other, choosing which cord will sit on the surface. Any pattern of any degree of complexity can be created, as well as three-dimensional effects more common in basketry.

# Northwoods

## Jan Hayman

### Towel in Summer and Winter and Plain Weave

## Design Process

The Northwoods towel was inspired by an Ojibwe elder sharing tales of her youth, including being shipped out to Indian school by the Canadian government. Her stories were all the more captivating because she spoke without rancor despite the injustices imposed on her and her family. The design celebrates the wildness of the north woods, its native peoples, and the moose, whose population numbers have declined in recent years.

The starting point was a sheep design by Georgean Curran (1990). The block arrangements in the threading and the treadling were modified to create the most realistic moose motif possible within the limits of the six blocks of summer and winter available on eight shafts. Vertical bands of patterning are created with a dukagång-style treadling. I used three repeats of the moose, separated by seven A blocks. Using weaving software to design in the drawdown for figures in 8-shaft summer and winter has also proven instructive for creating more complex original motifs for the drawloom. For more information on summer and winter, see Sullivan (1991).

Using two colors in the warp, one for the tie-down threads on shafts 1 and 2, and a different color for the pattern threads on shafts 3 to 8, adds greater richness to the plain weave areas. The brown tie-down threads coordinate with the rust and oak pattern weft colors.

## Weaving Information

Size: 31" x 22"

Warp: 8/2 unmercerized cotton, 3360 ypp, medium brown and jeans; 20 epi

Weft: 8/2 unmercerized cotton, 3360 ypp, royal (tabby and plain weave); 5/2 mercerized cotton, 2100 ypp, oak and light rust (pattern); 20 ppi including tabby in summer and winter border, 12 ppi in plain weave body

Source: Original draft

Weave Structures: Summer and winter in dukagång-style and plain weave, 8 shafts

Finishing: Handsewn 0.6" hem. Machine washed in warm water with mild detergent. Machine dried in moderate heat, removed while still damp and laid flat. Pressed on cotton setting.

Take-Up and Shrinkage: Warp 17%, weft 10%

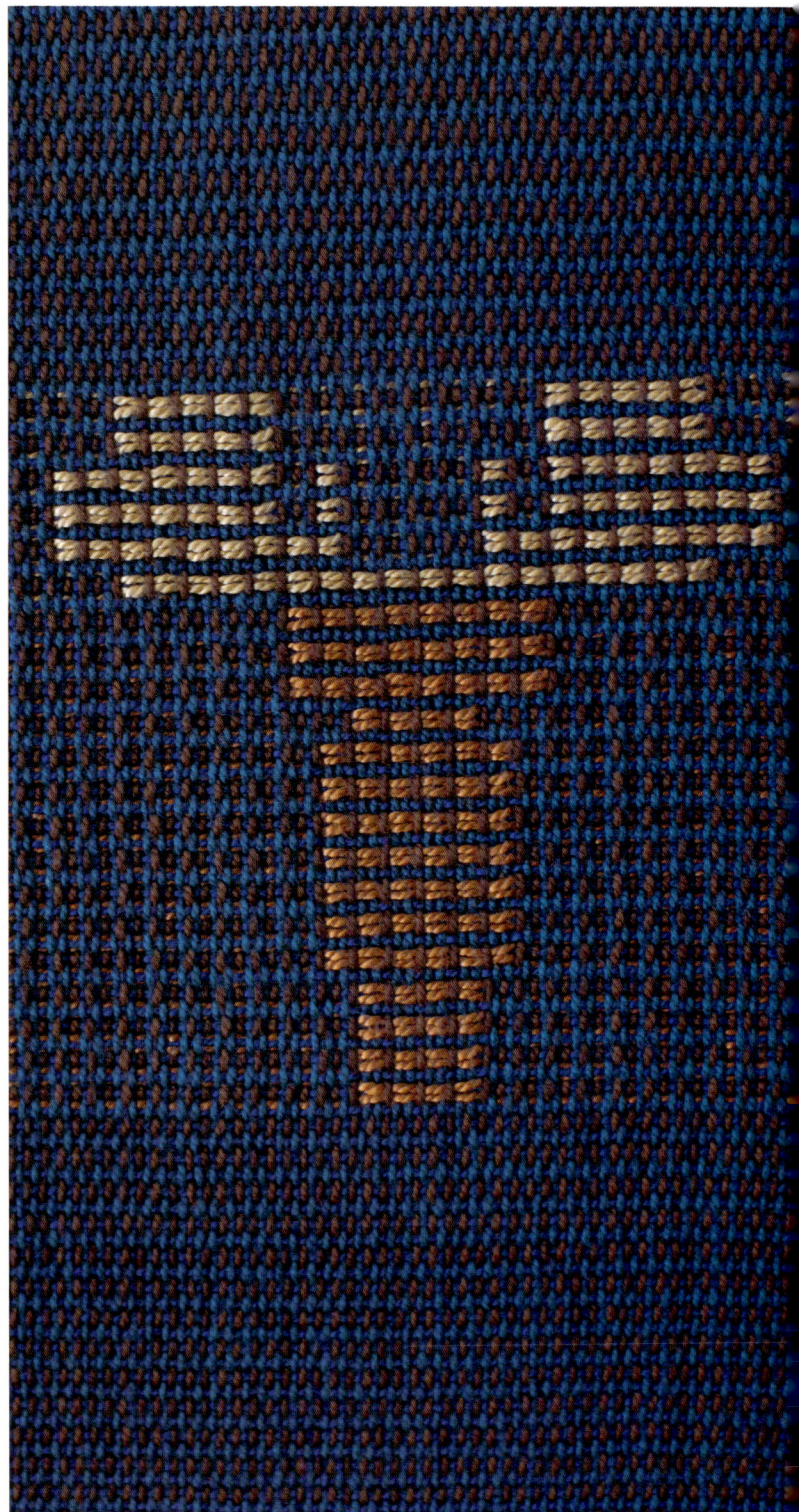

## Tips

• When weaving summer and winter in dukagång style, each pattern treadle is tied with shaft 1 in addition to the selected pattern shafts. The dukagång-style of treadling frees up two treadles commonly used as the tie-down treadles. Additionally, it eliminates the need for a skeleton draft (double treadling). The weaver can then have more treadles for pattern if desired, or left free for future design modifications.

• Combining two or more close colors for warp and/or weft rather than using a single color creates a richer and more interesting cloth.

• When weaving figures, a bit of careful planning may allow you to add detail to the figure with color. Here, the light-brown antlers set off the dark moose head.

• There is no need to pattern the entire surface. These figures are more interesting as a single patterned band on a plain body than they would be as an all-over pattern.

Balance | Repeat

2A | 2B | 5C | D E | 4F | E D | 5C | 2B | 2A

2C
2BCE
BCDE
CDEF
3DEF
F    Repeat
7EF
4F

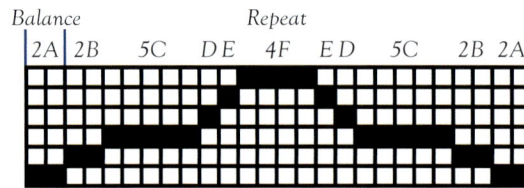

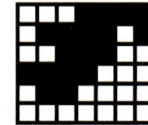

*Profile Draft. Increase or decrease the number of A blocks in the threading to adjust the distance between moose motifs or to create wider selvedges. The actual piece uses seven A blocks (28 warp ends) at the selvedges and between the moose but only two are shown in both drafts.*

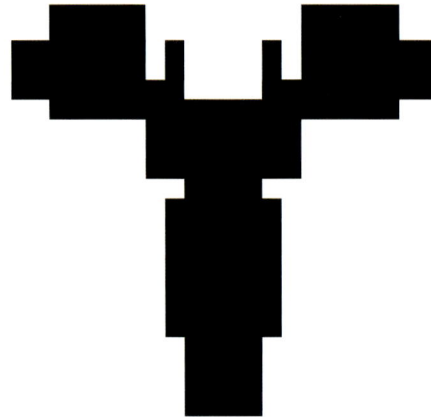

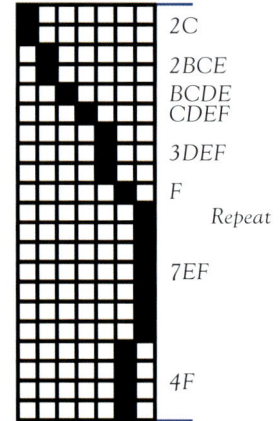

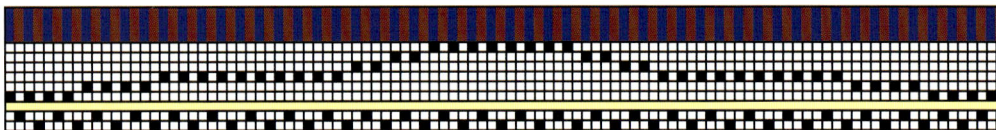

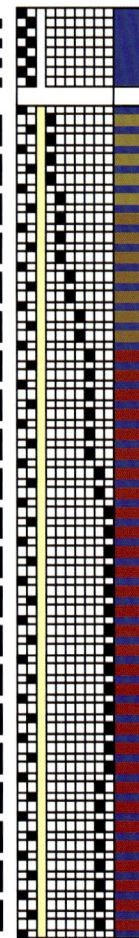

Plain weave

Pattern

*Threading Draft. Summer and winter forms the pattern bands (use tabby, shown) with plain weave body and hems. Dukagång-style treadling is used, with the same tie-down (on shaft 1) on all pattern picks. The draft was expanded to separate the pattern shafts and treadles from the tie-downs and tabby. The colors were altered to be more visible on the page.*

# Autumn Leaves
## Edna Devai

### Scarf in 4-Color Double Weave

### Design Process

Two years of intensive study of 4-color double weave led me to publications and workshops by Marian Stubenitsky (2014), Marguerite Gingras, Bonnie Inouye, and Su Butler. In the midst of this study, I interpreted the 4-shaft Blooming Leaf pattern from Davison (1944) as 4-shaft 4-color double weave. That project then inspired me to start playing with other leaf design possibilities of my own.

This 8-shaft leaf pattern takes full advantage of the color possibilities of 4-color double weave. Repeating the leaves without reversing (mirroring) them stops the formation of the complementary star motif which occurs in the traditional Blooming Leaf pattern. I used a more open sett of 60 epi to achieve a softer hand and better drape. The pattern direction reverses in the middle of the scarf treadling so that it is symmetrical when worn. Instead of a fringe, I opted for a regular double weave hem.

I enjoy all the movement in this design and the high degree of iridescence.

### Weaving Information

Size: 64" x 6.75"

Warp: 60/2 spun silk, 14,880 ypp, hand-dyed lapis lazuli and red; 60 epi

Weft: 60/2 spun silk, 14,880 ypp, hand-dyed golden apple and wine berry; 79 ppi

Source: Original draft

Weave Structure: 4-color double weave (interleaved echoed twills) with double weave hems, 8 shafts

Finishing: The double weave hem layers are turned in and secured with invisible stitches by hand. Hand washed and rinsed in warm water first with Dawn, then again with Eucalan without rinsing and blotted on towel. Blocked and air dried. Pressed on silk setting when damp.

Take-up and Shrinkage: Warp 5%, weft 13%

## Tips

• Fine threads often look a bit sparse or are less durable when left as fringe. Using a double weave hem with fine threads and a sett higher than one would use for plain weave gives a clean, durable finish, which is still flexible and elegant at this scale.

• Leaves come in many varieties, with both smooth and serrated or shaped edges. Most of the traditional western leaf designs produce smooth-edged leaves, constructed with invariant mathematical precision. Adding small changes helps to both shape the leaf and give other edge forms. Here, a series of small points create serrated edges, and one larger point makes the lower lobe.

• Pictorial designs are often more life-like when they do not reverse on every repeat in warp and weft or along the diagonal. Secondary motifs which form with reversals, such as the star mentioned earlier, can take focus away from the main motif.

• The asymmetry of this leaf gives the sense that you might be seeing it at an angle rather than flat. It might be in motion or imperfect, both more natural in feeling.

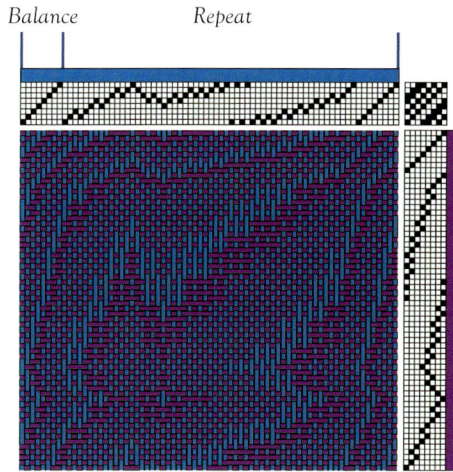

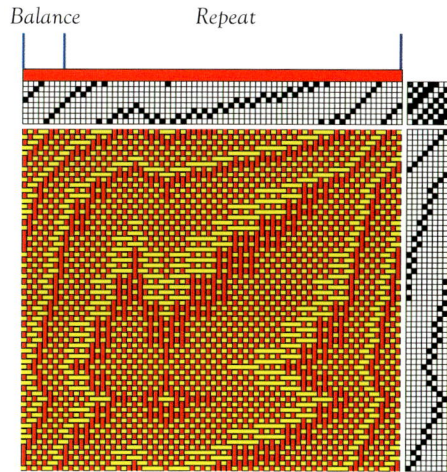

Component Drafts. The threading and treadling are networked on an initial of 2. The blue warp component is woven with a 1/1/1/1/2/2 regular twill tie-up which gently shades the motif. Starting on the right, the red warp is the same threading, moved down by four shafts, and woven with the same treadling on a 2/1/1/1/1/2 regular twill tie-up. The two tie-ups are related by inversion, so the shading is on opposite sides.

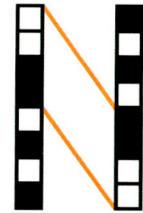

First treadle of each component. The pattern area is moved down four shafts and the opposite shafts are lifted.

The blue warp component's first treadle is tied for plain weave on the first four shafts and 2/2 twill on the second four shafts, then moved up by one on each treadle. This arrangement places the weft floats beside the warp floats.

The red warp is woven on opposites from the blue warp. The component's first treadle is tied for 2/2 twill on the first four shafts and plain weave on the second four shafts. This arrangement places the weft floats to the other side of the warp floats.

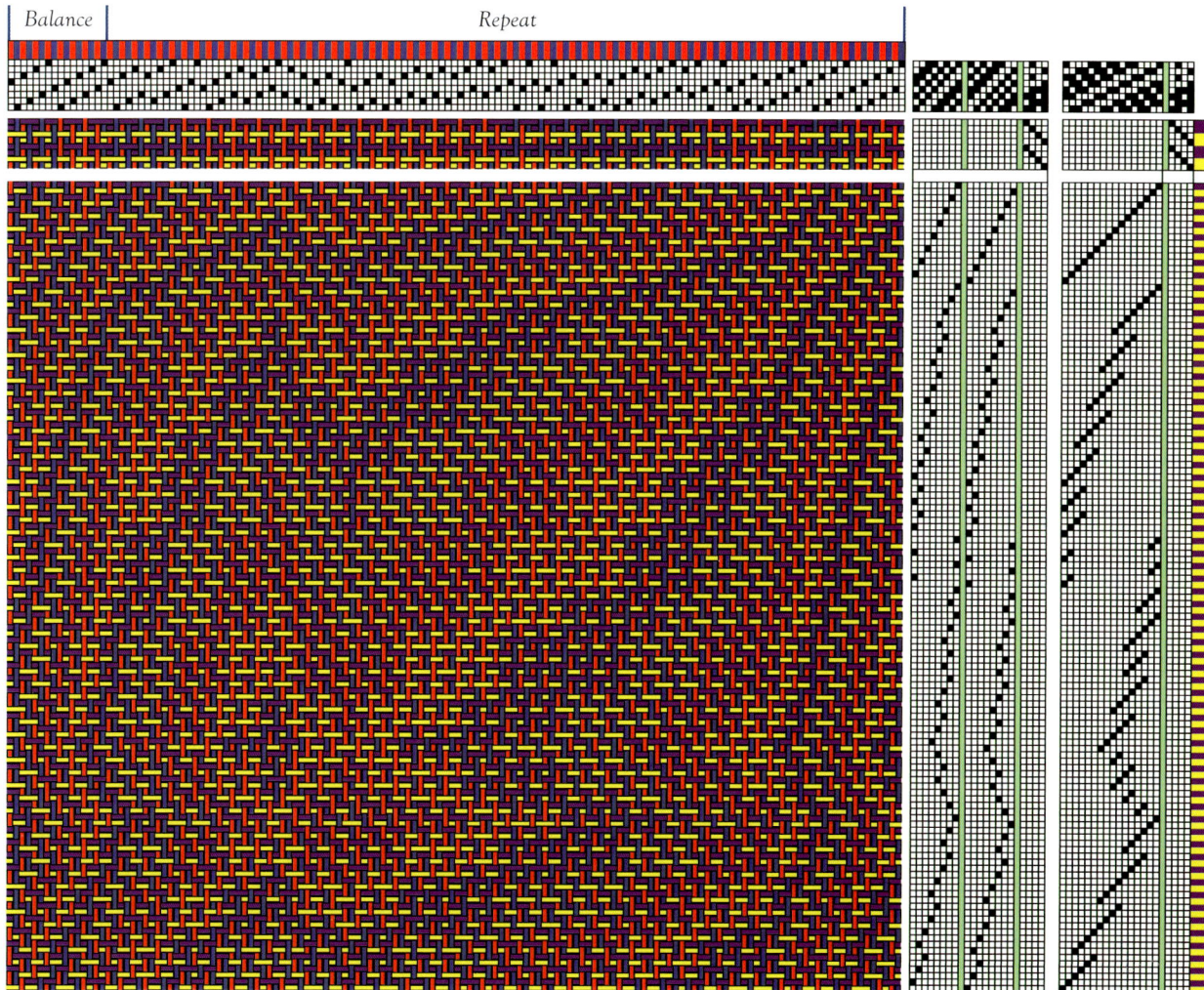

Hems

Pattern

Threading Draft. The two components are interleaved in warp and weft. Curved lines and the small reversals in warp and weft create the leaf image. The hems are double weave (plain weave), with shafts 1 to 4 on the top layer.

Two treadlings are shown, one with the components separated and a simpler one with the components integrated. The integrated treadling falls on a network initial of 4. The draft was expanded to separate the parts.

# Inside Out
## Alice van Duijnen
### Scarf in Double Weave (Twill)

## Design Process

The idea of a turned tube came to me when playing with a piece of fabric and asking our famous "What if?" question. My first prototype on a piece of cloth gave the best results when alternating the openings left and right. I tried different variations of sizes of the tube sections compared to the opening sections and in the end settled for equal sizes, 7.5" each. This gives a nice drape and does not make the scarf too stiff, while still showing sufficient changes between inside and outside. Prototypes taught me that the colors should differ strongly for maximum effect. I chose tomato red against black. The scarf has been turned inside out through each of the openings so the red inside warp-dominant side alternates with the black outside weft-dominant side. For more information about double weave, see Arn-Groschott (1999).

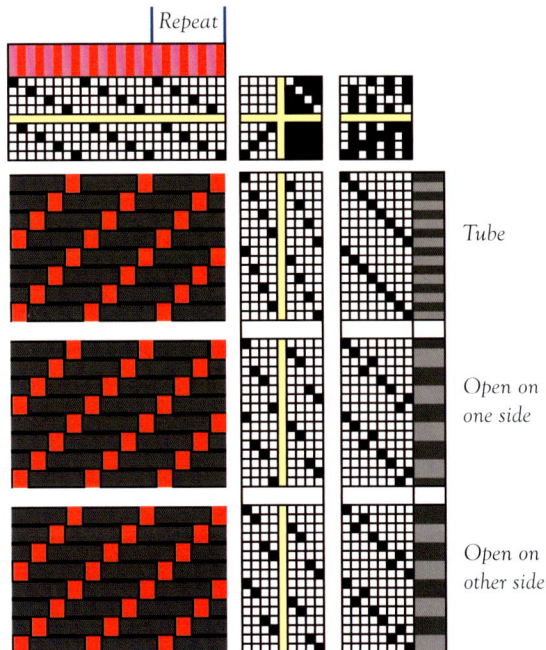

*Threading Draft. Only the top layer of double weave is shown in the drawdown. As woven, the outside of each layer is a 4-shaft regular 1/3 twill. The three treadlings change only by how the double weave edges connect or not. The first tie-up separates out the layers and the second one is designed for easier treadling. The draft was expanded to separate the layers.*

## Weaving Information

Size: 78.5" x 7.5" plus 5" fringe on each end

Warp: Alpaca/silk (70/30%), 4000 ypp, tomato red; 50 epi

Weft: Alpaca/silk (70/30%), 4000 ypp, black; 50 ppi

Source: Original draft

Weave Structure: Double weave (1/3 twill), 8 shafts

Other Weaving Information: Openings in the tube were woven alternating on right and left side. All openings measure 7.5" long with 7.5" tubes in between.

Finishing: Two-ply fringes with two ends per ply. Hand washed with mild wool detergent in lukewarm water. Scarf has been turned inside out through each of the openings so the inside red warp-dominant side alternates with the outside black weft-dominant side.

Take-up and Shrinkage: Warp and weft, 10%

## Tips

• If you weave a twill tube, make sure to leave out the last end of the back side in order to make the twill pattern continuous.

• Experiment to find the optimum size, spacing, and left or right placement for openings for your materials and design.

• The concept of turning the tube inside out will work with many structures. For maximum effect, choose a structure whose back side (the inside) is dramatically different from the front side (the outside). That includes 1/3 or 3/1 twills in any form, from straight as here, to point, herringbone, undulating, broken, etc.; Atwater-Bronson lace and spot Bronson; tied unit weaves such as summer and winter; and surface weaves of many types such as cannelé, Moorman technique, corduroy, and rya.

• Working with a striped warp and/or weft will have interesting effects.

• If you don't mind discontinuity around the tube, the two layers may be different structures and/or the shafts distributed unevenly between the layers.

# Weaving Words and More

## Inge Dam

### Shawl in Crepe and Tablet Weaving

### Design Process

When I think of a pattern to use in a fabric combined with tablet weaving I often go to handweaving.net. The draft I have modified for this shawl was found in Christian Morath (1784-1810). I thought this pattern would work well with the tablet techniques I had chosen for the bands. To enlarge the pattern, I extended the twill in warp and weft.

I love the idea that I can weave words in tablet weaving so I decided to weave words related to weaving in two of the bands. The letters are from a book by Linda Hendrickson (2003). The other two tablet bands are woven using the Kivrim tablet weaving technique. There are many pattern possibilities with the Kivrim technique so I have designed some that I thought would work well with the fabric pattern. These tablet-woven bands are woven at the same time the loom-controlled part is woven (Dam, 2013), rather than woven separately and sewn on.

By weaving this piece I got an idea for weaving a piece for my grandchildren, with words related to their world. It will be very colorful, with colors that my granddaughters love such as purple and yellow.

### Tips

• When working with a group of complex elements, it helps to have the elements take different weights. A visual hierarchy calms and melds the ingredients. Here, the green bands with words take your eye first, followed by the striping of the other tablet bands and the painted warp. The 8-shaft crepe pattern is the least obtrusive, furnishing a textured surface for the painted warp, while the geometric bands pick up a smaller number of colors and a simpler, more forceful version of the blurred diagonals in the crepe.

• To give a piece depth and interest, try having different optimum viewing distances for different features. Often, color patterning is the most obvious feature at a distance, with woven pattern second, and the intricacies of the interlacement only obvious on closer perusal. These words are large enough to read at the same distance as the overall color striping. Only when the viewer is quite close do all the details become obvious.

• Combining a published draft with modifications and your own flourishes makes it your own.

## Weaving Information

Size: 73" x 23.5" plus 12" fringe on each end

Warp: 30/2 Tencel (tripled), 12,600 ypp, hand dyed; 28 epi

Weft: 10/2 mercerized cotton, 4200 ypp, navy; 26 ppi

Source: Original draft, combined with draft modified from handweaving.net, Morath (1784-1810), #18048.

Weave Structures: Crepe and on-loom tablet weaving, 8 shafts

Other Weaving Information: Four tablet-woven bands were incorporated into the fabric. Two of the bands were woven using the Regular Double-Faced Tablet Weaving technique (Hendrickson, 2003) and two using the Kivrim technique (Gehlhaar, 2003).

Finishing: Beads were added to the fabric fringes while they were being twisted. Hand washed in hot water with Downy for five to ten minutes. Laid flat to dry until damp and steam pressed.

Take-up and Shrinkage: Warp 10%, weft approximately 15%

*Threading Draft. Enlarged points in threading and treadling are woven with a randomized crepe tie-up for allover texture. One repeat is shown.*

# Stars of Saint Mary

## Kati Reeder Meek

### Funeral Pall in Twill Blocks and Atwater-Bronson Lace

### Design Process

Working with a committee for this commission was an interesting process. In September, I began with a member familiar with my work. Though the church society budget was not generous, I wanted to be. They offered to pay for materials in addition to the final sum and I said, "I'll try." The first sample was a 4-shaft twill, but the priest didn't like the 'plaid' look of the cross stripes. Then, I tried the drawloom with its great patterning capacity in 8-shaft satin. There were three more sample warps, through the winter, trying to get a beautiful (not plaid!) design for the cruciform stripes. Matching the proportions warp-wise and weft-wise proved beyond my rusty drawloom skills and errors were too difficult to see to achieve the professional look I wanted.

This 'Stars of Saint Mary' pattern came about as I played with an idea seen on handweaving.net. At the final meeting in April I brought samples of the 'Stars of Saint Mary' and everyone was quite pleased with the weight and hand of the cloth as well as

the design. I had made a second sample of the same design with fatter yarns and they agreed that cloth was too heavy. I think it was beneficial to present a sample that they could reject. The Rosary Society also wanted the phrase, "*HOLY MARY MOTHER OF GOD PRAY FOR US SINNERS*" from the Rosary to adorn the lower sides with decorative curves and crosses. These bands were woven separately side by side for perfect matching on 12 shafts each (total of 24 shafts) in 36/2 wool in Atwater-Bronson lace. See Piroch (1990) for the lettering technique on eight shafts. The lettering bands were finished and appliquéd onto the finished pall.

My policy on handwoven cloth is that no machine stitching should ever be visible. There was no machine stitching at all on the pall. All mine! The cotton plus wool is not as wrinkle-resistant as I had hoped, though the finished pall weighs barely over three pounds. I believe I would use all wool for a pall or any large piece in the future.

## Weaving Information

Size: 10' x 6'

Warp: 16/2 Egyptian cotton, 6700 ypp, natural and four light shades of blue; 40 epi

Weft: 2/36 worsted wool, 7500 ypp, natural and three shades of blue; 40 ppi

Source: Original modification of a found draft

Weave Structures: Twill blocks, 8 shafts; separately woven Atwater-Bronson lettering bands (no instructions given), 12 shafts per band

Finishing: Soaked in bathtub with tepid water overnight, added one tablespoon clear shampoo and fulled with clean, bare feet for 20 minutes. Rinsed three times with white vinegar in first rinse, hung over rod until stopped dripping. The pall was blocked over a linen sheet, anchored with hand weights, and left until nearly dry. Steam pressed gently on wool setting. When dry, the two halves were sewn with back stitch using the 24/2 cotton warp yarn. The seam was steamed open and seam allowances secured on each side. The ends were pressed, then hemmed, mitering the corners. The lettered woven bands were attached after finishing.

Take-up and Shrinkage: Warp 10%, weft 7%

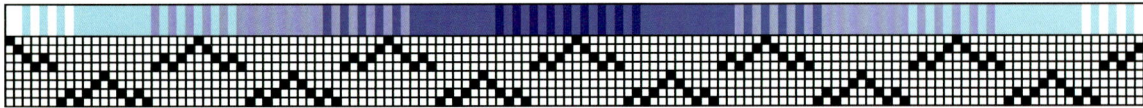

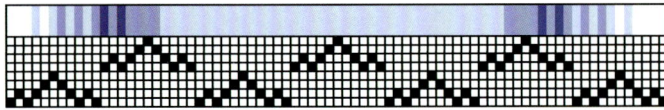

*Threading Stripes. The graded warp color sequence for the center (above) and side (left) stripes are given.*

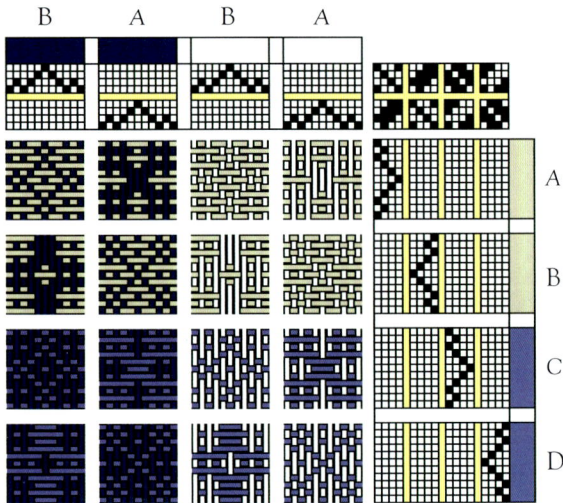

*Threading Key. The 4-shaft twill blocks alternate between two irregular twill tie-ups. The A threading block always weaves crosses and the B, diamonds. In each treadling block warp- and weft-dominant blocks are adjacent. In the B and D treadlings, the decorated point figure inverts. In C and D, the face changes. The draft is expanded to separate the blocks and colors are modified to help see the interlacement.*

## Tips

• Make matching panels easier by warping with a trapeze (Meek, 2005), weaving with live-weight tensioning, using a computer-aided loom, and using a temple moved forward every inch (marked on the computer program with a color-change reminder). A Tyvek tape measure, with attached supplementary paper notes, can indicate reversal points, color changes, and major pattern changes (as in the colored cross-bands of this piece).

• Blocking, ironing, and handsewing a piece this large can be challenging. Block by stretching a king-size linen sheet over two banquet tables with athletic weights and supporting the middle space with an adjustable ironing-board. Anchor the damp pall squarely with small athletic weights and leave until nearly dry. Iron with a padded and linen-covered 2' x 4' ironing board. Slide and move the board as needed under the sheet supporting the pall, steam-pressing gently on wool setting. Align the two sides and join with a small backstitch using 24/2 cotton on the same set-up. Steam open the seams and stitch the seam edges with small running stitches. Miter the corners and hem, then handstitch lettering bands.

• Changing face when there is a major color change can make the pattern seem more continuous or integrated. Here, the weft bands change face to keep the white stars on blue ground consistent with the warp-wise stripes.

• Kati advises, "Don't agree to include lettering on a large piece of handwoven until and unless all factors and techniques, including take-up and shrinkage, are familiar methods in combination."

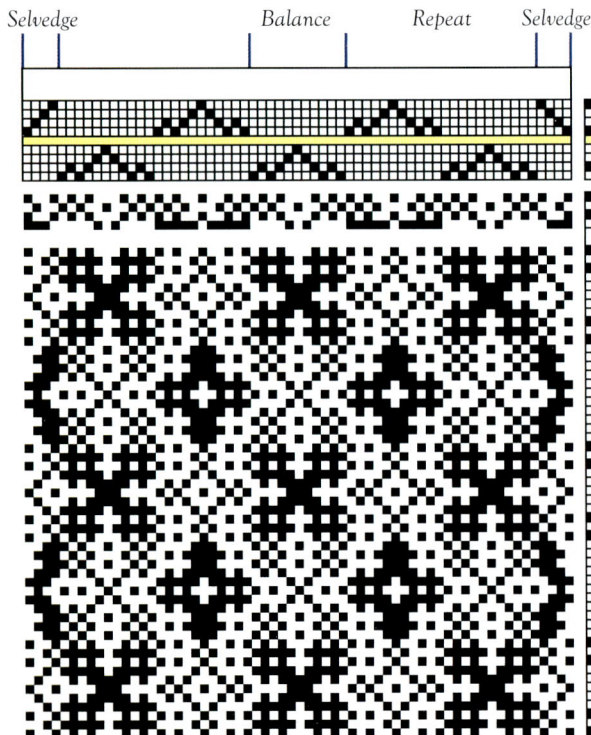

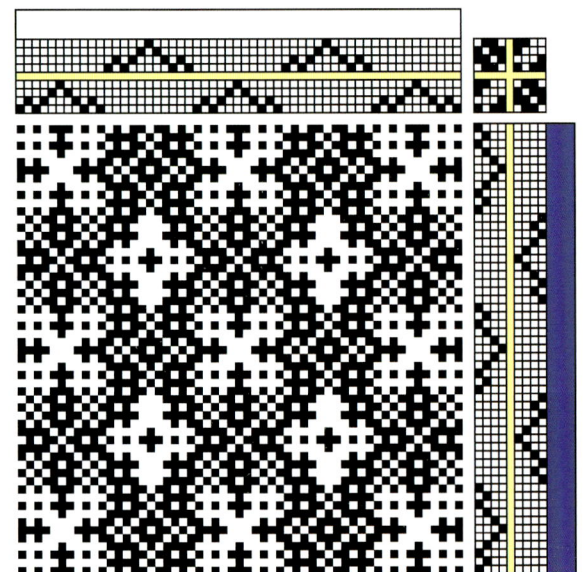

*Threading Drafts. Structure drawdowns to show how the motifs connect. Left, body with treadlings A and B. Right, face reversed for colored weft, using treadlings C and D. The drafts are expanded to separate the blocks.*

112

# For Christopher
## Charlotte Lindsay Allison

### Blanket in Skillbragd

### Design Process

When I first cradled my baby boy, I was told he was from Northern European roots. Later, I learned he is of Norwegian descent. When first introduced to weaving, I was drawn to Northern European looms and textiles, all because of my deep, abiding love for Christopher.

Within the pages of Johansson (1984), there is a section on the weave structure Smålandsvav which intrigued me. The chapter is well written and easy to follow. Skillbragd is the name for this weave structure in Norway. In a book of skillbragd blankets and coverlets by Sandstad (2002) I saw a drawdown I fancied for a blanket. I modified my warp and pattern weft to be different from the published drawdown, making it my own. The blue pattern weft is 6/2 wool to match the color of Christopher's eyes. Yes, when I look into those clear blue eyes, it is as though I am looking through a window into heaven. Typically in Norway (and Sweden), a sheepskin is sewn to the back. However, living in Texas, I opted to back the cloth with cotton.

For Christopher's 8-shaft throw, I wove on a modified countermarche loom. It has two tabby ground shafts and six pattern shafts. Plain weave is threaded through normal heddles on the back shafts. The pattern shafts are closest to the front of the loom and are threaded in units in long-eyed Opphämta heddles. Each filled-in square is threaded with a unit.

I love the intrigue of this weave structure. It was a thrill for me to see the pattern unfold before my eyes. Such a fun project!

### Weaving Information

Size: 66" x 31"

Warp: 16/2 cotton, 6720 ypp, bleached; 25 epi

Weft: 16/2 cotton, 6720 ypp, bleached (tabby); 6/2 Tuna wool, 1600 ypp, bluebell (pattern); 25 ppi

Source: Sandstad (2002, p. 132)

Weave Structure: Skillbragd (Smålandsväv or treadled opphämta), 8 shafts on modified countermarche loom

Finishing: Washed in tepid water with Synthrapol. Blanket was soaked to make certain that it was completely wet, then agitated for three minutes. Spun until the water was out of the machine and refilled. Pressed on low with a large towel until barely dry, then hung until dry.

Take-up and Shrinkage: Warp 9%, weft 6%

Each 2-thread unit has one thread on shaft 8 and one on shaft 7, with regular heddles. The two threads then pass as a pair through zero to six long-eyed pattern heddles on shafts 1 through 6 (in this example, shafts 1, 2, 3, 4, and 6). The back two shafts are hung at a distance from the front six in order to allow room for proper movement through the front shaft heddles. Elastic bands help return the Glimåkra's front pttern shafts to starting position (Blair, 2021).

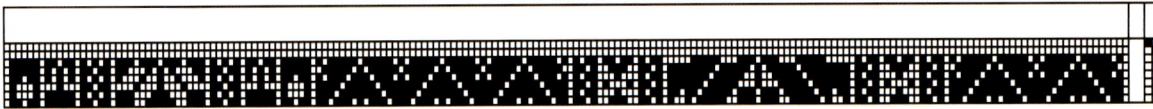

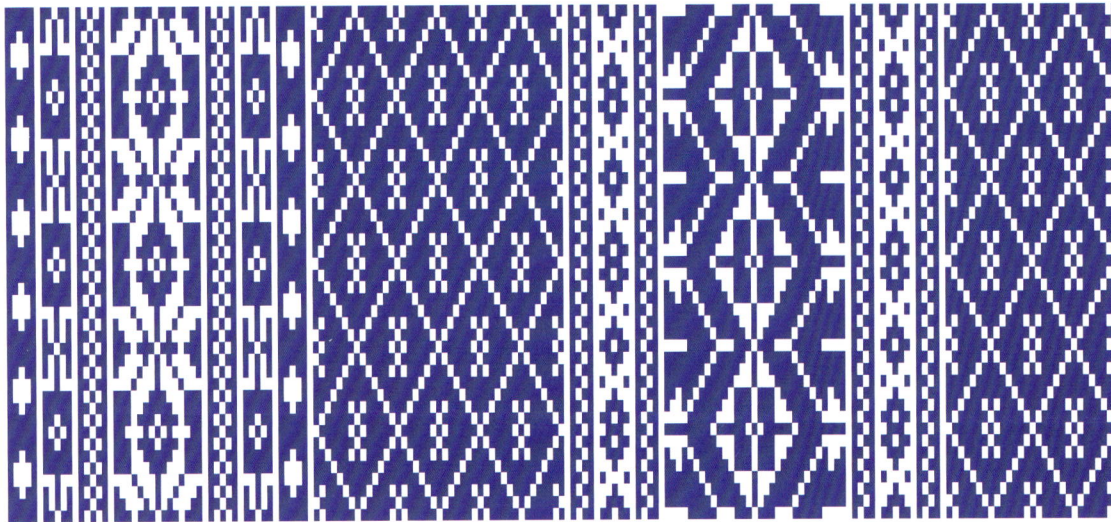

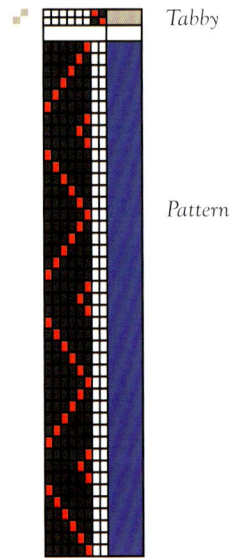

Modified Shaft-Loom Profile Draft. Skillbragd (Smålandsväv or treadled opphämta) woven on a modified countermarche floor loom. Each 2-thread warp unit is woven with four picks, consisting of two pattern picks alternating with two tabby picks. To weave plain weave, shafts 7 and 8 are used alternately alone. The weft-float pattern threads are formed by the shafts which sink (red in treadling), with the shafts not forming pattern remaining up (dark gray). For example, if shaft 6 is treadled down and shafts 1 to 5 remain up, all pattern units threaded through shaft 6 will weave pattern. The pattern sheds will be shallower than the tabby sheds and may require a thinner shuttle. The tabby color is actually bleached white rather than the tan shown.

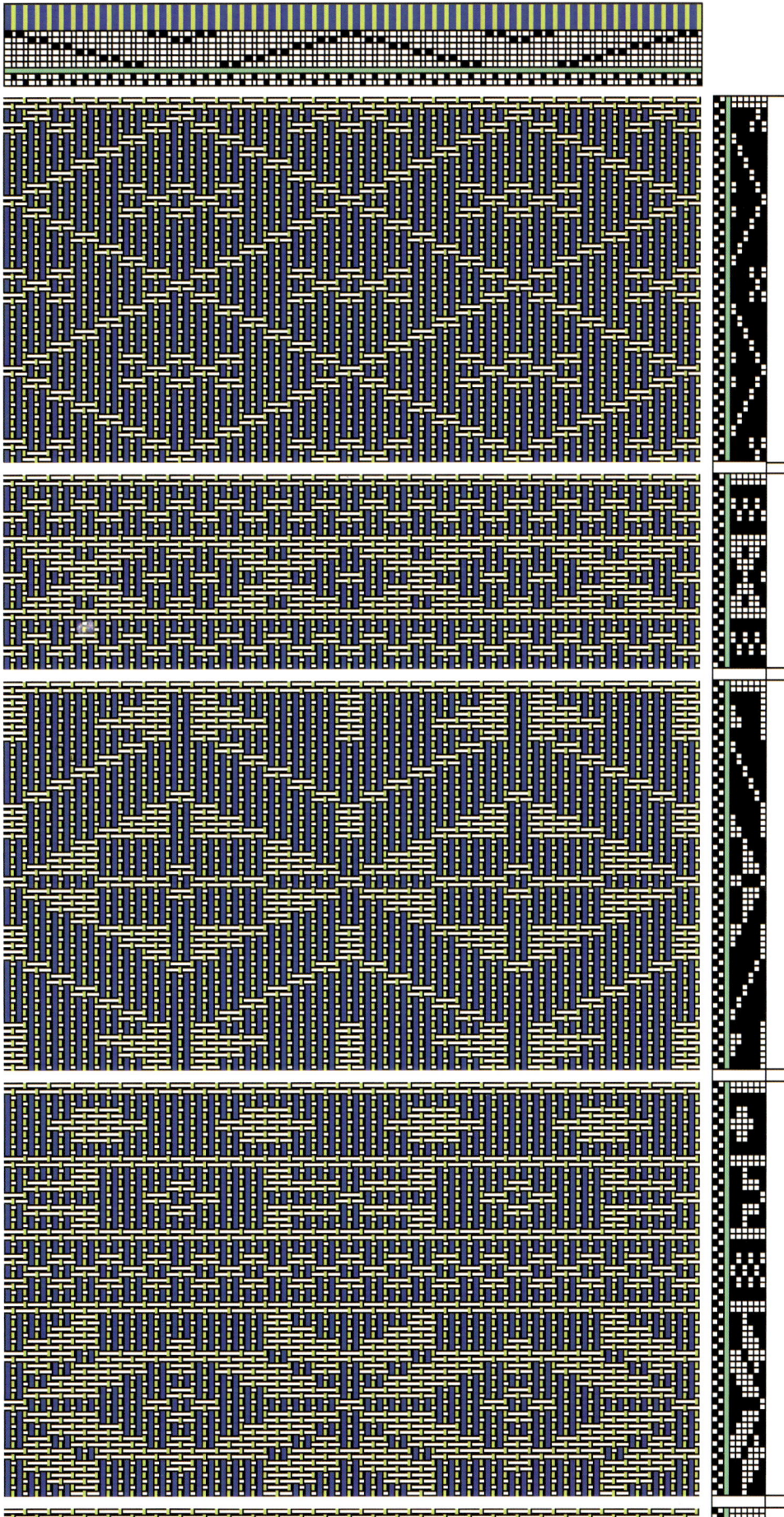

## Tips

• To hide the stitches when attaching the backing fabric, work carefully from the back to tie the back to the front, hiding all of the joins.

• While inspiration can come from anywhere, try exploring your own family's ethnic traditions.

• Modifying a loom in this manner opens up a large number of new design possibilities for the 8-shaft weaver.

• This type of draft can be turned to weave the stripes of patterns in the weft direction in warp floats on an unmodified loom. It will require a dobby, computer dobby, table loom, or changing the tie-up as new sheds are needed (very often in this design).

• Charlotte advises, "With graph paper in hand, have great fun exploring your own designs - especially when you let your heart guide your inspiration."

*Threading Draft. Alternative drawdown for an unmodified 8-shaft loom, made by turning the draft. In the turned draft, the pattern is formed by warp floats rather than weft floats. A liftplan is needed as there are far too many shaft combinations for a usable tie-up. Repeat treadlings as desired. The draft was expanded to separate the pattern from tie-downs and tabby.*

# Ode to Wanda

## Barbara J. Walker

### Shallow Basket in Ply-Splitting

### Design Process

Wanda Shelp's book (Shelp and Wostenberg, 1991; p. 75) was my place to begin; I wanted to ply-split one of her drafts. I liked the look of #4.101 but added changes of direction in the twill line to show more movement. I wanted to evoke brush strokes and preferred the back view of the original drawdown. As an 8-shaft draft, this undulating twill has a 1/3/3/1 regular twill tie-up; as a ply-split piece that is irrelevant to the process.

Gradual color changes across the piece show movement and are more interesting than using only one color in the warp-wise cords. Three different colors were used for the warp-wise cords, with one or two colors per ply changed to achieve the blending. The weft-wise cords are one color and considered to be background. A trac border finished the basket rim.

The joy of ply-splitting a drawdown lies partly in the fact that the number of shafts has no bearing at all. It is just as easy to ply-split a 40-shaft design as it is to ply-split a 4-shaft design.

*Threading Draft. The undulating twill pattern is shown as a draft for an 8-shaft loom, with the full pattern given for warp and weft. It acts as a cartoon for the basket. The finished piece is not made this way, nor is there a twill structure in the basket.*

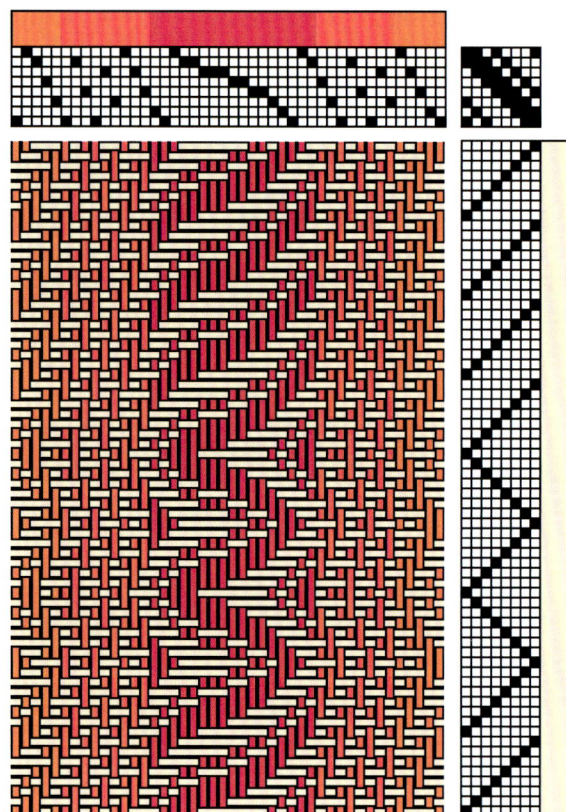

### Weaving Information

Size: 9" x 6.25" x 1"

Warp: Artist-made 4-ply cords, mixed linen sizes

Weft: Artist-made 4-ply cords, mixed linen sizes

Source: Modified draft #4.101 (Shelp and Wostenberg, 1991)

Structure: Ply-splitting

Finishing: A trac border finished the basket rim.

## Tips

• Ply-splitting from the center of the drawdown outward allows you to center the length of each cord.

• Shaft-weaving designs are a rich source of patterns for ply-splitting (Walker, 2012). Only the drawdown portion of the draft is used for ply-splitting. The threading, tie-up, and treadling are irrelevant. Without a shaft constraint, it is a fascinating technique to use for designs which would require more shafts than you own.

• Float length in shaft weaving is irrelevant in ply-splitting.

• Confining color changes to only one direction lets the other serve as a unifying element.

• Blend colors smoothly by changing only one or two colors per ply in each cord as you move across the piece.

# Illusion Revealed
## Gudrun Polak
### Band in Card Weaving

### Design Process

The design of this card-woven band is the outcome of cross-pollination in the fiber arts. While the techniques of loom weaving and card weaving are very different, the images that are created can be similar. Weaving patterns with diagonal lines lend themselves to being adapted to the technique of warp twining in card weaving.

Simple twill patterns are easily replicated in card weaving. Regular 2/2 twills, 3/1 twills, and even diamond and leaf shaped patterns have their obvious equivalents in card weaving. Plaited twill patterns translate into more complex card weaving patterns. The reward is a body of more interesting designs.

The pattern of this band was inspired by an 8-shaft weaving pattern for a plaited twill (Strickler, 1991; #356, p. 100). Typically, a card-weaving pattern is designed to have a certain image on the front side. What shows up on the back side can be a surprise. It may be nothing recognizable at all. It may be a fuzzy version of the front side, the front pattern upside down, or a completely new pattern. In the case of this band, the pattern on the back looks a lot like another plaited twill pattern from the same source (Strickler, 1991; #360, p. 101).

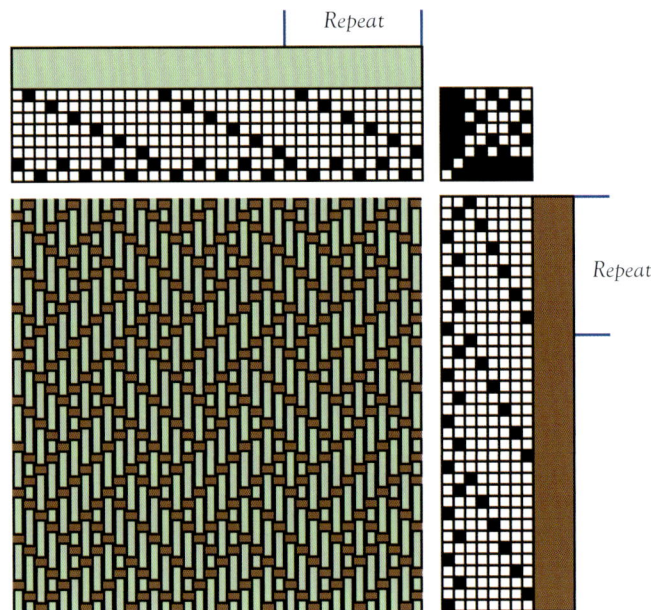

*Threading Draft. Plaited twill as woven on an 8-shaft loom. Based on draft #356 in Strickler (1991), it is similar to the front of the band. The band is not made in this way and does not have a twill structure.*

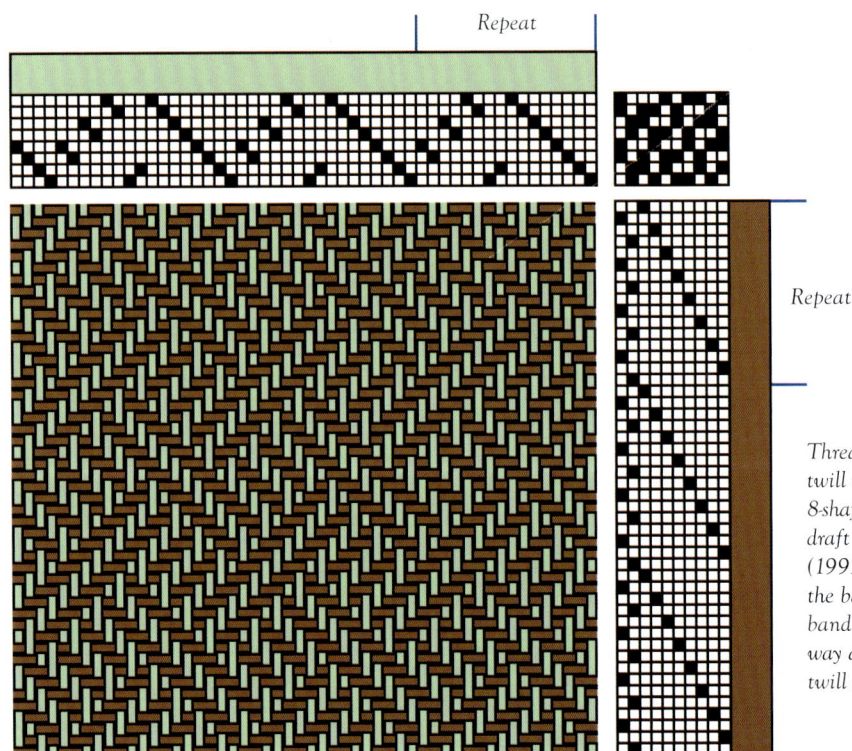

*Threading Draft. Plaited twill as woven on an 8-shaft loom. Based on draft #360 in Strickler (1991), it is very similar to the back of the band. The band is not made in this way and does not have a twill structure.*

118

## Weaving Information

Size: 50" x 0.75"

Warp: Sewing Machine Silk Twist, green and brown; 26 cards

Weft: Sewing Machine Silk Twist, brown; 20 ppi

Source: Original draft inspired by Strickler (1991) #356

Weave Structure: Warp twining using 4-hole square cards

Finishing: The band itself needs no finishing. It is ready to be turned into a band for a musical instrument, a strap for a handbag, or a reversible belt.

Take-up: Warp 20%

## Tips

- Simple and complex twills from shaft weaving are a good source of design ideas. The diagonal twill lines are natural elements for card weaving.

- Drawing out a twill pattern on graph paper is a good first step to designing a similar pattern for card weaving. With the cards threaded as for this project we know that turning a card backwards will create a forward slash (/) in the woven band; turning a card forward creates a backslash (\). If you turn the left half of the cards forward and the right half of the cards backwards (or vice versa) you will weave a herringbone pattern. Changing the turning direction for some cards at any pick will create a more complex pattern. A good starting point for understanding the design steps is to use simple diamond twills like (Strickler, 1991; #369, #370, p. 103). For more information on designing in tablet weaving see Polak (2004 a and b, 2006).

- Play and experiment! The pattern possibilities are intriguing and endless, making card weaving a fascinating technique.

The weaving draft grid is numbered 16 through 1 from top to bottom on both the left and right sides.

*Above, Weaving draft for cards. The direction of the turn is shown for two repeats of the 8-thread sequence. Cards turned in one direction (backward) have a gray background; cards turned in the other direction (forward) have a white background.*

| # | 1 | 2 | 3 | 4 | 5 | 6 | 7 | 8 | 9 | 10 | 11 | 12 | 13 | 14 | 15 | 16 | 17 | 18 | 19 | 20 | 21 | 22 | 23 | 24 | 25 | 26 |
|---|---|---|---|---|---|---|---|---|---|----|----|----|----|----|----|----|----|----|----|----|----|----|----|----|----|----|
| A | | | | | | | | | | | | | | | | | | | | | | | | | | |
| B | | | | | | | | | | | | | | | | | | | | | | | | | | |
| C | | | | | | | | | | | | | | | | | | | | | | | | | | |
| D | | | | | | | | | | | | | | | | | | | | | | | | | | |
| T | S | Z | Z | Z | Z | Z | Z | Z | Z | Z | Z | Z | Z | Z | Z | Z | Z | Z | Z | Z | Z | Z | Z | Z | Z | Z |

*Left, Threading draft for cards. Cards 1 and 26 are threaded with brown in all four holes, while the other cards alternate brown and green.*

# Part II: Extending to 8-Shaft Components

# II.1  8-Shaft Drafts as Profiles

Unlike a simple threading draft which shows the interlacement of individual threads, a profile draft is a form of shorthand drafting for block weaves. It indicates the placement of pattern and background (or a second or third pattern) in the cloth. That is, each square indicates the design effect of a group of threads which always work together rather than the actions of single threads.

This compact form of drafting makes it simpler to see the design in the cloth independently from the structure. It is faster than drafting the placement of each thread and makes it easy to transfer a pattern from one structure to another. Profile drafts can be converted to threading drafts in any block structure which is compatible with the design constraints. The choice of structure provides a way to enlarge patterns, control float lengths, and add complexity to the design, as well as to change the hand, etc.

Any threading draft may be used as a profile draft, however, the opposite is not true. The examples each use a single structure, but translation to multiple structures can lead to interesting cloth.

*Top Right, Original 8-shaft undulating twill draft showing thread-by-thread interlacement. There are 38 warp threads per repeat and the maximum float length is seven threads in the warp, eight in the weft. A regular 2/1/1/1/1/2 twill tie-up is used.*

*Second Right, 8-block profile draft made from the twill draft with the warp floats arbitrarily chosen as pattern, shown as black squares.*

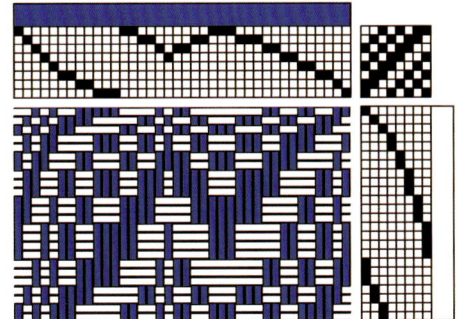

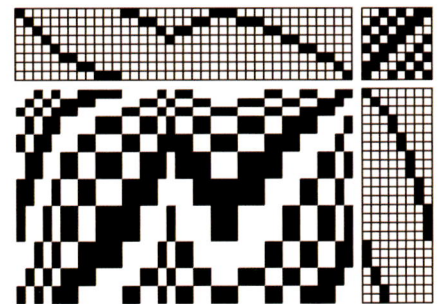

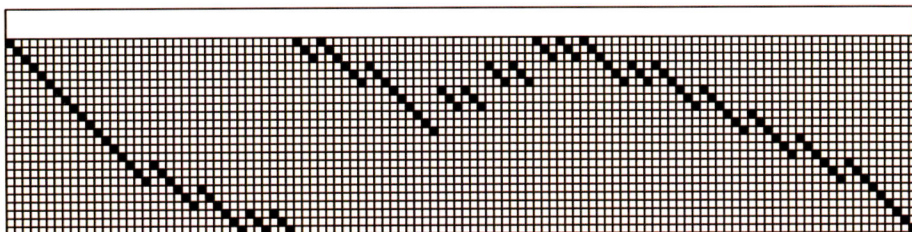

*Above, Tie-ups for the 3-shaft 1/2 twill pattern and 2/1 twill background (second pattern) blocks.*

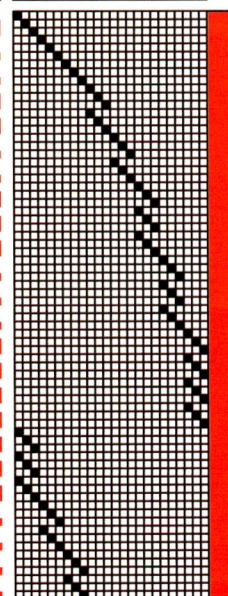

*The profile draft converted to a 24-shaft threading draft for turned 3-thread twill blocks. Maximum float length is two threads.*

122

The profile draft converted to a 12-shaft straight 4-tie tied weave with half treadling blocks and a skeleton tie-up (tabby not shown). Maximum float length is seven threads.

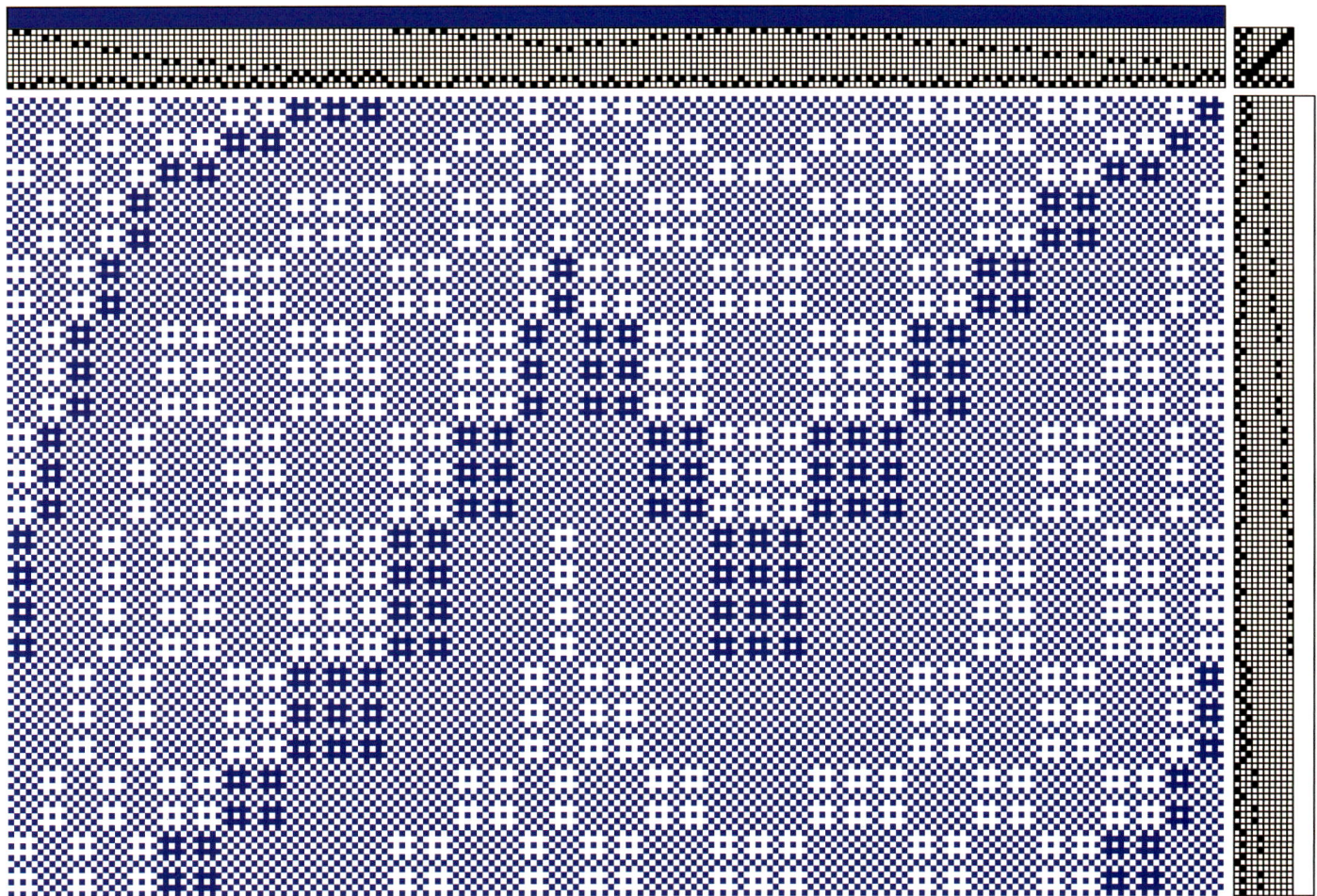

The profile converted to a 10-shaft threading draft for Swedish lace. Note that the warp and weft floats combined make up the pattern. Maximum float length is five threads.

# Field of Green

## Betty Alexander

### Pillow in Crackle Variant

### Design Process

Our guild, Western Weavers, decided to honor past member Wanda Shelp by using a point twill threading from an 8-shaft draft in Shelp and Wostenberg (1991; threading #3, page 32) as a profile threading. Each of the six weavers used the same profile threading and plugged in the structure, tie-up, and treadling of their choice, creating a study in using a profile draft.

I chose crackle for my piece and used Fiberworks to substitute the threading and liftplan. I modified the draft until I arrived at a result which was pleasing to me. Incidentals were added, the loom threaded, and sampling done. I decided on a non-traditional crackle variant without tabby (Wilson, 2011). It is a one-shuttle weave that produces a stable fabric. After weaving three pillows with different colored wefts, I shall no doubt weave more decorative pillow covers!

*Threading Draft. An 8-shaft crackle threading with a regular 2/1/1/1/1/2 twill tie-up. The treadling combines a straight twill line of five which advances by one, then mirrors, with simple points across all eight shafts. Right half shown.*

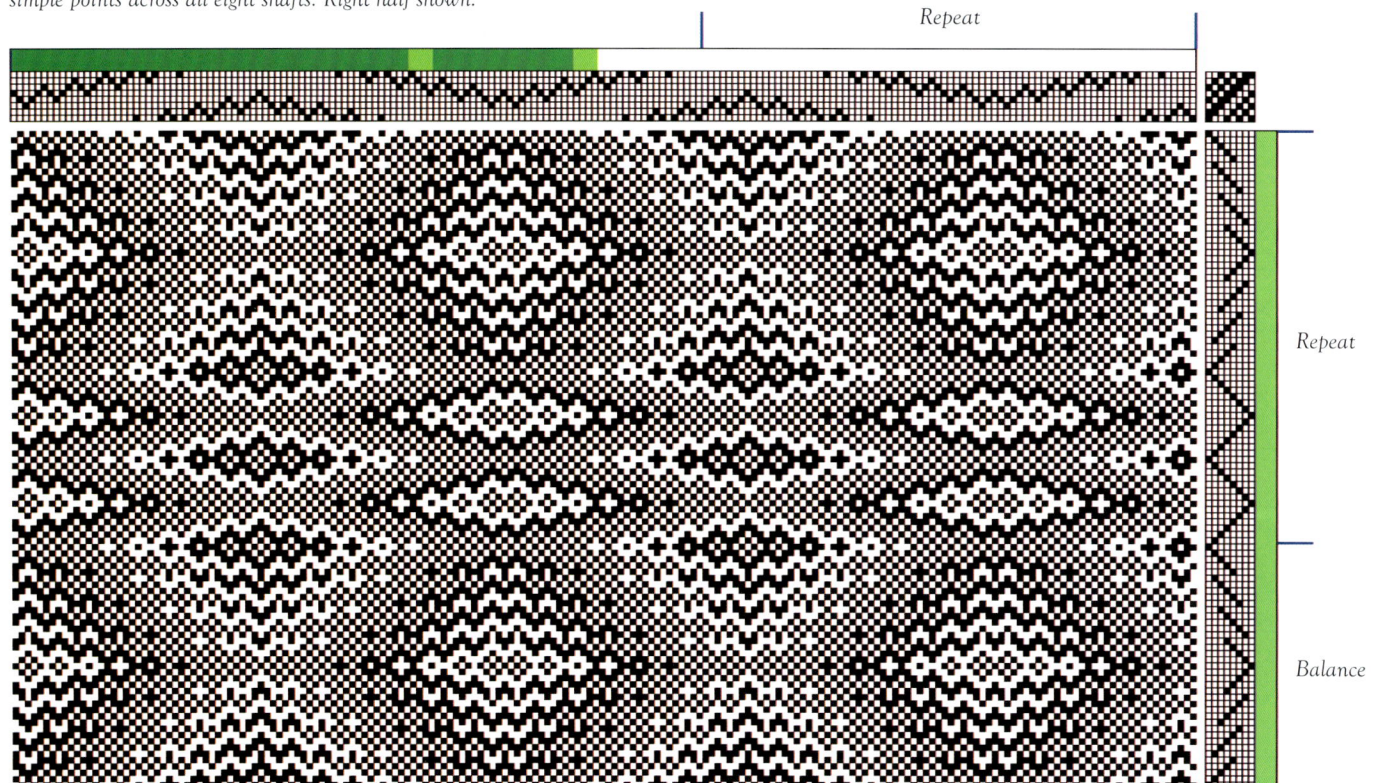

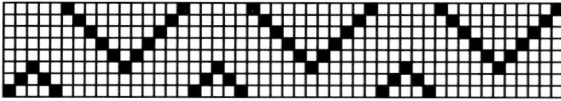

*Profile Threading. Derived from 8-shaft draft in Shelp and Wostenberg (1991).*

## Tips

• One can find many ways to finish a pillow top on the internet. Pick one that suits you and go for it!

• Twills are an excellent source of profile drafts for other structures.

• Consider offering a change in pattern information to the viewer at different viewing distances. Varying the contrast between warp and weft is a way to break up a strong pattern and to give the viewer something different to see at different distances. The darker warp stripe patterns will be more visible across the room, while pattern in the low contrast areas requires a more intimate viewing distance.

• "Punctuation" can add spice and unity to a design. Here, the narrow light green bands in the warp break up the large darker green area and serve as bridges to the lighter edges of the pillow.

## Weaving Information

Size: 18" x 18"

Warp: 8/2 mercerized cotton, 3200 ypp, natural, bright dark green, white, and light green; 18 epi

Weft: 8/2 mercerized cotton, 3200 ypp, white (detail photo), light green (whole pillow photo), or light pink (not shown); 17 ppi

Source: Modified from Shelp and Wostenberg (1991)

Weave Structure: Crackle woven as twill, 8 shafts

Finishing: Secured with a machine zigzag stitch on each end prior to fulling. Hand washed in hot water with mild detergent, soaked for 20 minutes, gentle agitation, then rinsed in warm water. Blocked to size and laid flat to dry until just damp; pressed with pressing cloth until dry.

Sewing: No pattern was used. The pillow is made with one piece of fabric and fastened on the back with a 16" strip of 0.5" Velcro.

Take-up and Shrinkage: Weft 3% take-up, warp and weft shrinkage negligible

# Wyoming Sagebrush

## Kay Strike

### Napkin Set in Atwater-Bronson Lace

## Design Process

Joining Western Weavers with Wanda Shelp and Carolyn Wostenberg has led to the new challenges of joining Complex Weavers (2016), using computer weaving software and weaving this project. The guild chose threading draft #3 on page 32 of Shelp and Wostenberg (1991) as our starting point in a profile draft. Having never used computer weaving software, I purchased Fiberworks because of its compatibility with my Mac computer. I inserted the threading, tie-up, and various treadlings from page 32 into the program and began to play. The most pleasing structure to me was an Atwater-Bronson lace weave based on the treadling of draft #2.59.

I decided to use a 16/2 cottolin, and experimented with shades of white, light tan, dark tan, and sage green. After inserting various color combinations in Fiberworks, I chose light tan for the warp. I then sampled all of the other colors as weft to determine which weft color would best display the Atwater-Bronson lace warp threads. While all the colors displayed them equally well, I still wasn't pleased with the overall effect. At that point, I doubled the 16/2 weft threads and discovered the sage green displayed the most defined lace pattern.

## Weaving Information

Size: 17" x 17"

Warp: 16/2 cottolin, 6720 ypp, light tan; 24 epi

Weft: 16/2 cottolin doubled, 6720 ypp, sage; 24 ppi

Source: Modified from Shelp and Wostenberg (1991)

Weave Structure: Atwater-Bronson lace, 10 shafts

Finishing: Hems were hand sewn. Machine washed in warm water in mild laundry detergent with medium spin, machine dried 15 minutes until damp. Pressed with damp cloth.

Take-up and Shrinkage: Warp and weft 15%

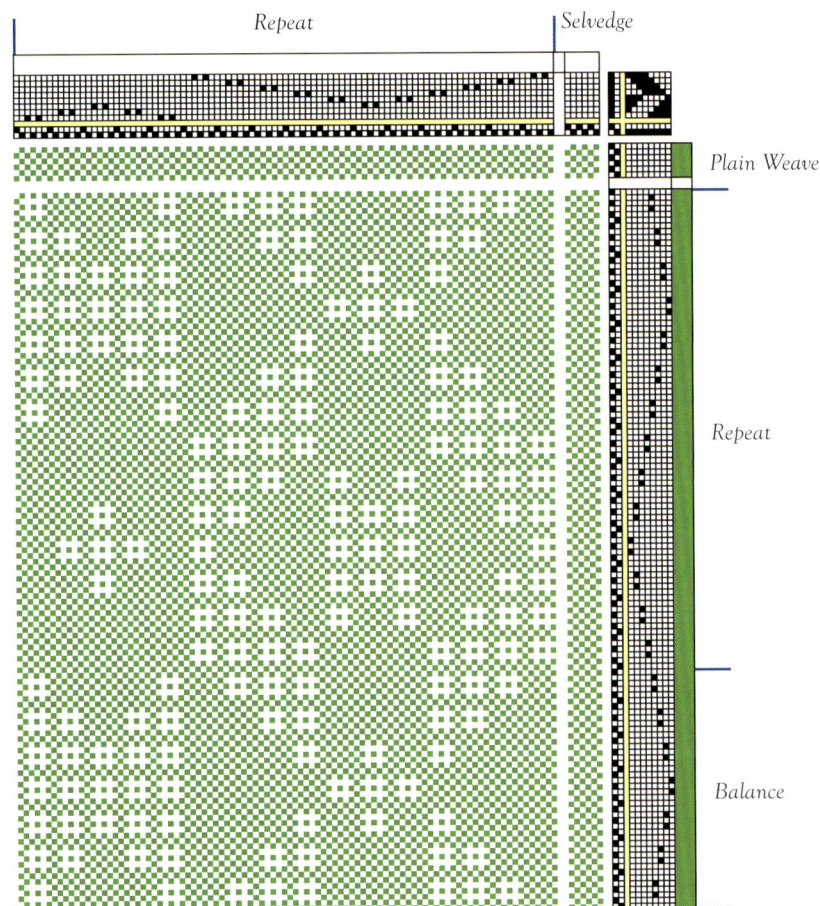

*Threading Draft. The profile has been converted to 6-thread Atwater-Bronson lace blocks woven with warp floats. The plain weave selvedges are formed by alternating the two tie-down shafts. The draft has been expanded to separate the tie-down shafts and tabbies from the pattern shafts and picks.*

*Profile Draft. Profile threading derived from 8-shaft draft in Shelp and Wostenberg (1991). The tie-up divides the blocks into two sets (A to D and E to H) with opposite patterns for sharp breaks. A simple point forms the treadling.*

126

## Tips

• Combining the color view of a drafting program with actual sampling can lead to improved color selection.

• Doubling or using a heavier weft thread makes differences in warp and weft more pronounced. In a traditional treadling of Atwater-Bronson lace, where all the floats are in the weft direction, a heavier or doubled weft will make the weft pattern floats more visible, and there are no warp floats of a different weight to distract the eye. If the less common warp float side is used as the top, as here, the doubled weft provides a firmer background, with a higher proportion of its color relative to the warp color. This distinction also helps the floats to stand out, though more delicately than on the weft float side.

• In other laces with both warp and weft floats, the difference between a heavier (or doubled) warp or weft and a lighter weft or warp could be used with care to make the heavier direction dominant, with a secondary or shading pattern in the lighter direction.

# Crossing Paths
## Roxanne Zahller

### Table Runner in Summer and Winter

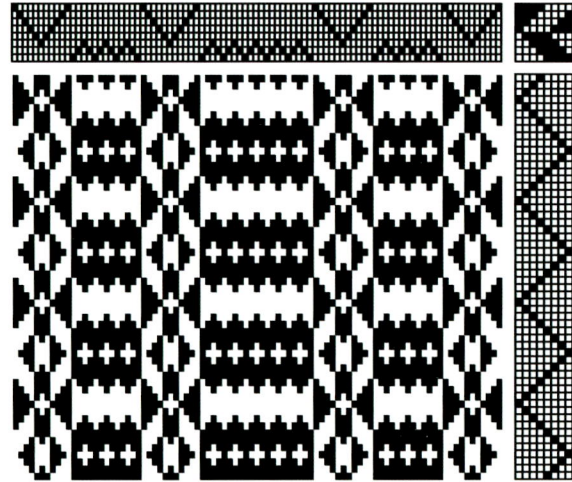

*Profile Draft. The original Shelp and Wostenberg (1991) threading was changed by repeating the small points three or five times rather than once. The tie-up divides the blocks into two sets (A to D and E to H) with opposite patterns for sharp breaks. A simple point forms the treadling.*

## Design Process

The members of Western Weavers in Wyoming chose a random point twill 8-shaft threading from Shelp and Wostenburg (1991; page 32, threading #3) as our profile threading. Then, we each picked a different block weave structure for our projects.

In my profile draft, I retained the tie-up from page 32 and used treadling #2.60 on the same page, repeating some sections of blocks. I decided to use summer and winter for the structure, and treadled in Dukagång fashion. Wanting to add some color interest, I gave each of the two block motifs in the warp its own tone. I based the colors on a lovely pottery bowl that I have, finding yarns in my stash to coordinate with the bowl. I was very pleased with the results.

I named my piece Crossing Paths because I feel very fortunate to have crossed paths with Wanda Shelp, who was such an inspiring and helpful teacher and mentor.

## Weaving Information

Size: 44.5" x 14" plus 1.5" fringe on each end

Warp: 10/2 mercerized cotton, 4200 ypp, natural and tan; 24 epi

Weft: 20/2 mercerized cotton, 8400 ypp, natural (tabby);10/2 mercerized cotton doubled, 4200 ypp, dark brown (pattern); 28 ppi

Source: Modified from Shelp and Wostenberg (1991)

Weave Structure: Summer and winter, 10 shafts (plus two optional)

Finishing: Ends were secured with Italian hem-stitching, over five ends and up five picks. Soaked in warm water with Castile soap, rinsed warm. Laid flat to dry until damp and steam pressed until dry.

Take-up and Shrinkage: Warp and weft 15%

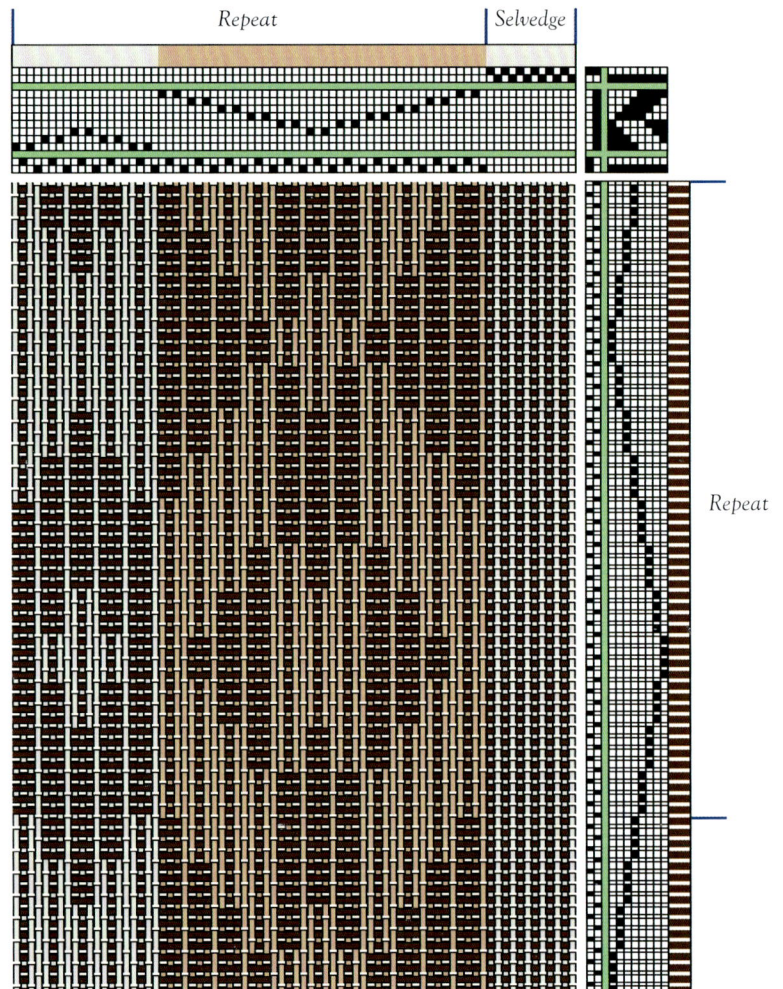

*Threading Draft. The profile was translated to summer and winter with Dukagång-style treadling. Plain weave selvedges were threaded on two additional shafts (optional). The draft has been expanded to separate the tie-down shafts and tabbies from the pattern shafts and picks.*

## Tips

• Use a favorite item or photograph to inspire your color choices.

• Dukagång-style treadling of summer and winter, with its vertical columns of floats, makes a strong, graphic statement. Here, the simple vertical lines complement the diamond patterning without the distracting effects of the more complex blurring one would get with paired O or paired X style treadlings.

• Color can be changed to emphasize a change in pattern or motif, or kept constant to join the different sections, lessening their differences. A third choice, changing the color within patterns or motifs, can create more design possibilities. Choosing one of these coloring options can add rhythm and unity to the piece as it defines a single, consistent way for the viewer to see the pattern. Alternatively, two or all three coloring schemes may be used in one piece to create more pattern options and a more complex result from a single repeating structural pattern.

• Sometimes a design looks better when a section is repeated more or less than initially planned. Play with your design options before committing to a final draft.

• Patterns with strong diamonds can take on ethnic connotations from many different cultures.

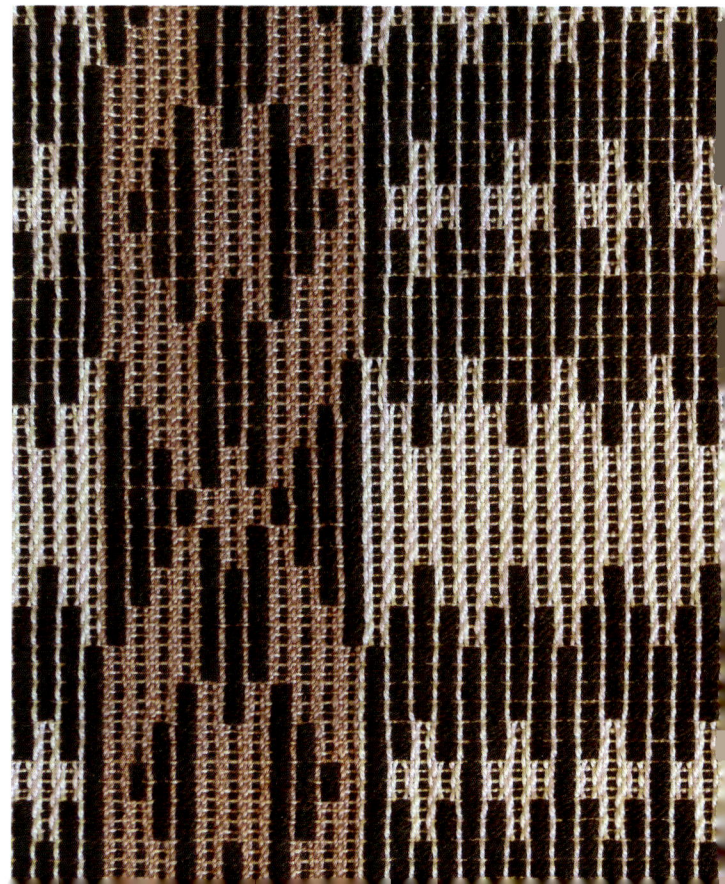

# Diamonds in Squares

## Carolyn Wostenberg

### Table Runner in Quigley

### Design Process

Our Western Weavers group decided to use Wanda's and my book (Shelp and Wostenberg, 1991) as a group effort to honor Wanda's memory. Cheri Shelp suggested an 8-shaft point twill draft threading (#3, page 32) to be used as the profile threading. Each member would then choose a different weave structure for their entry.

Previously, the Western Weavers had done a study of tied weaves and I had woven Quigley several times. I knew that I could plug the threading units into this type of profile draft. I used van der Hoogt (1993, p. 89) as a reference for converting the profile draft to a Quigley threading draft with straight order of tie-downs on shafts 1 to 4 and pattern threads on shafts 5 to 12. The tie-downs are lifted in a 1/3 twill pattern, and reverse direction at strategic points in the treadling. I had to weave this design several times before I completed a piece that squared up and was without threading errors.

*Profile Draft. Profile threading derived from 8-shaft draft in Shelp and Wostenberg (1991). The points in the rosepath-style treadling are doubled so the tie-down direction can change symmetrically when woven in Quigley. The tie-up, with its simple triangle and opposite pattern on treadles one versus two, keeps the pattern bold and sharply defined.*

*Portion of runner, with warp horizontal.*

*Threading Draft. The profile has been translated to Quigley, a straight single 4-tie weave. The direction of the ties reverses at turning points in the treadling. Shown as a skeleton draft with 14 treadles for a 12-shaft loom. Use tabby (not shown). The draft has been expanded to separate the tie-down shafts and tabbies from the pattern shafts and picks.*

## Weaving Information

Size: 52" x 17.5"

Warp: 20/2 mercerized cotton, 8400 ypp, multi-colored brown/black; 30 epi

Weft: 20/2 mercerized cotton, 8400 ypp, multi-colored brown/black (tabby); pattern, 5/2 mercerized cotton, 2100 ypp, white (pattern); 40 ppi including tabby

Source: Modified from Shelp and Wostenberg (1991)

Weave Structure: Quigley, 12 shafts

Finishing: Machine washed and dried. Pressed using cotton setting.

Sewing: Ends were serged, folded under and hand stitched.

Take-up and Shrinkage: Warp 11%, weft 8%

## Tips

• Less common than summer and winter, Quigley has more tie-down pattern options, but works in a similar way.

• Choosing a supplementary tied weave structure with four tie-down shafts instead of a simpler pattern of two tie-down shafts increases the size of the blocks and the scale of the design. It may or may not increase the float length, depending on the tie-up chosen for the tie-down threads.

• The choice of tie-up for the tie-down pattern makes a lot of difference to the look and clarity of the overall pattern. Commonly, a 1/3 regular twill tie-up is chosen for the four tie-down shafts in Quigley. The opposite side will reverse to a 3/1 regular twill pattern for the tie-downs, and the pattern and background blocks will be strongly differentiated from each other and between the two sides. A 2/2 tie-up will be more subtle, with the back also a 2/2 tie-up. The 2/2 tie-up also obscures more of the difference in pattern and background blocks.

• Changing the direction of the tie-downs used in the treadling is a way to add additional interest to a design. Aligning the change in direction with the center of a pattern figure or at mirrors in the pattern treadling adds a feeling of unity and order to the changes. Here, the direction changes at the center of the large diamond and the center of the narrow bands in between the large diamonds.

# Traditions
## Amy Buchan

### Table Runner in Uneven Tied Overshot Variant

### Design Process

This piece started as a guild project to honor the memory of one of our members, Wanda Jean Shelp. The group began with an 8-shaft point twill threading (Shelp and Wostenberg, 1991; threading #3, page 32) to be used as the profile threading.

Wanda and I were both members of the Complex Weavers Early Weaving Books and Manuscripts study group, so I chose a traditional structure, uneven two-tied overshot, for my interpretation of the profile draft. During the design process, I referred back to the notes and samples that Wanda had shared with the Western Weavers guild on tied overshot. To keep the pattern smaller and the floats shorter, I used 3-thread blocks of uneven tied overshot rather than the more common 5-thread blocks.

The threading profile was changed a bit to suit the design. I also introduced some variations in the tie-downs at one of the two turning points, changing the alternation and the spacing with pattern threads, and used stripes of silver in these areas. In the tie-up, the pattern portion of the tie-up on shafts 3 to 10 follows an irregular twill pattern for ten treadles rather than eight. The pattern treadles change four ties on shafts 1 and 2 to become a small area of pattern themselves (see the small tie-up analysis figure).

## Weaving Information

Size: 35" x 15" plus 1.25" fringe on each end

Warp: 10/2 mercerized cotton, 4200 ypp, bleached, silver; 30 epi

Weft: 10/2 mercerized cotton, 4200 ypp, bleached (tabby); 5/2 mercerized cotton, 2100 ypp, soldier blue (pattern); 30-32 ppi

Source: Modified from Shelp and Wostenberg (1991)

Weave Structure: Uneven tied overshot variant, 10 shafts

Finishing: Fringe was knotted with 12 ends. Machine washed with detergent for 30 minutes and rinsed in warm water. Machine dried on medium heat until slightly damp, shaking often to prevent wrinkles. Hard pressed by hand on high using a pressing cloth until dry.

Take-up and Shrinkage: Warp 13%, weft 9%

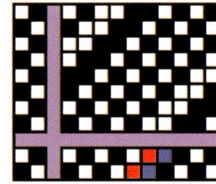

*Threading Draft Tie-up. Enlarged to show the two ties which have changed from the expected (marked in red) to an unusual variant (marked in blue). Expanded to separate the tie-down shafts and tabby treadles from the pattern area.*

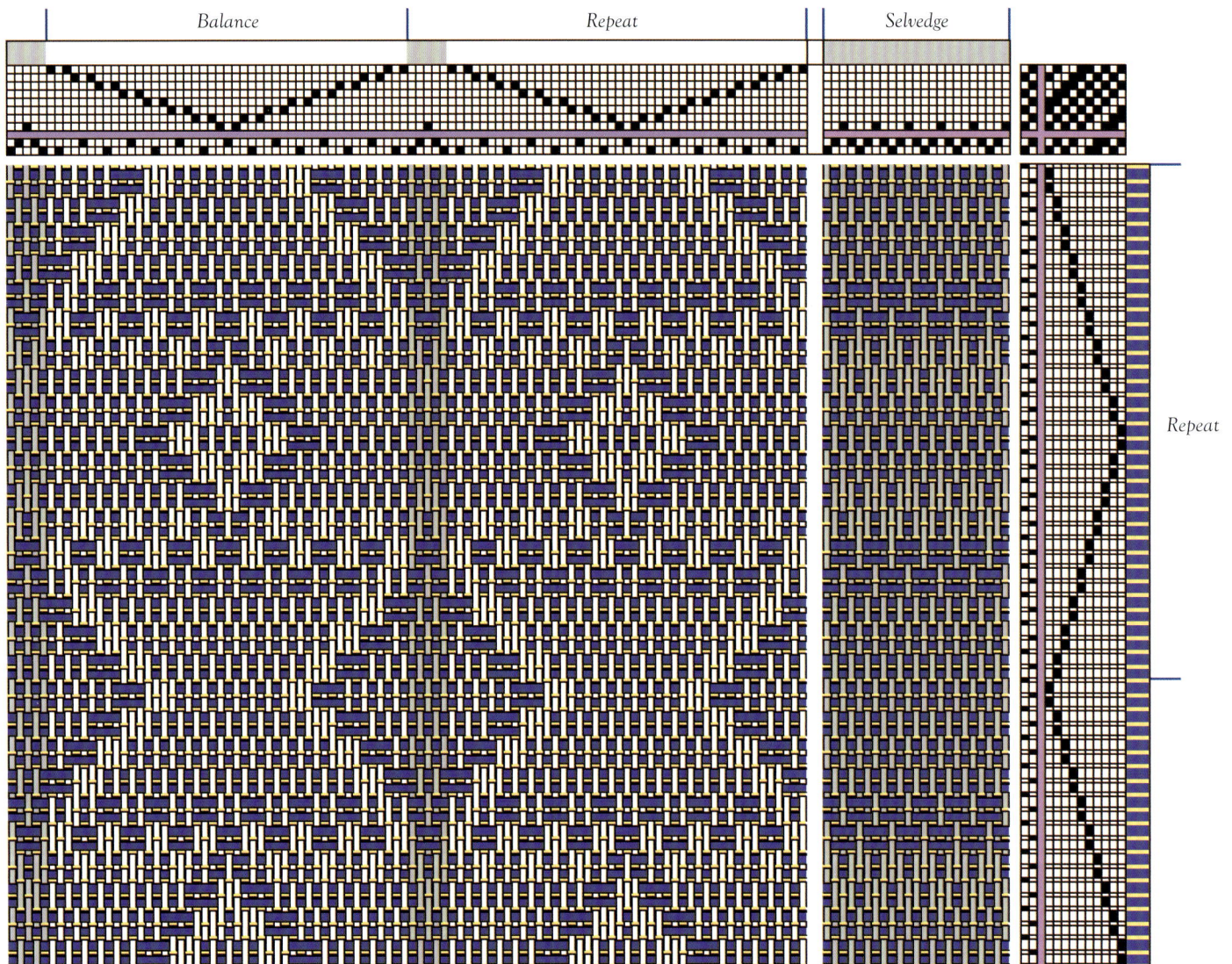

*Threading Draft. The unusual part of the threading in the selvedges and small points of the body is marked and woven in silver warp threads. Weave with tabby as shown. The draft has been expanded to separate the tie-down shafts and tabbies from the pattern area.*

## Tips

• Many structures allow the weaver to change block size to control float length and pattern size. In uneven two-tied overshot, any odd number of threads per block, which does not exceed the desired float length or other design constraints, may be used. Commonly, 5-thread blocks are used, but 3-, 7-, and sometimes 9-thread blocks are also useful. A 3-thread substitution uses only 60% of the number of threads in a 5-thread block, allowing for shorter floats, a more compact pattern, more repeats, and other design possibilities. Blocks of lace weaves, Ms and Os, some of the tied weaves, satins, some twill blocks, and other structures can be expanded or contracted in this manner.

• In structures such as this, where repeating blocks causes the floats to lengthen, block sizes can sometimes be combined to mimic the effect of repeating blocks. Using 3-thread blocks for single blocks and 5-thread blocks for doubled blocks is not quite consistent, but is an interesting option to evaluate if needed. This particular draft had only single blocks, so changes in block size were not needed.

• Making small, careful changes to a regular sequence of tie-downs and their usage in the tie-up is an ingenious way to create greater pattern options. Here, the changes to the pattern treadles result in interesting small horizontal stripes, punctuating the overall design rhythmically.

• There is no reason that one has to stick to a regular twill patterning in the tie-up or to any tie-up of the pattern area with the same number of pattern treadles as blocks. If your loom has enough treadles (or has levers, or a dobby), or you can devise a skeleton tie-up, consider exploring options requiring more sheds.

# Half-Shattered Diamonds
## Cheri Shelp

### Scarf in Twill

### Design Process

Our guild, Western Weavers, decided to take one profile draft and make it our own. For me it seemed only appropriate that the starting point be my mother's book (Shelp and Wostenberg, 1991). We began with threading #3 on page 32, an 8-shaft point twill variant. We each then went to the drawing board, or more precisely our computers, and began the process of designing.

I love a good twill and was hoping to come up with a twill threading with a network treadling. For the warp, I substituted straight 3-end blocks into the profile draft, for a 24-shaft piece. Experimentation with tie-ups from handweaving.net led to the tie-up choice. In the end, I didn't care for the any of the networked treadlings I tried, so I continued to play in Fiberworks until I came up with my final draft.

When we started the project I wasn't sure how much variety there would be in our final pieces. Amazingly, the pieces are so different that if you didn't know they came from the same profile draft threading, you would never guess.

### Weaving Information

Size: 76" x 12" plus 3" fringe on each end

Warp: 16/2 bamboo, 1620 ypp, sage green; 36 epi

Weft: 16/2 bamboo, 1620 ypp, dark green; 36 ppi

Source: Modified from Shelp and Wostenberg (1991)

Weave Structure: 3-end twill block variant, 26 shafts

Finishing: Twisted fringe with three strands per ply and finished with overhand knots. Hand washed in warm water with mild detergent, then rinsed. Laid flat to dry and hard pressed.

Take-up and Shrinkage: Warp and weft 10%

## Tips

• Because the tie-up and treadling chosen do not match the "twill block" (or 3-end block) warp, the final interlacement is much more complex than simple twill blocks. Combining parts from different structures and different drafts can lead to completely different or hybrid structures, with much more complexity than is present in any of the original drafts. It can take quite a bit of exploration to find pleasing combinations, but is worth the effort.

• The "half shattered" effect is caused by not reversing the block threadings at points (reversals) in the draft. This disrupts the symmetry, creating one smooth side and one "shattered" side, stepped by threes. If the structure were simple 3-thread turned twill blocks, the pattern would be blockier but consistent within the blocks, with the twill always in the same direction. Combining the 3-thread warp blocks with a tie-up not intended to be broken into 3-shaft groups makes the consistent direction in the warp blocks act differently on opposite sides of the point. This effect can be far more interesting than simply mirroring at the points, taking a piece from the expected to something more exciting, as in this example. Use care, however, as in some cases the asymmetry is more disturbing or confusing than interesting.

Repeat    Selvedge

Repeat

Threading Draft. The profile threading was used to place straight 3-shaft blocks in the warp.
The tie-up is similar to those used for manifold (interleaved) twills. Separate plain weave
selvedges were added. The treadling is a simple point. The draft was expanded to separate the
selvedge shafts from the pattern.

# Purple Haze
## Elaine Dimpelfeld

### Scarf in Atwater-Bronson Lace

### Design Process

The starting point of this design was a desire to work with both lace and a profile draft, inspired by Laurie Autio's lectures. I had never used Atwater-Bronson lace so I decided to try it. I also wanted a design that had some diagonal flow. As soon as I saw Bonnie Inouye's version of an advancing Wall of Troy (Inouye, 2000; p. 45), I knew it would be the inspiration for the profile draft. I loved the results of converting the profile to Atwater-Bronson lace with 6-thread units; it looked like complex kimono fabric. To make a scarf at my chosen sett, however, I had to limit the number of blocks. I selected an area which would show some diagonals and added a plain weave border.

I played with various tie-ups, colors, and treadlings, encouraged to try different ideas by my teacher, Janney Simpson. In the end, I kept the tie-up, but simplified the treadling to an advancing point, which made it easier to see the pattern change shape across the scarf.

Another goal was to have one end be a different color than the other. The weft on the first quarter is black, and on the last quarter is eggplant. The middle half forms the transition between the two. It alternates picks of black and eggplant, planned so that all the weft floats are eggplant and the lace appears more purple on that side. I finished with plied fringe and added purple and green seed beads randomly.

This profile would also be interesting in another weave structure, such as summer and winter. Some day, I would like to try a similar approach on a wider piece, such as a shawl or blanket, so I can see the entire repeat of the threading blocks.

# Tips

• Beading the fringe adds weight to help a light scarf hang smoothly. It also can add a bit of sparkle or other interest.

• In laces, a plain weave border on all four sides functions to hold the lace open after finishing. By providing a firmer edge to beat against, the plain weave edges also make it easier to get a good, even beat, and to weave neat selvedges.

• Using two alternating colors in the weft of Atwater-Bronson lace is a useful design tool. Because the blocks in this structure always have an even number of threads (here, six threads per block), and the weft floats are always on the even numbered picks, simple alternation will always put the same color on the pattern picks, no matter the block size used.

• If desired, when alternating two colors in the weft in Atwater-Bronson lace, change the color on the pattern picks by throwing two picks in a row of the same color. Generally, the pattern is altered at a change in blocks, but can be done within the block, with care, for special effects.

• Picking the right size for the blocks is critical. Swapping to a 4-thread block rather than using a 6-thread block would allow more blocks across the piece. However, particularly at this sett and in these lower contrast colors, the pattern would be much less obvious.

*Detail showing the three weft colorations.*

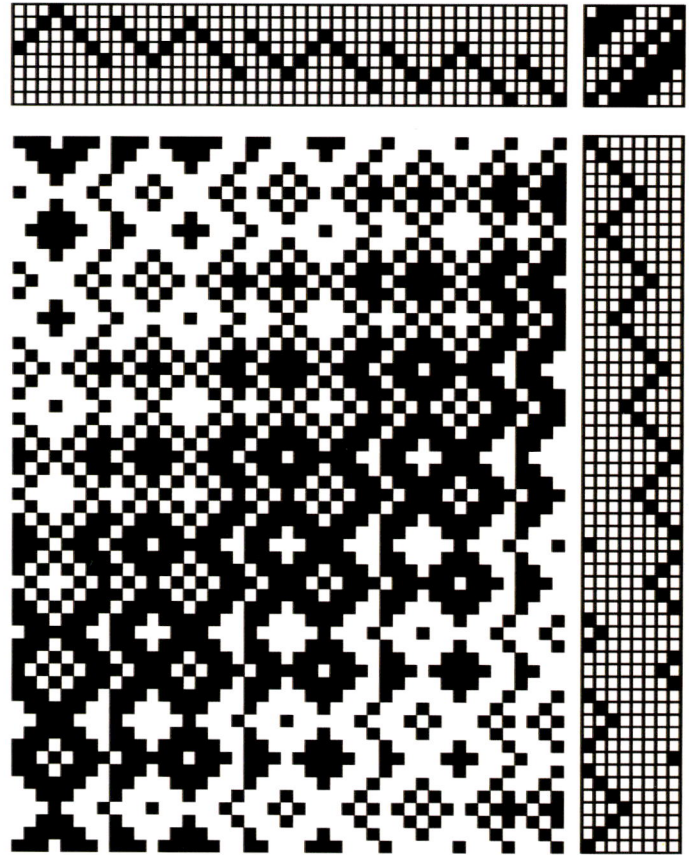

## Weaving Information

Size: 66" x 12.5" plus 4.5" fringe on each end

Warp: 8/2 Tencel, 3360 ypp, olive; 20 epi

Weft: 8/2 Tencel, 3360 ypp, black and eggplant; 28 ppi

Source: Modified from Inouye (2000) to use as a profile draft with different treadling.

Weave Structures: Atwater-Bronson lace, 10 shafts

Other Weaving Information: In the middle section, the black and eggplant wefts were alternated, with the eggplant in the pattern picks so that the lace on that side would appear more purple.

Finishing: Hemstitched over three ends and up three picks. Plied fringe finished with overhand knots. Purple and green seed beads were randomly added to the fringe. Hand washed with mild detergent for three minutes and rinsed in warm water. Laid flat to dry and lightly steam pressed.

Take-up and Shrinkage: Warp 3%, weft 4%

*Profile Draft. Wall of Troy threading advanced by one for each repeat in threading. The treadling has a 5-block point advanced by one on each repeat. A regular 1/3/3/1 twill tie-up was used.*

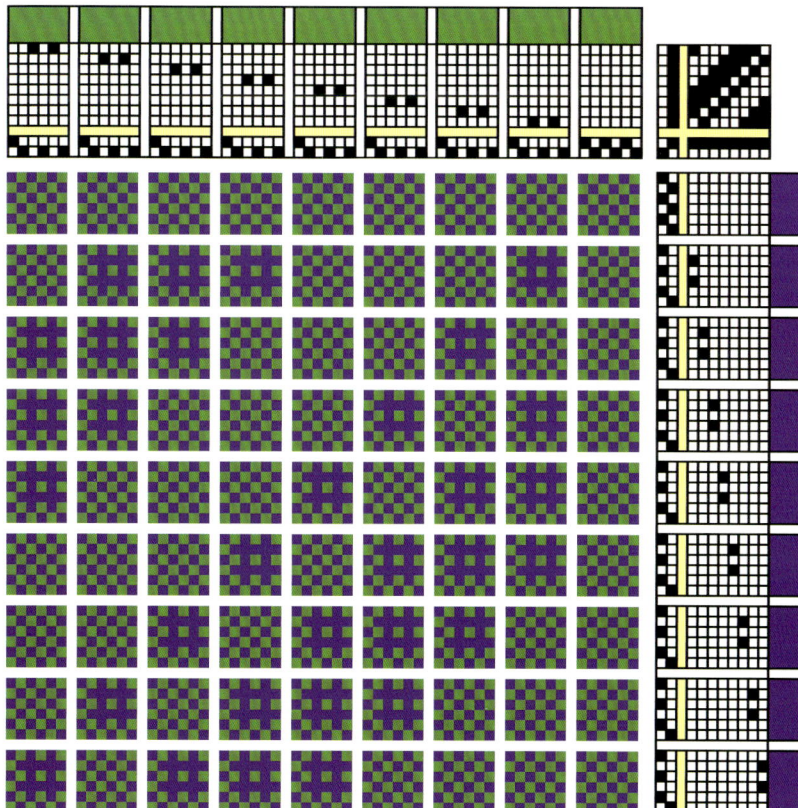

| H | G | F | E | D | C | B | A | Selvedge |

| | | | | | | | | |

Plain Weave

AEFG

BFGH

ACGH

ABDH

ABCE

BCDF

CDEG

DEFH

*Key to Profile Draft. The draft has been expanded to separate the tie-down shafts and tabby treadles from the pattern area.*

# Stairway in Blue

## Linda Tilson Davis

### Scarf in Bateman Blend

## Design Process

More than the other Bateman weaves, Bateman blends lend themselves to going beyond eight shafts (Harvey, 1983). I have woven a number of pieces in various Bateman blends but previous work primarily involved imagery. For this piece, I wanted to use a twill profile, which is more similar to what Dr. Bateman used (Harvey, 1982). Of course, in his work, he was limited to eight shafts, and my eight blocks require eleven shafts.

I found an 8-shaft advancing point twill in VÄV (van der Venne, 2011) which I liked as a profile draft with Bateman blend #1-A in 6-thread blocks (Harvey, 1982). Then, I wove a long sampler with thirteen variations to try combinations of ties and treadling styles for both pattern and tabby picks as outlined in Davis (2017). The textures and patterning vary considerably. I chose this combination because each side looked different, and the difference was more than an inverse representation. The treadling was as drawn in and required two to four repeats per pattern block.

Originally, I thought I would weave this piece in "hot" colors to represent the colors of the Grand Staircase of the Escalante, but in the sampling I didn't find this as satisfying as using blue. This blend, like all I have woven previously, was a wonderful and pleasant surprise!

## Weaving Information

Size: 56" x 12.6" plus 3" fringe on each end

Warp: 2/24 Alpaca/Tencel/nylon (45/45/10%), 6800 ypp, natural; 36 epi

Weft: 2/24 Alpaca/Tencel/nylon (45/45/10%), 6800 ypp, natural (tabby); 2/14 Alpaca/silk (80/20%), 3472 ypp, French blue (pattern); 43 ppi including tabby

Source: Advancing point twill (van der Venne, 2011) used as a profile draft.

Weave Structure: Bateman Blend #1-A, 11 shafts

Finishing: Hem stitched. Hand washed in lukewarm water with mild detergent. Line dried and steam pressed.

Take-up and Shrinkage: Warp 2%, weft 1%

## Tips

• When using a complex structure, such as Bateman blends and other Bateman structures, sampling combinations of structural variables is invaluable to making the best design choice for your current piece. The sampler will also be helpful for future work in the same threading system.

• Be sure to examine both the front and back of the cloth when evaluating options for treadling and tie-up. While many structures are simple inverses on the two sides, others, like the Bateman blends, have more extensive possibilities.

• Scarves, and other items which are meant to be seen on both sides or which are reversible, present an opportunity to use contrasting effects on the two sides. Check that they work together in the way you would like them to be seen.

• Bateman blends are particularly versatile in treadling options. For example, this threading could be tied up and treadled to produce a true Atwater-Bronson lace or spot Bronson piece. Improvising at the loom within a tie-up provides additional interesting design possibilities.

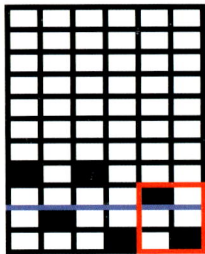

*Repeat*

*Repeat*

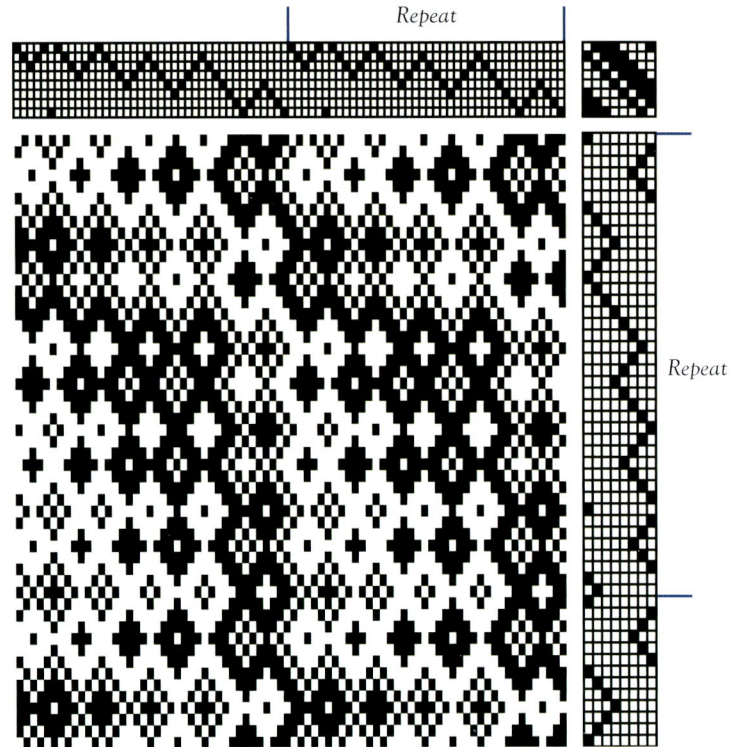

*Threading block. In Bateman Blends, the two ends which begin each block are on shafts 1 and 3. This pair forms what Bateman called a "tie group" (Harvey, 1983), outlined in red. The ends on shafts 1 and 2 form the tie-downs, and shafts 4 and up, the pattern.*

*Profile Draft. The profile threading and treadling show how uneven points advance irregularly. A regular 3/3/1/1 twill tie-up is used. The aspect ratio of the blocks matches the woven scarf.*

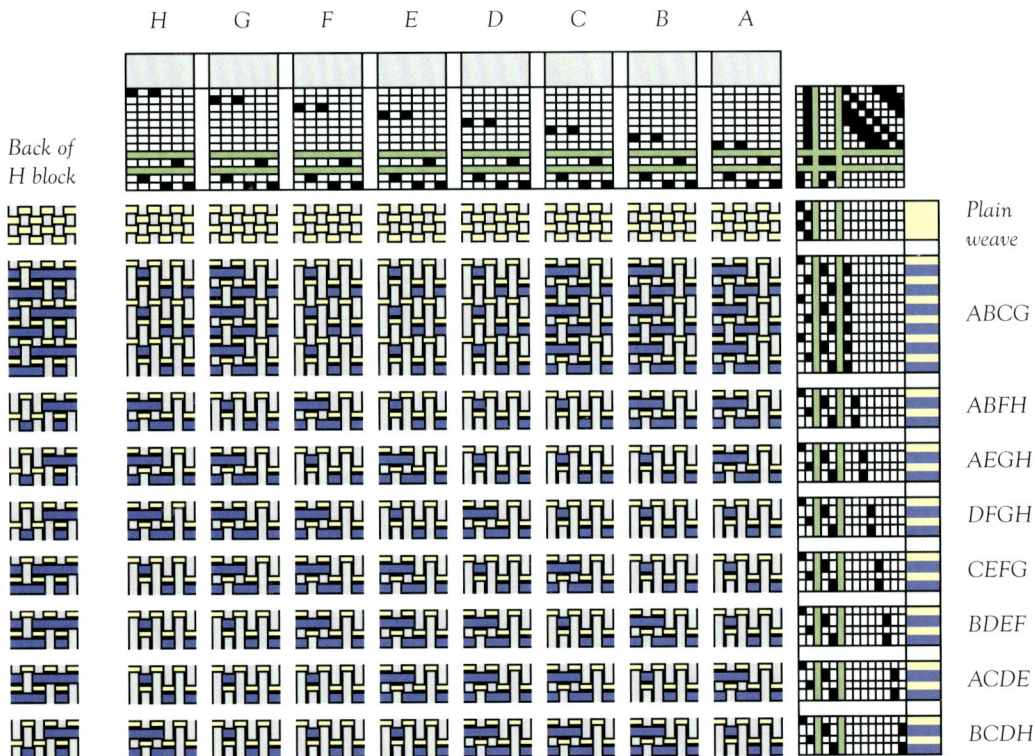

Back of
H block

H    G    F    E    D    C    B    A

Plain weave

ABCG

ABFH

AEGH

DFGH

CEFG

BDEF

ACDE

BCDH

*Key to Profile Draft. As shown, tabby alternates with pattern picks. Like summer and winter, the two pattern picks alternate tie-down shafts. Each treadling block is woven three times in the piece, as spelled out in the first pattern treadling (pattern in ABCG).*

*The back and front are quite different, with 2- and 3- thread floats on the front and 3- and 5-thread floats on the back. At the far left, the back of the H block is given for comparison.*

*Shown as a skeleton draft. The draft has been expanded to separate the tie-down and tie-group shafts and tabby treadles from the pattern area. In the piece the warp and tabby weft are the same; here the coloring of the two are different for clarity.*

144

# II.2  8-Shaft Blocks or Sections

With 16, 24, or 32 shafts, drafts of any complexity or structure on eight shafts can be combined sequentially on their own set(s) of shafts. Of course, divisions with other numbers of shafts and unequal numbers of shafts are also possible.

As on eight shafts, there is no need to use straight draw for the sections, or to treadle them tromp as writ. Nor do all the sections need the same threading, treadling, tie-up, and/or repeat length. While it is most common to use variants of the same structure and pattern in each section, it is interesting to combine structures and/or patterns.

These examples alternate between two simple threading and treadling patterns, but as many possibilities as you can imagine can be created, especially when using a liftplan.

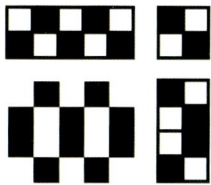

*Simple 2-block profile used for placement of pattern changes in both threading drafts.*

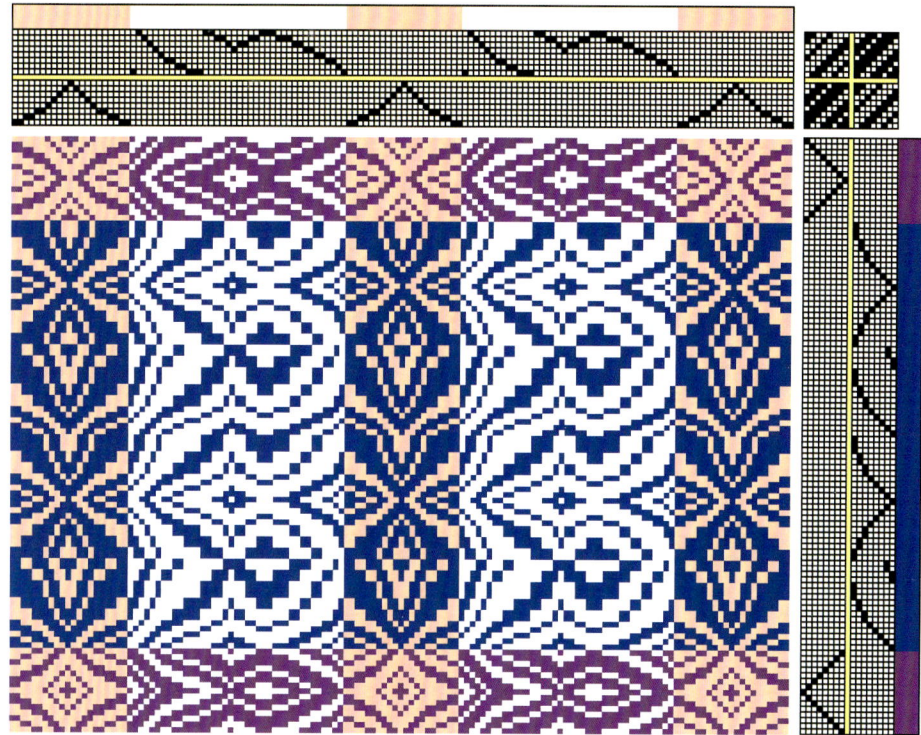

*Two 8-shaft sections with two different undulating threadings and point and undulating treadlings. Both weave undulating twill everywhere, and alternate between a 3/1/2/2 regular twill tie-up and its opposite, a 1/2/2/3 regular twill tie-up. Use tabby (not shown). Note the reversal in the second "A" treadling to change the point direction.*

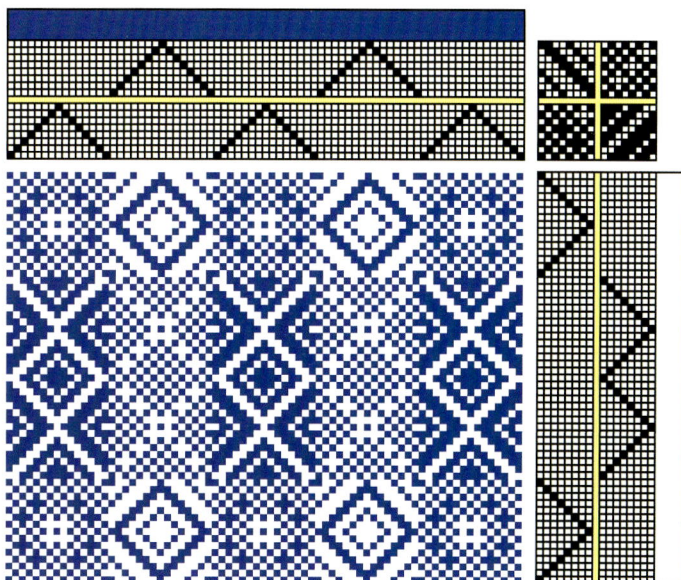

In the standard two-option depictions of profile drafts, the black and white squares may or may not give a good idea of the final cloth design. At left, the black squares of the profile are woven as twills and the white as laces. In two colors, as shown, the cloth will have a warp-wise striping of warp- versus weft-dominant areas which is not obvious from the profile draft. Nor does the profile give a good idea of the complexity resulting from the four different tie-ups, or the different threadings and treadling above.

*Point threadings and treadlings for both 8-shaft sections, with the tie-up creating the different structures and patterns used in the two sections. When the A section weaves lace with mostly warp floats, the B section weaves twill with more weft floats. When the A section weaves twill with more warp floats, the B section weaves lace with only weft floats.*

# Shimmering Chevrons

## Sara von Tresckow

### Scarf in Satin Damask

### Design Process

I have worked with the drawloom for over ten years now, mostly with linen and cotton at setts of 50-60 epi for firm runners, upholstery, table linens, and clothing. Most of my earlier pieces were done in 5-end satin, which gives an unusually smooth surface and solid feel. I wanted to design fabric using an 8-end satin, which has longer floats, and to use half units. That is, the ground structure has eight threads, but the pattern blocks change halfway through the block, allowing finer detail. Also, stepping away from the usual cotton and linen threads sounded interesting.

I found some 20/2 silk remaining from a clothing project, custom dyed at Treenway, and decided to pair it with Jaggerspun Zephyr wool/silk blend in two shades of red to give it a shimmer. I chose an 8-end satin with a counter of 5. On the drawloom, once a structure is chosen, it is possible to design the dimensions, threads, and sett without a specific pattern in mind. As the satin needed a close sett, I chose 30 epi for the warp. The draw harness was set up with 106 pattern half units of four threads on each lingo in a point threading. I then designed four or five different patterns which could be drawn on that point threading.

I often use what looks like a weave structure rendered in "pixels" of pattern and background structure in a damask design. The chevron point twill effect in the pattern is developed by drawing the image of a 6-shaft extended point twill with a regular 3/3 twill tie-up on graph paper and developing it into a liftplan for the drawloom. Those interested in learning more about drawloom weaving may find Johansson (1982) and von Tresckow (2014) helpful.

The results were scarves with a luscious hand, delicate, with subtle patterning. The 8-end satin definitely gave the fabric a softer feel than 5-end. As a result of this project, I am currently working on 100% Zephyr scarves on the single-unit drawloom and they are developing beautifully.

### Weaving Information

Size: 68.5" x 12.5" plus 4" fringe on each end

Warp: 2/18 wool/silk (50/50%), 5040 ypp, cinnabar and real red; 30 epi

Weft: 20/2 silk, 5000 ypp, custom dyed red; 22 ppi

Source: Original draft

Weave Structure: 8-end satin damask, drawloom

Finishing: Twisted fringe with two plies of four threads. Hand washed gently and rinsed with warm water. Placed dripping wet on drying rack and steam pressed on silk setting.

Take-up and Shrinkage: Warp 7%, weft 10%

## Tips

• Longer floats often require a tighter sett. The 7-thread floats of 8-end satin or 1/7 twill may require a different sett from 5-end satin or a 1/4 twill, which have 4-thread floats. Additionally, the fabric is apt to be softer and more reflective with longer floats.

• A simple point of pattern blocks is a versatile threading for symmetric patterns or figures, whether on a drawloom or shaft loom. Many different pleasing designs may be made by changing only the tie-up and treadling.

• Using a threading draft as a profile draft is a useful trick. There's a fractal feel when you use the same structure as the final piece, and a weaverly sense of fun when going from one structure as the base of the profile to another in the woven piece.

• Half units, whether on the drawloom or a shaft loom, allow the weaver to scale down a design and create smoother (less pixelated) patterns or figures.

• This scarf could be made on a shaft-draw drawloom with as few as seven pattern shafts and eight ground shafts, although the threading would not be as versatile as the simple point on the single-unit draw system.

• On a regular shaft loom, half units of 8-end satin take 32 shafts for this pattern. Switching to 4-end turned broken twill would take 28 shafts, or to 5-end satin would take 35 shafts.

• If one wanted to weave the same design on an 8-shaft loom without pick-up, the structure could be changed to one which allows seven blocks on eight shafts, or one with six blocks and a background option (such as Atwater-Bronson lace or huck lace), or adapted to fewer blocks to fit other structures. Some of the structural characteristics of the satin damask (e.g., float length or float directions) could be retained but not all.

147

Profile Draft. Drawloom set up, with pattern shafts on a large point.

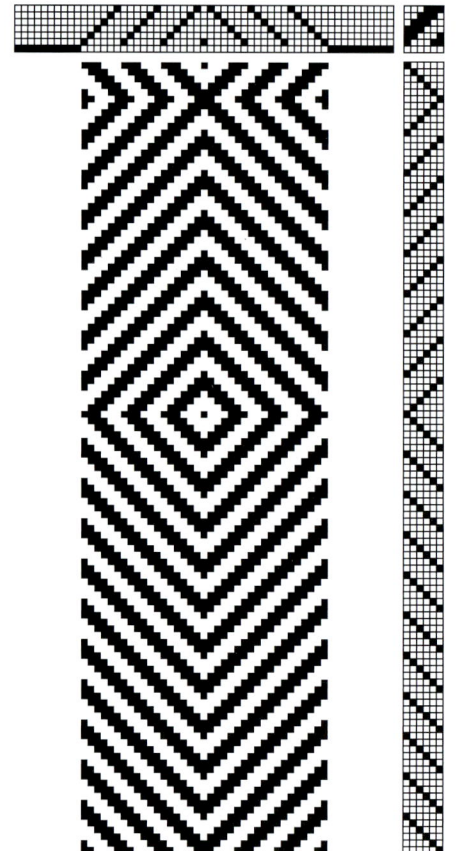

Profile Draft. Portion of the profile reduced to seven blocks, in shaft-loom fashion.

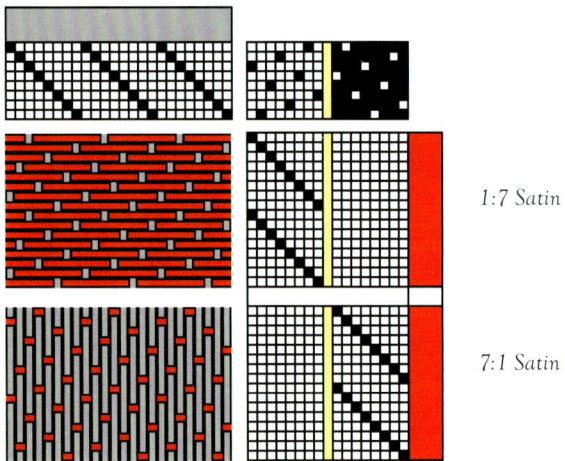

1:7 Satin

7:1 Satin

Above, Component Threading Draft. The two 8-end satins of the base weave are shown as they would be woven on an 8-shaft loom. The pattern changes after every four picks (half units) rather than on the full repeat.

Left, Drawloom Tie-up. The black shafts rise and the red ones sink.

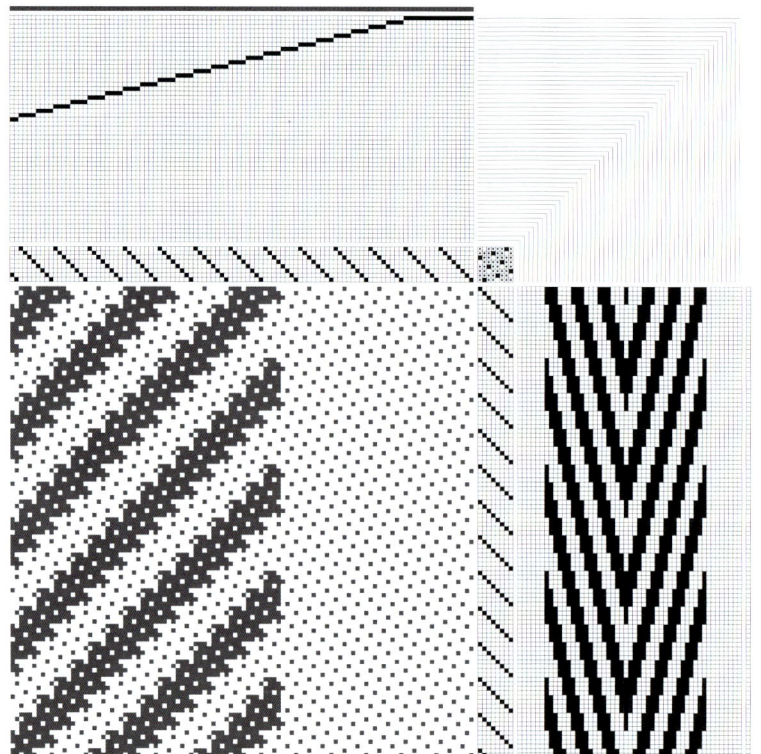

Threading Draft. Section of drawdown on the drawloom.

148

# Winter Solstice
## Susie Hodges

### Scarf Set in Summer and Winter

### Design Process

A modern approach to summer and winter (a.k.a. single two-tie unit weave) may be used to create curves and figures on eight shafts or more. For the past few years, I have used this approach to create a series of special occasion scarf sets featuring figurative stripes. Although I weave them on sixteen shafts, I always begin a design with 8-shaft drafts of images appropriate to the occasion. Because only one set of tie-down shafts is needed, a 16-shaft draft can accommodate two different 8-shaft summer and winter designs, with two shafts left over for a simple third stripe or extra pattern units. In my "Winter Solstice" scarves, the stripe designs are made more interesting by threading and treadling each of the three stripes in a different way.

Full 4-end units are used in the threading for the point pattern of the full moon image and for the two units which form background. In full unit threadings, the pattern shafts change only at the end of units (1, $P^a$, 2, $P^a$; 1, $P^b$, 2, $P^b$; where 1 and 2 are tie-down shafts, and $P^a$ and $P^b$ are pattern shafts). Half units form the straight order pattern of the narrow crescent moon. In half-unit threadings, the pattern shafts may change in the middle of the unit (1, $P^a$, 2, $P^b$). The brick-style (alternating tie-downs) treadling is unusual in that the pattern shafts change on almost every pattern pick to create finer detailing and smoother curves.

Additional interest is sparked by using the warp-dominant option for the full moon patterns, the background of the crescent moon, and the lavender dividing stripes. The crescent moon and background of the full moon are made in blue weft pattern floats. As always, in summer and winter the pattern and background areas reverse on the opposite side. Since scarves need a two-way design, the images rotate 180° when repeated.

I like to make each stripe a different color. Analogous colors are easiest to use, but I often prefer a broader range of colors that share a common undertone. In this case, the lilac, white, and ice blue share a pale blue cast. It helps if the pattern weft shares in the color scheme, too, but for good contrast, it needs to be of an opposite value (dark or light) from the warp colors. These scarves use darker blues for the pattern wefts. The thinner tabby weft should be a color that gives up its identity to the other colors, in this case a soft, pale blue merino. This delicate balance of yarn qualities means that potential weft colors always need to be auditioned on the loom.

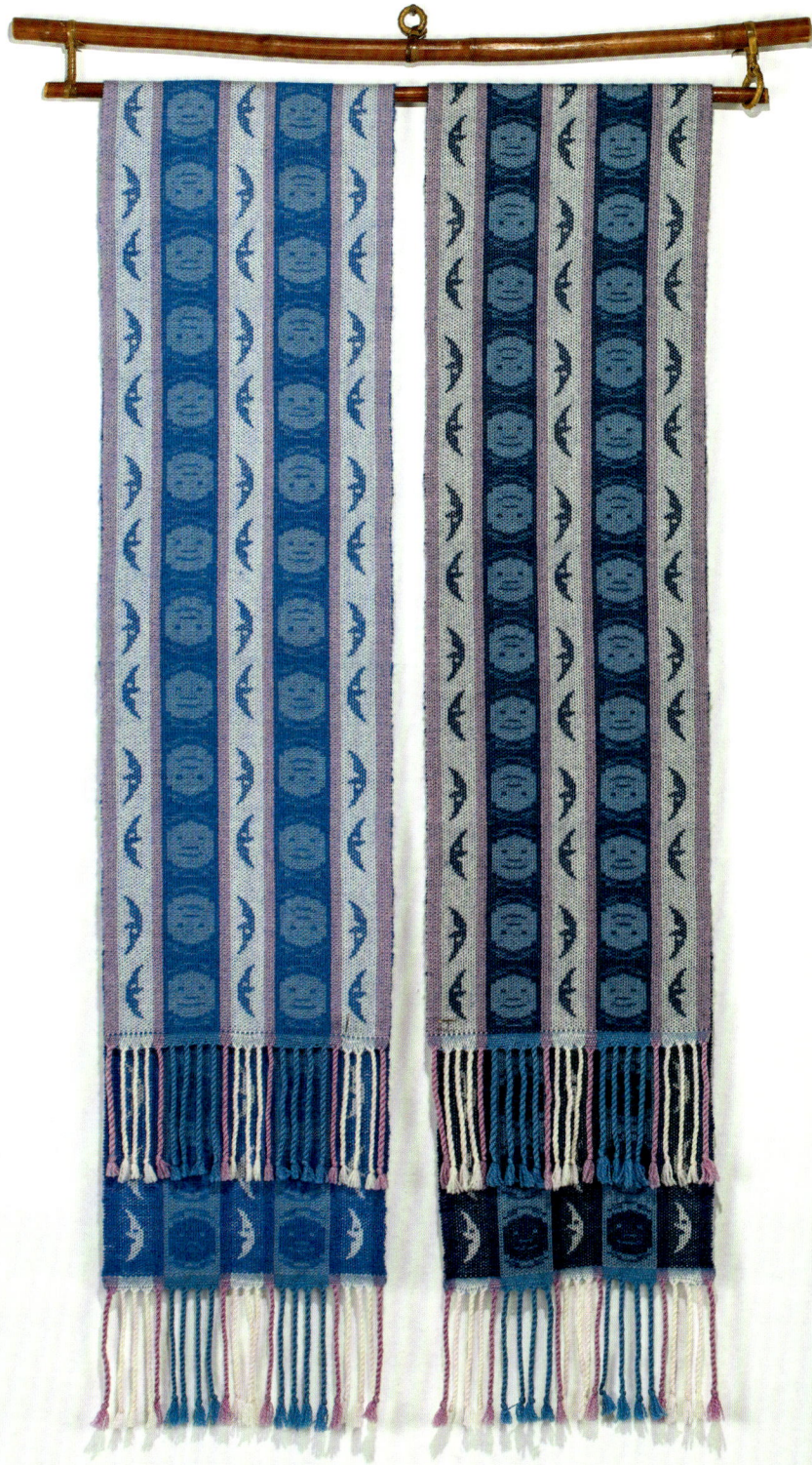

# Tips

• For best results, sample the fiber, grist, and color of pattern and tabby weft yarns on the loom. Add an extra yard or more of warp for this purpose.

• Rotating designs 180° on repetition is a graceful way to make the scarf read the same on both ends when worn. Here, it also adds motion to the line of crescent moons.

• For greater color unity or harmony, pay attention to the undertones in the yarns chosen.

• It is easier to draw motifs in a liftplan form of the draft without showing the required tabby.

• Although not as commonly used, half units of summer and winter allow for a finer scale and smoother, less pixelated edges to a design. Combining half and full units is a way to manipulate scale and pixelation within a piece.

• A brick-style treadling helps half units move and blend more smoothly in the design. The common paired O and paired X treadlings may look oddly interrupted and choppy with half units.

• Small details like the eyes and noses in this draft are affected by the tie-down warp with which they are paired. It may help to move a bad-looking detail up or down a row in the treadling. Occasionally, it also helps to shift the starting point of the tabby sequence by one.

• Combining 8-shaft, etc. drafts in the same structure may result in bonus pattern shafts as long as any tie-downs present are used in the same way in both drafts and can be used in common for both sections. If one desires the tie-downs to be used differently, for example, paired O in one stripe and brick-style in another, they need separate shafts.

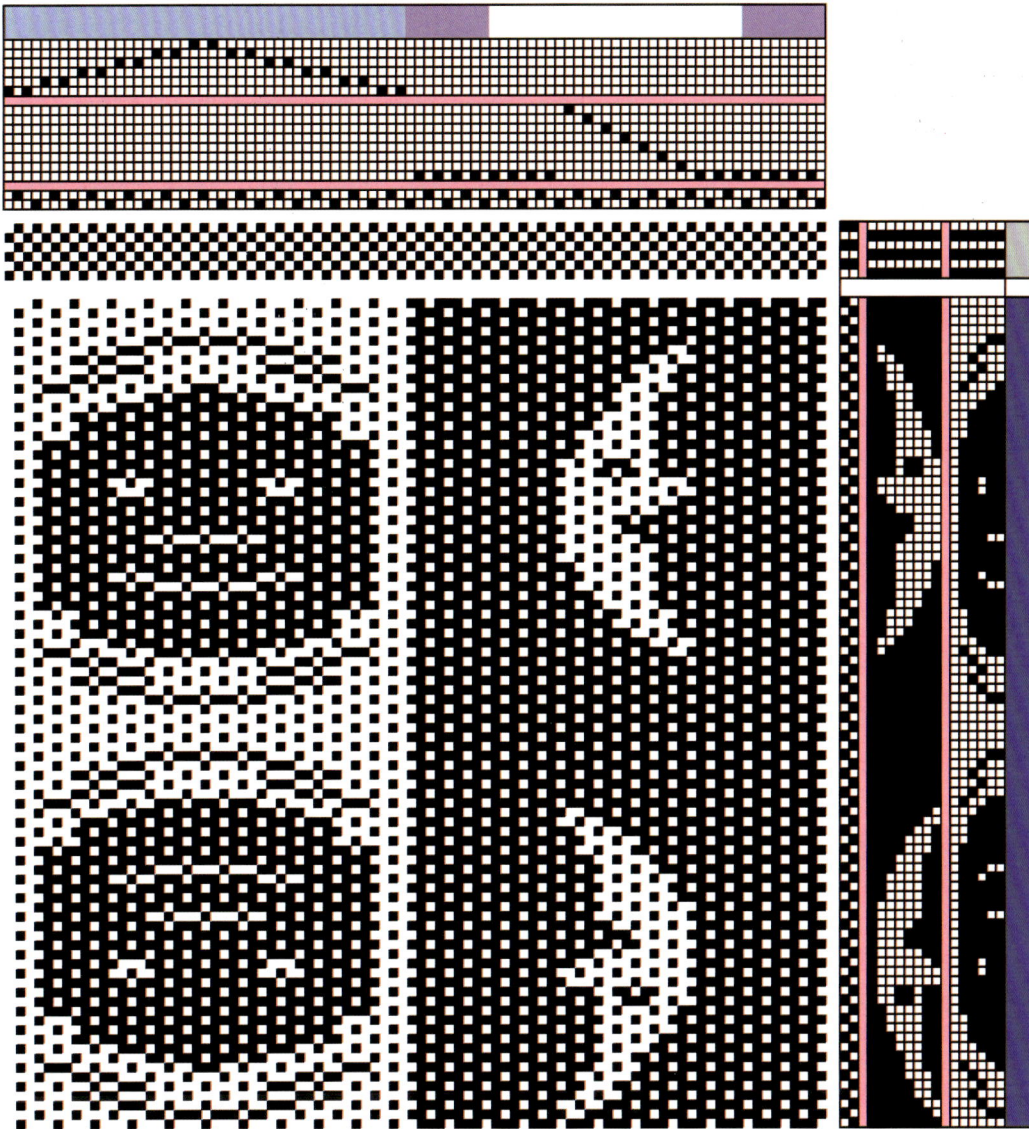

*Plain weave*

*Pattern*

*Threading Draft. Each stripe is threaded on its own set of pattern shafts. The full moon is mirrored, while the crescent moon is not. Both rotate 180° to complete the design. One pattern unit is set aside to always weave background (unit A), and one to always weave pattern (unit I). The full moon uses full 4-end threading units of summer and winter. The crescent moon uses half units. The full moon image is formed by background and is more warp colored. The crescent moon is formed by pattern and is more weft colored. The treadling is brick-style (alternating), with the pattern shafts shifting on almost every pattern pick.*

*Tabby (not shown) is used in the pattern area. The draft is expanded to separate the tie-downs from the two pattern areas.*

## Weaving Information

Size: 63" x 8.5" plus 6" fringe on each end

Warp: 2/18 wool/silk (50/50%), 5040 ypp, white, ice blue, and lilac; 24 epi

Weft: 2/18 wool/silk (50/50%), 5040 ypp, royal blue; 2/18 merino wool, 5040 ypp, Williamsburg blue; 2/20 merino wool, 5600 ypp, Aurora blue; 24 ppi

Source: Original draft inspired by Kim Bunke (in van der Hoogt, 2010).

Weave Structure: Summer and winter, 16 shafts

Other Weaving Information: Weave a narrow band of plain weave to begin and end. Threading patterns are a combination of repeated full units, straight (half units), and point (full units) orders. The liftplan creates warp-dominant and weft-dominant stripes on both sides of the fabric.

Finishing: Two-ply fringes of 10 to 12 threads were twisted and plied prior to wet finishing. Machine soaked in hot water and mild detergent with two towels. Spun on medium cycle. Rinsed in same way with a cup of 5% vinegar. Machine dried on air cycle with towels for 10 minutes and rolled in a towel. Ironed with press cloth while slightly damp on wool/silk setting. Polished with dry iron to bring up silk sheen. Lightly brushed with rat-tail hair brush to improve hand.

Take-up and Shrinkage: Warp and weft 3%

# Bursts of Pink

## Peg MacMorris

### Scarf in Snowflake Twill

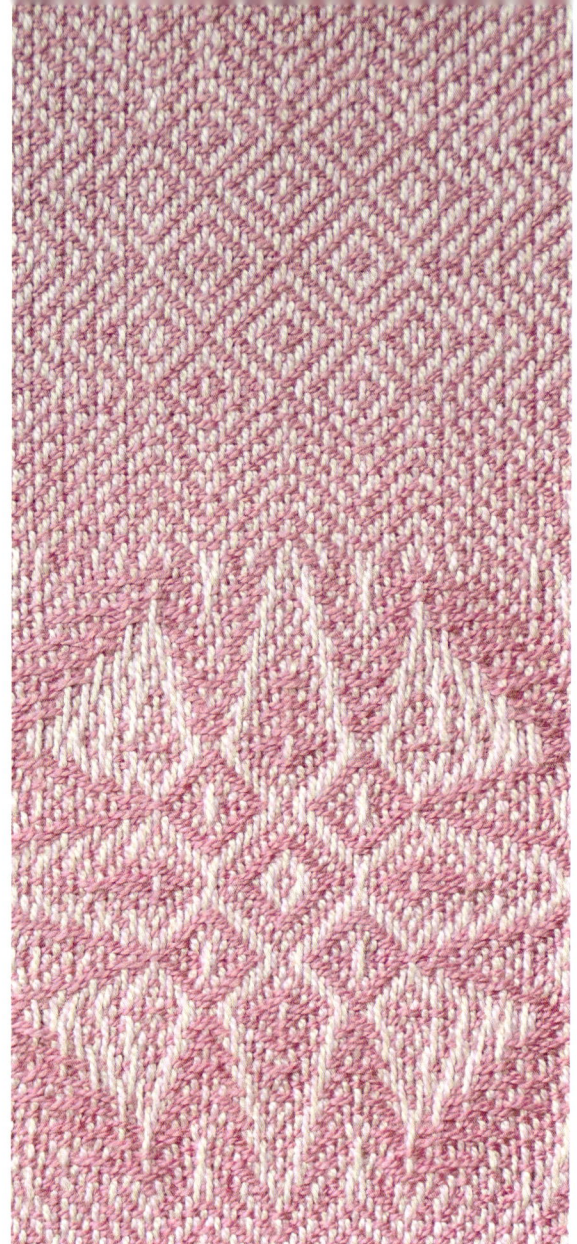

### Design Process

This scarf was woven to be donated to a benefit auction to raise money for the care of low-income breast cancer patients. I looked for a design that I could weave in shades of pink for that purpose, and decided on a "tiled" 8-shaft snowflake twill motif (modified from Keasbey, 2005; p. 98) which I had used previously for shawls and scarves. The design would be visually appealing and showcase pink as a statement.

When I wove shawls with a similar draft several years ago, the goal was to highlight the woven motif by alternating the design and its complement across the width and down the length. When a 16-shaft loom is used, an 8-shaft design can be threaded on the first eight shafts for one block and the second eight shafts for the second block. When used as the primary block, the tie-up is a bolder 3/1/1/3 regular twill tie-up, with longer floats. When used as the secondary block, the tie-up is a more subtle 2/2/2/2 regular twill tie-up (which effectively changes the snowflake pattern from eight shafts to four) in the opposite direction, with shorter floats. Alternating between the two options creates the muted checkerboard effect. Weaving the two blocks to emphasize one at a time gives fabric that surrounds each design block with a quieter space, enhancing the presentation of the design. Additionally, a 16-shaft point was added to each edge as a border and woven trompe as writ to start and end the piece.

Understanding how to use the 16-shaft loom to accomplish this "alternately tiled" pattern was a step forward in my grasp of multi-shaft weaving. The concept is one I use frequently in my work.

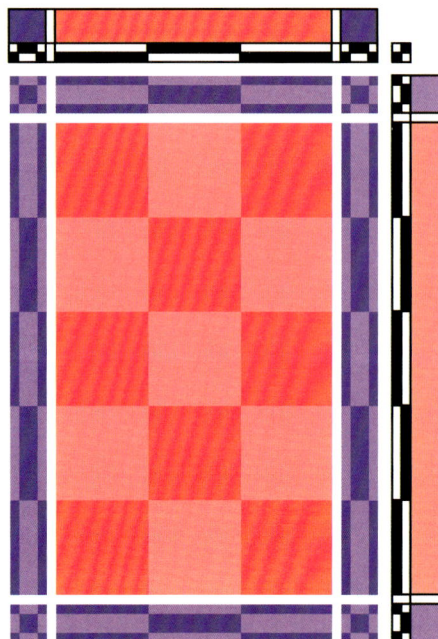

*Profile Draft. The colors correspond to structures rather than actual colors, with the darker colors assigned to the bolder pattern. The A section occurs on shafts 1 to 8 and the B section on shafts 9 to 16. Repeat as needed, ending on the A section. The borders, on a less complex point threading and treadling, are separated and shown in purples.*

### Weaving Information

Size: 65" x 9" plus 6" fringe on each end

Warp: 16/2 soy silk, 6400 ypp, pale pink; 30 epi

Weft: 16/2 soy silk, 6400 ypp, fuchsia; 30 ppi

Source: Original draft inspired by Keasbey (2005).

Weave Structure: Snowflake twill, 16 shafts

Finishing: Fringes twisted in bundles of four warp ends per ply, then tied with overhand knots with beads added to every third bundle. Hand washed in lukewarm water with mild detergent and rinsed. Hung to dry. Steam pressed on rayon setting.

Take-up and Shrinkage: Warp 3%, weft negligible

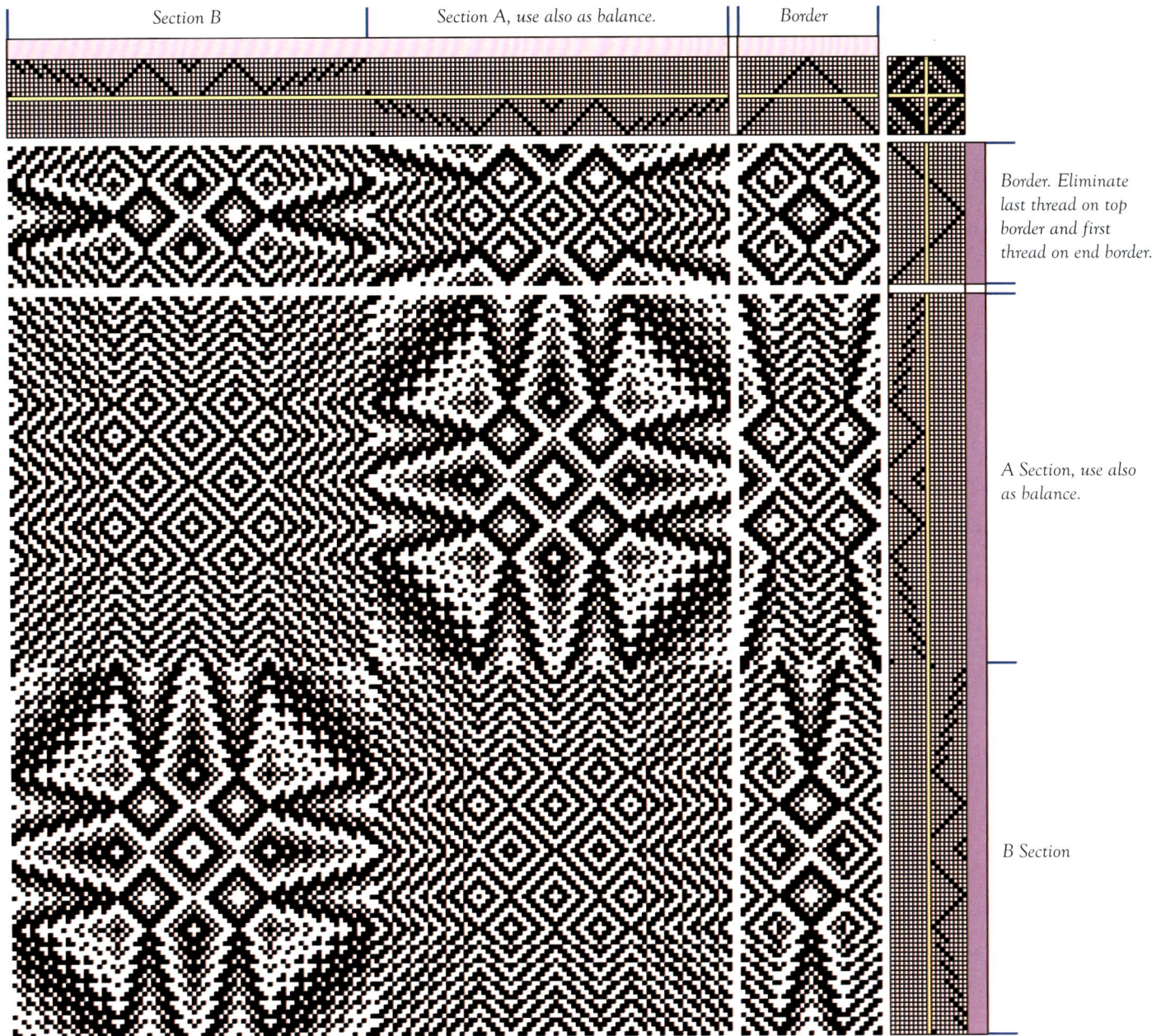

Section B | Section A, use also as balance. | Border

Border. Eliminate
last thread on top
border and first
thread on end border.

A Section, use also
as balance.

B Section

*Threading Draft. Portion of draft showing
the two sections and one border. Each section
is threaded the same. Changing the tie-up
in quadrants from a regular 3/1/1/3 to
a 2/2/2/2 twill tie-up (enlarged below)
changes the "loudness" of the pattern in
alternating sections. Switching the twill
direction in the quadrants creates a subtle
star and rose effect. The draft has been
expanded to separate the sections.*

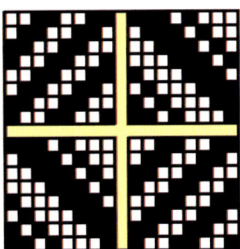

## Tips

• Because the motifs are striking, it is important to beat evenly to ensure that each motif is square.

• When combining blocks or sections on different shafts, each pattern can be very complex if desired. That is, one is not limited to straight draw sections or straight order of blocks within a section.

• Muting one pattern relative to the other allows the eye to focus on the main pattern and have a resting place around it. The degree and composition of the muting is an important part of the design. Two striking patterns used together can also be interesting, but they often recombine visually to appear as a single, larger whole and will usually not have the resting quality of the partially muted version. Experiment with a variety of tie-ups to create the effect you want.

• Adding a small border which combines simpler sections of shafts and treadles from both blocks can be a nice complement to a more complex body design.

154

# Dot, Dot, Dot, Dash
## Marlene Golden

### Scarf in Crepe, Twill Blocks, and Plain Weave

### Design Process

This scarf was designed as part of a series. One of my goals was to create a versatile threading which could be used in a variety of ways with quick changes to the accent colors or tie-ups. I think of this pattern as a combination draft, with four parts working together. The body is an 8-shaft crepe from Oelsner (1915, #803, p. 176; also available on handweaving.net) with accent stripes of turned twill blocks in 3/1 versus 1/3 twills, with a slight variation in the threading. These are bounded by a colored block in 2/2 twill on four shafts. Two ends of plain weave were inserted between the 2/2 twill and the crepe to ensure a clean break between the structures.

The colored stripes of 2/2 twill were not beamed so that the color of the stripes could be changed for every scarf woven. The "dot dot dot dash" pattern of the turned twill serves as an accent and punctuation for the piece. In addition to changing the color of the accent stripe, the treadling and/or tie-up of the crepe and/or twill block sections can be changed. So, many different scarves can be woven on this one warp using different colors and different treadlings.

This is a versatile draft that can be used again and again with different looks to individualize a long warp.

### Weaving Information

Size: 54" x 7.75"

Warp: Suave cotton, 3900 ypp, black; 8/2 cotton, 3360 ypp, black; 8/2 slub rayon, 3100 ypp, black; 20/2 Tencel, 4200 ypp, cobalt, quadrupled; 30 epi

Weft: 20/2 spun silk, 4930 ypp, white; 30 ppi

Source: Original draft, inspired by Oelsner (1915).

Weave Structures: Turned twill variant (1/3 twill and 3/1 twill), crepe weave, 2/2 twill, and plain weave, 22 shafts

Finishing: Hems woven in not-quite-plain-weave double woven tube (not shown), then folded in, fused with Steam-a-Seam, and hand sewn closed. Hand washed in warm water with mild detergent, rinsed in cool water. Rolled up in towel, laid flat to dry. Hard pressed with iron on silk setting.

Take-up and Shrinkage: Warp 4%, weft 5%

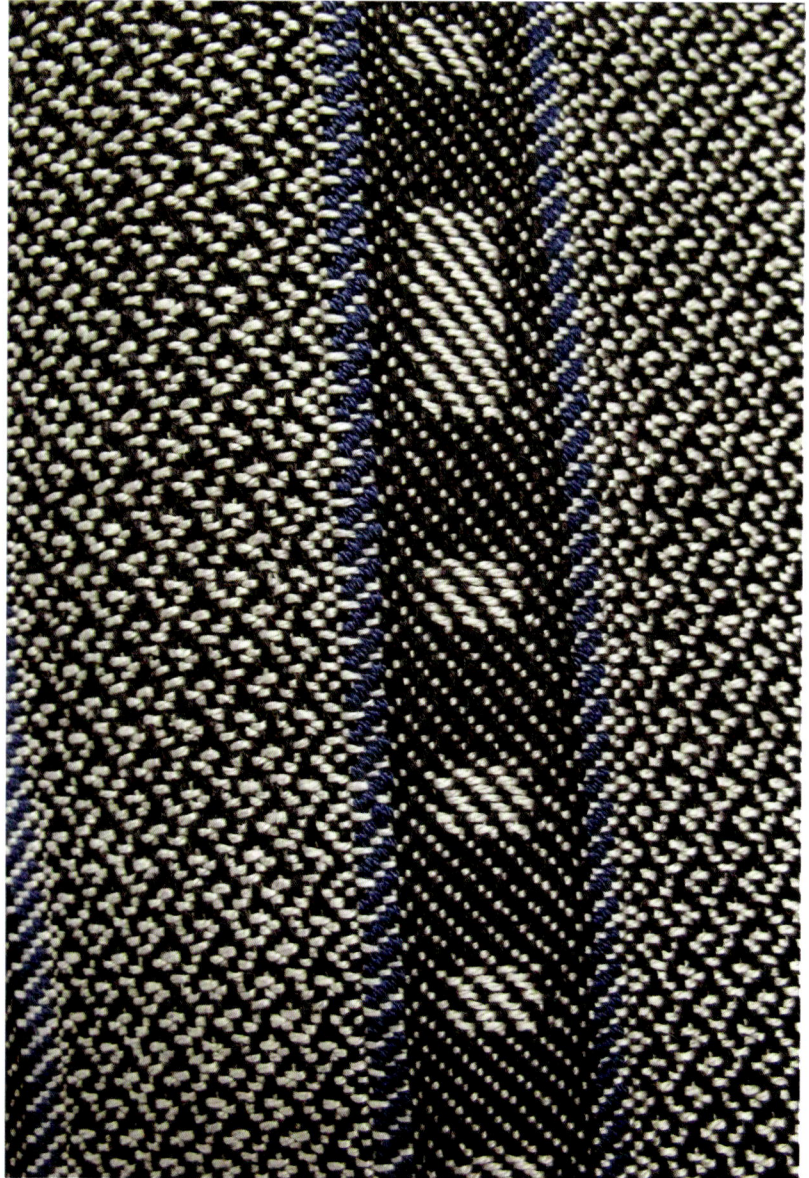

155

## Tips

• Using sections of warp which are not beamed, whether there is a structure change or not, allows the weaver to make quick changes to the color scheme by tieing in the new threads. For instance, if a black warp is long enough for four scarves, one can use a different color scheme for each, e.g., a red accent stripe in the warp with white weft, an orange warp accent stripe with a blue weft, a purple warp accent stripe with a moss green weft, etc.

• Changing the tie-up and/or the treadling for the main body and/or the secondary parts between pieces creates more variation in a series. For this example, any number of very different scarves could be woven using different Oelsner tie-ups in the body and different colors for the supplementary warp stripe and/or weft.

• When combining structures, be sure to adjust setts or yarns as needed so that the same beat (ppi) works across all sections. Structures with similar take-up and shrinkage (two twills with similar float lengths, for example) are easiest to use together. With care, very different structures may be combined. Ignoring all rules may lead you to an intriguing fabric with ripples, ruffles, and other effects.

• Coding words, as can be done in Morse code in the turned twill stripe, is a fun way to personalize a message for the wearer.

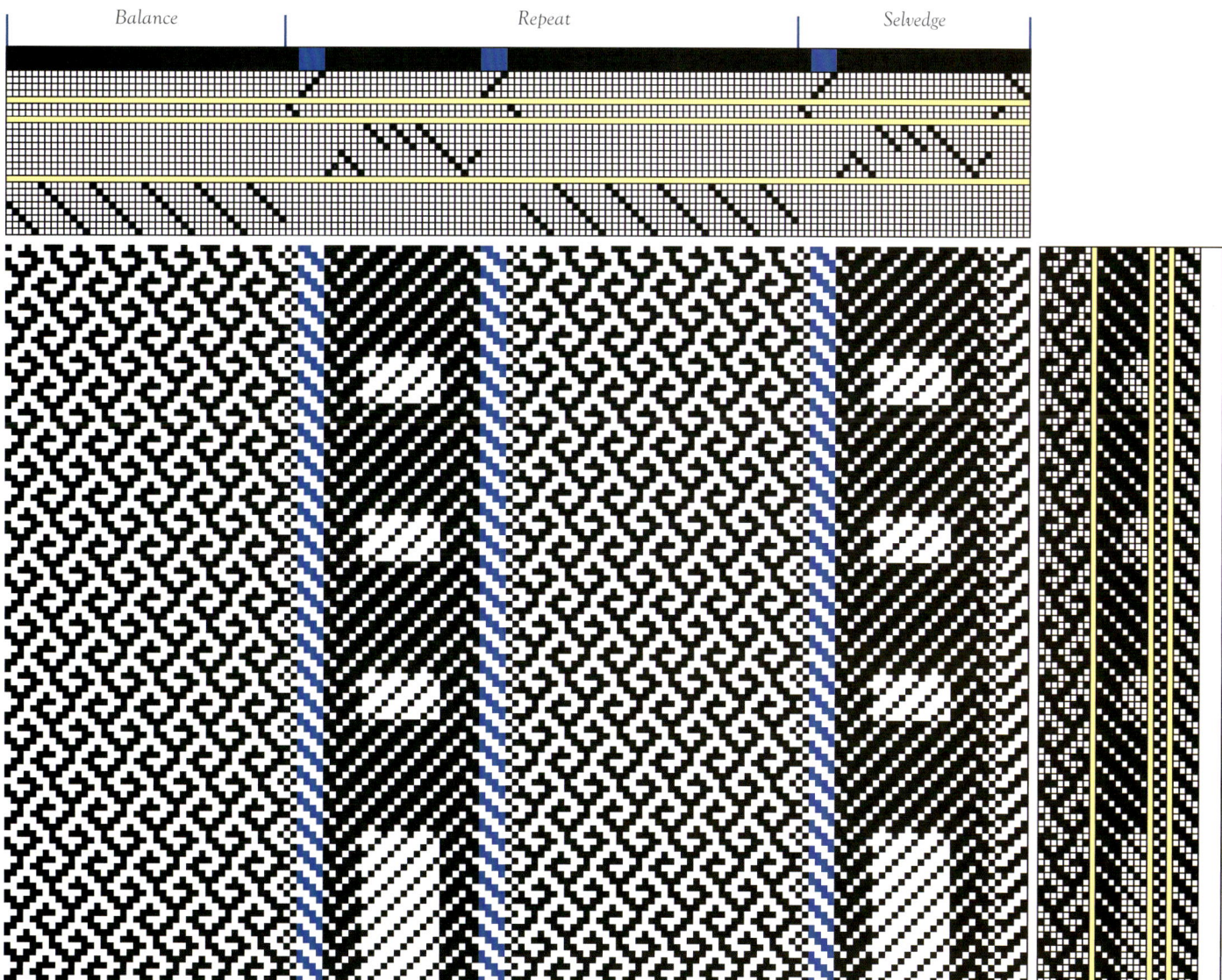

*Threading Draft. Crepe, forming the background, is woven on shafts 1 to 8, with stripes of turned twill on shafts 9 to 16, transitional plain weave on shafts 17 and 18, and a colored block in 2/2 twill on shafts 19 to 22. The draft, shown as a liftplan, has been expanded to separate the parts.*

157

# Waffling About

## Stacey Harvey-Brown

### Shawl in Waffle Weave and Plain Weave

## Design Process

Having attended a CW Study Day with Rosalie Neilson in the UK, and getting a sneak preview of her new design book (Neilson, 2017), I decided to use her block design method for a series of exchange samples for the 2017 Collapse, Pleat, and Bump Complex Weavers Study Group. The samples were designed to have surface relief through the use of waffle weave. Six different 3-block motifs across the width crossed three different 3-block treadling motifs. In the samples, the motifs were separated by bands in the warp and weft.

I was exploring a fine angora/wool yarn and planned to adapt the design for a shawl length after taking the exchange samples from the loom. In the initial planning of the threading drafts, I wanted to ensure that the design flowed for a shawl as well as gave interesting stand-alone motifs for the sample exchange. The limited re-threading for the shawl entailed removing the separating bands between motifs and adjusting the threading to remove repeated blocks.

In order to keep an odd/even progression in the warp, a thread has been irregularly left or extracted at the ends of the blocks. This results in the waffles varying in width from 13 to 15 threads wide with some mirrored and some asymmetric. It would be possible to make them all alike (1 to 8 to 2, slightly asymmetric), but I like a more fluid approach as I never know precisely how it will turn out. I am always striving to get a more organic look rather than a precisely geometric look. The pattern portion of each treadling block begins and ends on a pick based on the same tabby. The opposite tabby then ends the block to preserve the plain weave alternation.

The weaving was straightforward apart from having to check each pick for clinging threads. A gentle finishing suited the shawl, but more vigorous finishing would create more bloom in the angora and more dimensional texture, as well as greater shrinkage. The fabric then becomes suitable for a very warm and cuddly lightweight baby blanket or knee throw. The fabric is fully reversible with both sides having distinct designs.

## Weaving Information

Size: 70.5" x 22" plus 4" fringe on each end

Warp: 2/26nm angora/wool, 6448 ypp, ecru; 22 epi

Weft: 2/26nm angora/wool, 6448 ypp, ecru; 24 ppi

Source: Original draft, inspired by Neilson (2017).

Weave Structure: Waffle weave and plain weave, 24 shafts

Finishing: Hemstitched on loom, 2-ply fringe alternating five and six strands per ply and tied with overhand knots. Hand washed in lukewarm water with detergent for five minutes. Rinsed twice in lukewarm water, with conditioner in final rinse. Tumble dried for 15 minutes, then hung to dry.

Take-up and Shrinkage: Warp 12%, weft 17%

## Tips

• With sticky yarns, like this angora-wool blend, you may need to check every pick for clinging threads and clear the shed where required.

• Finishing is a critical part of design. Small changes can result in very different fabrics, suited to different uses. Sample your finishing technique before committing the full length of cloth to a process.

• Many structures which are not normally woven as blocks in a design, such as waffle weave, can be turned into a block weave. Decide on a compatible weave to form the background, and substitute the needed tie-up into the blocks. Structures with different characteristics such as shrinkage, as in the waffle and plain weave of this piece, will alter each other. The shrinkage is not as much as a piece with all waffle weave, nor as little as one would expect of all plain weave. Additionally, the waffles are not as deep and the plain weave is not as flat as in a single structure piece.

• The strong contrasts in texture between the waffle and plain weave blocks allows the complex pattern to be elegantly visible even in a fuzzy yarn with warp and weft of the same color.

• The number of designs possible with just three blocks is impressive. This small sampling of motifs using just three blocks in warp and weft entices further exploration.

*Profile Draft. This is the starting profile draft with the motifs separated for clarity.*

160

Component Threading Draft. The plain weave and waffle weave components are shown as they might be woven on an 8-shaft loom.

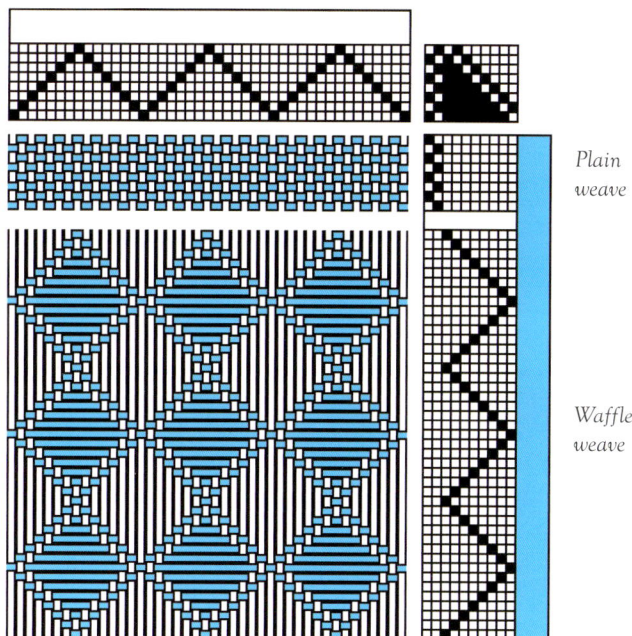

Plain weave

Waffle weave

Profile Draft. Final 3-block profile after removing spacers and adjusting block interfaces.

Threading Draft. Portion of the draft corresponding to the first motif in the upper right of the profile draft on the opposite page. Notice the small differences in the block threadings, introduced to provide a more organic feel. A pick of plain weave ends each treadling block. The draft is expanded to separate the blocks.

# Spring Samaras
## Georgia Hadley
### Runner in Twill, Plain Weave, and Flossa Knots

*Detail, oriented as woven.*

## Design Process

The starting point for me in any design venture is trying to make new connections with standard known formats. In this case, I combined my love of twill with my fascination with flossa (shorter, more closely spaced rya) knots. Early spring is a perfect time for roaming about, observing natural wonders. The colors used in the knots were inspired by the early spring samaras (winged maple seeds) in my yard. These delicate seeds were especially beautiful and their exuberant clusters transferred well to three-dimensional knots. The veining of the leaves brought to mind a variety of twill lines. Using a point threading, but separating it into 8x8 blocks allowed me to create a complex whole from simple 8-shaft twill tie-ups. In the past, I have completed a series of tablecloths on 32 shafts using 8x8 blocks, so the thought of breaking the point tie-up that way came naturally.

The flossa knots are set into the plain weave areas. Each knot is made of three strands of multiple colors, carried as loose strands rather than on a shuttle or bobbin. The flossa knots (Collingwood, 1978) were lifted by hand rather than done over a stick. I find it easier to pull the knots to size individually and the slight irregularities in height add to the organic feel of the design. The loops are not cut. Unfortunately, my warp wasn't as long as I thought. In the end, the knots I wove horizontally looked better in a vertical position.

In the future, I will continue my experimentation and observation, developing a series of one-of-a-kind pieces. Belief in all things beautiful matters greatly in this life.

## Weaving Information

Size: 30" x 21"

Warp: 12/2 mercerized cotton, 5040 ypp, bark; 28 epi

Weft: 20/2 mercerized cotton, 8400 ypp, pistachio and cocoa; 10/2 mercerized cotton, 4200 ypp, cocoa; knots, 20/6 mercerized cotton floss, 2800 ypp, pistachio, maroon, and burgundy; 20/2 mercerized cotton, 8400 ypp, lime; 10/2 mercerized cotton, 4200 ypp, cocoa; 8/2 rayon, 3360 ypp khaki; 28 epi; four rows of knots per inch.

Source: Original draft

Weave Structures: Twills, plain weave, and flossa (rya) knots, 24 shafts

Other Weaving Information: The uncut knots were done freehand and stick up about 1/8" when relaxed, 1/4" when pulled tight. There are roughly four rows of knots per inch, with each knot made of three different strands worked over four warp ends.

Finishing: Handsewn hems, backed with iron-on interfacing to hide knot threads. Not washed.

Take-up and Shrinkage: Warp and weft, 0%

162

Threading Draft. Because the tie-up and treadling are separated into coherent blocks, the simple point also functions as three blocks. In the warp, the B block always weaves as a straight line (left or right), and the A and C blocks always weave as points. In the weft, the B and C blocks always weave as points, and the A block as straight. The tie-up blocks consist of irregular twills and plain weave. The draft has been expanded to separate the blocks.

## Tips

• Combining loom-controlled weaving with hand techniques, such as knotting, twisting, brocading, etc., is fertile ground for exploration. Although more commonly combined on four shafts, there is no reason not to pursue the idea on more shafts.

• Look at the world around you for color and design inspiration. A close examination will often find unusual but pleasing color combinations. Consider the lines in your inspiration item and explore how to transfer some of their aspects to your piece. Here, the diagonal twill lines of varying weights capture some of qualities of the angled vein lines in the maple leaves.

• Texture is often overlooked, but can be an important tactile part of design. Looping, knotting, using textured yarns, etc. add to the dimensionality of the design, inviting the viewer to touch and appreciate the cloth in a different way.

• Uncut flossa loops reflect light differently and have a completely different tactile effect from the more typical cut pile. Sample both cut and uncut loops for your project, as well as combinations of cut and uncut, loop height, and loop spacing.

• Although a point threading and treadling like this would most often be used with a 24-shaft regular twill tie-up, breaking the tie-up into smaller blocks adds greater complexity and interest.

• The plain weave areas are perfect for hand-manipulated effects of many kinds.

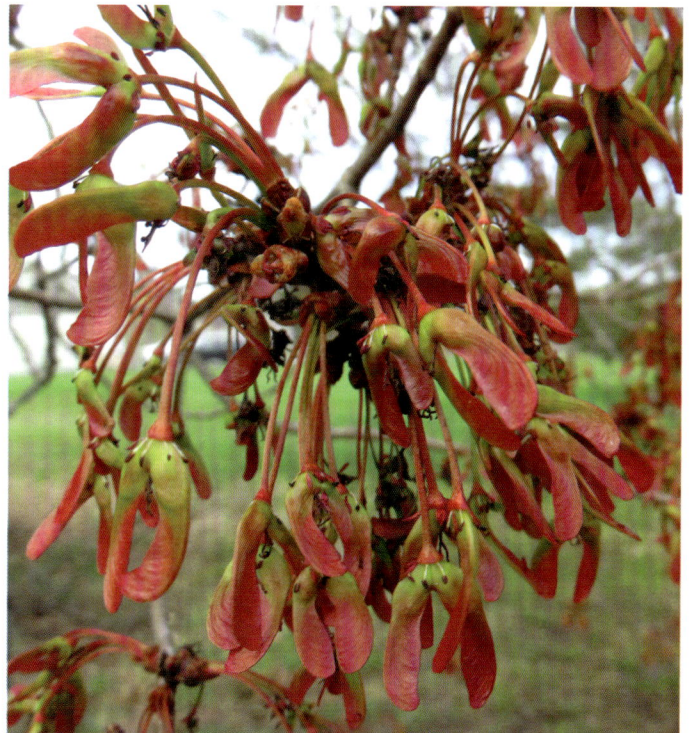

*Component Threading Draft. There are eight different block tie-ups used. This draft in liftplan form shows how each block would look if repeated in straight treadling order on an 8-shaft loom.*

# 3-D Triangles

## Sally Eyring

### Vest in Point Twill and Extended Rep

### Design Process

The world isn't flat, so why should my weaving be flat? I spent years learning the rules of two-dimensional weaving; then, I learned how to break those rules to weave three-dimensional sculptural forms. My techniques and loom devices allow me to weave a shape into the cloth without depending on differential shrinkage or sewing for the shape. For example, the fabric for an earlier jacket had one 54" and one 11" selvedge. My techniques require special devices to control the warp tension and the extra length of woven cloth at the front of the loom.

I am constantly trying to extend my techniques to new and different shapes and forms. I developed the vest pattern first, and then wove the cloth to fit the pattern. I placed the pattern piece for the gathered section on the diagonal, then determined the placement of the black vertical gathering stripes on a straight threading. The front diagonal piece is woven three-dimensionally, with the gathers created as the piece is woven. I had to invent several loom devices to control the tension at the back of the

loom and the gathered cloth at the front of the loom in order to create this three-dimensional effect (Eyring, 2020).

I threaded the warp with an irregular 8-shaft point twill on the first eight shafts as the body. The narrow black straight draw selvedges form the gathering bands, and are threaded in opposite directions. These bands are sleyed at 60 epi, twice the sett of the body. Sometimes they weave as a flat twill, and sometimes they serve as places to form the woven gathers. To form the gathered front panel of the vest, I opened up a tabby shed on one side of the piece and left the same shed open for 50 picks while weaving twill across the rest of the panel. Then, I pulled in the gathers, changed the tabby shed, and wove another 50 picks. I wove four such groups before switching to gathering on the other selvedge. When I changed the side of the gathering, I changed the weft colors at the same time to accentuate the triangles. The rest of the vest was woven in the normal fashion on eight shafts without the side gathering bands.

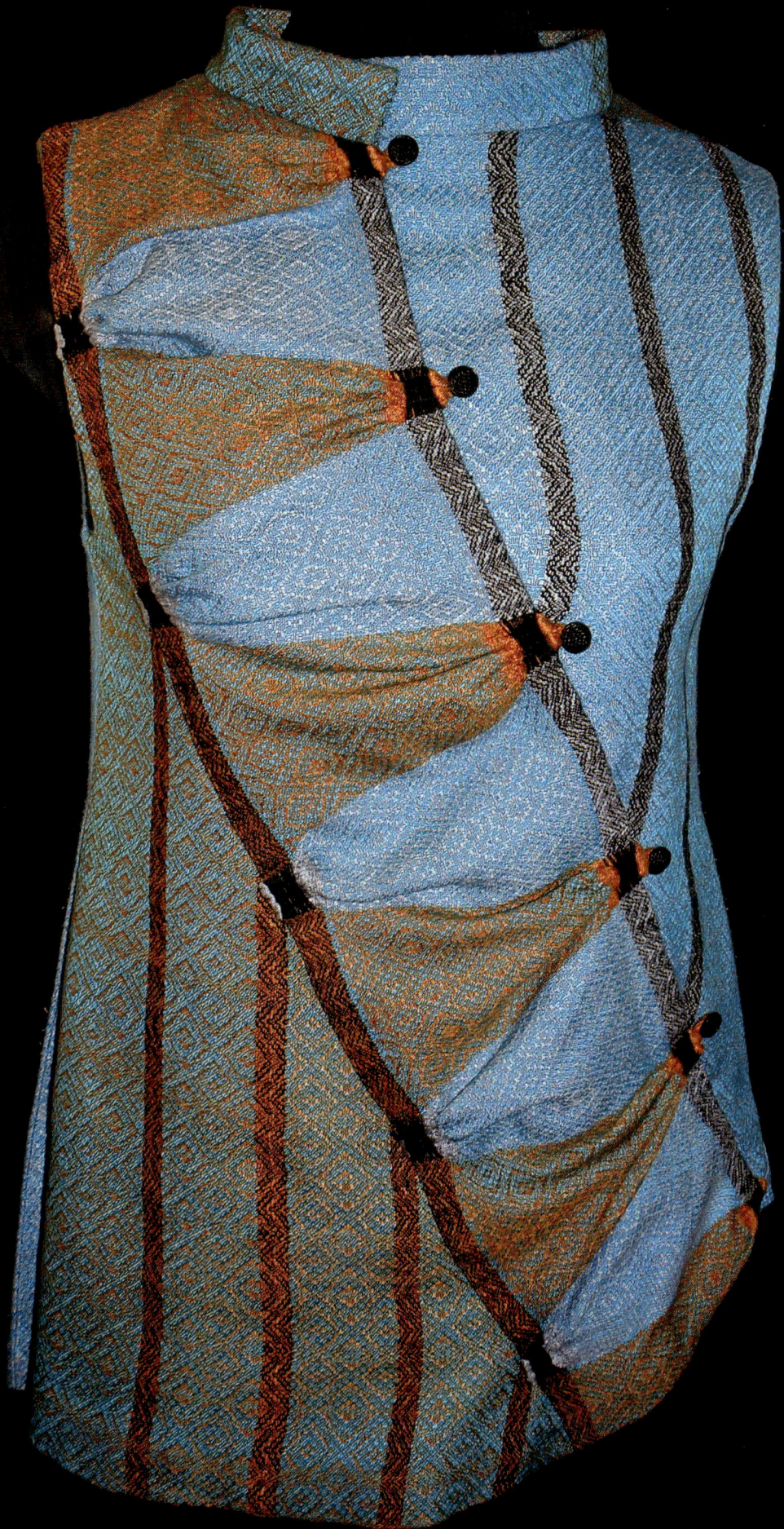

*Threading Draft. A portion of the drawdown is shown in liftplan view. The black warp areas are where the gathering occurs, alternating sides. The red picks on the draft mark where a rod is put in to pull in the fabric to create the gathers. These rods are temporary and removed once weaving starts again. Only two of the four gathering picks per section are shown. The draft is expanded to separate the parts.*

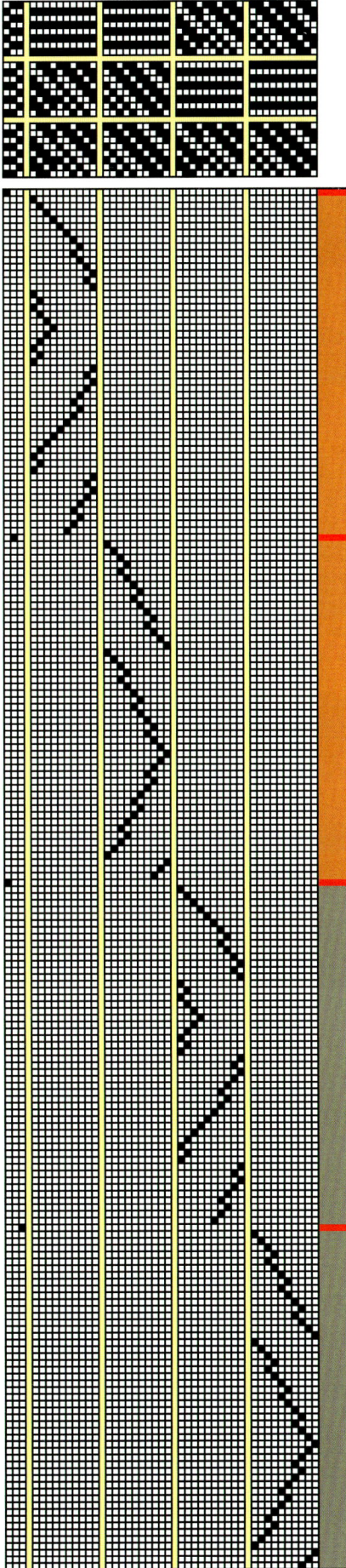

## Weaving Information

Vest Size: US 10-12

Warp: 20/2 silk, 4900 ypp, turquoise; 20/2 linen, 3000 ypp, black; silk, 30 epi and linen, 60 epi

Weft: 20/2 silk, 4900 ypp, rust and silver; 32 ppi

Source: Original draft

Weave Structures: Irregular point twill and extended rep, 24 shafts

Other Weaving Information: The red picks on the draft mark where a rod was put in to pull in the fabric to create the gathers. These rods are temporary and removed once weaving starts again.

Finishing: Hand washed, spun in washing machine to damp dry and pressed.

Sewing: The vest is lined with commercial silk fabric.

Take-up and Shrinkage: Warp and weft, 12%

## Tips

• Don't be afraid to experiment with entirely new techniques to create your own new effects!

• Why should cloth be flat?

• Looms are a tool. Modify your tools to suit your needs.

• While differential shrinkage, pulled thread techniques, and structural changes can create some pleating, ruffling, and shaping, this technique allows precise placement of effects anywhere while weaving.

• Changing the sett and/or picks per inch for different sections can create a large variety of interesting and unusual effects.

• For extensively detailed information on modifying your loom and weaving three-dimensional pieces, see Eyring (2020).

*Threading Draft. Treadling for the draft on the opposite page shown as a tie-up and treadling instead of a liftplan. The draft is expanded to separate the parts.*

# II.3 Layers

Double-, triple-, and more-layered cloth is created by interleaving two (or more) drafts, usually in a 1:1 ratio. Other ratios may be used, e.g., when the setts are different. The layers may be in any structures which work with the loom and pattern chosen, and joined at the edges or not.

In the draft at right, the last two treadles are used to raise the top layer when the bottom layer is woven. When the top layer is woven, the bottom layer(s) stays down (an empty white section in the tie-ups). When the bottom layer is woven, the top shafts are lifted (a solid black section in the tie-up). If layers are stitched together, the stitchers will appear in these parts of the tie-up. While the examples given have even distribution of shafts between layers, many interesting effects may be had by splitting the shafts unevenly.

All of the drafts on these two pages have a total of eight shafts used for each layer. In the 2- and 4-block drafts, the shaft combinations of the layers change. The tie-ups on the 2- and 4-block drafts have color added to the tie-up to show the top layer warp and weft colors. These drawdowns are shown in double weave view, top layer only. The shafts and treadles have been rearranged from their usual simpler order, colored, and expanded to make the creation of the layers more obvious.

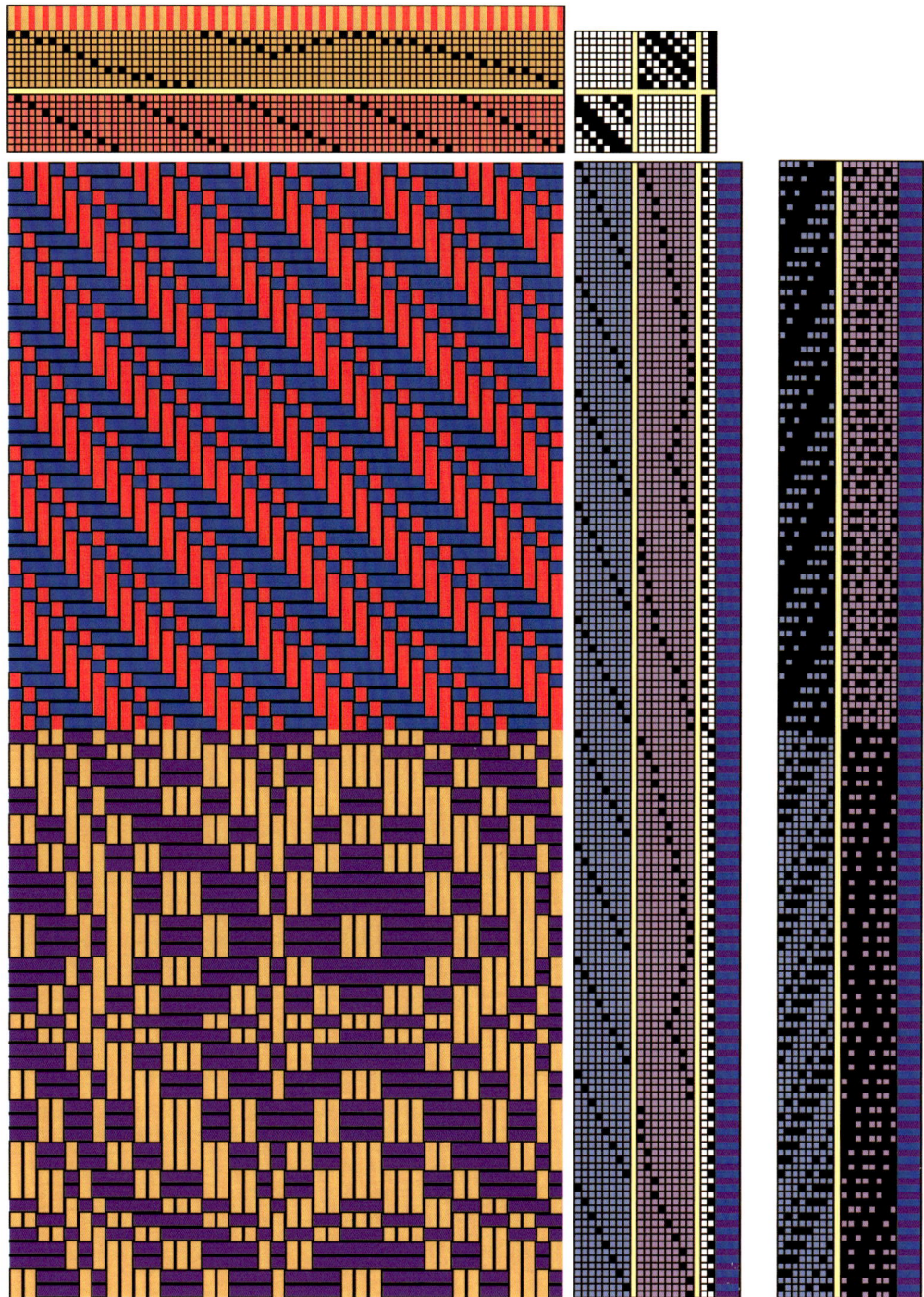

*A single block with eight shafts in each layer can be woven in weft-wise stripes of each pattern/structure. In order to make this draft work on a 16-shaft treadle loom, a skeleton tie-up (as well as a liftplan) is shown. The back is the opposite face from the front, though otherwise identical.*

*To make the back the same as the front would require 16 more treadles. Use a heavier weft yarn for the orange and purple layer to account for the looser interlacement. The treadles and shafts are color-coded and separated to help distinguish the layers.*

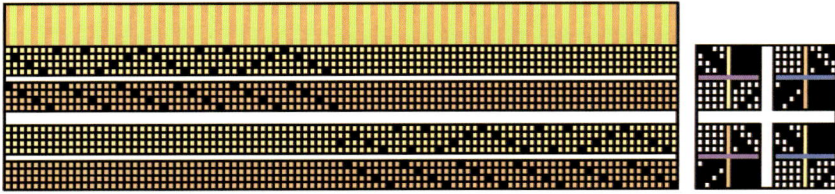

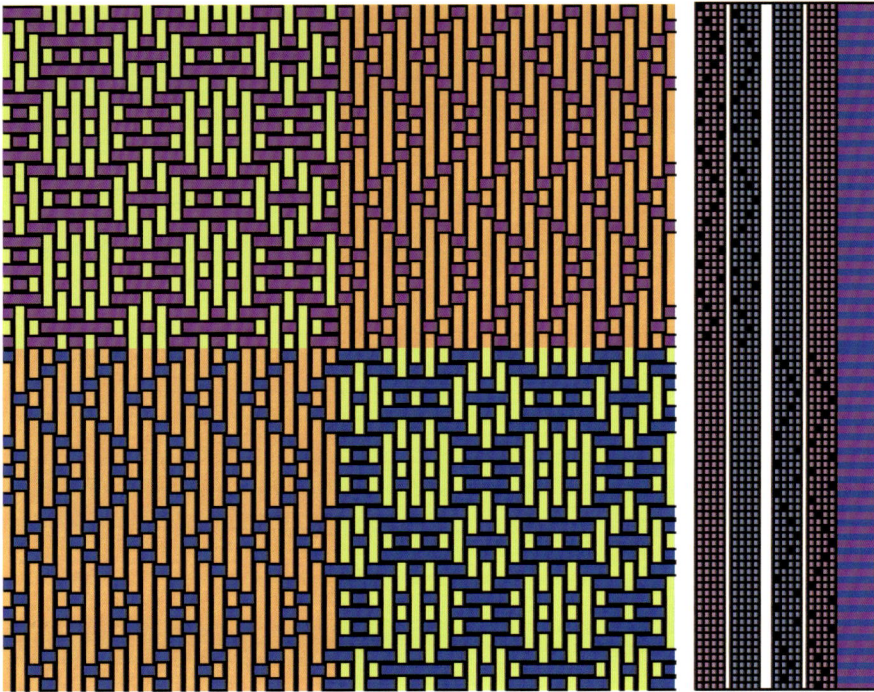

Dividing the shafts into two blocks allows weft-wise and warp-wise switching of layers on the surface. Using an even division of the 8-shaft layers, only four shafts are available for each layer in each block. Note that the color order has been switched in the second treadling block to put the blue weft on the top surface. It is also possible to have both blocks weave diamonds or both weave zigzags (larger tie-up, not shown).

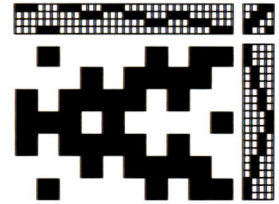

Profile for the 4-block draft.

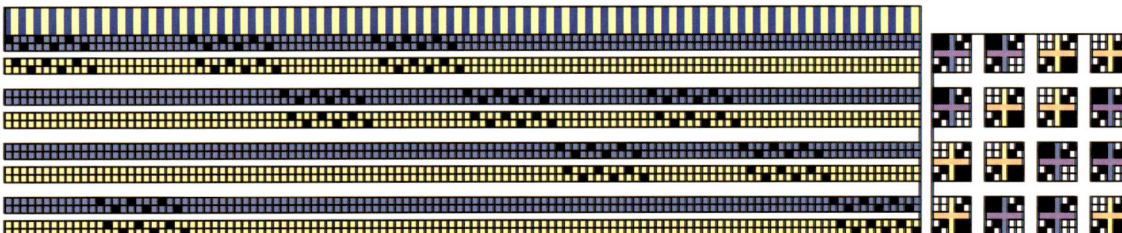

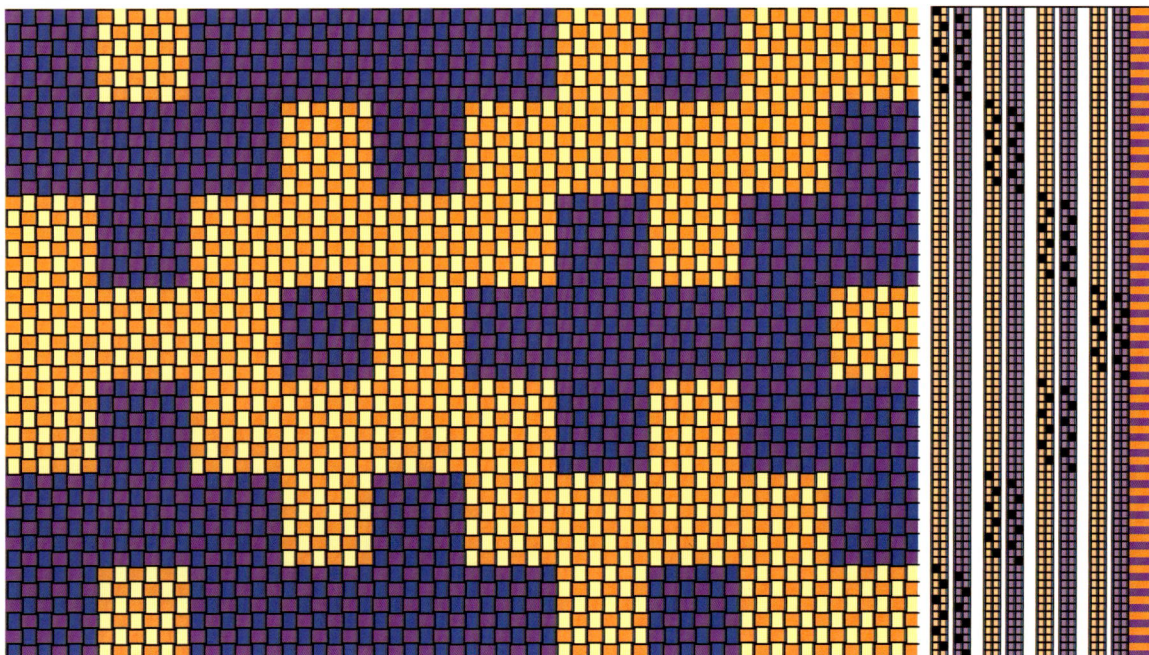

Dividing the shafts into four blocks allows only four shafts per block, with two per layer within each block. As shown, this is a unit weave version, with any blocks able to weave pattern together. While strongly limiting the structural possibilities, the increase in block design possibilities, and sometimes in clarity and stability, can be an advantage.

171

# Portholes on a Restless Sea of Color

## Bonnie Kay

### Wall Art in Double Weave (Monk's Belt, Twill, and Overshot)

### Design Process

The starting point for this design was a photograph of a piece by Ted Hallman (O'Connor, 1996, p. 49). I had been weaving double weave with plain weave and twill and liked the idea of including more 4-shaft structures, different from the ones used by Hallman. In this piece, monk's belt is woven in one section and Primrose overshot in the other. Various combinations of these two structures alternate with a regular straight 2/2 twill with tabby.

In one section, twill and traditional Primrose overshot were threaded on shafts 1 to 4 and 5 to 8 respectively. In the other section, twill and monk's belt were threaded on shafts 9 to 12 and 13 to 16 respectively. At any given time, eight shafts form each layer of the cloth, though which shafts are grouped can change. I used three treadlings: shafts 5 to 8 and 13 to 16 on top (overshot and monk's belt), shafts 5 to 8 and 9 to 12 on top (overshot and twill), and shafts 1 to 4 and 13 to 16 on top (twill and monk's belt). The combination using twill in both blocks on top (shafts 1 to 4 and 9 to 12 on top) is possible, but did not seem as interesting.

### Weaving Information

Size: 36" x 11"

Warp: 8/2 Tencel, 3360 ypp, light gold, burnt orange, poppy, teal, and sapphire; 40 epi

Weft: 20/2 Tencel, 8400 ypp, black (tabby); 8/2 Tencel, 3360 ypp, light gold, burnt orange, poppy, teal, and sapphire (pattern); 48 ppi including tabby

Source: Original draft inspired by Ted Hallman (O'Connor, 1996).

Weave Structures: Double weave (monk's belt, 2/2 twill, and Primrose overshot), 16 shafts

Finishing: Ends were hand sewn. Cloth loops were sewn at top of piece and a Pyrex tube was inserted for hanging. Hand washed in lukewarm water with mild detergent for five minutes. Rinsed in cold water. Laid flat to dry until damp and hard pressed with steam iron.

Take-up and Shrinkage: Warp 3%, weft 1%

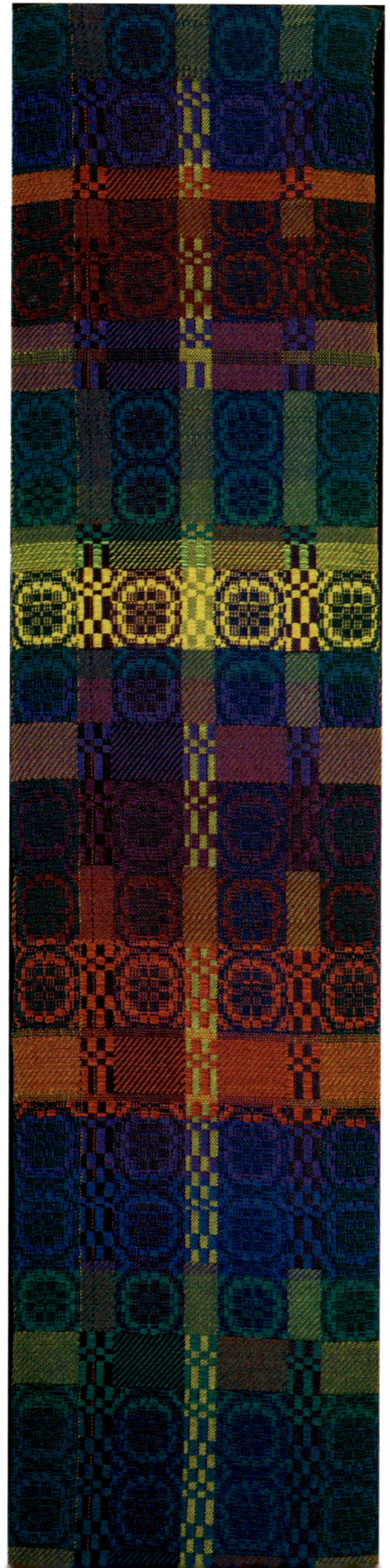

## Tips

• One or more picks of plain weave at places where the layers exchange may be used to tie the two layers together more firmly.

• In a complex treadling like this one, using a table or dobby loom may be easier than retieing the treadles repeatedly.

• The use of bright, contrasting colors adds drama and allows the patterns to stand out.

• When combining structures, consideration needs to be given to the tabby requirements. If you combine structures where the tabbies do not occur on the same picks or choose one structure with a tabby and one without, then adjustments may be needed. In this piece, the overshot and monk's belt require tabby, but the twill does not. By adding tabby to the twill, the twill sections work smoothly with the other structures. If tabby were not added to the twill treadling, alternating floats would be thinner and black, a very different effect.

• When combining patterns it may help to use one or more as the focal point and the rest as background. Here, the overshot, monk's belt, and twill all have different scales. This creates a visual hierarchy, with the overshot serving as a focal point, the monk's belt quieter and less prominent, and the twill a softer background note. Each stays as a distinct pattern of its own. When all the patterns combined are the same "loudness" (for example, using three different overshot patterns), the individual patterns may recombine visually rather than staying distinct. It may still be interesting and good design, but gives a very different result.

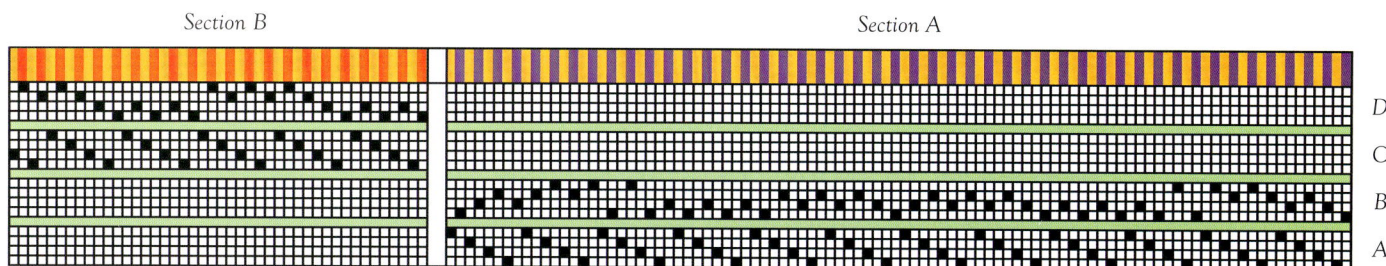

*Threading Draft. In this threading, each layer uses four shafts per section. Layers A (shafts 1 to 4) and C (shafts 9 to 12) are threaded straight draw. Layer B (shafts 5 to 8) is an overshot threading, and layer D (shafts 13 to 16) is a monk's belt threading. The two sections alternate, ending with section A. The draft is expanded to separate the layers.*

173

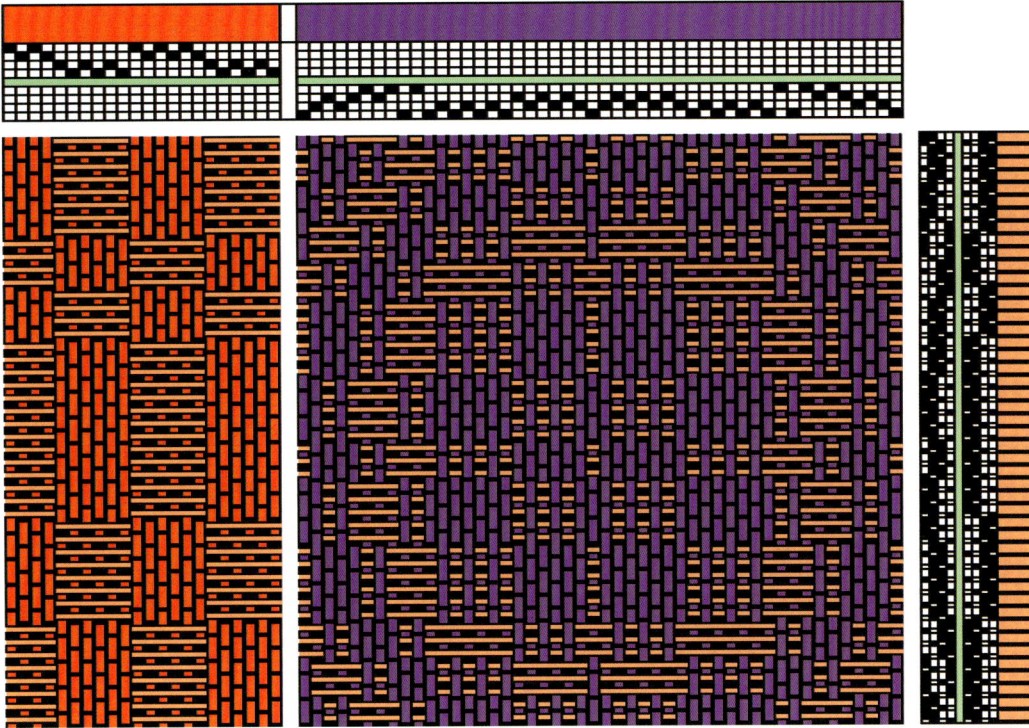

Component Threading Drafts. The first treadling option is shown in two drafts (in liftplan), as if it were two single-layer 8-shaft drafts. The drafts are expanded to separate the two blocks.

Above, Section A weaves overshot and section B weaves monk's belt on the top layer.

Below, Sections A and B weave 2/2 twill with tabby on the bottom layer.

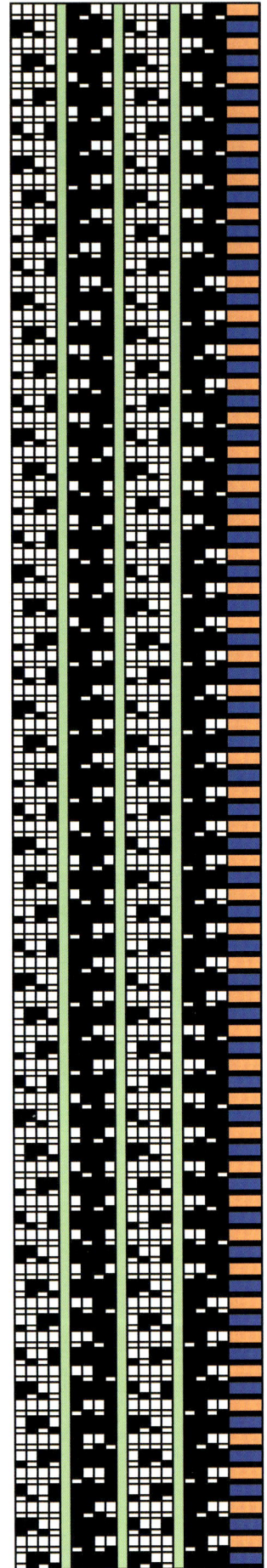

Right, Actual 16-shaft liftplan for the first option, with overshot and monk's belt on the top layer (shafts 5 to 8 and 13 to 16) and 2/2 twill with tabby on the bottom layer (shafts 1 to 4 and 9 to 12). Two picks are woven on each layer before changing to the other layer.

*Left, Actual 16-shaft liftplan for the second treadling option, with overshot and 2/2 twill with tabby on the top layer (shafts 5 to 8 and 9 to 12) and twill with tabby and monk's belt on the bottom (shafts 1 to 4 and 13 to 16). The cloth is woven with two picks on each layer before changing to the other layer.*

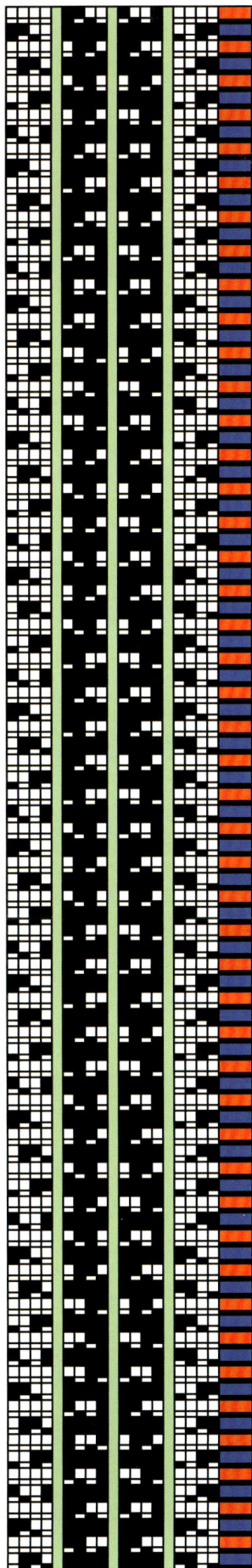

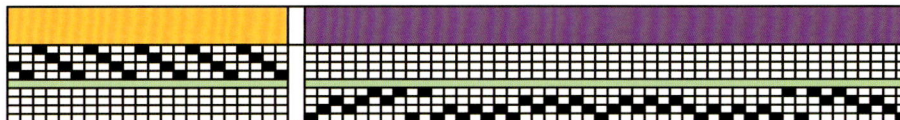

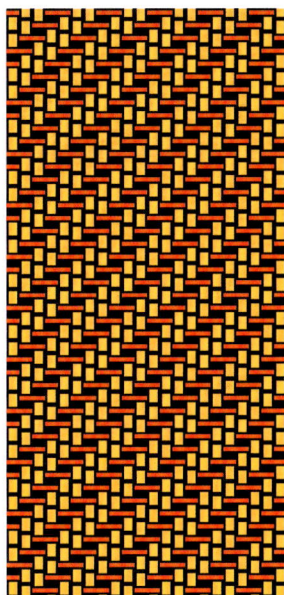

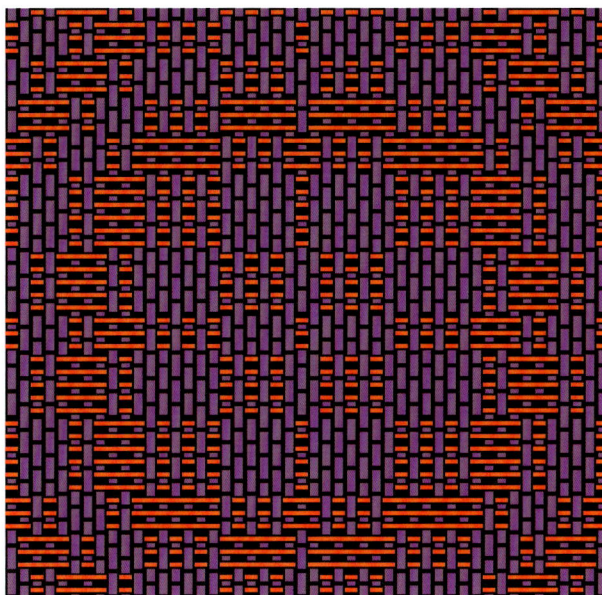

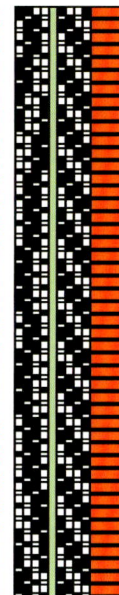

*Component Threading Drafts. The second treadling option is shown in two drafts (in liftplan), as if the layers were two single-layer 8-shaft drafts. The drafts were expanded to separate the two blocks. The third treadling option swaps these two layers (not shown).*

*Above, Section A weaves overshot and section B weaves 2/2 twill with tabby on the top layer.*

*Below, Section A weaves 2/2 twill with tabby and section B weaves monk's belt on the bottom layer.*

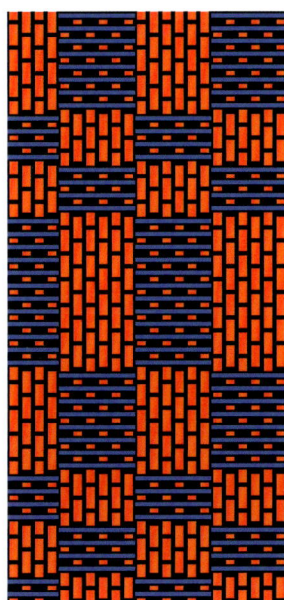

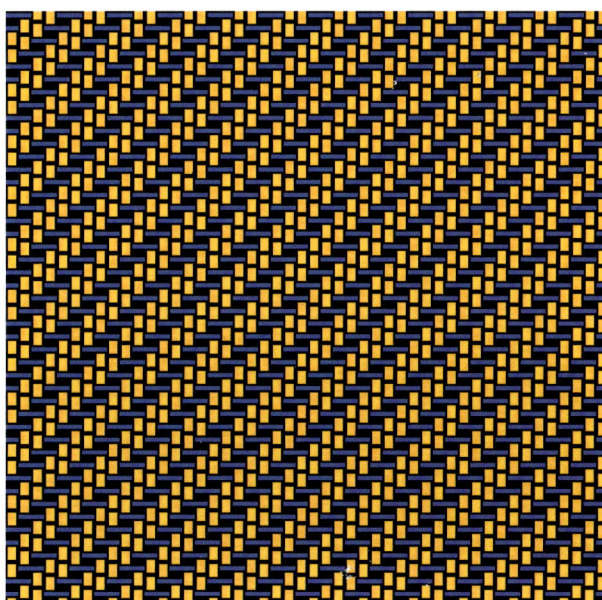

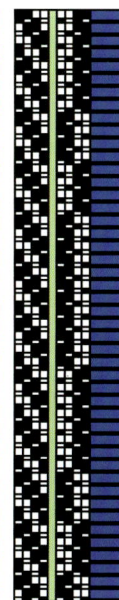

# Through the Looking-Glass

## Cally Booker

### Scarf in Double Weave (Huck Lace)

## Design Process

I first became interested in weaving double cloth in huck lace when I realized that the warp and weft floats would allow me to stitch two layers together invisibly. As I started to weave and exchange layers, I found that I liked the way the lace structure softens the edges of a block design. When exchanging layers, huck becomes quite a shaft-greedy structure, needing two shafts per half unit. On my 16-shaft loom I can manage only two blocks of huck per layer, giving me just four half units to work with. Fortunately, I discovered I could easily maintain the required odd-even order of the huck half units if I used four-shaft twill threadings as profile drafts, and have found these to be a rich source of design options.

For this piece I chose a high-contrast red and black colorway, a departure from my usual style. I wanted to complement the scheme with a pattern that is bold but not busy, so I turned to one of my favorite designs, the shaded 4-shaft twill, with 1/3, 2/2, and 3/1 areas. This design poses a practical challenge for my mechanical dobby, as I am limited in the number of lags available. I was able to set up a chain for the first part of the design and then adjust it for each subsequent section.

To contrast the regularity of the twill-based design, I placed it asymmetrically on the piece. This gave me a predominantly black side with a red pattern at one end and a predominantly red side with a black pattern, so it can be worn either way. This reversibility, and my hunch that the Red Queen might well wear a dramatic over-sized scarf such as this, gave me the title: "Through the Looking-Glass."

## Weaving Information

Size: 66.5" x 12" plus 4" (red) and 6" (black) fringe on each end

Warp: 2/18 merino/silk (50/50%), 5040 ypp, ebony and cinnabar; 33 epi

Weft: 2/18 merino/silk (50/50%), 5040 ypp, ebony and cinnabar; 33 ppi

Source: Original draft

Weave Structure: Double weave (huck lace), 16 shafts

Finishing: Hemstitched on the loom in groups of ten warp ends (five from each layer). A two-ply fringe was made for each layer separately, using alternating hemstitched groups. Hand washed in hot water with mild detergent. Rinsed in warm water, followed by cool water. After washing, the red fringe was trimmed to four inches and the black fringe to six inches.

Take-up and Shrinkage: Warp 15%, weft 17%

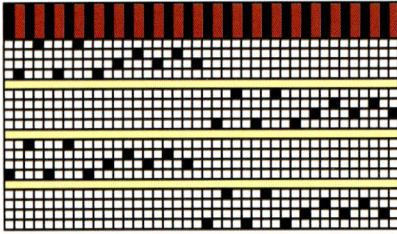

*Threading Draft. Only the top layer is shown, with the treadling given as a liftplan. Colors are slightly different in the warp and weft to better show the structure. The first two blocks (section 1) weave all black on the top surface and the last two (5) weave all red on the top surface. Sections 2, 3, and 4 show the 12 distinct block patterns used to weave the red/black combinations required for the twill-like pattern shown in the profile draft below. Expanded to separate the blocks.*

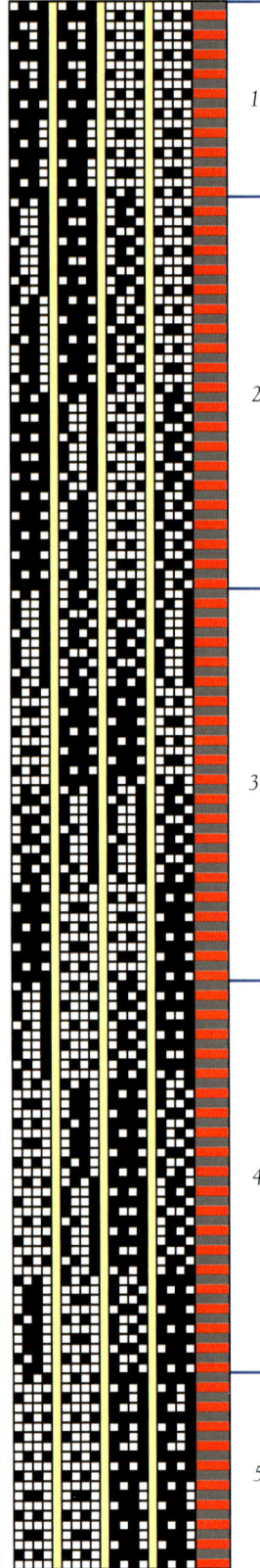

## Tips

• If you want "holes all the way through" then double weave huck lace needs a wider sett per layer than you would usually use for a single layer of huck lace. If you have a suitably-sized reed, leaving an empty dent between half units can help. A yarn with a bit of "tooth" is also an asset with the wider sett, helping to keep the cloth from becoming sleazy.

• For the selvedge, use half-basket weave, weighted separately. To form a support for hem-stitching, use two picks of plain weave in each layer at each end.

• The important key to double weave huck is maintaining the odd-even tabby order. As long as that is kept, each section can be repeated as many times as desired and partial repeats are fine.

• Stitchers are helpful in the plain part of the draft where the same layer stays on top for a long distance (Keasbey, 2006). In the patterned part, the layer exchange is sufficient to link the two layers together, though stitchers may be added if desired.

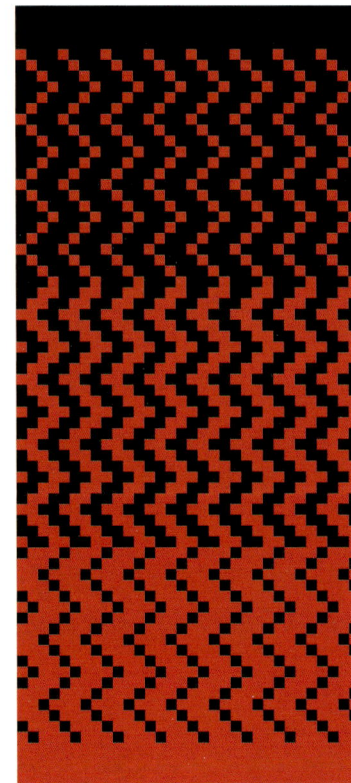

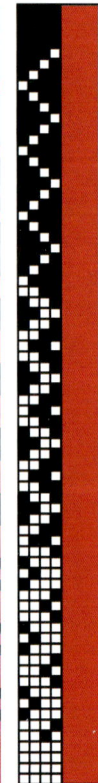

*Profile Draft. Shows placement of the four pattern blocks, in twill-like zigzag pattern progressing from 4 black/0 red, to 3/1, 2/2, 1/3, and ending with 0/4 (all red).*

178

# Spring into Autumn
## Patricia Foster

### Yardage for Curtains in Double Weave (Beiderwand)

## Design Process

I have a preference for geometric patterns and in recent years have used beiderwand and lampas to achieve this effect. The starting point for this design was the ratio of 1:3. The structure for both layers is beiderwand (Keasbey, 1993), each with its own pattern. The two different patterns were designed so that the size of the repeat on the first side (the turned "T" motif) is three times wider but the same height as the repeat on the second side (the "box" motif). Then, when layers are interchanged or panels with opposite sides up are joined, a row of boxes from side two lines up exactly with one T from side one.

The larger scale pattern, in simple gold warp and brown weft, has an autumn look, while the smaller scale pattern, in an array of finely mixed combinations of yellow, green, blue, and purple warps with the brown weft speaks of spring. The larger patterns become abstract leaves, set against the small circles evoking spring flowers.

Eventually, the yardage will be made into lined and hemmed curtains. Each wide curtain will consist of three panels, with the central section featuring side two (shown right), while the two outside panels showcase side one (not shown).

I have never tried anything as difficult as this, although I have woven beiderwand and lampas on 32 shafts. This is probably the most complex weaving I have ever attempted. As to any ideas for the future, I won't do this again, and will go away to lick my wounds!

## Weaving Information

Size: 110" x 24.5" plus 4" fringe on one end

Warp: 12/2 cotton, 5040 ypp, primrose yellow (back cloth); 10/2 bamboo, 4200 ypp, multiple colors (front cloth); 24 epi

Weft: 12/2 cotton, 5040 ypp, primrose yellow, (tabby, back cloth); 10/2 bamboo, 4200 ypp, various colors (tabby, front cloth); 22/2 cottolin, 3170 ypp, dark brown (pattern for both cloths); 24 ppi

Source: Original draft

Weave Structure: Double weave (beiderwand), 16 shafts

Finishing: Briefly machine washed. Air dried outside. Pressed with steam iron.

Take-up and Shrinkage: Warp 6%, weft 8%

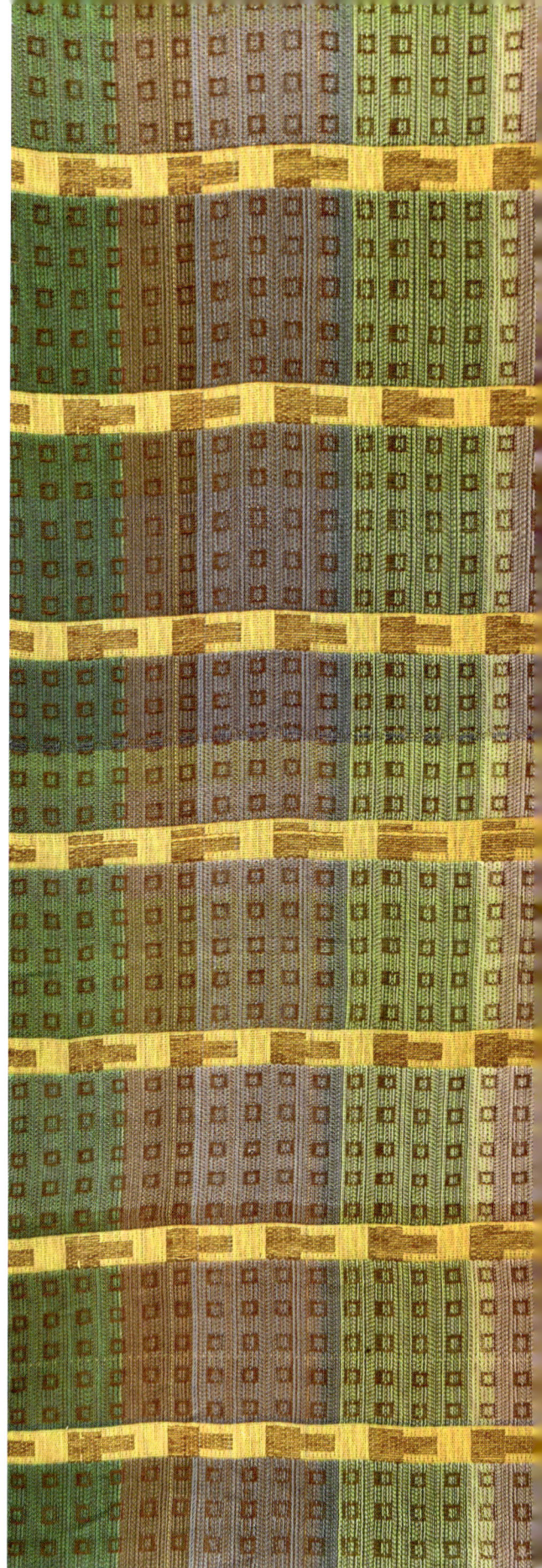

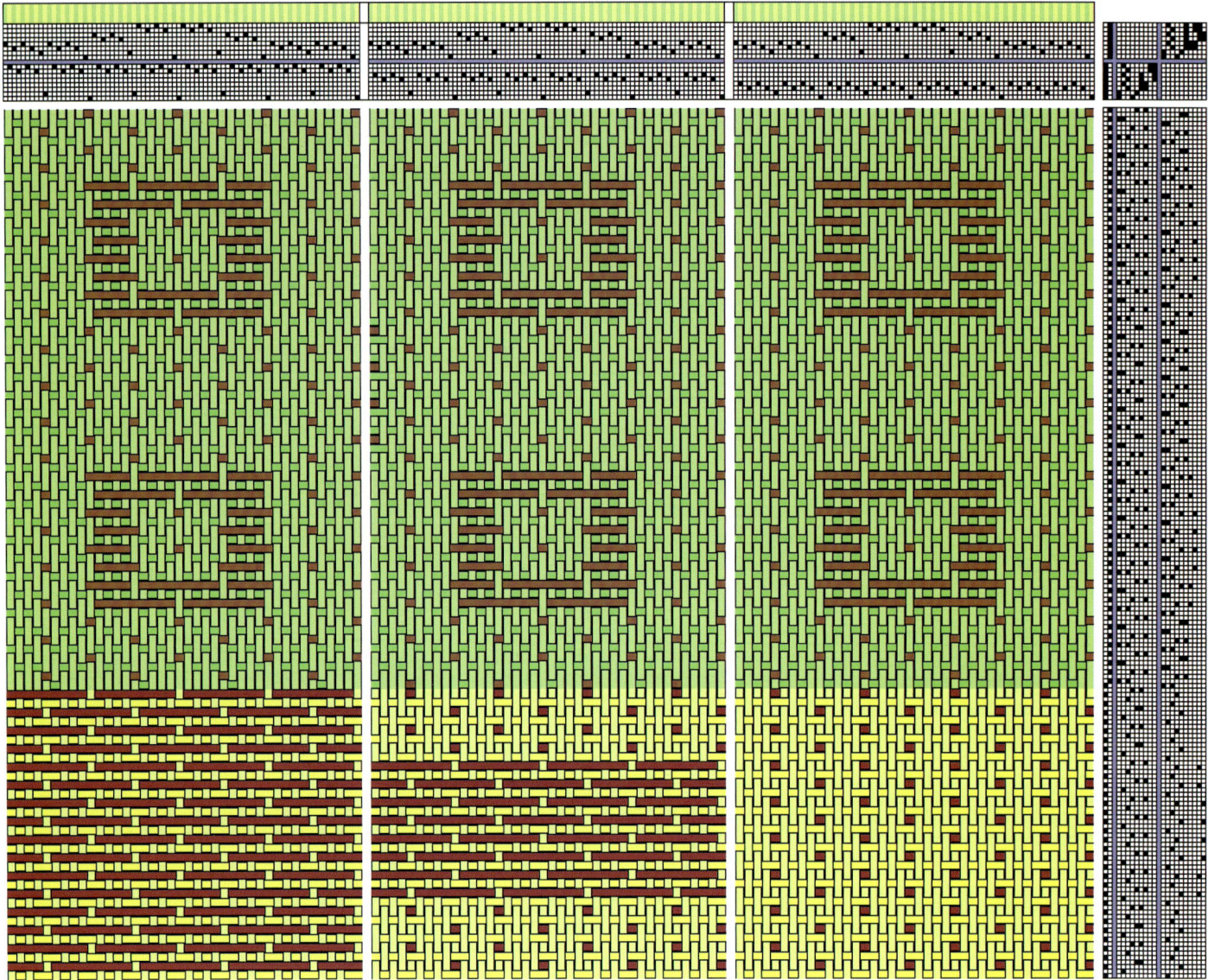

*Threading Draft. Two 8-shaft layers of 4:1 beiderwand. In the A layer (shafts 1 to 8), each warp section uses only one of the three possible blocks. The B layer (shafts 9 to 16) is exactly the same in each warp section, using all three blocks in each section. The first section of the draft has the B layer on top, and in the second part of the draft, the A layer is on top. Note the dots of brown stitchers in the background areas. Shown with skeleton tie-up, and expanded to separate the parts of the draft.*

## Tips

• Placing each warp on its own beam allows the two different warps to be wound separately and more quickly. It may also simplify complex threadings by having each layer on its own lease sticks, as well as help to control differential take-up or tensioning from two different patterns or interlacements.

• Planning two patterns so that they will meet or join exactly is an artform. Although it is more common to have the two repeats be the same length, planning a multiple of one to match one repeat of the other is a good design choice. The change in scale allows one pattern to dominate and be the focal point, and may also help disguise small mismatches in the weaving.

• Using a theme, such as the seasons, is a handy way to organize designing. The theme need not be expressed literally. Using color and abstract patterning to express an idea is often as or more effective, allowing viewers to develop their own interpretations.

• Tackling a new combination, even in structures you know well, can present unexpected challenges. Fun, or full of frustration, stretching yourself is always a useful learning experience.

*Threading Draft Liftplan. Same treadling as previous page's skeleton draft, with color bar. Expanded to divide the blocks.*

# Pieces of Eight and Two-Bits

## Sandra Hutton

### Shawl in Double Weave (Plain Weave) with Supplementary Warp

## Design Process

The concept for this book brought to my mind "pieces of eight." Unlike the gold coins depicted by the trunkful in pirate movies, pieces of eight were silver, approximately 1.5" in diameter. Of Portuguese origin, they were used all over the world, and remained legal tender in the U.S. until the Coinage Act of 1852. A pie-shaped quarter of the coin, known as "two-bits," could be cut or broken off and used in trade for items requiring an amount smaller than the whole coin.

Three 8-shaft supplementary warps (Walker, 2016), used to depict the coins and quarters, were interlaced on one surface of an 8-shaft double weave fabric (van der Hoogt, 1993; p. 108). The long floats characteristic of the reverse side of supplementary warps were hidden between the two layers. The layers were exchanged in the warp approximately every 2" to keep them together and minimize one layer stretching more than the other. The double weave was threaded on shafts 1 to 8, with the full coins on shafts 9 to 16, one quarter on shafts 17 to 24, and the other quarter on shafts 25 to 32. Longer floats between the quarters were tacked to the reverse layer on random picks so they wouldn't bunch and create lumps. The supplementary motifs are offset to one side of the scarf rather than centered or repeated.

A great deal of sampling was done to design the coin, break off quarters, and select an appropriate weight of metallic yarn for the supplementary warp. I did not want the metallic yarns to distort the drape of the shawl. I sampled three options and decided on four ends of #105 cord in a heddle. Two ends of #4 braid could have worked equally well, but #8 braid was too stiff and wouldn't have draped as well. The slightly over-twisted silk/wool blend in the body of the scarf is a joy to work with and snuggles into the weave structure with wet finishing.

## Weaving Information

Size: 85" x 15.75" plus 5.5" fringe on each end

Warp: 60/2 bombyx silk/wool (60/40%) doubled, 6400 ypp, hand dyed red; cord 105c, rayon/polyester, quadrupled (72/28%), silver; 52 epi

Weft: 60/2 bombyx silk/wool (60/40%) doubled, 6400 ypp, hand-dyed red; 52 ppi

Source: Original draft

Weave Structure: Double weave (plain weave) with supplementary warp, 32 shafts

Finishing: Groups of eight yarns (four of each layer) were hem stitched and then two groups were plied and tied with overhand knots. Hand washed using mild detergent and rinsed in medium temperature water. Laid flat to dry. Pressed on synthetic setting with steam iron.

Take-up and Shrinkage: Warp 8%, weft 3%

*Threading Draft. In this abbreviated portion of the drawdown, only the patterned part of the top layer is shown, with the supplementary warp pattern threads in white. These threads are interleaved with the 8-shaft base double weave cloth at a rate of two base to one supplementary thread. Each of the three patterns is placed on its own eight shafts, for a total of 32 shafts*

*with the base. The supplementary warp stitchers in unpatterned areas can be found as untied shafts in the liftplan on the opposite page. The two blocks of the double weave base are shown in red (block A) and orange (block B) for clarity. In the actual piece they are all red.*

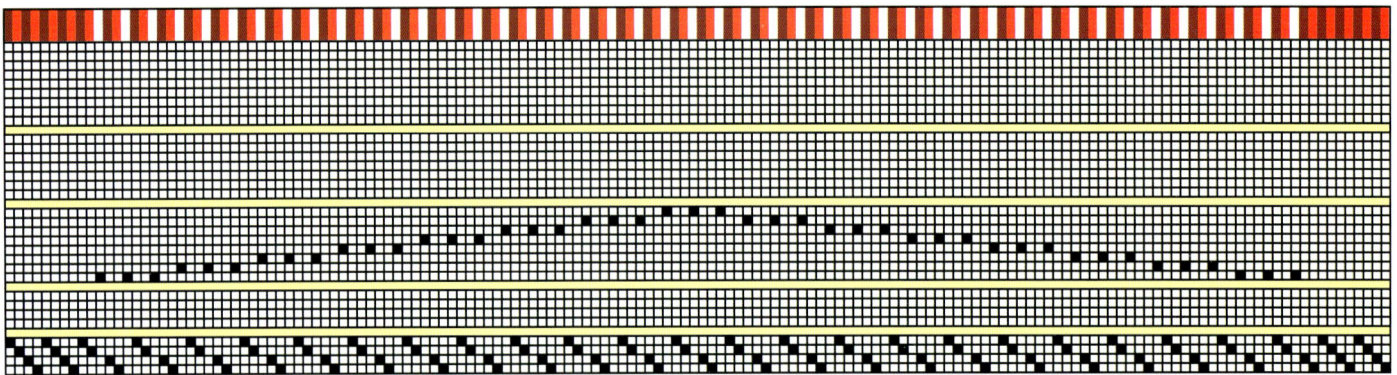

*Threading. Section of threading showing how the full piece of eight motif on supplementary warp threads fits into the base. The other two quarter motifs work similarly. The two base layers in this block are shown in red and orange for clarity but are actually both red. The threading is expanded to separate the parts.*

*Component Threading Draft. The double weave base consists of two 4-shaft blocks on eight shafts. Each block weaves two plain weave layers, one threaded on even shafts and the other on odd shafts. The layers exchange in the warp about every 2". The color has been changed from all red to help visualization. Only the top layer is shown and the draft is expanded to separate the blocks.*

2B  2A

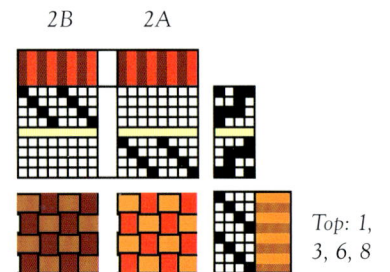

*Top: 1, 3, 6, 8*

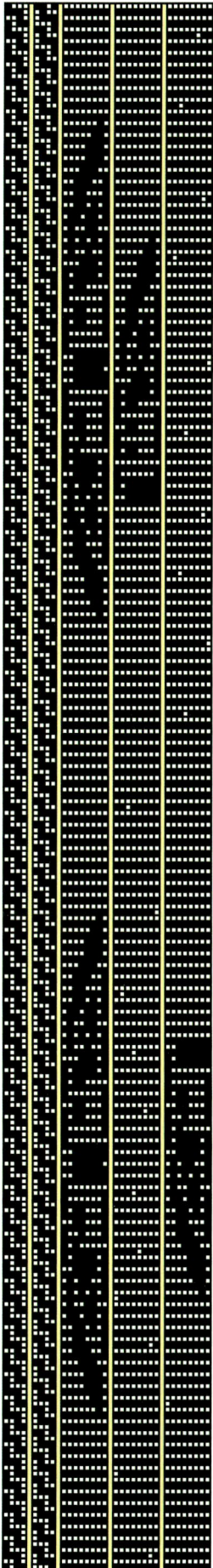

## Tips

• Double weave is an effective way to encase long floats on the back of a cloth. It protects them from snagging and increases durability for many uses.

• Finer threads may be needed in double weave pieces to maintain the desired weight and drape of the final piece.

• Tieing two layers of double weave together at relatively small intervals will help prevent differential lengthening and shifting of the layers. Exchanging in the weft (not done here) also works to help lock in any supplementary warp threads. Use the same color in both layers to minimize the visual effect, or contrasting colors to make a different, bolder design statement. In one color, the subtlety of the change becomes a feature visible only at a more intimate distance.

• Adding an occasional single-thread tacking tie to the back layer for the supplementary threads helps to stabilize the long back floats of the top layer. It will not be extremely obvious, particularly amongst soft, fuzzy main yarns.

• Designs do not need to be centered and/ or mirrored to be effective and pleasing. Consider the way a piece will be used, including how it drapes on the body or the angles from which it may be viewed to find non-symmetric arrangements. Because they are less common, asymmetric designs are often more exciting and modern appearing. They often convey a sense of movement not present in a mirrored, centered design.

*Component Profile Drafts. Three 8-block drafts showing the placement of the supplementary pattern threads. The supplementary threads fall on shafts 9 to 16 in the full coin, 17 to 24 on the upper right two-bit quadrant, and 25 to 32 on the lower left two-bit quadrant.*

*Threading Draft Liftplan. Enlarged for better visibility, the liftplan has been expanded to separate the components.*

# II.4  Interleaved and/or Networked

## Interleaving

Interleaving simply means alternating between the threading, treadling, and/or tie-up of two or more drafts. It is a design technique rather than a structure per se. Many names, each with its own set of conditions, have been applied to drafts which use interleaving. These include parallel, echo, manifold, interlocking, shadow, moiré, offset, 4-color double weave, etc. Note that many more drafts could be also considered interleaved, including layered cloth, some tied weaves, beiderwand, and lampas. The process of interleaving has many variables, including:

- Number of drafts (or copies of one draft) interleaved
- Part(s) interleaved (threading, treadling, and/or tie-up)
- Structure(s) interleaved (combined as desired as long as the float lengths are acceptable)
- Positioning (on same shafts/treadles or on their own set)
- Pattern correspondence (parallel, echo, offset, unalike)
- Interval (the distance between similar lines)
- Ratio of interleaving threads (usually 1:1, others possible)
- Coloring (single color to blend the lines, or lines separated into their own colors)
- Tie-up(s) (can be used to shift color placement)
- Balance of warp and weft (balanced weave, warp emphasis, weft emphasis, warp-faced, or weft-faced)

*Above, Threadings from two different 8-shaft drafts interleaved at a 1:1 ratio. Both drafts share a 16-shaft regular 4/1/3/4/1/3 twill tie-up and point treadling.*

*Below, The two interleaved 8-shaft threadings have been separated out to show the different patterns. The threading and tie-up have been expanded to separate the two sets of eight shafts. Although both threadings use the same 16-shaft tie-up and treadling, they sample different parts of the tie-up on any given treadle. That is, the tie-up for the first eight shafts is the same as the tie-up for the second eight, but shifted by eight treadles.*

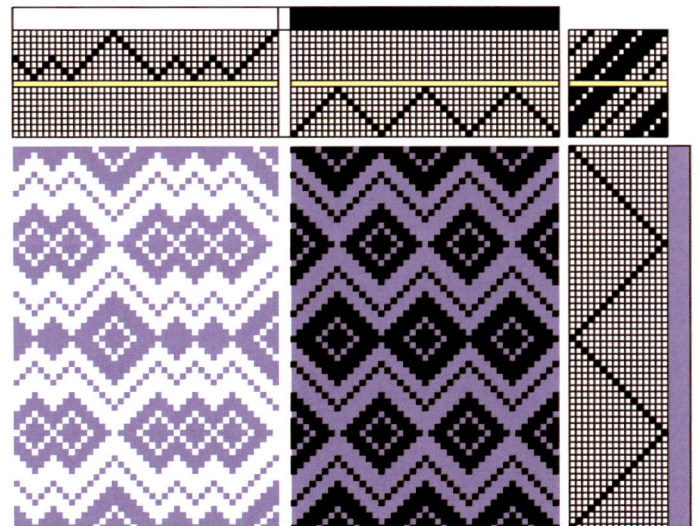

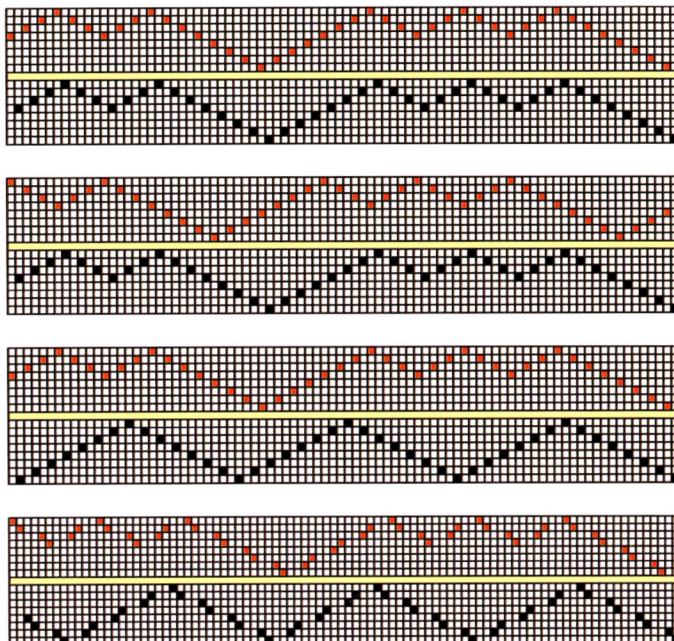

*Above, four interleaved threadings, with each interleaved pair on their own set of eight shafts (shown separated with a yellow line).*
  *Top, Echoed, 1:1 ratio.*
  *Second, Starting point offset by four ends, 1:1 ratio.*
  *Third, Two different patterns, 1:1 ratio.*
  *Last, Two different patterns, 2:2 ratio.*

186

# Networking

A networked threading or treadling is built on an underlying pattern, generally with fewer shafts or treadles than the final draft. Building blocks called initials are stacked and repeated to form a network grid which represents all the possible threading (or treadling) positions within the underlying pattern. To network a draft, lay the threading or treadling to be networked on the network grid, and move the points which do not fall on the network onto the network in a regular fashion. The resulting draft can be used as a threading draft or profile draft.

Network drafting can be used to limit the float length, interpret long, smooth curves, and to add a different design look (often more geometric). However, it can also lose detail and blur boundaries.

The initial is often referred to by the shape and the number of shafts needed for it. A "straight initial of 8" has a basis in 8-shaft straight draw. The initial is often based on straight draw, points, or satin threadings, but any threading or treadling can be used. Smaller, simpler initials tend to preserve more of the detail of the original pattern.

The cleanest, clearest networked drafts will occur when the tie-up is matched to the initial (bottom right).

*Right, Straight initial of 8 and the 24-shaft network built by stacking and repeating the initials.*

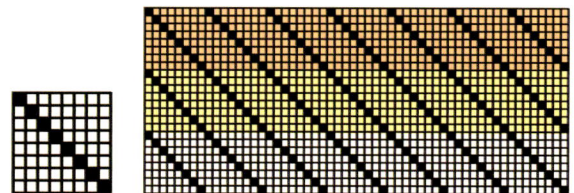

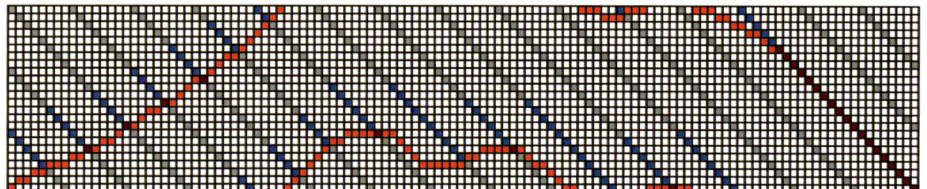

*Above, A curve in red superimposed on the network, shown in gray. Points on the curve which fall on the network are marked in dark red. These points do not move. Points which fall off the network are moved up to the nearest point on the network, shown in blue. The blue and dark red points become the new, networked threading.*

*Above, Original curved draft, with regular twill tie-up of 5/1/1/1/3/1/1/3/1/1/1/5. It has long floats with any tie-up and is generally more suited to be a profile draft.*

*Right, The same draft networked on a straight initial of 8 in warp and weft, with the same tie-up. The details of the curves are simpler, and the pattern characteristically more fractured and "fuzzy" than the original. This tie-up can be broken into three regular 8-shaft twill sections which work along the diagonal: 5/1/1/1, 3/1/1/3, and 1/1/1/5. With the match of these choices of tie-up to the straight initial of 8, there are no floats longer than five threads.*

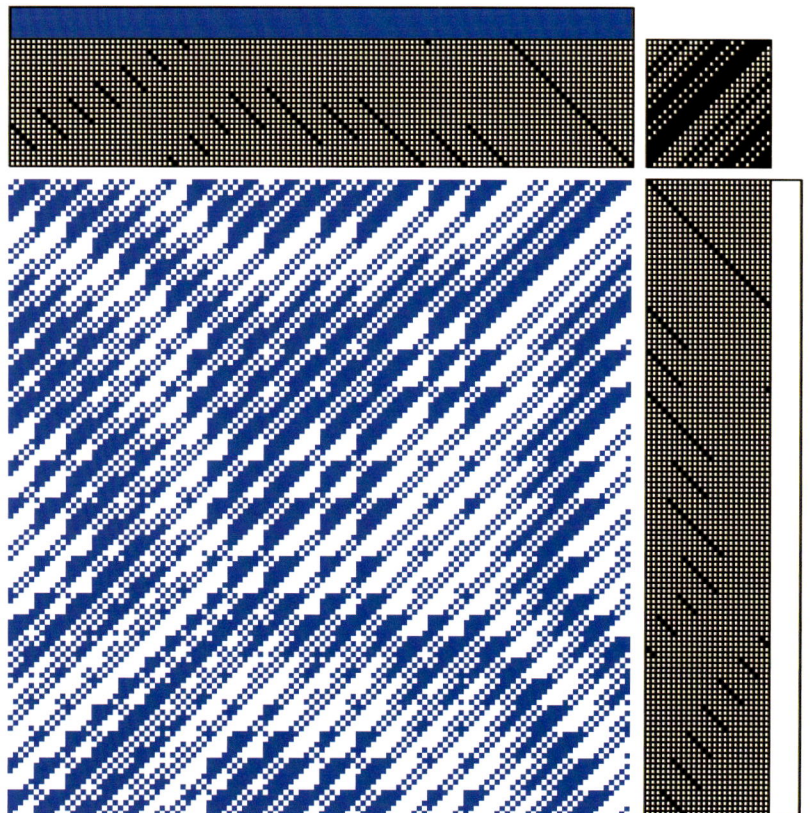

187

# Good Friends

## Marguerite Gingras

### Greeting Card in Double Weave (Turned Swivel)

## Design Process

When I selected turned swivel (Gingras, 2003) for an overshot sample exchange, I was planning a turned taqueté warp for another group, and looking for a way to combine both projects. I chose four warp colors to use for flowers and Christmas motifs, to weave greeting cards on the same warp. On 32 shafts, I threaded each color in parallel (echoed) on eight separate shafts. The four colors make a complementary plain weave structure with the weft. The long floats on the back were woven with a different weft to give a second complementary, attached layer.

Angels are among my favorite motifs for Christmas cards, and I have woven them in many structures before. This time, I had four colors to play with in the Fiberworks sketchpad. They allowed me to color the wings, sleeves, hair, and to decorate the dress in solid colors. By combining red and yellow, I had a fifth color option to use for the face and hands. These new angels have horizontal arms, with wings extending behind them.

I worked on a few versions to improve the proportions and face, and tried different haircuts. I was limited to eight squares (half the symmetrical figure), but I like designing a recognizable image with a small number of pixels, refining it progressively by adding or removing a point at a time, and giving it a personality.

Each color was isolated and put in the profile liftplan on eight shafts corresponding to its threading (see drafts on page 191). The face and hands appear twice because they are formed by a combination of two colors. I also added horizontal borders using each color in turn. The colored squares in the profile liftplan became plain weave for the top layer tie-up, and this tie-up pasted over the opposite plain weave gave the bottom layer tie-up (see page 190). The threading and treadling can be lengthened or shortened, but must keep alternating odd and even shafts and treadles, a further constraint upon the design.

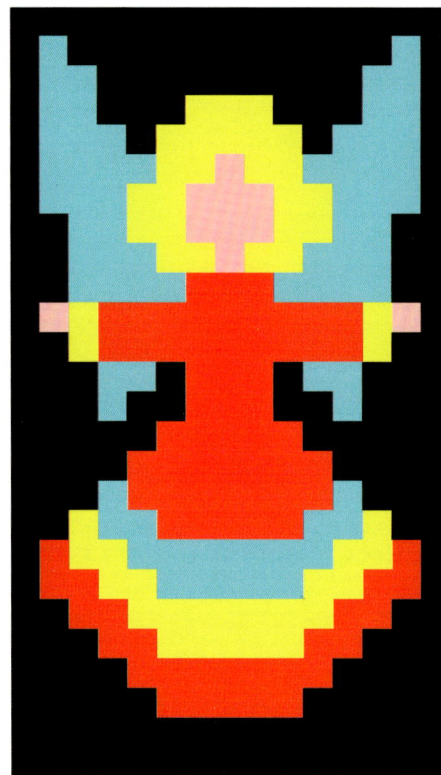

*Cartoon. Top surface placement of the four simple colors (black, yellow, red, and aqua) plus peach (blended red and yellow) for face and hands is indicated.*

## Weaving Information

Size: 5.83" x 4.13"

Warp: 10/2 mercerized cotton, 4200 ypp, black, yellow, red, and aqua; 80 epi

Weft: 10/2 mercerized cotton, 4200 ypp, black; 20/2 mercerized cotton, 8400 ypp, violet blue; 38 ppi

Source: Original draft

Weave Structure: Double weave (turned swivel), 32 shafts

Finishing: Machine stitched on four sides. Soaked successively in lukewarm water with soap, then with vinegar, and finally just clear water to remove possible dye excess. Machine washed in warm water with mild detergent for about 15 minutes. Rinsed in cool water twice, first with vinegar, then spun on shortened cycle. Rolled in a towel to remove excess water and dye. Steam pressed with and without press cloth and laid flat to dry after pressing. Softened in dryer on air fluff for ten minutes.

Take-up and Shrinkage: Warp 11%, weft 8%

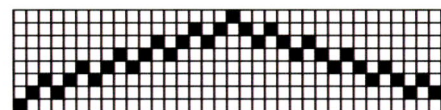

*Draft Component. Design line for threading. This 8-shaft line is interleaved with three copies of itself, each on its own set of shafts and in its own coloring, to form the threading.*

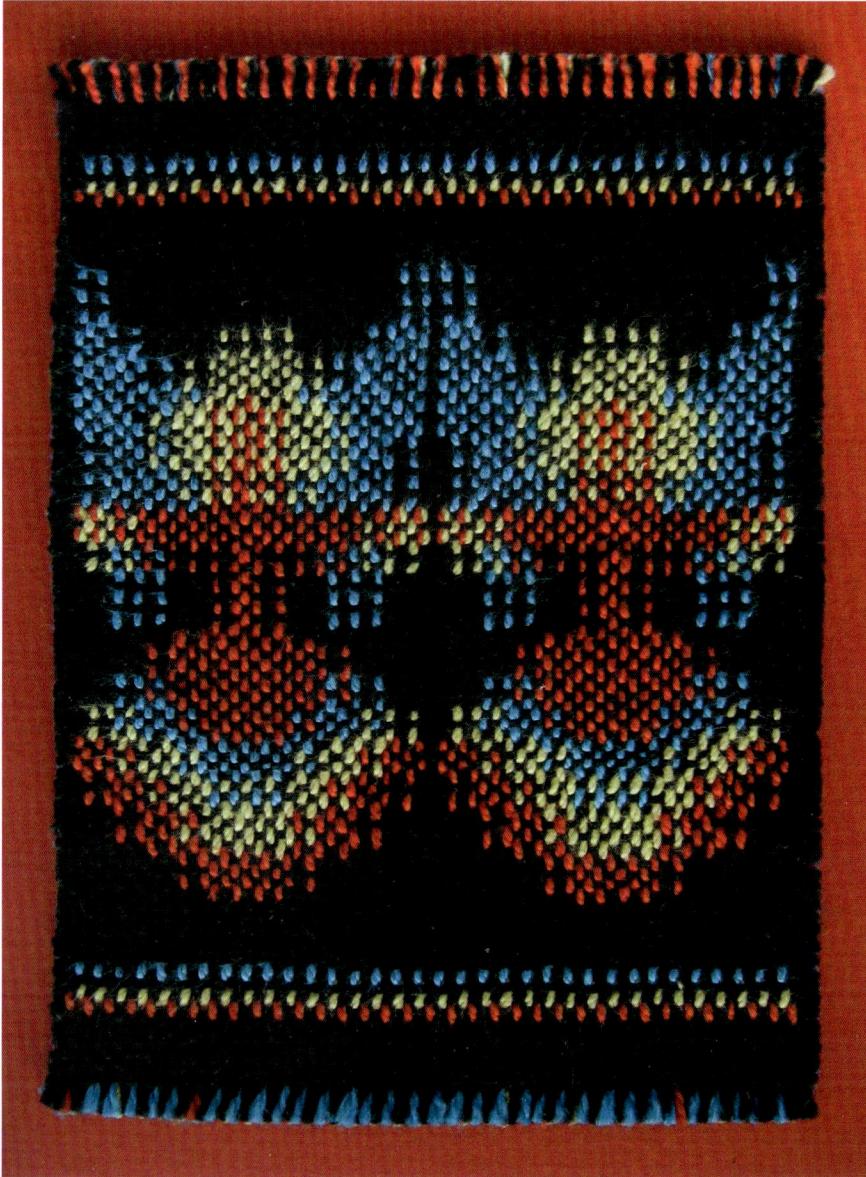

*Card, top layer of fabric.*

*Back layer of fabric, showing more of the possible complex color mixtures.*

## Tips

• When winding the warp, be careful not to tie a Z-twist thread to an S-twist thread. Here, the yellow and black ends are Z-twist and the red and aqua are S-twist. The difference adds a subtle bit of liveliness to the fabric.

• To avoid unwanted color dots of neighboring threads when weaving at this sett, separate some warp colors in the reed, and, if needed, lift one at a time before it is used on the top. A stick put in the shed near the woven fabric also helps.

• When changing the colored squares of the profile liftplan to plain weave, the choice of odd or even shafts to start the pattern can affect the details of the design significantly.

• With this type of threading or treadling, four color lines can be combined up to three at a time, making fourteen possible color combinations. Each color may be used by itself, or with one or two other colors (more groupings are used in the fabric back, above).

• The same design could be woven on eight shafts with four weft colors by turning the structure. With an additional eight shafts, a second complementary layer could be woven as in the card. Or, if desired, a simpler second warp on just two additional shafts could be added to weave the long floats as a different integrated layer in the back, or with its own weft for a completely separate plain weave layer, covering the long floats.

• Although abstract designs, often with flowing curves, are more common, exploring imagery with parallel or echoed threadings can be a fruitful venture. Taqueté, samitum, swivel, polychrome, etc., and their turned variants work well with imagery in parallel wefts or warps respectively. Swivel provides a delicate, pointillist look which requires some finesse to use most effectively.

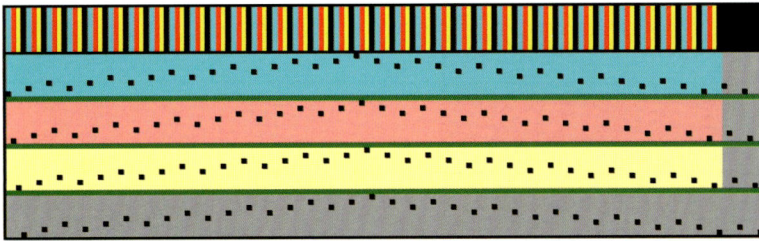

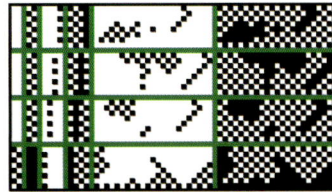

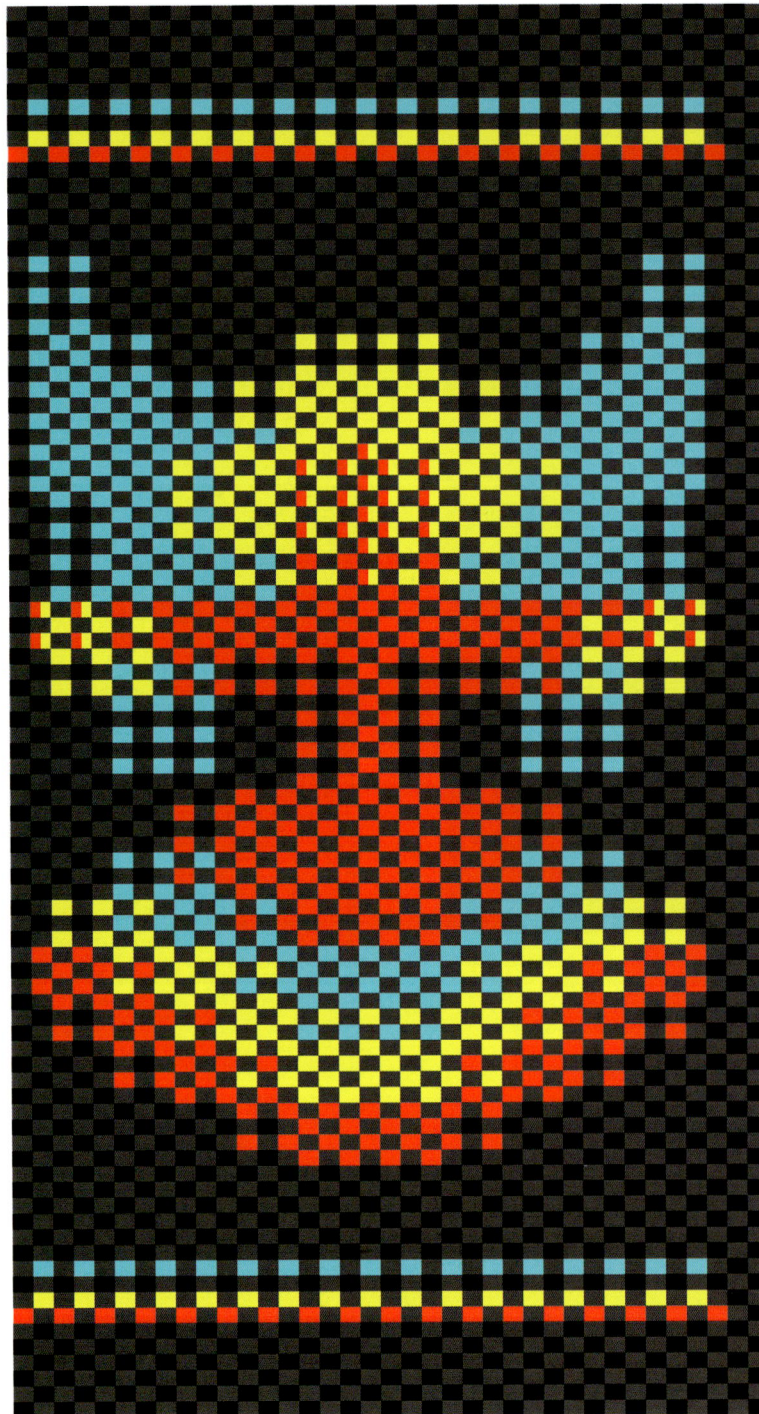

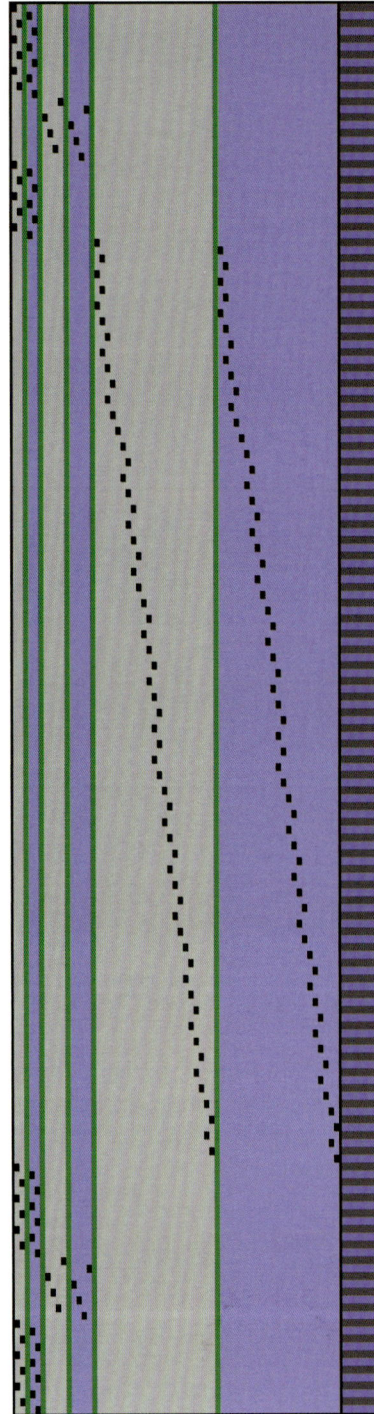

Threading Draft. Only the top layer is shown in this two-layer turned swivel drawdown. In order to better see the structure, the black weft of the top layer is shown as dark gray in the drawdown.

In the threading, shafts controlling black threads are shaded gray; yellow threads, yellow; red threads, pink; and aqua threads, aqua. The treadles shaded in gray control the top layer. The treadles shaded in purple control the bottom layer and are woven with a violet blue weft.

Four warp ends (one each of black, yellow, red, and aqua in the threading pattern area) work together to complete one column (normally formed by a single end) of the plain weave or plain weave variant in both the top and bottom layers.

The draft has been expanded to separate the four 8-shaft lines (each with its own color), and the different parallel parts of the tie-up and treadling. Several treadles are duplicated to make the treadle patterning clearer.

Profile Liftplan. Each group of eight shafts is colored to indicate which threads they control. The pattern areas, which become plain weave for the top layer, are shown in the main color, with the back layer threads in white or gray.

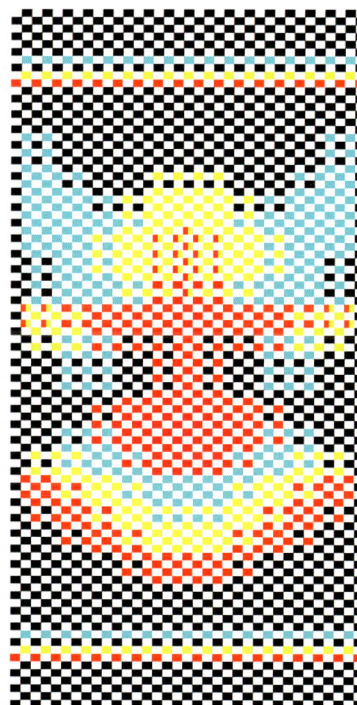

Above, Compound Component Draft. Only the warp pattern of the top layer is shown. The white squares in the drawdown will be filled by the black weft. The plain weave effect is a result of using a turned swivel scheme of pattern creation. In this type of compound plain weave, more than one color is used to complete one column of the drawdown.

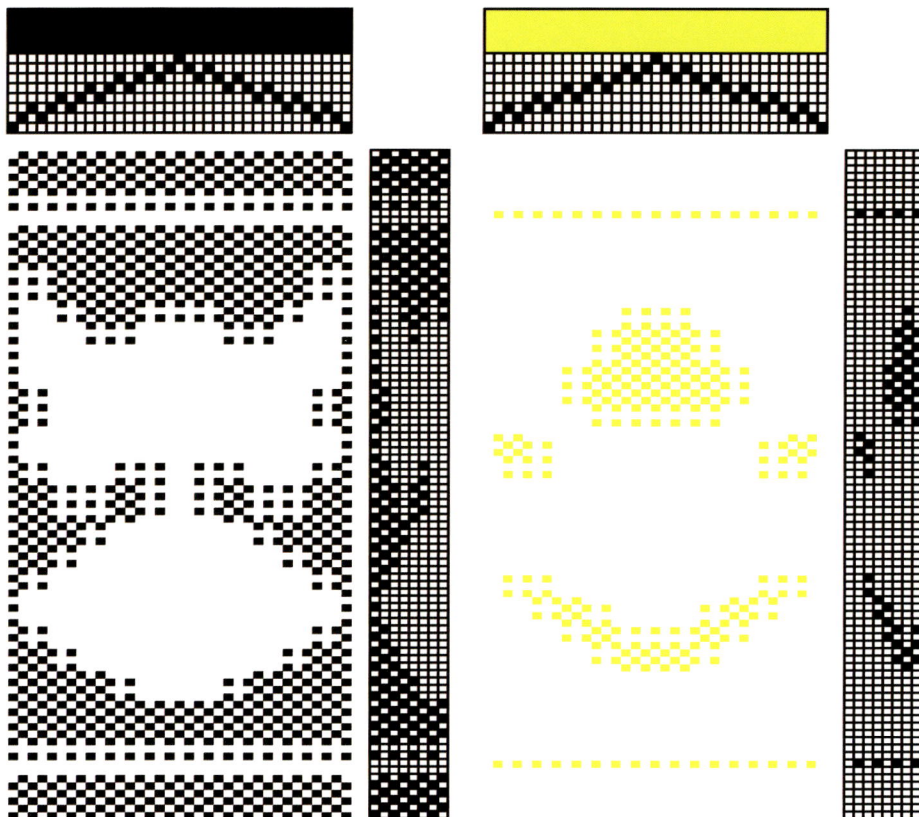

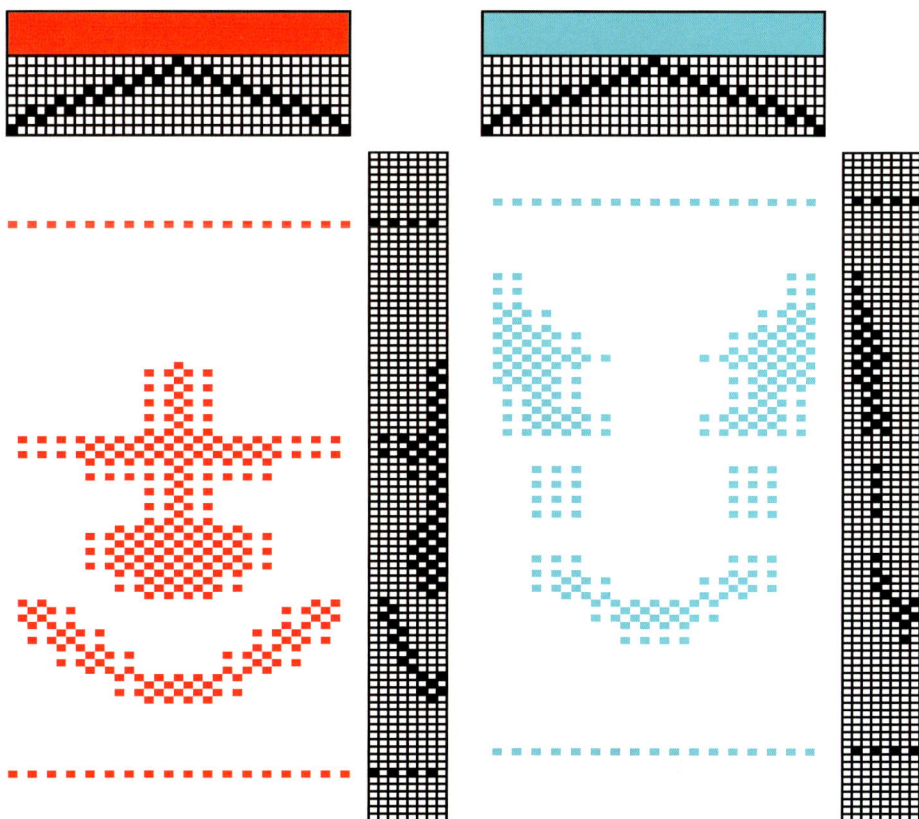

Above, Component Drafts. Each warp color in the drawdown on the preceding page has been separated out onto eight shafts. In the full draft, the black ends are controlled on shafts 1 to 8, yellow on shafts 9 to 16, red on shafts 17 to 24, and aqua on shafts 25 to 32. Only the warp threads creating pattern on the top layer are shown in this view. In the face and hands, yellow and red overlap to form a blend. To create the full image, all four drafts are stacked together (right).

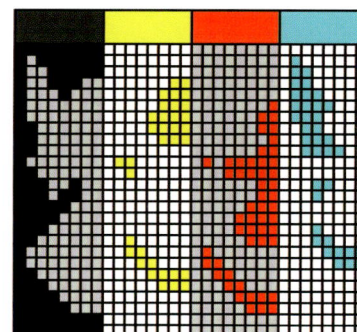

# Sky Fills the Heart

## Beryl Moody

### Scarf Set in Networked Twill

## Design Process

I like network twills a lot, but had never used an 8-end initial (straight initial of 8) in my design work as I find the lines to be a bit jagged for my taste. However, for this particular project I decided to utilize that appearance to mimic a shibori-dyed textile in both warp and weft.

I use WeavePoint software in almost all my design work. I usually work with the threading and the treadling first, then work out a tie-up that looks good with the first two components. I started by drawing a curve on 24 shafts because I needed a multiple of eight shafts for my network to work properly. Instead of mirroring the starting curve, I converted my threading to the networked 8-end initial and then mirrored it so that I would have a sharp V in the design. For the treadling, I experimented with a variety of curves before I networked the treadling line, also with a straight initial of 8. Having completed one liftplan, I worked on several others, then choose my favorites to weave. When there are rough parts in the liftplan that don't seem to flow, or threads that look out of place, I can spend much time refining it - thread by thread. A basket weave selvedge on four additional shafts was added to the draft.

## Weaving Information

Sizes: Scarf #1: 84" x 8.25" plus 6" fringe on each end; Scarf #2: 70" x 7.75" plus 6.5" fringe on each end; Scarf #3: 71.5" x 8" plus 3.5" fringe on each end

Warp: Cabled bamboo, 6400 ypp, hand dyed with fiber reactive dye in a low water immersion bath, various blues; 40 epi

Weft: Scarf #1: 14/2 mercerized cotton, 5880 ypp, off white; 25 ppi; Scarf #2: 20/2 Tencel, 8400 ypp, white; 26 ppi; Scarf #3: 80/2/5 mercerized cotton, 6720 ypp, off white; 30 ppi

Source: Original draft

Weave Structures: Networked twill and basket weave, 28 shafts

Finishing: Scarf #1: Hemstitched. Twisted two-ply fringe, with off-white crystal beads on some fringe strands before twisting. Scarf #2: Hemstitched. Twisted fringe, no beads. Scarf #3: Hemstitched. Twisted fringe with blue seed beads added to some fringe strands before twisting. Hand washed in mild detergent. Rolled in towels to remove excess moisture, then air dried on rack. Pressed while still damp with very warm iron.

Take-up and Shrinkage: Warp 10%, weft 8%

*Detail, Scarf #3, back side.*

*Scarves #1, 3, and 2.*

## Tips

• A hand-dyed warp adds additional depth.

• For the basket weave selvedge to work in these drafts, start your shuttle on the right side in the first pick.

• Although common, the starting curve for networking does not have to cover more shafts than are planned for the final project.

• Picking an initial which divides evenly into the number of shafts desired will give the cleanest results (Schlein, 1994).

• Changing the tie-up and treadling can create very different designs on the same warp. Keeping some of the parameters constant provides unity to the group. Here, the similar color choices, constant straight initial of 8 in the weft, float lengths, and the scale of the three designs are similar. Variety comes from how the floats and background are used. In the first scarf, there is a plain weave background with warp and weft floats forming patterns in opposite directions, creating a braided look where they intersect. In the second scarf, weft floats alone form pattern on a plain weave background. The third scarf uses a complex interplay of warp and weft floats without a plain weave background.

*Details, Scarf #1 (above) and Scarf #2 (right).*

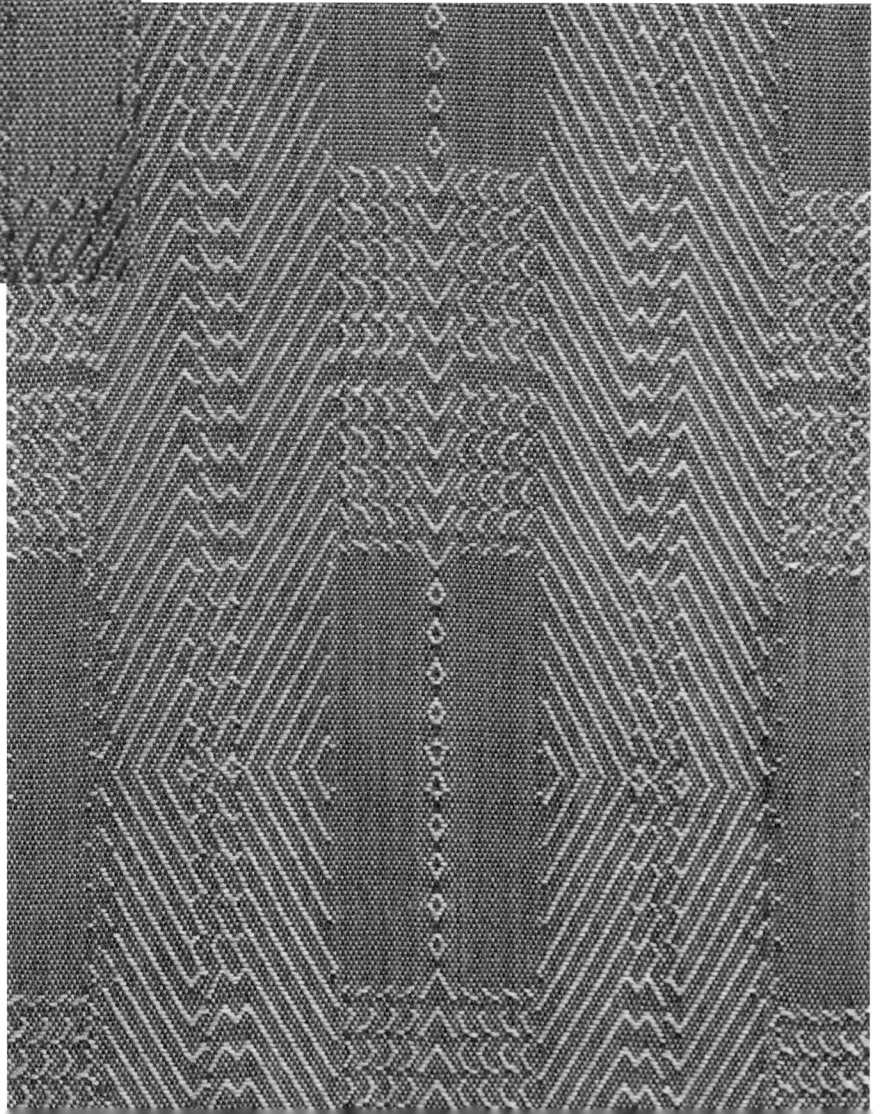

194

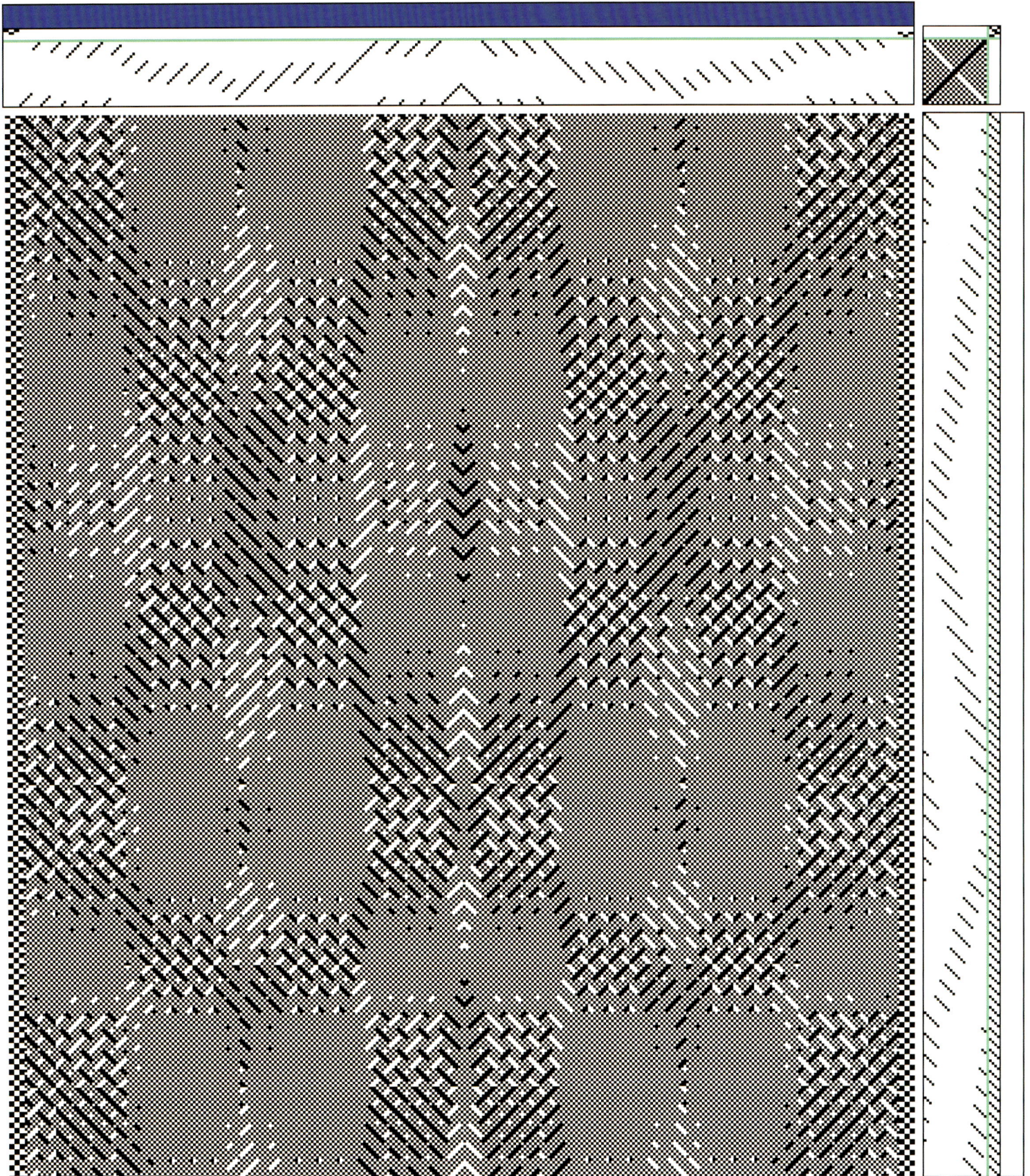

*Threading Draft for Scarf #1. Full width of draft shown with partial treadling. Basket weave selvedges are on shafts 25 to 28. Networked on a straight initial of 8 in warp and weft. Using a plain weave background, the warp floats work in star-fashion, while the weft floats work in rose-fashion. Expanded to separate selvedges from body, with a skeleton treadling.*

*Threading Draft. Portion of threading draft for scarf #2 (full threading with selvedges shown in the draft for scarf #1). Weft floats form complex twill patterns on a plain weave background. The treadling is networked on a straight initial of 8. Unlike the treadling for the first scarf, it has true mirrors at reversal points, similar to the warp.*

*Threading Draft. Portion of threading draft for scarf #3 (full threading with selvedges shown in the draft for scarf #1). This treadling started as a networked twill on an initial of 8, with true mirrors in the treadling. It was then adjusted extensively by working in the drawdown. Unlike scarves #1 and 2, there is no plain weave background. Areas of greater concentrations of weft floats contrast with areas of greater concentrations of warp floats. Within areas, smaller changes from warp to weft floats and mirroring in warp and weft provide focus.*

# Spot Check
## Sara Nordling

### Scarf in 4-Color Double Weave (Networked Twill)

### Design Process

The design process for "Spot Check" started with a curiosity about networked 4-color double weave, a structure new to me. I knew, with the resources at my disposal and my weaving software, I could figure it out. It was a trial and error process. My first designs were more networked 4-color twills, nice, but not what I wanted. While reading various notes on the topic in the Complex Weaver's Double Weave Study Group, I encountered a comment by Bonnie Inouye stating that the network needs to be on a 4-end initial. That stipulation made all the difference for the number of shafts and type of shift I was contemplating. The design process was also greatly aided when I discovered how to use my Weavemaker software to interleave and shift a draft, creating an echo. This is a technique that the manual says is possible but for which there are no directions. The helpful people at AVL were able to explain the process to me.

Once I had designed an 8-shaft networked line on an initial of 4, I expanded to 16 shafts and echoed it. After playing with various mutations, I shifted the first motif up eight shafts, causing a shift in the colors. I then made a 16-treadle networked pattern on an initial of 4. Shifting this pattern by sixteen treadles (for a total of thirty-two treadles), and using a different tie-up completed the pattern. The first set of sixteen treadles fall on a regular twill tie-up of 1/1/1/1/1/1/1/1/4/4 and the second set on an inverse tie-up of 1/4/4/1/1/1/1/1/1/1. The warp and weft were immersion dyed using fiber reactive dyes. Two colors alternate in the warp, and two in the weft. The pattern was repeated two and a half times in the warp.

I see many more possibilities with this design, exploring the mutation and shifting of more motifs as well as different color combinations. Part of the fun of weaving this project was having extra warp at the end to try different color combinations from my yarn stash.

### Tips

• The motifs can be color-shifted by changing the order of the warp and/or weft colors. Here, the switch in the threading is accomplished by having two threads in a row from the same range (for example, shafts 1 to 8 or treadles 1 to 16), rather than perfect alternation from two separate ranges (e.g., shafts 1 to 8 and 9 to 16).

• Unlike a simple networked twill, interleaving a networked twill and its echo on separate shafts and treadles allows you to use tie-ups which would create long floats if used alone, but not when used in combination. That is, the tie-up does not need to match the initial (Schlein, 1994). Without interleaving, these drafts would have floats up to eleven threads long. Interleaved, there are no floats longer than four threads.

• The particular combination of tie-ups used switches the placement of long floats and plain weave in the two components, tieing down any long floats. Additionally, the placement of the warp and weft floats is reversed so that all four colors can be seen.

• Small changes in patterning and/or repeat length can lead to a more complex and interesting cloth.

## Weaving Information

Size: 70" x 8" plus 1" fringe on each end

Warp: 20/2 mercerized cotton, 8400 ypp, white, hand dyed using fiber reactive dyes; 48 epi

Weft: 20/2 mercerized cotton, 8400 ypp, white, hand dyed using fiber reactive dyes; 48 ppi

Source: Original draft

Weave Structure: 4-color double weave (networked twill), 16 shafts

Finishing: Hemstitched on the loom. Machine washed with mild detergent and line dried. Pressed with iron on cotton setting.

Take-up and Shrinkage: Warp 9%, weft 10%

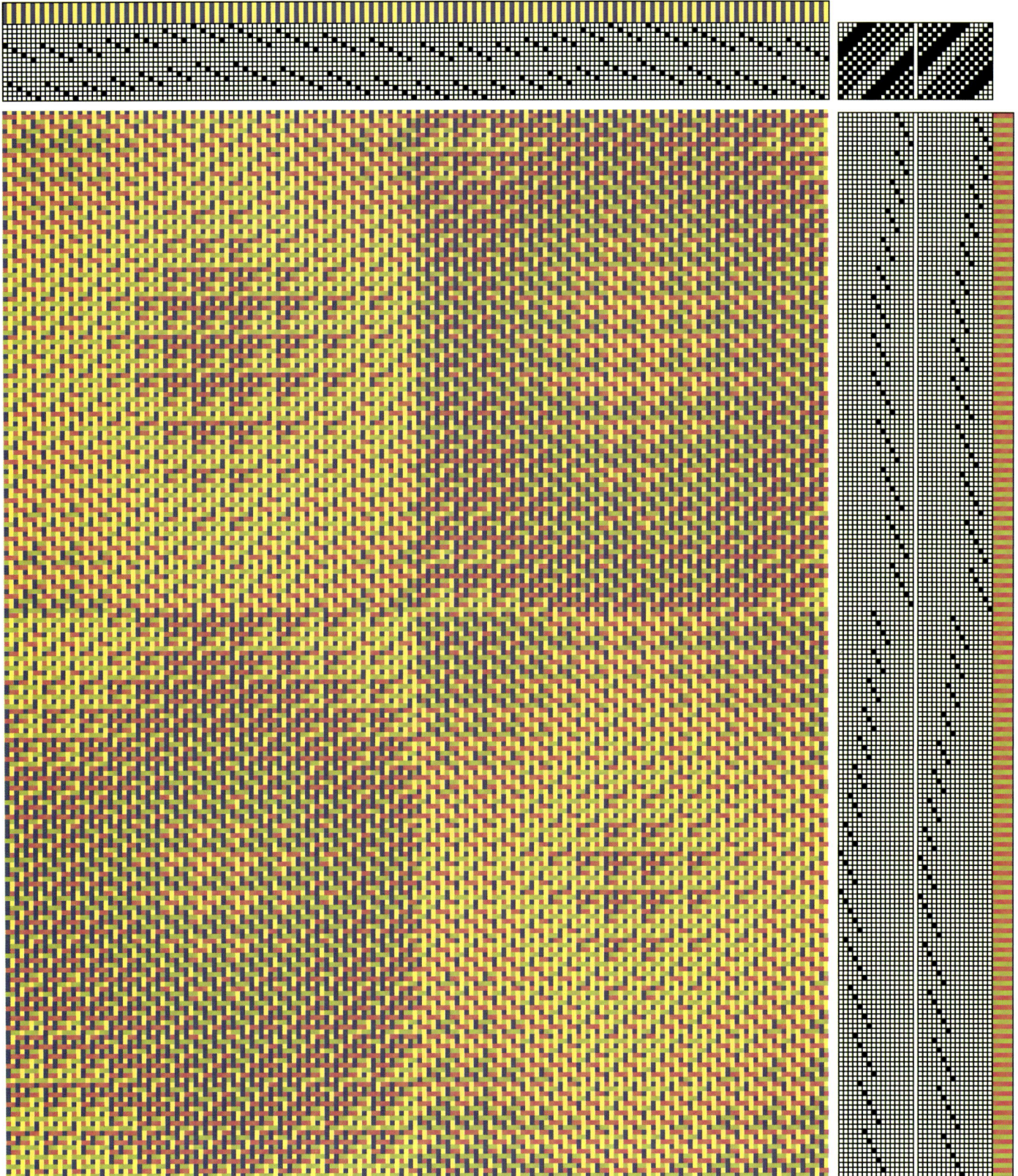

Threading draft. An 8-shaft twill networked on an initial of 4 is interleaved with a copy of itself on a second set of eight shafts for a total of 16. The treadling is also networked on an initial of 4 but over 16 treadles, with an interleaved copy on another 16 treadles with a different tie-up. The first set of treadles use a 1/1/1/1/1/1/1/1/4/4 regular twill tie-up, and the second set, a 1/4/4/1/1/1/1/1/1/1 regular twill tie-up. The colors shift position on the warp repeat where two ends from the same set of shafts repeat, rather than strictly alternating. This changes where the colors fall on each section.

Component Draft. The threading draft has been pulled apart to show the components in color. Two repeats of the profile are shown, including the color swap which occurs from changing order on the second one. Each of the four motifs on the previous page is composed of four interleaved components. The interval of interleaving is 8, that is, identical copies of the 8-shaft threading are on their own shafts (1 to 8 and 9 to 16).

In contrast, within a tie-up, though echoed exactly, the two treadlings are not exactly alike, and overlap occurs in the treadles. Unlike the threading, the treadling does not switch sequence at the color change. The components are networked on an initial of 4 in threading and treadling. Though the tie-up is not optimized for a twill network of 4, it is perfect for 4-color double weave.

Component Drafts.
A closer look at the
eight different 8-shaft
structures which
are interleaved in
the final threading
draft. Both threading
and treadling are
networked on an
initial of 4. The
threads on shafts 1
to 8 (left) sample a
different portion of the
two 16-shaft tie-ups
from the threads on
shafts 9 to 16 (right).

Compared to the
second and fourth
treadlings, the first
and third treadlings
are shorter (62 vs.
69 picks) and cover
fewer treadles (9 vs. 11
treadles).

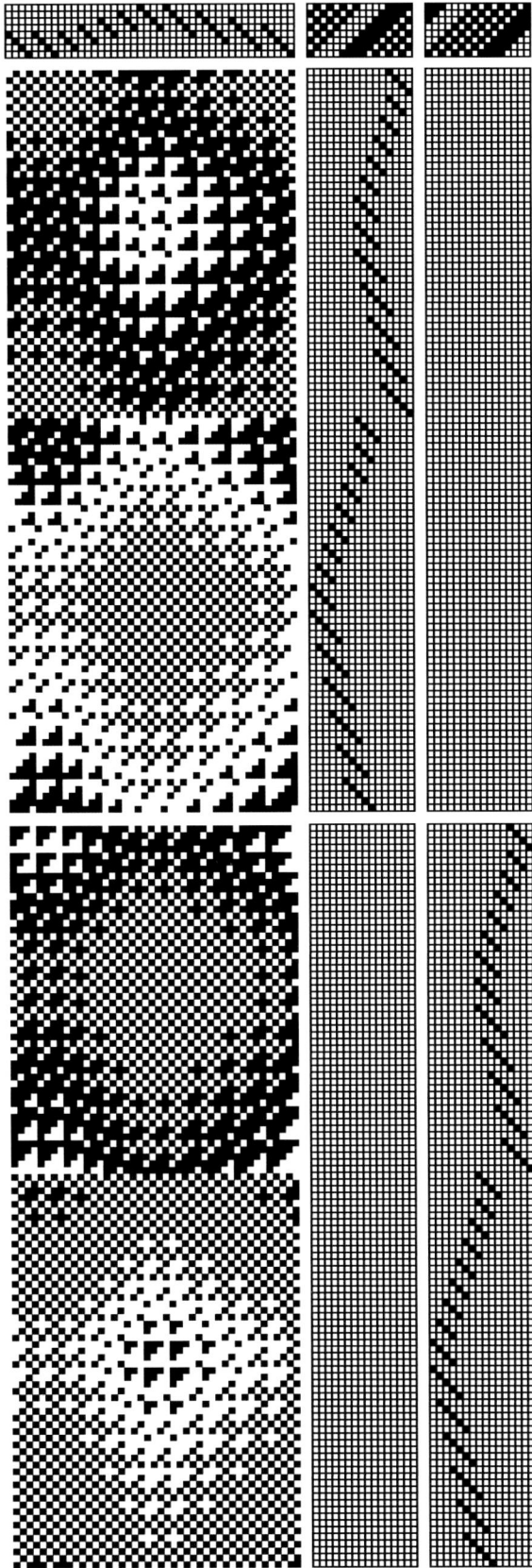

Component Draft. Shafts 1 to 8.                    Component Draft. Shafts 9 to 16.

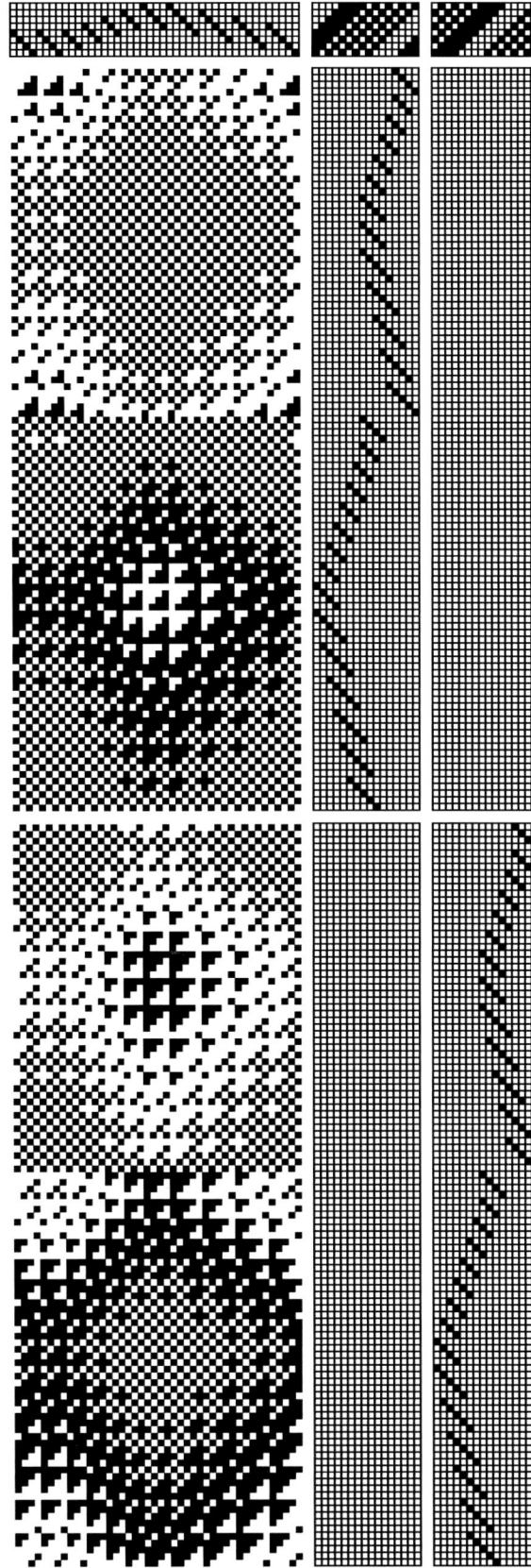

202

# II.5  8-Tie Weaves

Supplementary weft 8-tie unit weaves work exactly the same way as summer and winter, with its two ties, works. In the warp, tie-downs alternate with pattern threads; in the weft, tabby alternates with pattern threads, which form weft floats. More tie-down shafts allow greater complexity in the portion of the design created by the tie-downs, adding nuance to the cloth.

Any 8-shaft weave which gives an acceptable float length may be used for the tie-downs. Of course, the technique may also be used with any number of shafts desired for the tie-downs.

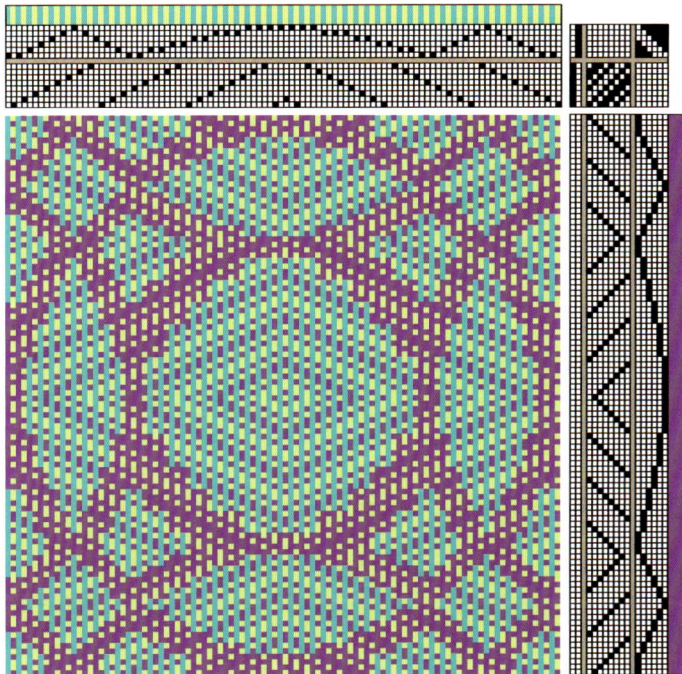

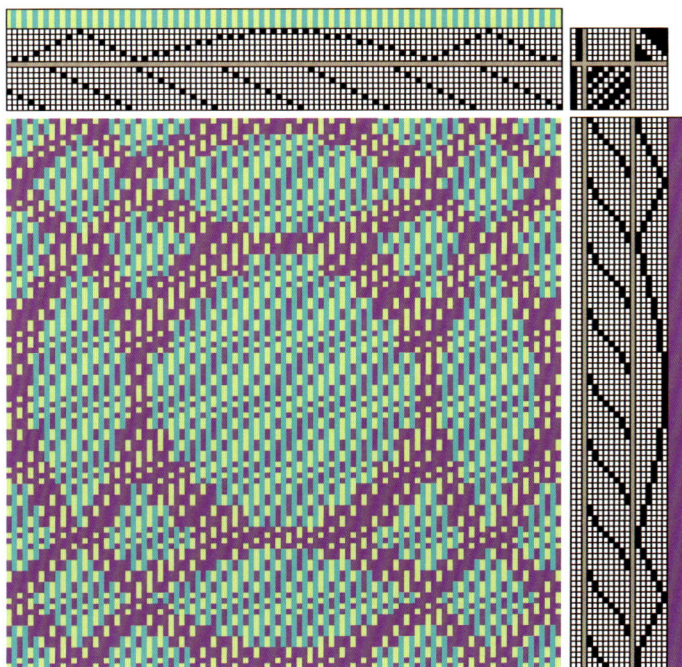

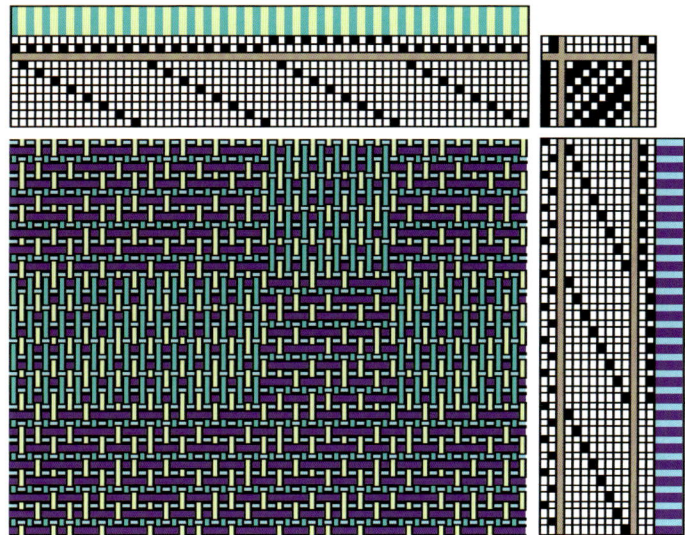

*Above, A standard 2-block, 10-shaft version of a single 8-tie unit weave, with a regular 1/2/1/1/2/1 twill tie-up for the tie-downs, and one pattern shaft per block. This skeleton draft has been expanded to separate the tie-downs and tabby from the pattern shafts. As always, the number of weft threads required to square the block will vary with the materials used.*

*Far left, Two "unblocked" 8-tie weaves with six pattern shafts. Tabby is needed (not shown) in these expanded skeleton drafts.*

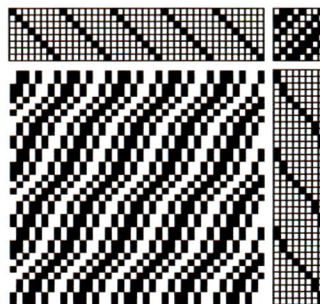

*Tie drafts (near left and above it) and the pattern draft (above) for the two drafts to the far left are shown separately.*

"Unblocking" the pattern shafts in the warp is an old but less common trick for reducing patterns and making them more graceful (less pixelated). In this sense, unblocking means that the pattern shafts may not change where the tie-down design repeats. The technique also allows the opportunity to have a varied tie-down design in the warp, rather than one with simple repeats.

In the top draft to the left, a diamond tie design changes direction with pattern reversals, contrasting with the pattern curves. In the bottom draft, an undulating tie design complements the pattern curves and adds a ripple-like movement.

# Diamonds in Blocks

## Kay Faulkner

### Scarf in Double 8-Tie Unit Weave and Plaited Twill

### Design Process

I like the texture of a more complex tie-down pattern in a tied weave design. In background areas, it gives a much more interesting fabric than just a plain weave arrangement of the tie-downs. Multi-shaft tied unit weaves allow for pattern to occur in two places – the tie pattern and the pattern blocks. Both are critical to the overall design. Additionally, the use of half tones in the motif adds an extra dimension by allowing the positive and negative parts of the pattern to have a transitional element which acts like a shadow.

This project explores the combination of a plaited twill with an 8-tie unit weave incorporating shadowing "half tones." The ends of the scarf are woven in a plaited twill treadling, requiring two unshared shafts for each pattern block. Alone, this twill could be woven on ten shafts. Without the plaited twill ends, the draft for this scarf could have used just twelve shafts, with pattern blocks sharing four shafts. Instead, to create the half tones, the two pattern shafts from the main pattern block are joined in the tie-up by one of the two pattern shafts in each of the adjacent blocks. At any given time, there will be a pattern block (positive), a background block (negative), and two half-tone shadows, which rotate through the weaving length.

An added bonus in the finished scarf was the three-dimensional quality to the surface of the scarf. This effect was caused by the differing float lengths from the half tones and tie-up, and was evident when tension was released after it came off the loom. Surprisingly, it was maintained after laundering.

### Weaving Information

Size: 67" x 8" plus 6" fringe on each end

Warp: 2/20 silk, 5000 ypp, natural; 25 epi

Weft: 2/20 silk, 5000 ypp, natural (tabby); 2/20 silk (doubled), 5000 ypp, peach (pattern); 36 ppi over plaited twill, 60 ppi in pattern area, including tabby

Source: Original draft

Weave Structures: Double 8-tie unit weave and plaited twill, 16 shafts

Finishing: Two-ply twisted fringe with four strands per ply. Machine washed on normal cycle with pH-neutral detergent. One teaspoon vinegar added to final rinse. Line dried until damp, then cool tumble dried. Hand pressed.

Take-up and Shrinkage: Warp 15%, weft 20%

## Tips

• Half-tones or shadows can add extra dimension to a design by creating a smoother bridge between pattern and background areas and/or forming their own patterns.

• Having two separate pattern shafts per block, rather than sharing pattern shafts, allows the half tones to be placed as desired or eliminated completely, much like 4-block 8-shaft overshot. That is, the blocks function completely independently. Several scarves were woven on this warp, so this threading was chosen as allowing the most versatility.

• Rather than using two identical motifs, try varying them. Here, the doubled blocks which occur on the repeat make the offset center pattern diamond motif larger and more blocky than the edge diamonds, an interesting effect.

• It is interesting to contrast a perfect mirror symmetry in the ties with some asymmetry of the pattern shafts, or vice versa. Here, slight asymmetry in the pattern shafts causes a change to a different, but seamlessly compatible, plaited twill as the center line is passed and a slight shading occurs in the main pattern area.

• Using an irregular twill tie-up for the tie pattern causes the diagonal twill lines of the ties to fracture (not continue smoothly) as repeats occur. It's a very effective addition to this piece, increasing the complexity in a way which complements the large pattern design. The technique also changes the float lengths, adding to the dimensionality.

*Above, Draft Component. Large 8-tie point as it might be woven on an 8-shaft loom. It has an irregular shaded twill tie-up which creates the broken grading effect.*

*Draft Component. Expanded pattern tie-up, separated into the 2-shaft blocks. A block with two white squares (no pattern ties lifted) weaves the weft-float pattern. A block with two black squares (both pattern ties lifted) weaves background, and a block with one black and one white weaves half-tones. Analogous to 4-block 8-shaft overshot, each can be placed as desired.*

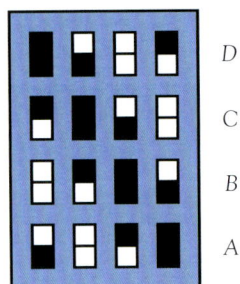

*Draft Component. One full repeat of the pattern draft as it might be given for an 8-shaft loom. The pattern tie-up weaves pattern in one full block and two half-tone blocks, and background in the fourth block. This pattern does not reverse (mirror) fully in the center, causing a shaded effect.*

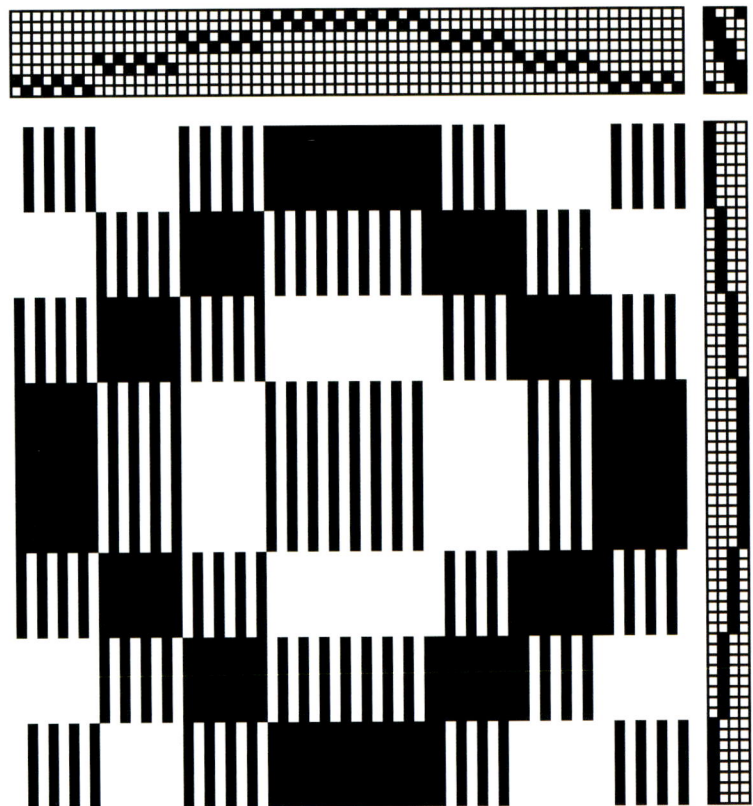

206

*Threading Draft. This 16-shaft 4-block draft is a double 8-tie unit weave. That is, there are two pattern shafts per block (shafts 9 to 16), and the blocks are used full size. The tie-downs reverse as a single point, while the pattern threads do not. This causes an interesting irregularity in the plaited twill end bands as the center is crossed. The draft has been expanded to separate the pattern, tie-downs, and tabby.*

*The skeleton treadling is divided into three parts:*

*Top, Plaited twill for end bands*
*Middle, A single block of the pattern as woven with tabby*
*Bottom, A large portion of the pattern alone (tabby needed but not shown)*

# Boxed In

## Penny Peters

### Scarf Set in Single 8-Tie Weave

### Design Process

A workshop with Kay Faulkner was the starting point of this set of scarves. Use more than four shafts for ties? Had never thought about it! In retrospect, this was a fairly easy draft to accomplish. The overriding pattern of the interlocking boxes was created in Photoshop (Schlein and Ziek, 2006). Then, it was imported into my weaving program where it took 14 pattern shafts. The design has the effect of floating a woven pattern above the background.

I chose three different 8-shaft tie patterns from handweaving. net for the three scarves: a crepe arrangement of broken squares (chosen to somewhat mimic the pattern thread design), a twill with weft floats outlining small rectangles of plain weave, and a plaited twill with more warp emphasis. Then, the ties were added to the pattern of interlocking boxes. The difficult part was learning how to manipulate the weaving draft program, and to meld the overall design with the ties. Interleaving the two drafts solved the issue. Finally, 4-shaft selvedges were added, for a total of 26 shafts.

Three colorways, pink, blue-green, and gold, further changed the appearance of the scarves in this set.

*Draft Components. The three different interlacements of the 8-shaft tie-downs are shown as they might be woven alone on an 8-shaft loom. The pink pattern is a crepe weave; the blue-green, a weft-float twill with plain weave; and the gold, a plaited twill. The draft has been expanded to separate the patterns.*

*Draft Component. Pattern threads shown alone, using 14 shafts in the warp and 11 treadles. The pattern shafts change independently of the repeat of the tie-down threads. That is, the design is not based on full 16-end units (eight of the same pattern thread alternating with eight tie-down threads). The pattern weft consists of paired picks on the same tie-down shed. Alternating two colors on two different pattern sheds forms the two sets of interlocking boxes.*

## Weaving Information

Size: 80" x 10"

Warp: 60/2 silk, 14,000 ypp, black; 60 epi

Weft: 60/2 silk, 14,000 ypp, various colors and black; 80 ppi

Source: Original draft

Weave Structures: Single unblocked 8-tie unit weave, 26 shafts

Finishing: Plain weave woven for 2" at each end and hand hemmed. Washed in warm water and rinsed. Rolled in a towel and dried until damp. Pressed dry.

Take-up and Shrinkage: Warp negligible, weft 10%

## Tips

• Combining profile drafting in Photoshop with structure details in a conventional weaving program can simplify the process of converting a design to a weaving structure for a shaft loom.

• In an 8-tie unit weave, keeping a straight order of ties allows flexibility in the tie-down pattern. Anything which can be woven on 8-shaft straight draw can become the tie-down pattern, as long as the float length suits the final usage.

• Make a pattern appear interlocked or woven by providing strategic small breaks to give the illusion of going over and under itself. Using two colors or textures for the interlocking pattern adds to the effect.

• When weaving a set, create unifying factors. Although the colors and tie patterns are very different, these scarves are united by the same large block pattern, background color, and materials.

• Find a way to lure the viewer in by changing what is visible at different distances. As a group, the scarves provide something different at three viewing distances. From afar, the weft pattern color is the dominant feature. At a moderate distance, the similarity in block pattern becomes obvious. Up close, the finer scale differences in the tie patterns are visible.

• Making the pattern repeat length different from a multiple of the tie-down repeat length adds interest to the design.

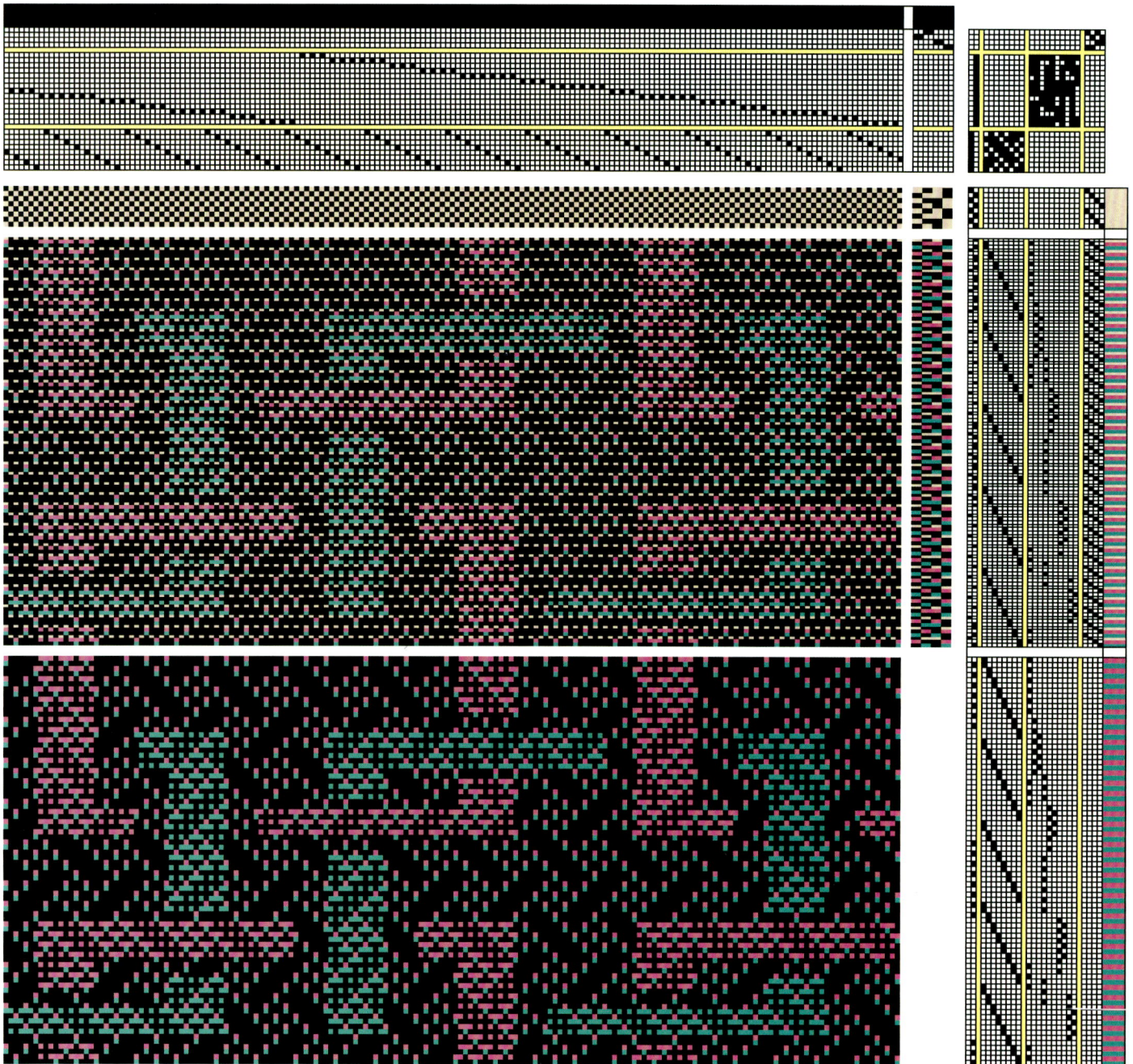

*Threading Draft. In this skeleton draft, the eight tie-down threads are arranged in straight order on shafts 1 to 8, with pattern threads on shafts 9 to 22, and selvedges on shafts 23 to 26. The pattern shafts do not form full 16-thread units with the tie-downs, but change wherever needed. The repeat length of the pattern is not an even multiple of the tie-down pattern. When one of the pattern picks weaves "no pattern" it uses the second tabby as the pattern shed. In the treadling, the tie-downs are used in straight order, twice for each, to accommodate the paired pattern picks. To weave the other variants, substitute the tie-up for their tie-downs into the appropriate section of the tie-up.*

*The draft is expanded to separate the tie-downs, pattern, selvedges, and tabbies. Where shown, the tabby (plain weave) picks are depicted in light tan for visibility, rather than the actual black. The skeleton treadling is divided into three parts.*

*Top, Plain weave plus selvedges*
*Middle, Full treadling with tabby and selvedges*
*Bottom, Paired pattern picks alone without the selvedges or tabbies*

212

# Silence

## Laurie Knapp Autio

### Table Cover in Single 8-Tie Weave, Summer and Winter, Atwater-Bronson Lace, and Plain Weave

## Design Process

Silence may have both positive (listening, growth, peace or centering in a noisy, distracting world) and negative (not speaking when one should, fear, death) connotations. When expressing an idea as a weaving, it is important that the weaving itself add something not available in other media, say, painting or photography (Ziek, 2007). One might choose to augment through color, fiber, texture, grist, and/or structure.

This Jacquard-woven piece starts with a profile derived from a 24-shaft fancy twill with lace tie-up that I designed for teaching. When used as a threading draft, the warp-dominant flowers have an irregular warp-float lace surrounding them and are centered with huck lace. The simple, geometric diamonds are weft dominant, surrounded by a regimented diamond of spot Bronson in weft floats and centered with contrasting spot Bronson in warp floats. As a profile, these become pattern and background areas rather than warp and weft floats.

From one end to the other, the structures, patterns, and colors change in loudness and exuberance. At the top of the piece, the profile was distorted into a large, exuberant pattern which grows from the edges to the center. An 8-tie supplementary weft weave fills the large distorted draft. The flowing ties, representing voices, run rather wildly in a unidirectional undulating twill, contrasting with the more static, symmetrical block pattern. In the center of this section, the ties change to those of summer and winter treadled brick-style, a much more subdued pattern compared to the undulating twill. The changed ties spell out the word "SILENCE" in a very subtle way, albeit with letters about 6" high (see techniques for drafting in Photoshop in Schlein and Ziek, 2006).

Next come three bands with four small repeats of the undistorted profile, separated by frames, emphasizing the flowers rather than the diamonds. The first row uses the undulating 8-tie weave, the next is in summer and winter treadled brick-style, and the third is Atwater-Bronson lace with 4-thread blocks to match the size of the tied weave blocks. For the last section, the word SILENCE is repeated at smaller size in Atwater-Bronson lace on a swath of plain weave. Placing the quietest part at the bottom is deliberately unbalanced and unsettling. Weaving a repeat of the Atwater-Bronson lace design with the rust brown pattern weft before going straight to the monochromatic Atwater-Bronson lace would have been less jarring.

I made this piece thinking of the negative aspects of keeping silent. On completion, I showed it to my friends, the cloistered sisters of the nearby St. Scholastica Priory. They were delighted with the celebration of the value of silence. I was enlightened by their insight, and the realization that the idea itself could be read in many ways. In light of this revelation, I decided to use the piece flat, on a table, where it could be read equally in different directions, rather than hung on a wall as originally planned.

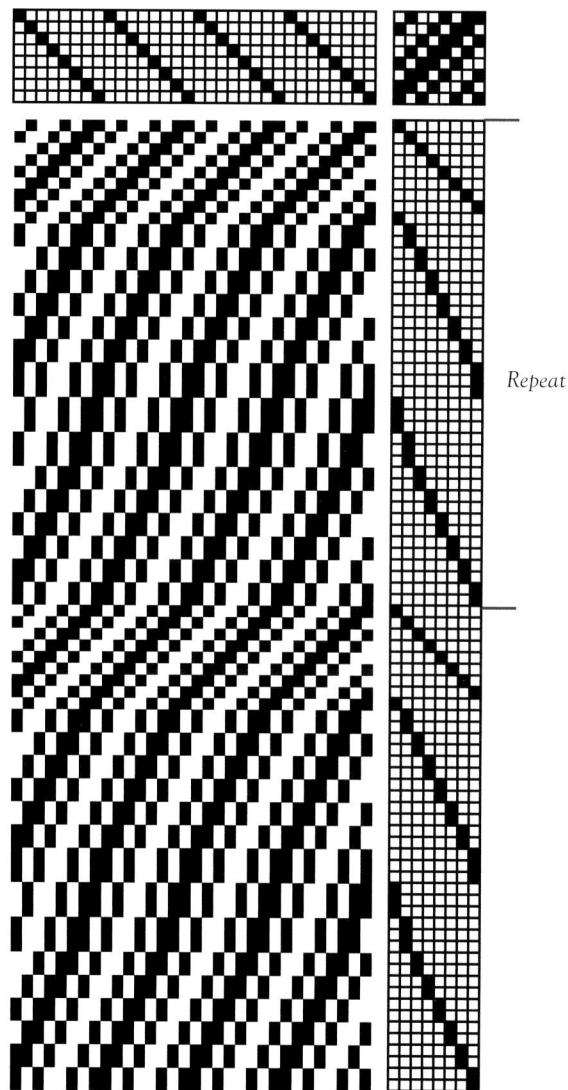

*Repeat*

*Draft Component. The 8-tie pattern is shown as it might be woven on an 8-shaft loom. This draft has a balanced 2/1/1/2/1/1 twill tie-up.*

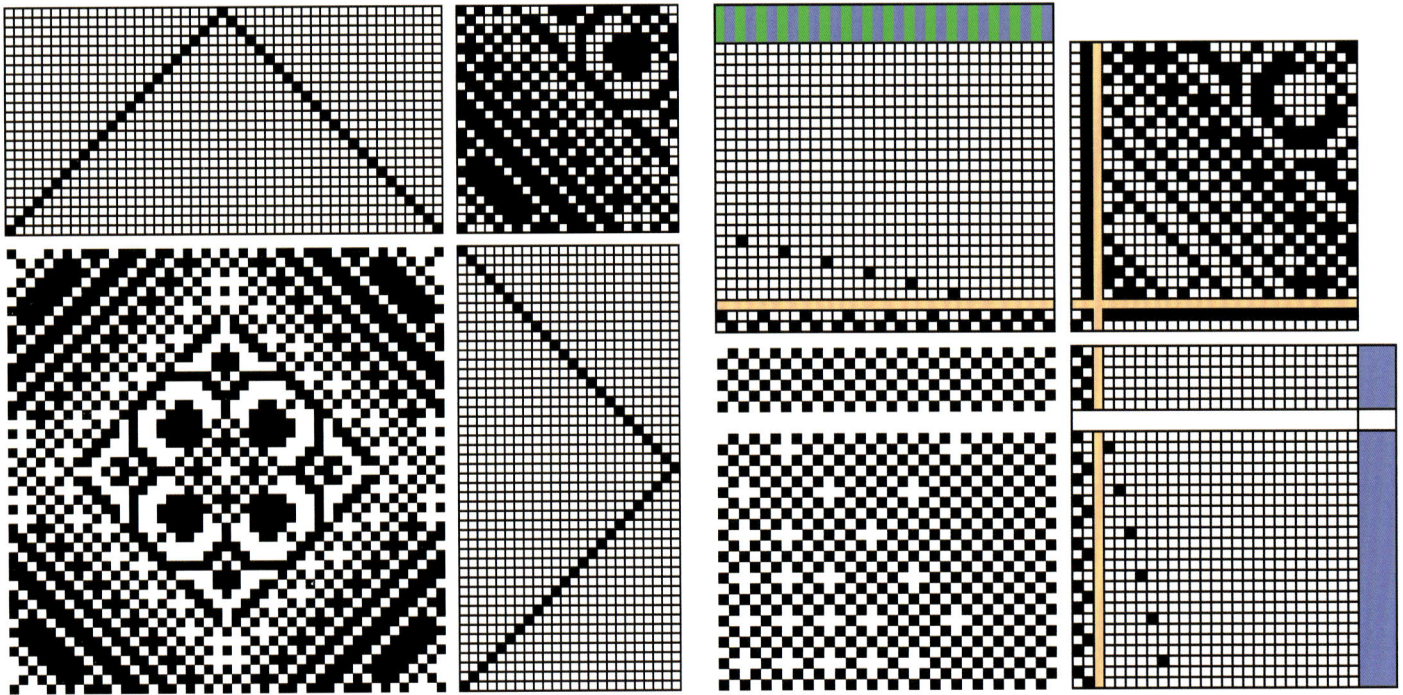

Clockwise from top left. Profile and truncated threading drafts (expanded to separate tie-down, pattern, and tabby areas). Shown as if woven on shaft looms.

Profile Draft. Undistorted 24-block motif for pattern bands.

Threading Draft. Atwater-Bronson lace, six blocks of 24 shown.

Threading Draft. 8-tie weave using quarter units, ten blocks of 25 shown. A larger section is given to show more of the tie-down patterning. Use tabby (not shown) with this skeleton draft.

Threading Draft. Summer and Winter, seven blocks of 25 shown. Alternating (brick-style) treadling. Use tabby (not shown) with this skeleton draft.

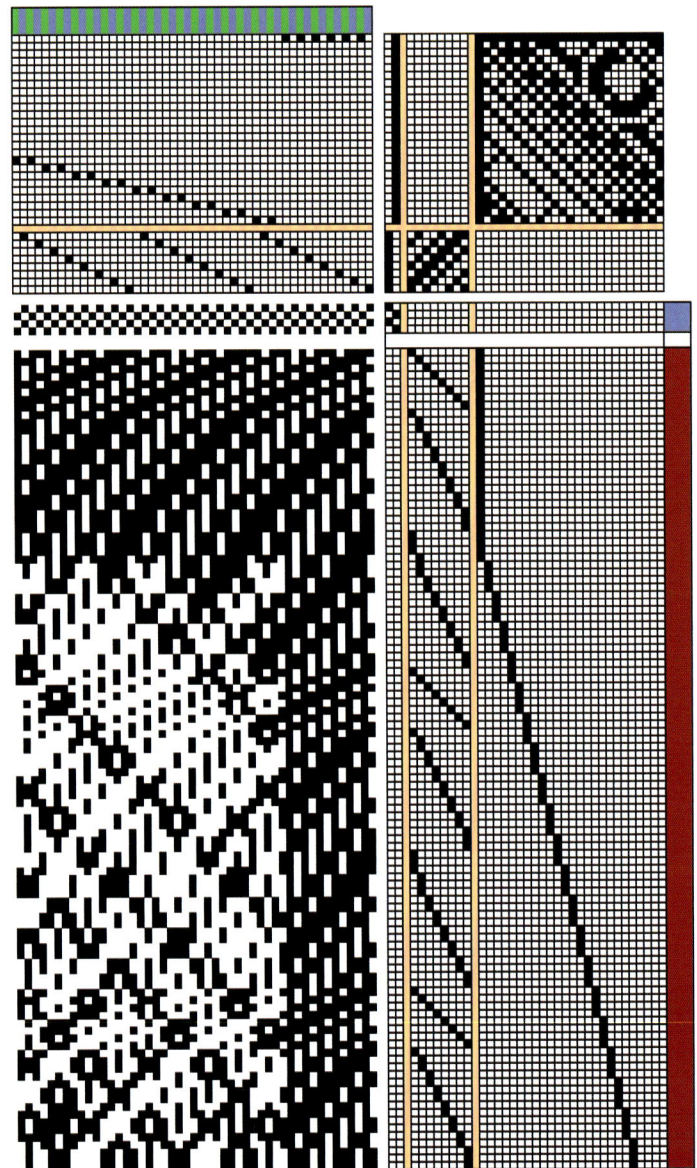

214

## Weaving Information

Size: 63.5" x 25.75"

Warp: 20/2 mercerized cotton, 8400 ypp, medium fern green and periwinkle blue; 30 epi

Weft: 20/2 mercerized cotton, 8400 ypp, blue (tabby); 20/6 mercerized cotton floss, 2800 ypp, cordovan; 30 ppi (lace, plain weave), 54 ppi (summer and winter, single 8-tie unit weave)

Source: Original draft

Structures: Single 8-tie unit weave as quarter units with undulating twill tie pattern, summer and winter with alternating (brick)-style treadling, Atwater-Bronson lace, and plain weave; Jacquard

Finishing: Hand hemmed on all sides. Hand washed in cool water with detergent for ten minutes, rinsed cool. Rolled in towels, then laid flat to dry until damp. Pressed on cotton setting while damp.

Take-up and Shrinkage: Warp 2%, weft 8%

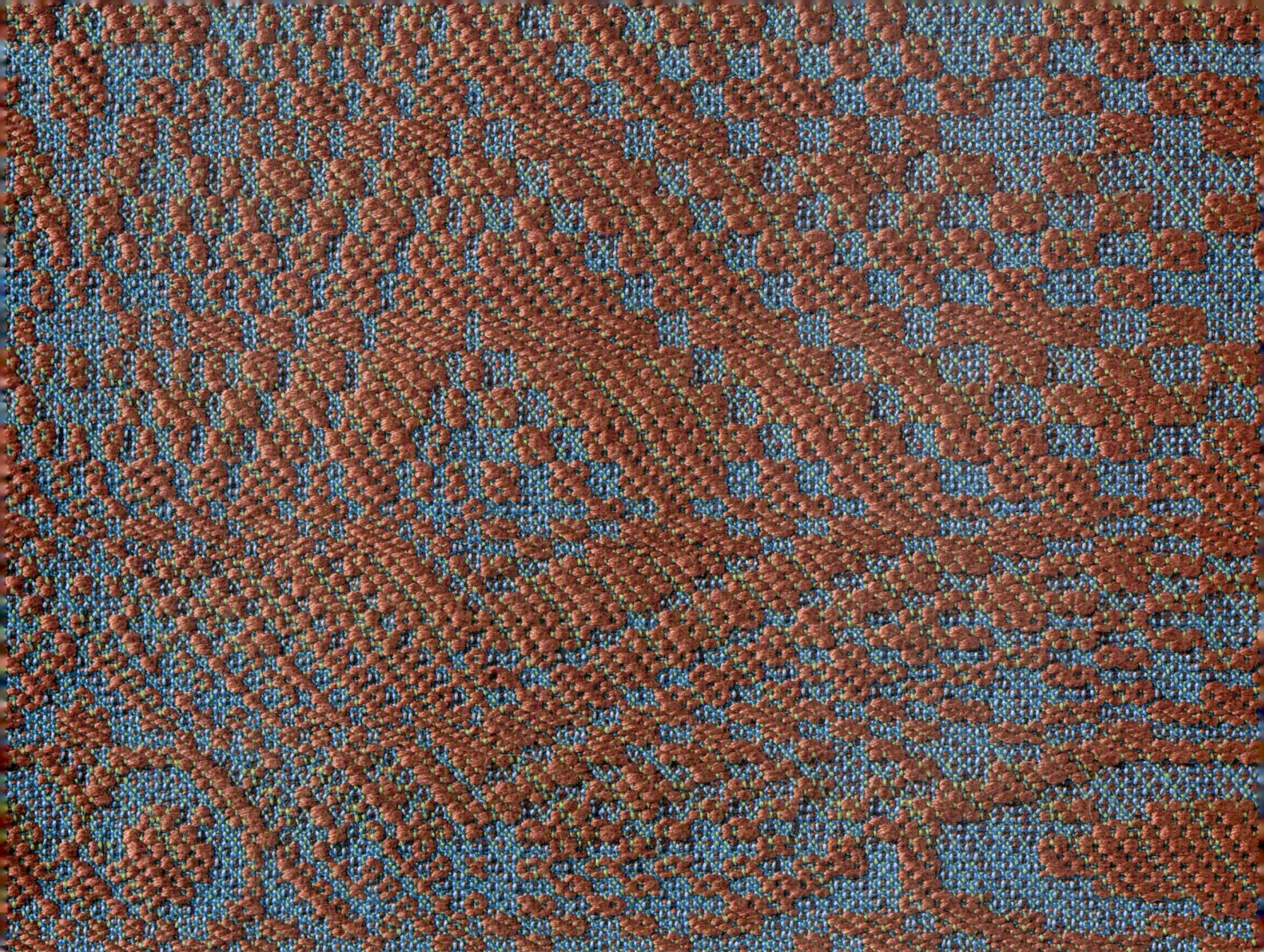

*Profile Draft. For the large 8-tie end section, the small 24-block motif was repeated three times, with the center repeat distorted. The curving distortion includes a change of scale, which gives the three-dimensional "louder" effect*

*Opposite, Details of the large 8-tie design (top), the summer and winter band (bottom left), and the Atwater-Bronson lace band (bottom right).*

## Tips

• It would be better to sett the piece at 27-28 epi to make it easier to square the tied weave portions and open the lace more. The weaver notes, "I was unable to square the tied-weave portions on this loom, though I had woven summer and winter at this sett with these materials before. I had to beat very hard (enough to move an 890 pound loom on rubber feet across the room) and had a lot of breakage on one selvedge. Special words were spoken to accompany the needling in of a zillion broken ends."

• Hemming selvedges can be a solution for any number of issues. Be sure to leave a wide enough margin if you plan in advance to hem the sides.

• Using 8-tie weaves as 4-thread quarter units makes the distorted design scale the same as the 4-thread summer and winter and Atwater-Bronson lace units. It also creates a less blocky, more graceful pattern.

• On a shaft loom, the quarter unit 8-tie weave can be woven in 4-thread Atwater-Bronson lace, summer and winter, etc. Many other structures can be woven on a straight 8-tie unit weave base.

• Be aware of being too subtle. Almost no one sees the 6" high word "SILENCE" in the exuberant top panel until the weaver points it out (find the "ILEN" above). It is very silent.

• Consider how the weaving itself can add to whatever idea you want to convey. Why weave it rather than collage or draw it? Can the choice of structure, texture, design elements, color, finger-manipulation, etc. augment or clarify the concept?

• Be open to other interpretations of your work. Others may see new ideas in your presentation, a bonus rather than a flaw.

• Use a dictionary. Study additional languages. Go to sea. Be sure you have the right cuss words.

# II.6  Graphic Techniques

Special graphic techniques allow the weaver to place structures freely within a liftplan or drawdown rather than being confined to blocks or stripes. Often accomplished with the help of Photoshop, placement of structures can also be done in other computer graphic programs, by hand, or in higher-level weaving programs such as ArahWeave and ProWeave.

While usually woven on a Jacquard loom, by limiting the width of the design area, dobby looms may use the technique. Additionally, using the results as a profile adds even more versatility with double harness looms (drawlooms) and dobby looms. The technique may also be used on any loom if one is willing to do pick-up, or treadled pick-up (changing the shed mid-pick as different structures are used).

*A 3-color cartoon, 32 pixels wide, for use as a 32-shaft liftplan.*

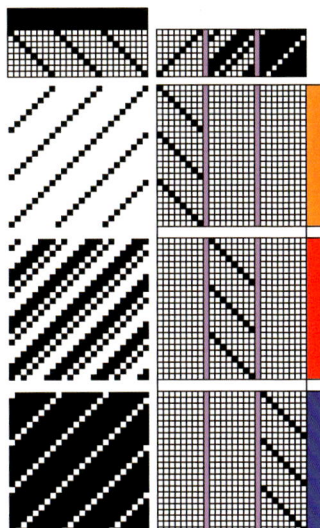

*Three 8-shaft twills (1/7, 3/3/1/1, and 7/1) for substitution into orange, red, and blue areas respectively.*

*Final draft with structures substituted into the liftplan.*

*Photo of Céilidh and Tiarella Autio reduced to six colors. Each color will be assigned a different interlacement in Photoshop.*

## Simplified Process

• Start with a pattern, photo, or drawing.

• Reduce colors to the number of structures desired.

• Reduce to number of pixels (threads or blocks) desired.

• Substitute the structures into the colored areas. This can be done by hand, in Photoshop, or in other programs.

• Weave using a dobby, drawloom, Jacquard, pick-up, or "treadled pick-up" technique.

# Color Play

## Pat Stewart

### Scarf in Double Weave (Twill)

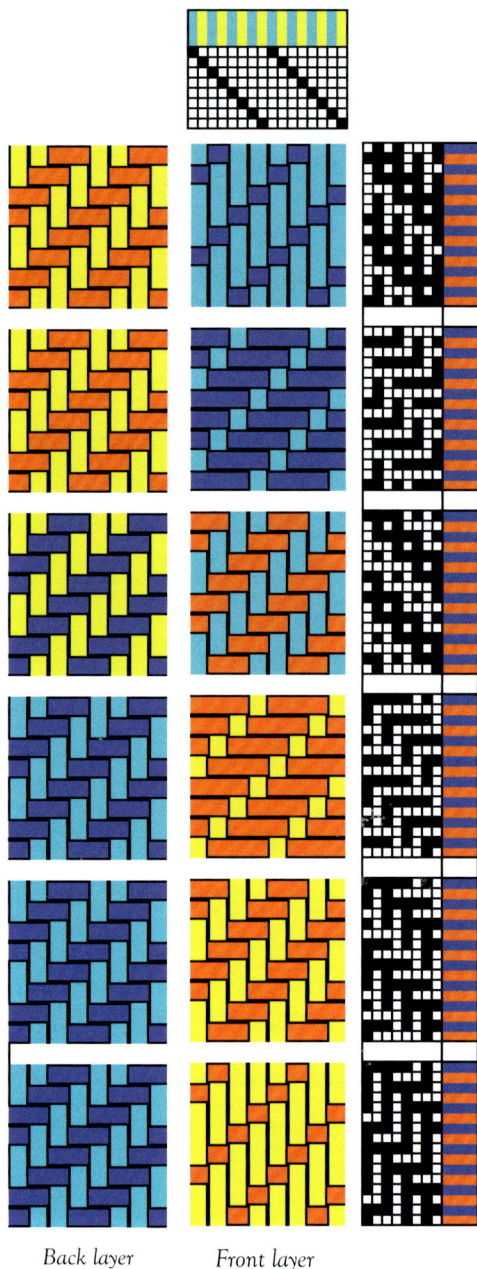

## Design Process

One block of double weave for two layers of straight 4-shaft twill requires eight shafts. Therefore, on my 24-shaft loom I can use three threading blocks of twill double weave. I began by making a digital "weave blanket" or sampler of a single layer of twills in weaving software to judge color interactions. I used various combinations of two alternating warp colors with two weft colors and tried the effects of 3/1, 2/2, and 1/3 regular twill tie-ups.

Using twills in double weave, I can change the color effect of the six stripes with only two alternating colors in the warp and two in the weft without changing the color order in warp or weft. I assembled the chosen color chips in a 3-block profile draft to judge the effect of the weaves on the face of the cloth. An over-under alternation imitating plain weave patterning was used as a design motif on the three blocks. Weaving the teal warp with the copper weft in 2/2 twill makes a neutral grayed color, which I used for the background. The vertical blue-lavender stripes are in 3/1 and 1/3 twills and the horizontal yellow-copper stripes are in 1/3, 2/2, and 3/1 twills. For this scarf, I chose to make the second (back) layer entirely in 2/2 twill.

For ease of visualization, the chosen twills were first constructed as double weave on a divided threading, then rearranged to a straight threading for easier threading on the loom. The hem is made of two layers of plain weave which mix the four colors on each side by weaving adjacent ends and picks together.

*Back layer          Front layer*

Component Threading Draft. In the final scarf, six of the twelve 4-shaft color blends were chosen for the top layer, and three for the back layer. The top and back layer of the six 8-shaft combinations are shown in doubleweave view with liftplans.

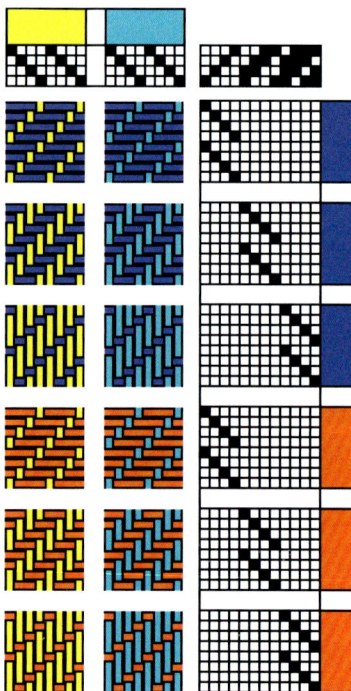

*Single Layer Component Draft. Using regular 4-shaft twills with 1/3, 2/2, or 3/1 tie-ups, twelve color blends can be created. Here, the yellow and teal warp ends are shown separately, each combined first with a blue weft and then with a copper weft. After the color options were evaluated, they were used in accordance with the cartoon shown on page 222. For ease of construction, the tie-ups of the components were first arranged in a divided draft as shown on page 223 and then rearranged in liftplans in straight threading and treadling blocks on 24 shafts.*

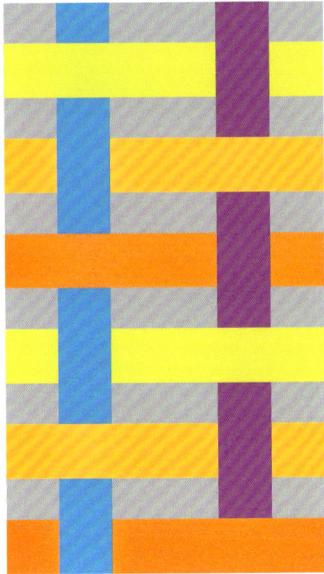

*Above, Cartoon. Each color is used to place a different structure and color option from the sampler. Gray areas use the copper weft with teal warp in 2/2 twill to create a neutral background. Blue and purple stripes use 1/3 and 3/1 twill respectively with teal warp and lavender weft. Yellow, light orange, and dark orange stripes use yellow warp with copper weft in 1/3, 2/2, and 3/1 twills to shift colors in three stripes.*

*Right, Threading Draft. One repeat of the final draft on 24 shafts with double layer plain weave hem at bottom. Only the top layer is shown in this double weave view. Red lines separate the three threading and liftplan blocks.*

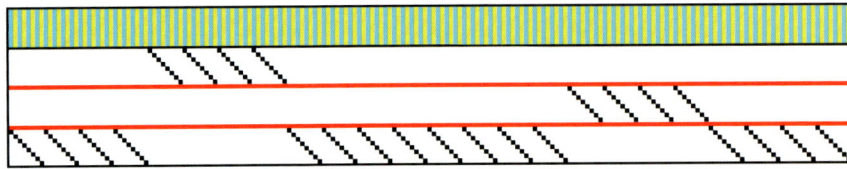

## Weaving Information

Size: 67" x 13"

Warp: 2/18 wool/silk (50/50%), 5040 ypp, teal;
2/20 worsted wool, 5600 ypp, marigold; 40 epi

Weft: 2/18 wool/silk (50/50%), 5040 ypp, copper
and violet; 37 ppi

Source: Original draft

Weave Structure: Double weave (twills), 24 shafts

Finishing: Two layers of double weave hem turned in
and slip-stitched closed. Hand washed in warm water.
Rinsed and laid flat to dry. Pressed while still damp.

Take-up and Shrinkage: Warp 9%, weft 4%

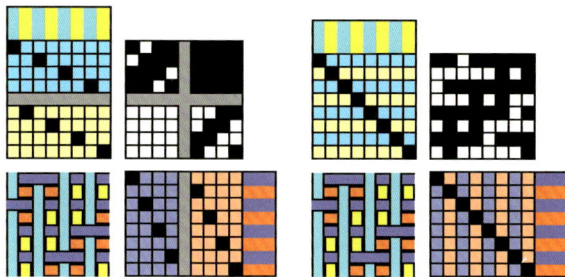

*Component Draft Options. It is often easier to design when the
shafts and treadles for one layer are grouped (left), and to weave
when they are rearranged into a simpler order (right).*

## Tips

• Creating a digital and/or woven sampler of possibilities in a single
block (or layer) is a good way to explore color and structural variations
systematically. Once the options are laid out, it is easier to choose how to
place them in a more complex final design.

• Placement into the final design may be made through digital graphic
techniques, such as Photoshop (Schlein, 2010), or by hand. Either way, you
may find it helpful to make a cartoon for placement of structures.

• Designing with a divided threading, one where the shafts for each layer
are grouped together (e.g., layer A on shafts 1 to 4; layer B on shafts 5
to 8; for a threading of 1, 5, 2, 6, 3, 7, 4, 8), makes it easier to see and
control how each layer interlaces. One may then rearrange into a simpler
threading, where the shafts from each layer alternate to form a straight or
other simple form (layer A on shafts 1, 3, 5, and 7; layer B on shafts 2, 4, 6,
and 8; for a threading of 1, 2, 3, 4, 5, 6, 7, 8). Nothing will change in the
drawdown in this process if it is done correctly. Some weaving programs
have tools or hacks to aid rearrangement.

• With two layers of 4-shaft straight twills, using 3/1, 2/2, and 1/3 tie-ups
creates warp-dominant, balanced, and weft-dominant areas, allowing the
color balances to shift as desired. With all three on the front layer and only
2/2 twill on the back layer, two very different sides to the scarf are created,
one with a larger color range, the other (back), more subdued.

# CW – The Ties That Bind

## Lynn Smetko

### Scarf in Summer and Winter and Tubular Double Weave

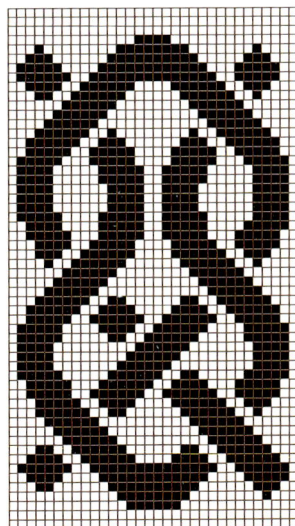

## Design Process

As the current CW President preparing a piece for this book, it seemed fitting to use the Complex Weavers' logo, a weaver's knot, as the motif for a scarf. While we may live all over the world and have diverse interests, we come together through our love of weaving, forging ties that bind.

First, the motif had to be designed. To include 8-end weave structures, the image's width and height had to be multiples of eight. Taking a .tif file of the CW logo into Photoshop, the size was reduced to 32 x 56 squares, adjusting the image as needed to get the best look (Schlein, 2010).

Selecting the weave structures was next. Several considerations guided the choice: the aspect ratio of the woven motif, the motif size in relation to the scarf width, the planned yarn size, and the number of shafts available (40). After substituting 1:7 and 7:1 satins into the profile draft, it was apparent that the motif would be too small in 60/2 silk. To achieve a larger motif, the 8-end satins draft became the new profile draft. That is, the Photoshop image served as the liftplan in a profile draft with a straight profile threading. After further sampling, summer and winter with alternating tie-downs was selected, requiring two tie-down and 32 pattern shafts. The warp, tabby, and pattern weft were roughly the same size, which increased the motif's lengthwise aspect ratio. Doubling the threading pattern blocks rebalanced that, but only two of the larger motifs fit across the scarf. Instead, I decided to use only half of the usual summer and winter treadling block: tabby a, 1+pattern, tabby b, 2+pattern. This resulted in a smaller motif with a good aspect ratio, and allowed four motifs to be placed across the scarf's width.

Last, the design of the scarf itself needed to be completed. Instead of having each row of motifs lining up vertically, alternating rows were offset by 50% horizontally. As a buffer between the pattern area and the selvedge on each side, a threading block with no pattern was created using Shaft 35. A plain border using only the background pattern was added to the beginning and end of the scarf. Shafts 36-39 controlled a 4-end tubular double weave selvedge.

*Cartoon. Complex Weavers knot.*

## Weaving Information

Size: 74" x 9" plus 7" fringe on each end

Warp: 60/2 Silk (15,000 ypp), dark blue; 60 epi

Weft: 60/2 Silk (15,000 ypp), navy (tabby); 3-ply Italian Chiné Silk, 12,500 ypp, variegated light blue (pattern); 55 ppi including tabby.

Source: Original draft

Weave Structures: Summer and winter (alternating-style half-unit treadling) and tubular double weave selvedges, 39 shafts

Finishing: Hand washed in a solution of mild detergent and lukewarm water, soaked for 15 minutes, and rinsed in cool water. Wrapped in towel to soak up extra water for 15 minutes and pressed dry on silk setting.

Take-up and Shrinkage: Warp 4%, weft 5%

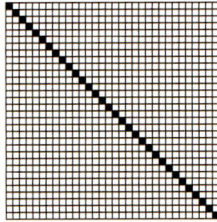

Component Profile Draft. Eight-shaft satins used to make the profile draft from the cartoon.

7:1 satin

1:7 satin

Cartoon. Transferred to 33 block liftplan. Second repeat offset by half.

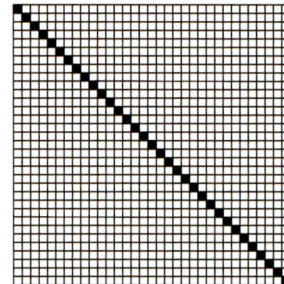

Profile Draft. The 7:1 and 1:7 8-end satins were applied to the light and dark areas of the cartoon liftplan. Created in Photoshop using 33 blocks.

## Tips

• Using graphic techniques to create a profile is less common but very useful. It allows the pattern to be scaled up (enlarged) by a multiple of the block size. Additionally, the process eliminates the occasional edge oddities which may cause longer floats where structures join.

• In summer and winter half of the heddles are on two shafts, generally 1 and 2. To assist the loom in keeping those shafts down when others are raised, you may need to add weights, bungee cords, or extra springs (to a spring pulley system) for the miscreant shafts.

• The decision of whether to separate motifs with background or continue them up to the edge of a repeat has a strong influence on how a design is perceived. Motifs which abut each other tend to connect and recombine visually, while motifs which are separated stay distinct. If you are operating at the limits of your shafts, it can be hard to convince yourself to give up a block for just background, but you may be able to find ways to offset the motifs differently to space them without the extra block.

• Offsetting rows of motifs by a set amount is a way to add more life to the design than can be found in strictly repeating rows and columns of motifs. With a straight order of blocks and a lever or dobby system, any offset desired can be used. A half offset is a classic, classy way to move patterns. Other offsets create different angles and motion effects. Generally, only the pattern moves, the structure does not. That is, the block threadings do not reverse, continuing seamlessly.

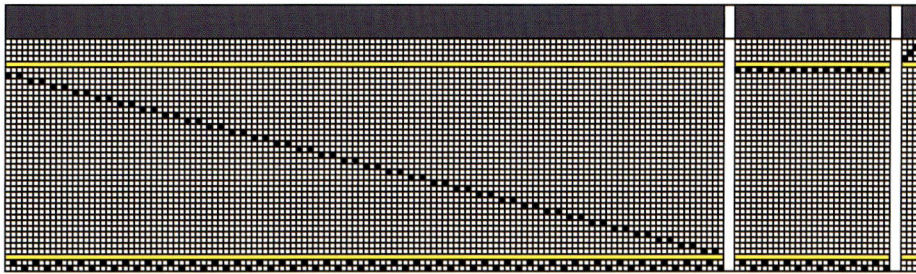

*Threading Draft. Portion of draft showing use of half units of alternating (brick-style) treadling. The next repeat will be offset by half horizontally. Use tabby in background and pattern areas (not shown).*

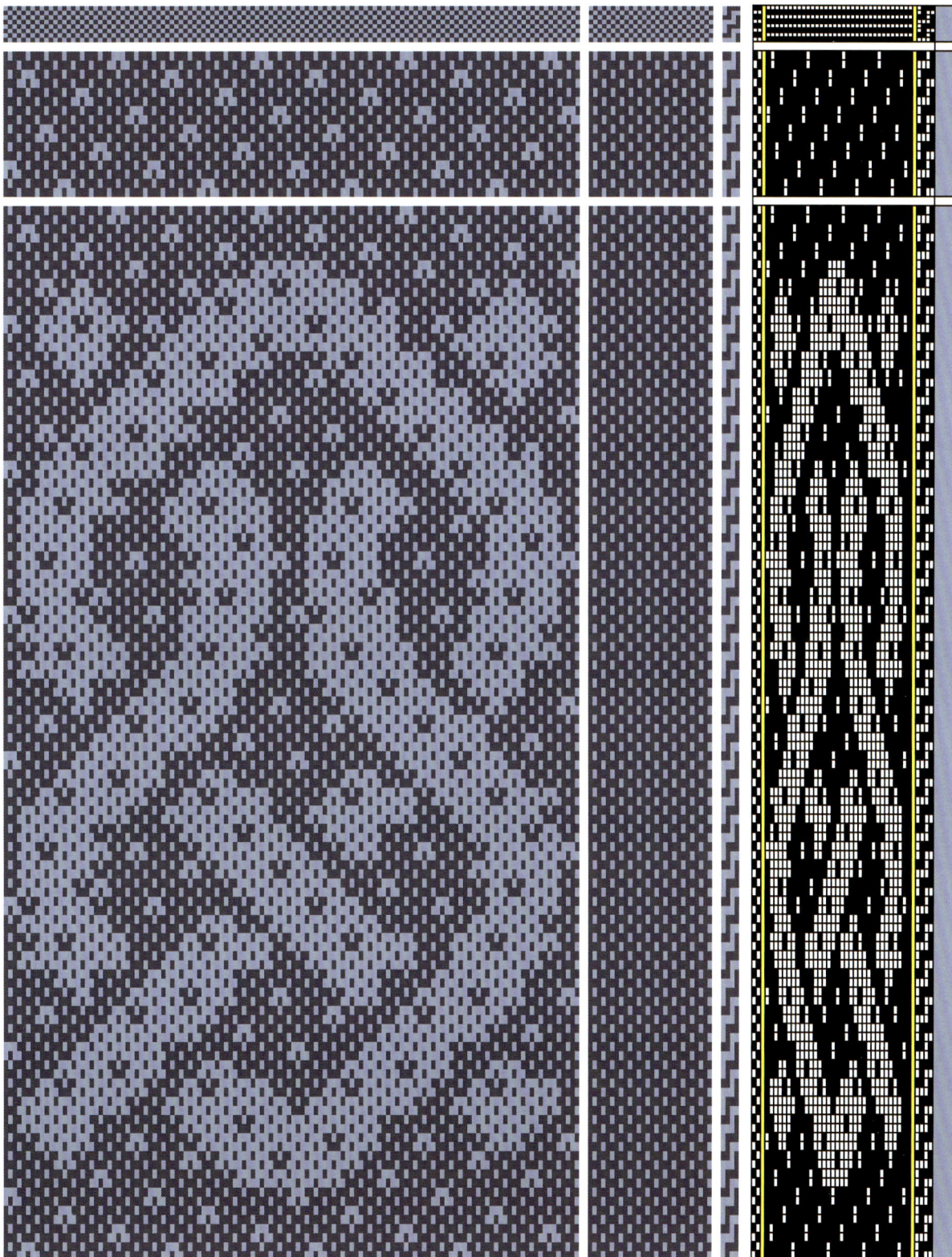

*Plain weave with tubular double weave selvedges*

*Background*

*Pattern, partial repeat. Tabby used but not shown. The draft has been expanded to separate the tie-downs and tabbies from pattern and selvedges.*

*When the tabby is added, the double weave selvedges follow an 8-thread repeat with each pick repeated twice (once on the pattern and once on the tabby). The doubled pick makes up for the lower thread density from splitting the warp into two layers.*

*Note: In order to preserve the aspect ratio of the woven motif when the tabby is not shown, the weft is portrayed as twice the width of the warp although similar yarn was used for both.*

# Northern Lights
## Lesley Willcock

### Scarf in Shaded Satin

### Design Process

The design of this scarf was inspired by images of the northern lights, which really appealed to me as I love to weave in swirls and curves. I decided that a selection of shaded 8-end satins would give the greatest contrast of the warp and weft colors whilst also allowing me to vary the color intensity.

From previous experience, I knew that using a networked threading could give me the desired dancing, swirling effect. I made a curve and networked it on a straight initial of 8. Once I had a 32-shaft threading I liked, I repeated it four times. On each repeat, the threading was advanced by eight shafts, which allowed the design to move on rather than simply repeat.

The liftplan was designed in Photoshop (Schlein, 2010) by drawing the swirling shapes and filling with different 8-end satins. To create the satin structure series, I started with a 1:7 satin and then increased the number of ends in the warp direction by one (e.g., 2:6). After sampling, the final version used varying amounts of six of the seven available satins (1:7, 2:6, 3:5, 5:3, 6:2, and 7:1; skipping 4:4). To allow the design to progress, the shape I drew was offset by eight treadles. That is, each repeat of the liftplan moved to the right by eight treadles, meaning that a full repeat was four times longer than the basic liftplan.

The final design decision was the choice of yarns. I knew the piece needed a fine silk, as with 8-end satins I would have some 7-end floats both in warp and weft. I had some space-dyed silk which perfectly represented the shades of blue, green and yellow of the Aurora Borealis, and used it with a purplish-grey for the inky night sky. My original sampling used the space-dyed silk as weft but it appeared too stripy. In the final piece I swapped the warp and weft colors.

### Weaving Information

Size: 63" x 11" plus 5" fringe on each end

Warp: 60/2 nm space-dyed silk (14,880 ypp), shades of greens and blues; 90 epi

Weft: 60/2 nm silk (14,880 ypp), gunmetal; 88 ppi

Source: Original draft

Weave Structure: Shaded 8-end satin, 32 shafts

Finishing: 2-ply fringe of 14 ends per ply tied with overhand knots. Hand washed in hand-hot water with Persil Silk Wash, rinsed in cooling water. Dried 20 minutes on low setting. Pressed while damp.

Take-up and Shrinkage: Warp 10%, weft 8%

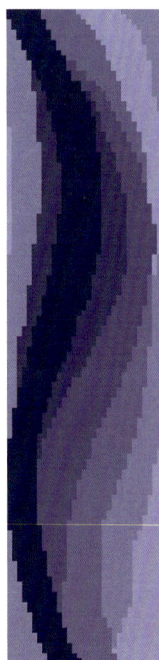

1:7 satin

2:6 satin

3:5 satin

5:3 satin

6:2 satin

7:1 satin

*Component Threading Drafts. Six of the seven possible 8-end shaded satins were used.*

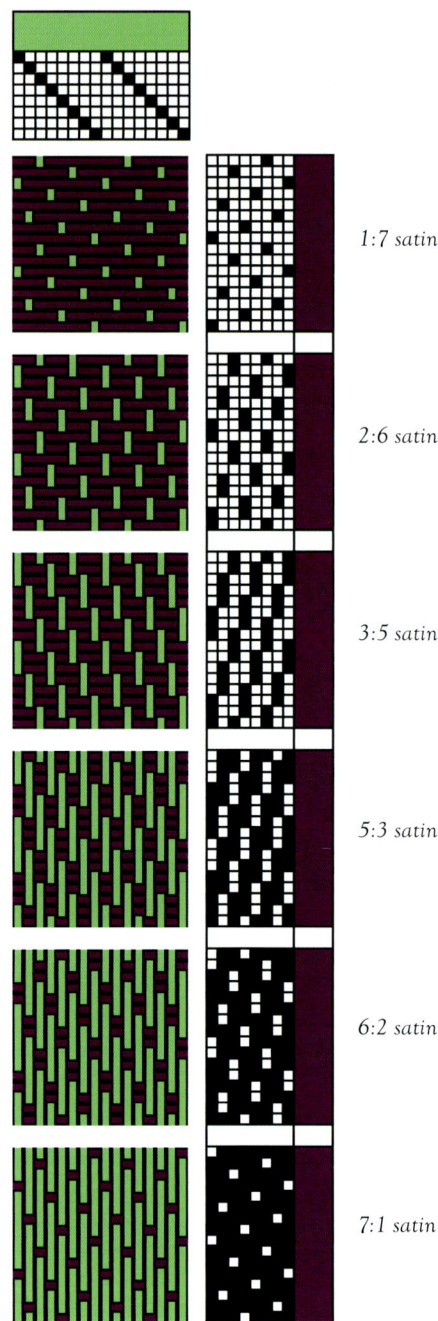

*Cartoon for Liftplan. The basic pattern, which is 32 units wide, is advanced by eight. Each color corresponds to a different 8-end satin interlacement.*

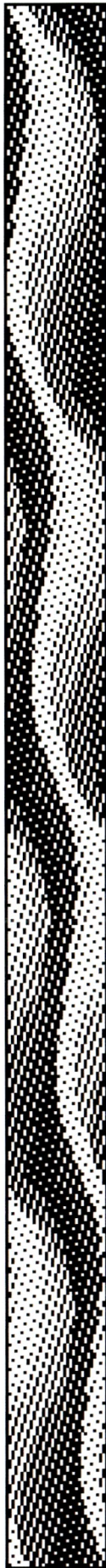

*Full Liftplan. The 8-end satins are placed into the cartoon liftplan and advanced to form the complete repeat.*

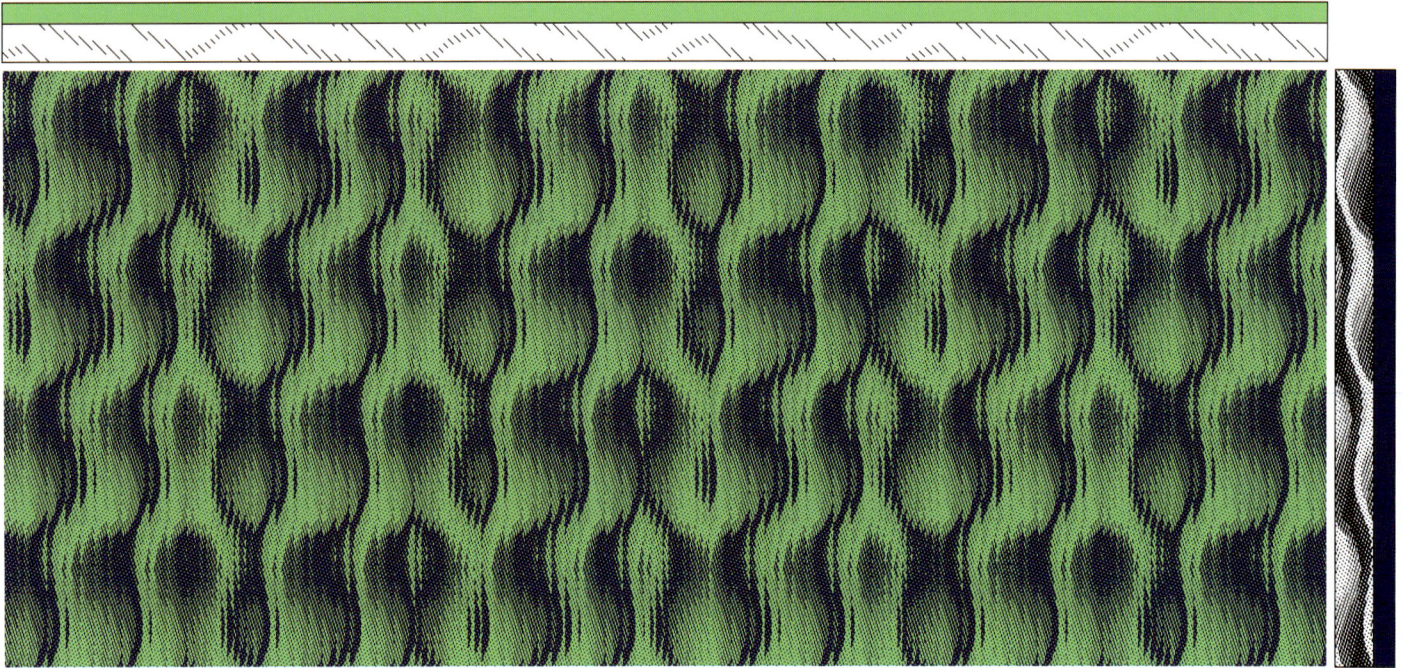

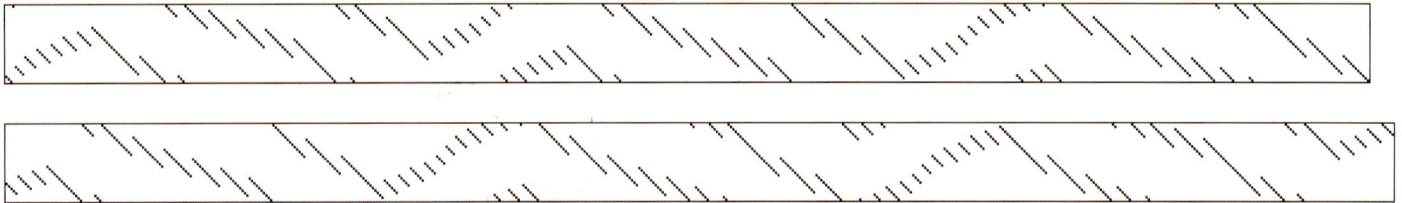

Top, Threading Draft. Full repeat in warp and weft.

Middle, Threading. Enlarged for visibility, 32 shafts.

## Tips

• It is not necessary to use all the steps of a sequence of structures. Here, the contrast between the northern lights and the night sky is enhanced by skipping the middle bridging step (4:4) of the 8-end satins used.

• While graphic techniques in the liftplan of a design for a shaft loom are often paired with a simple straight threading, more complex threadings can produce fascinating results. In this piece, advancing a networked threading allows a much livelier design than would happen with straight draw or a simple repeat. The result is more reminiscent of the movement of the northern lights.

• When advancing a networked threading or treadling, clean joins will be obtained by advancing by the number of shafts or treadles in the initial. With this initial of 8, an advance of eight puts the repeat back onto the network for a seamless merge.

• Matching the network initial to the satins used is key to making this variation work. If, for example, 5-end satins are chosen as the structure, then an initial of 5 in the networked warp combined with a number of shafts which divide evenly by five would give the cleanest results.

# "G" is for Giraffe
## Elaine Palmer

### Wall Hanging in Satin and Twill

### Design Process

As a graphic designer and photo art director, I have always been drawn to graphic, stylized, iconic images. I love animals, floral motifs, musical instruments, floor tiles, and using my travel photos as inspiration. A few years ago, I took a class with Madelyn van der Hoogt and wove her "Sunflowers" pattern on a lash-saving single-unit drawloom. At that point, I knew I wanted to learn more. Upon returning home, I took a week-long class on drawlooms with Becky Ashenden. Shortly after that, I bought an older Glimåkra standard loom, with the idea that one day I would convert it to a single-unit drawloom.

I volunteered for the local Engineers Without Borders student chapter, which has projects in Africa, so safari animals have interested me recently. For this piece, I went online and searched for "graphic giraffe." Vinyl Smith's "Giraffe Head Wall Decal" (Brown, n.d.) looked interesting. Using Excel, I took the giraffe's head and interpreted it into pixels. The image required some manipulation for the effect I wanted, particularly about the eye, the placement of the ears, and the horn on top of the head.

My first warp was 8/2 cotton with 8/1 tow linen as weft. I particularly liked the difference between the shiny tow weft in 7/1 regular twill and the dull cotton warp background in 8-shaft satin (Keasbey, 2005, p. 267). I was limited to weft colors which worked well with the purple warp. The color of the weft showed through slightly in the "satin" background portion, changing the hue of the purple. I found the red tow linen weft worked well. I wove three giraffes on the first warp, on the last adding the letter "G," styled after a child's wooden block toy.

After having woven several things on the first warp, I found the 8/2 cotton warp was too wide for my liking; the finished pieces were all too big. My second warp is 16/2 cotton in ivory. I am hoping I will like the size of those finished pieces better, but will I like the ivory warp? Zebras!

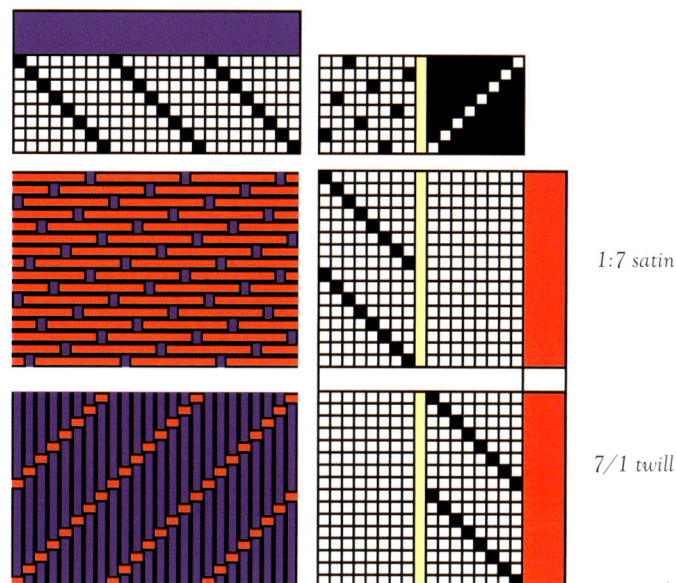

*1:7 satin*

*7/1 twill*

*Component Threading Drafts. An 8-end satin (1:7) and a 7/1 regular twill as they might be woven on an 8-shaft loom. The piece was woven with this, the back side, up.*

*Drawloom Tie-up. The black shafts rise and the red ones sink. Pattern is controlled by the use of drawcords, changing every eight weft threads.*

### Weaving Information

Size: 20" x 20" stretched, unframed

Warp: 8/2 cotton, 3224 ypp, dark purple; 35 epi

Weft: 8/1 tow linen, 2778 ypp, cardinal red; 35 ppi

Source: Original draft

Weave Structures: 8-end satin and 7/1 twill, single-unit drawloom

Finishing: Piece was not washed, serged top and bottom and stretched on canvas stretchers. Backing added after stretching.

Draw-in: Weft 2%

## Tips

• Sometimes it requires fewer draw pulls (or shafts to lift in a non-drawloom piece) to weave a piece back side up, as this one was.

• When designing a piece which is not exactly bilaterally symmetrical, and particularly if it has lettering, the pattern must be inverted and reversed.

• Try various finishing techniques before committing. In some wall art pieces, stretching without washing can be the best option. Sampling the finishing for this piece found that washing and mangling a similar piece blunted the desired contrast between the dull satin of the cotton and the luster of the tow linen.

• While often done in Photoshop or a high end weaving program, it does not take special equipment to make a graphic design and substitute in different structures. Find an image you like, enlarge or decrease size as needed, and use a transparent piece of graph paper to translate the pattern to weaving blocks. Coloring the blocks by hand or in a spreadsheet program and printing it out at large scale makes it easier to follow the pattern. Similarly, one does not have to weave these patterns on a dobby loom or Jacquard loom. The graphed pattern can be picked up by hand on any loom, or, in block designs, woven on a drawloom.

*Portion of Cartoon. This Excel cartoon covers the same section as the detail of the eye, above. Note that the cartoon is the reverse of the photo because the piece was woven back side up. The colored columns help the weaver keep track of the many cords. Darker squares mark the pulled cords. The numbers refer to how many of that group of five columns are pulled. Each row corresponds to one treadling block of eight picks.*

233

# The Sellin Family Tree
## Helen Sellin

### Wall Hanging in Satin Damask

## Design Process

During informal discussions at Complex Weavers Seminar 2014 in Tacoma, Washington, two different weavers, identities unknown, suggested weaving a genealogy tree as the obvious way to unite my weaving and genealogy interests. Why didn't I think of that? With an extensive genealogy database (the necessary information) and an Öxabäck drawloom with single heddle draw (equipment capable of a project requiring hundreds of independent design elements), a tree was certainly possible.

I started with the youngest family members at the top, rather than at the conventional bottom. This created an evergreen tree rather than a deciduous tree, which led to the border design and scattered trees in the main field. Ronald Schneider's "designer's eye" led me to several monumental improvements, starting with refinements to the title area. Then, inverting the border to a dark background with light trees converted a humdrum design to one with pizzazz. Finally, adding flourishes in the style of the name font to the ends of the lines connecting families unified the main field. Since each of the four main lines: paternal paternal, paternal maternal, maternal paternal and maternal maternal, had different international origins (Swedish, Finnish, Irish, and English respectively) the countries were added.

When a project is stimulating, the necessary patience and required time can be found to turn it into a labor of love. It took eight months to modify the loom hardware to single-heddle draw from 60-shaft pattern draw, then warp almost 2000 ends, each of which had to be threaded through pattern heddle, ground heddle and reed. Then, the weaving, all manual, took sixteen months. It was woven in half units of 8-shaft regular satin damask with clean cuts (Lillemor, 1982; Erikkson et al. 1995; Cyrus-Zetterstrom, 1977). The graphed chart was turned 90°, using 479 drawcords, with 900 pattern rows as woven. Four shuttle passes were made after each drawcord pull, i.e., the first half unit. Then, the next chart row was pulled and the four picks of the second half unit were woven. Having two sons, one tree was not enough so a second is underway!

In the future, I have two avenues I'd like to investigate: Can the design be changed so the joins between the half units improve in the actual weaving? Can different structures be used for pattern and background, given that the border is the inverse of the main field?

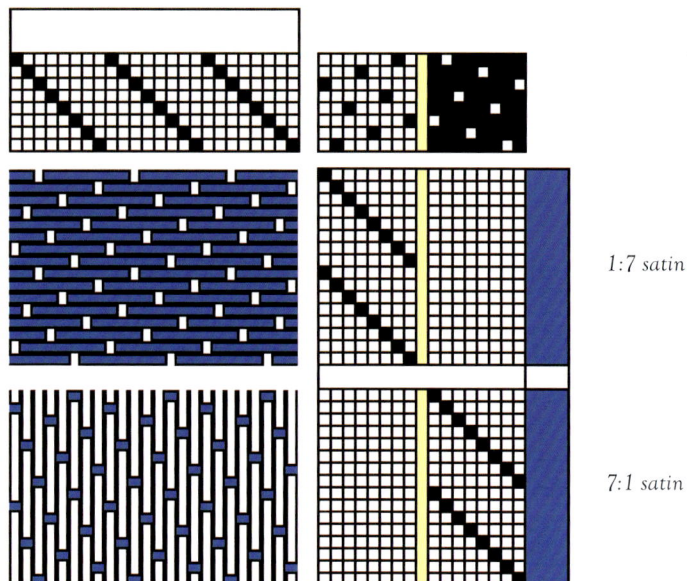

*1:7 satin*

*7:1 satin*

*Component Threading Drafts. Two 8-end satins (1:7 and 7:1) as they might be woven on an 8-shaft loom.*

*Drawloom Tie-up. The black shafts rise and the red ones sink. The pattern is controlled by the use of drawcords, changing every four weft threads (half units).*

## Weaving Information

Size: 30" x 54.5"

Warp: 20/2 mercerized cotton, 8400 ypp, natural; 60 epi

Weft: 20/2 mercerized cotton, 8400 ypp, charcoal grey; 60 ppi

Source: Original draft

Collaborator: Ronald Schneider refined the original design

Weave Structure: 8-end satin damask, single-unit drawloom

Finishing: Selvedge ends (long edges) turned and hemmed creating a pocket for a rod. Warp ends (short edges) turned under twice and hemmed. Machine washed in cold water with a mild detergent on gentle cycle for five minutes, rinsed twice, and rolled in a towel. Pressed dry.

Take-up and Shrinkage: Warp 9%, weft 6%

*Above, Small portion of cartoon.*

## Tips

• The drawloom shed with pulled pattern and accompanying risers and sinkers is quite narrow. Warp tension should be very tight, i.e., "as tight as an older woman can make it," to maximize the shed. Tension was released only for warp advance. A narrow shuttle with a moderately filled bobbin facilitates weaving. Particularly in the areas of trees, the clearance of sinkers was not always clean (the warp was somewhat "sticky" even though it was cotton). Therefore, before each pass of the shuttle, a check was made that the shed was clear.

• You may want to re-arrange the treadles from what is shown to a 'walking' order, from the outside in. In this case, the first half unit would use two treadles on outer left and two on outer right. The second half unit would use the center four treadles.

• Reversing pattern and background is an effective way to make a border if you have enough shafts and treadles, a drawloom, or a dobby loom.

• Using half units allows smoother curves and finer detailing.

• The addition of a small figure, in this case the evergreen tree, can bring unity to the borders and body of the piece.

• Use care in choosing fonts. The right one will add legibility as well as a sense of style and period to the piece.

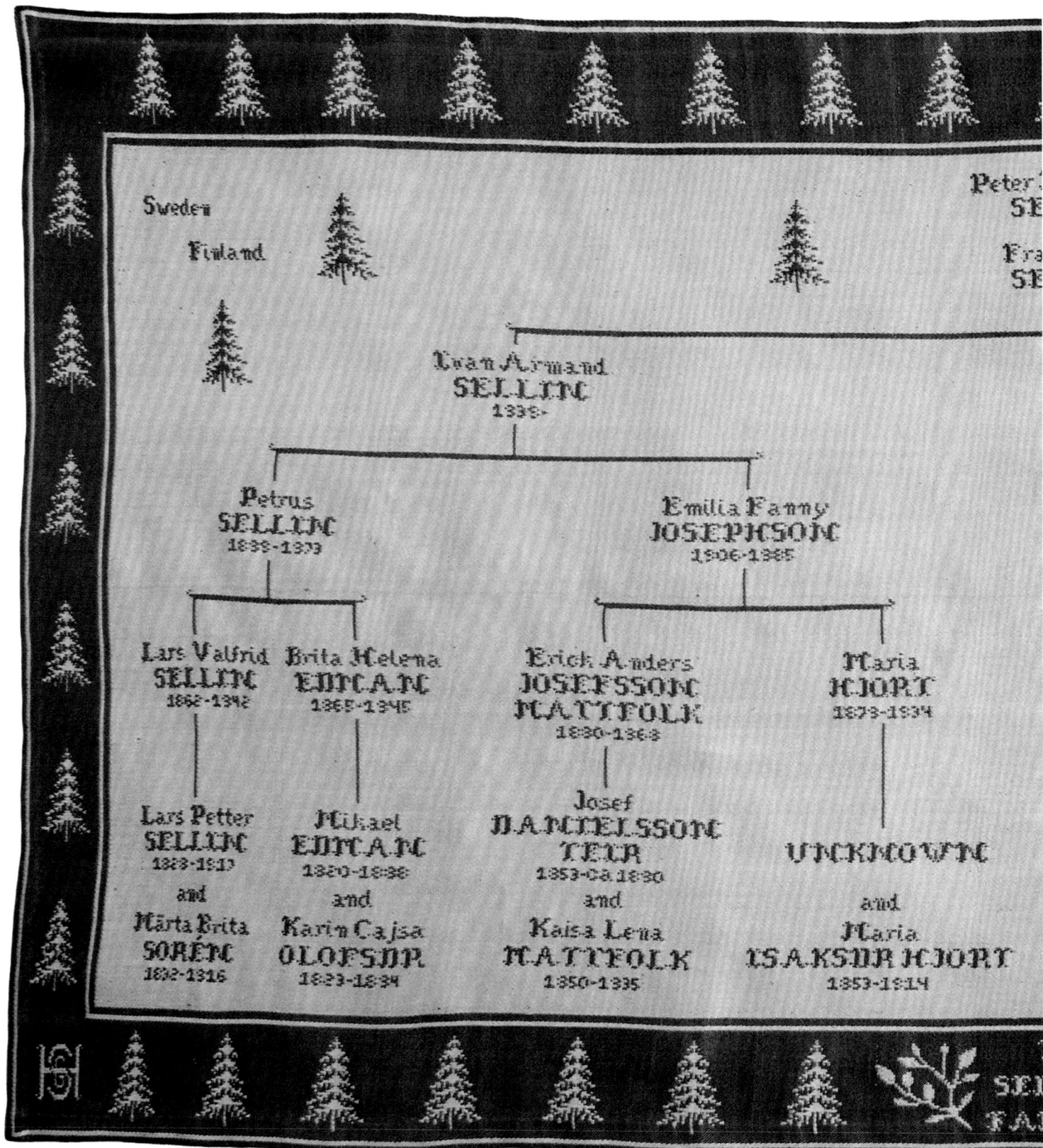

Sweden

Finland

Peter
SE...

Fra...
SE...

Ivan Armand
SELLIN
1935-

Petrus
SELLIN
1898-1979

Emilia Fanny
JOSEPHSON
1906-1985

Lars Valfrid
SELLIN
1862-1942

Brita Helena
EDMAN
1869-1945

Erich Anders
JOSEFSSON
MATTFOLK
1880-1963

Maria
HJORT
1873-1934

Lars Petter
SELLIN
1833-1917
and
Märta Brita
SORÉN
1832-1916

Mikael
EDMAN
1820-1838
and
Karin Cajsa
OLOFSDR
1829-1834

Josef
DANIELSSON
TEIR
1853-ca 1880
and
Kaisa Lena
MATTFOLK
1850-1935

UNKNOWN
and
Maria
ISAKSDR HJORT
1853-1914

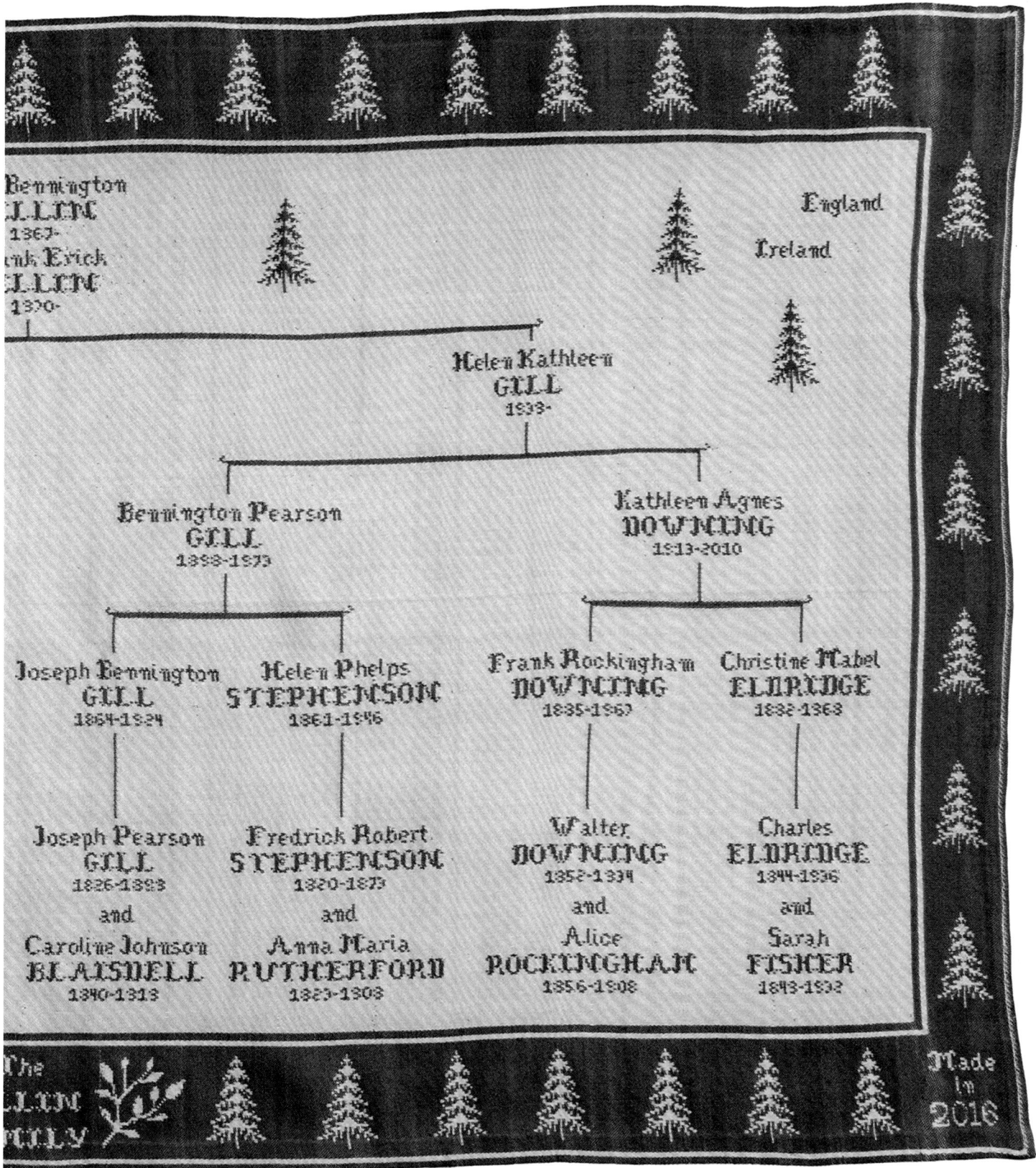

Bennington
GILL
1367-
Frank Erick
GILL
1390-

England

Ireland

Helen Kathleen
GILL
1893-

Bennington Pearson
GILL
1893-1979

Kathleen Agnes
DOWNING
1913-2010

Joseph Bennington
GILL
1864-1924

Helen Phelps
STEPHENSON
1861-1946

Frank Rockingham
DOWNING
1835-1967

Christine Mabel
ELDRIDGE
1832-1868

Joseph Pearson
GILL
1826-1893
and
Caroline Johnson
BLAISDELL
1840-1913

Fredrick Robert
STEPHENSON
1820-1873
and
Anna Maria
RUTHERFORD
1823-1903

Walter
DOWNING
1852-1934
and
Alice
ROCKINGHAM
1856-1908

Charles
ELDRIDGE
1844-1936
and
Sarah
FISHER
1843-1892

The
GILL
FAMILY

Made
in
2016

# Cloudscape

## Su Butler

## Wall Hanging in Irregular Satin

### Design Process

Being a new drawloom weaver, I had the desire to create realistic images in a weaverly manner. I started with images familiar to everyone - mountains, people, and sky. While I wanted enough realism to make the image recognizable, I also wanted it to feel like a woven piece of cloth with the characteristics of cloth, i.e. texture, pattern, etc.

Having researched drawloom weaving for a few years prior to purchasing my loom, I found I yearned for more visual depth than that presented in current work. Experimenting to that end, I chose to impose shaded satin structure onto the profile design of my work to create the desired end result. The cloud photograph was color indexed to six colors in Photoshop (Schlein and Ziek, 2006; p. 68). Then, I switched to grayscale, converting the colors to five values of gray plus pure white. For each value of gray, a pattern overlayment was created using five of the seven steps of an 8-shaft shaded satin for the design (2:6, 3:5, 4:4, 5:3, and 7:1; skipping 1:7 and 6:2). The white used no pattern (essentially, 0:8).

The profile was then used to weave blocks of 6-shaft irregular satin damask at the single-unit drawloom with the ground threaded straight draw on six shafts. There were nearly 700 pattern lines, each line requiring a new pull sequence of the 300 drawcords and six picks of the 6-shaft irregular satin to weave. The beginning and end borders were woven in unpatterned 6-shaft irregular satin.

I was pleased with the results after applying the shaded satin to the profile in Photoshop, but it was not until I removed the piece from the loom that I realized the full impact of my choice. I was very pleasantly surprised at how well the process worked. Armed with that success, I am designing many more pieces using the same idea.

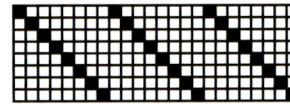

0:8

2:6 satin

3:5 satin

4:4 satin

5:3 satin

7:1 satin

*Profile Draft Components. Five of the seven possible 8-end shaded satins, shown as they might be woven on eight shafts, were applied to the shaded areas in the profile draft. Additionally, "no pattern" (0:8) was applied to the white areas.*

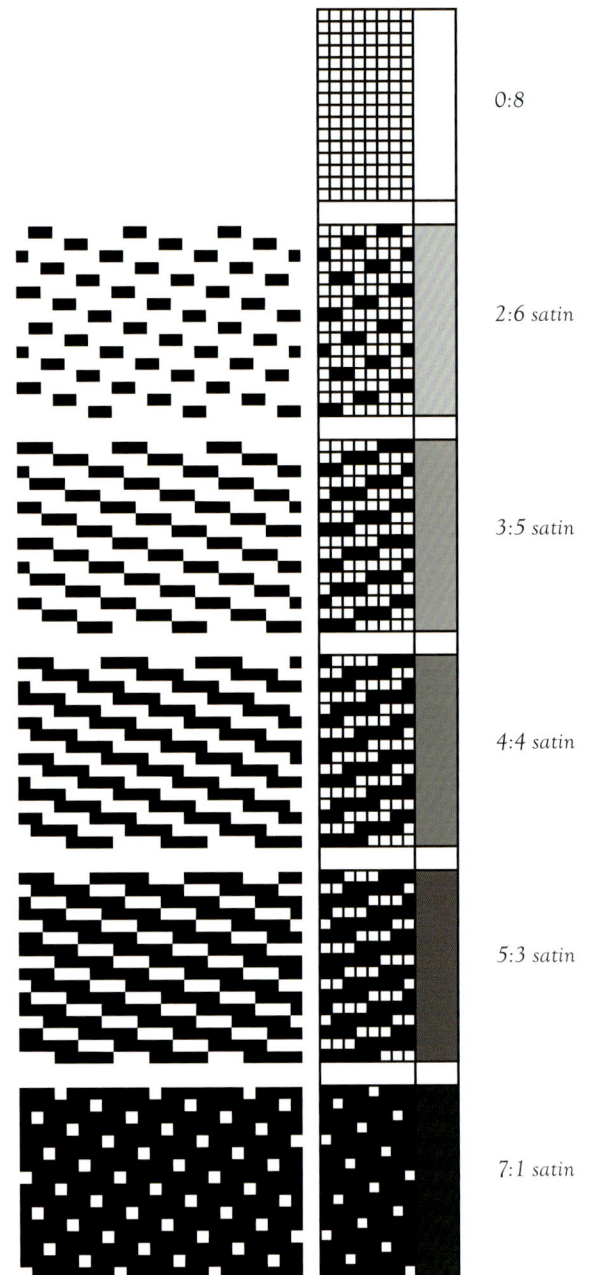

*Drawloom Tie-up. The black shafts rise and the red ones sink. Pattern is controlled by the use of drawcords, changing every six weft threads.*

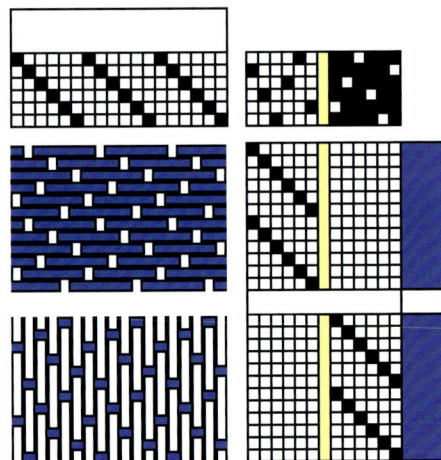

*Component Threading Drafts. Two 6-end irregular satins (1:5 and 5:1) are shown as they might be woven on a 6-shaft loom.*

1:5 irregular satin

5:1 irregular satin

238

*Below, Photo reduced to five shades of gray plus white to place the shaded satins and unpatterned areas for the profile draft.*

*Above, Original photo.*

## Weaving Information

Size: 31" x 68"

Warp: 16/2 mercerized cotton, 6720 ypp, white; 36 epi

Weft: 16/2 mercerized cotton, 6720 ypp, dark turquoise; 36 ppi

Source: Original draft

Weave Structure: 6-end irregular satin damask, single-unit drawloom

Finishing: Hand hemmed. Loop side of Velcro attached to bias tape and hand sewn along top edge of piece. Hook side of Velcro stapled onto a piece of oak, 0.25" by 66" long. One inch at each side is left free to hide the hanging mechanism. Machine washed in warm water on gentle setting for 20 minutes. Rinsed in cold water. Dried on low heat in tumble dryer until dry. Pressed with a steam iron.

Take-up and Shrinkage: Warp and weft 5%

## Tips

• When using a structure to create a profile draft, remember that some options (for example, all shafts down or all shafts up) which do not work in a threading draft can be perfectly viable and useful in a profile draft. This draft uses the 8-shaft (8-end) shaded satin series plus the option of no pattern (no warp threads up in the original 8-shaft satins) to create an area of pure tone.

• It is not necessary to use every step of a series (here, shaded satins) when using graphic techniques. A skip may help match values more closely to an original series of values in the starting design or help emphasize the difference between pattern and background areas.

• When creating imagery, keep in mind your reasons for doing a particular image as a weaving rather than a photograph or painting. Think about how you can use the unique characteristics of yarn and cloth to add to the interpretation. Structure, texture, reflectivity, grain, drape, dimensionality, etc. may all play a hand in enriching a woven image.

# Fishes
## Belinda Rose
### Shawl in Waffle Weave and Twill

## Design Process

My Jacquard loom is typically dressed with a 4-end rotation of softly contrasting neutrals, alternating light and dark. This sequence is quite versatile for double weave, turned taqueté, and weft-faced weaves. I wondered how it would work with waffle weave. Traditionally, waffle weave is woven on a solid color warp, or one which has differently colored ends placed to emphasize the longer warp floats and contrast them with the shorter ones.

For weft, I chose two analogous and tonally close colors, placing seven picks of blue where the weft floats were longer, followed by seven picks of green where the weft floats were shorter on the face. The resulting fabric had a subtle blue face and a green reverse amid deep indentations. The color rotation of the warp averaged out and did not distract from the weft color effect.

I filled a background layer with waffle weave in Photoshop, then drew an abstract fish design on a new layer (Schlein and Ziek, 2006). The diagonals of the fish nestle into the diagonal of the background waffle. As the usual resizing technique in Photoshop distorted this, I did not resize to adjust the warp to weft aspect ratio when weaving. I made a second version of the waffle, offset by seven (half of the repeat) horizontally and vertically. In the offset weave, the wefts reverse dominance, the green weft showing more on the front, the blue on the back.

I applied this weave to the fish, making green fish on a blue background. Alone, the background weave or its offset could be woven on an 8-shaft point threading.

To maintain neat edges, I used a modified 4-shaft broken 2/2 twill for the selvedges. As my test piece lost 25% in length, I wove a shawl 122" on the loom. To my surprise the warp loss was only 19%, producing an unexpectedly long shawl.

I would love to try this way of contrasting a waffle weave background with an offset version for pattern on a warp with a 14-end color repeat: seven ends of color A, seven ends of color B. A 32-shaft loom threaded with four blocks would give plenty of scope for designing pattern.

## Weaving Information

Size: 94" x 20"

Warp: 16/2 mercerized cotton, 6720 ypp, white, silver-gray, ecru, and slate gray; 45 epi

Weft: 16/2 mercerized cotton, 6720 ypp, eau de nil and peppermint; 31.5 ppi

Source: Original draft

Weave Structures: Waffle weave and modified twill, Jacquard

Finishing: Heading of rib trimmed close and overlocked with sewing machine. Soaked for 60 minutes, machine washed in 105° water, air dried over rack, washed again at 140° and air dried.

Take-up and Shrinkage: Warp 19%, weft 31%

## Tips

• In placing the design, it is important to consider how two weave structures will join to avoid awkward floats at the meeting points. In the case of waffle weave, aligning the diagonals of the pattern motifs with the diagonal in the background weave pattern works well. This means an offset of seven, half the repeat length.

• It is sometimes difficult to see how to apply an idea from Jacquard weaving to shaft looms. In this case, each block of waffle weave will take eight shafts. If one were to choose a smaller waffle weave pattern, for example, on four shafts, then two blocks could be woven on eight shafts, and eight blocks on 32 shafts. The complexity of patterns which can be designed increases with the 4-shaft waffle, though the waffles are smaller and less dramatically indented than the 8-shaft version.

• Experiment with changes in the color sequence to create some of the same effects. Color changes are not independent, unlike shifting the block to a new set of shafts. That is, all the blocks on the same threading are fixed relative to each other, even if the color changes.

*Right Top, Component Threading Draft. Blue-dominant waffle weave as it would be woven on eight shafts.*

*Right Middle, Component Threading Draft. Offset green-dominant waffle weave as it would be woven on eight shafts.*

*Right Bottom, Component Threading Draft. Broken twill variant selvedges (dark blue in cartoon) as they would be woven on four shafts.*

*Left Top, Cartoon showing placement of the fish and one selvedge (dark blue).*

*Left Middle, Placement of blue-dominant background waffle weave.*

*Left Bottom, Placement of fish in green-dominant waffle weave with weft color striping added. The red line indicates approximately where the two structures meet.*

243

# Telltale

## Anie Toole

### Tea Towel in Twill, Waffle Weave, Brighton Weave, Woven Shibori, and Basket Weave

## Design Process

I have been testing different structures which distort when off the loom and sampling woven shibori in specific zones on the Jacquard loom. On the Jacquard looms, I tend to try out a bunch of things, all at once. We have two at school, threaded to a fixed width and needing to be reserved ahead of time. I'll be wanting to test different unrelated structures, shapes, joins and fibers for dyeing. I throw them all together into one Photoshop file and try it as is to maximize my weaving time. Sometimes I get a nice surprise, sometimes I need to read the elements separately. I use a lot of 8-shaft structures because they are quick to write out yet still interesting in their results.

My first thought for this project was to design a festive tea towel, an everyday object. I was thinking picnic gingham, another layer of polka dots, the date, and some absorbent spots. I made it to reflect the happy chaos of weeknight dinners with my family. I have three young boys and the intense family life affects all of my art projects in space and time. This towel looks pre-stained, and it is drawn like a child's drawing with a large paintbrush. Part of my process is to embrace the chaos and use found objects on my floor as shapes for extensively researched work. It is done somewhat ironically, including the two extremes of my academic and family lives.

The structures I used are straight 1/7 regular twill in the stripes, 8-shaft waffle weave in the "smudges," 8-shaft Brighton weave (honeycomb variant) for the date, balanced 2/2 chevron twill for the background, offset basket weave selvedges, and 4/4 twill for the hems, to be turned and top-stitched. The 1/7 twill decorative border uses a half-bleached hemp weft which was indigo resist-dyed, then used for every pick which included 1/7 twill, even if it was only one warp end. The hemp was tied with ikat tape as resist, then dipped in an indigo vat (Dean and Casselman, 2010; Maiwa Handprints Ltd., n.d.). The shibori pull threads are in a large 1/7 zigzag twill-type pattern, interspersed between the ground threads of the other structures. After dyeing, these polyester threads are removed (Ellis, 2016).

This was my first self-directed natural dyeing project. I look forward to more exploration and making the process more efficient. I will also be testing organic shapes and crimp cloth shibori in areas on the Jacquard looms.

## Weaving Information

Size: 27" x 24"

Warp: 16/2 mercerized cotton, 6720 ypp, black; 40 epi

Weft: 16/2 hemp, 6720 ypp, natural, half bleached, indigo dyed; 8/2 polyester, 3360 ypp, white (for shibori pull threads, removed after dyeing); 36 ppi

Source: Original

Weave Structures: Twill, waffle weave, Brighton weave, woven shibori, and basket weave; Jacquard

Finishing: After the woven shibori threads were pulled, the piece was scoured with Synthrapol soap for one hour and rinsed, then simmered 45 minutes with tannin: 8% WOF (weight of fiber) pomegranate extract; rinsed, simmered 45 minutes with mordant: 15% WOF alum; and rinsed, simmered 45 minutes with 6% WOF weld extract, and rinsed. Left to dry overnight; pull threads removed. Washed in warm water with Synthrapol and rinsed. Pressed when dry.

Take-up and Shrinkage: Warp 10%, weft 3%

Cartoon. Each color will have
a different structure.

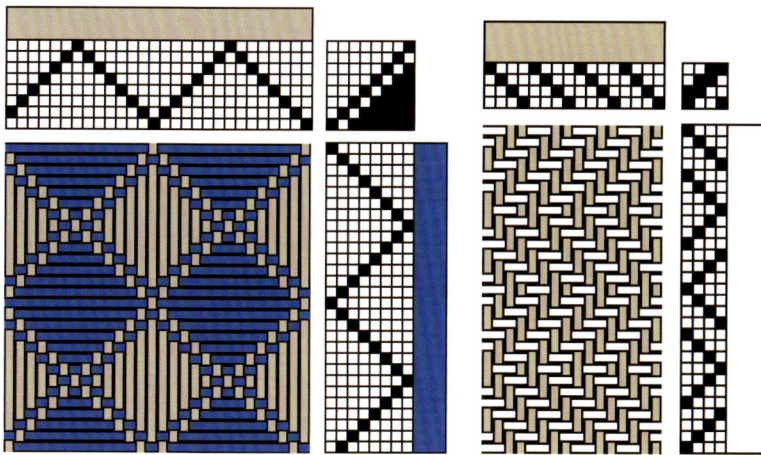

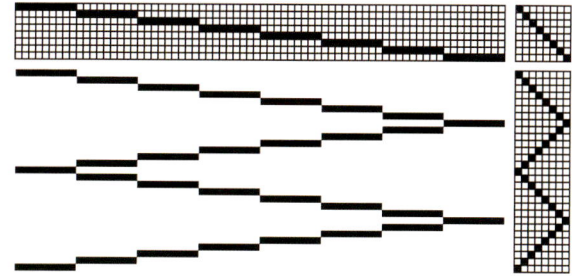

*Draft Component. Pattern for shibori pulling threads. In the final draft, the individual picks are interleaved with the other drafts after every eight picks. These threads are removed after dyeing.*

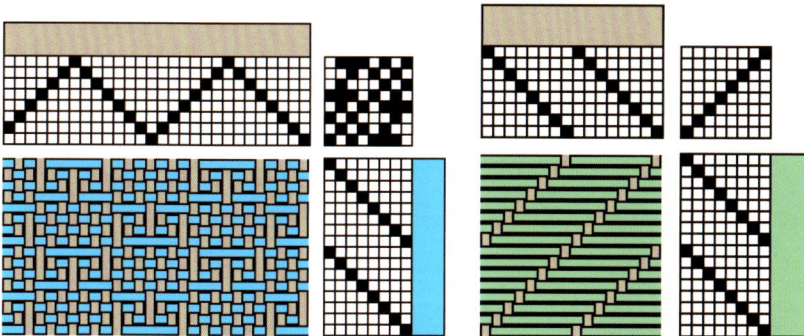

*Component Threading Drafts. Clockwise from upper left, waffle weave for "smudges," 2/2 chevron for background, 1/7 regular straight twill for border stripes, and Brighton weave (honeycomb) for date as they could be woven on a shaft loom. The weft colors relate to the area in the cartoon which they fill, not the actual weft colors. Separate drafts for basket weave selvedges (red in the cartoon) and 4/4 twill hems are not shown. The piece was woven sideways.*

## Tips

• Put tape or band-aids around your fingers before you get blisters when pulling the threads for the shibori resist. Double them if needed. Roll the thread around a bobbin to keep it tighter and pull as tight as possible.

• Find inspiration in the intersection of different aspects of your life. Cross-pollination is fertile ground for original work.

• Combining pre-resisted or painted warp and/or weft with loom-controlled shibori is a way to layer more patterning without extra shafts.

• Create texture through the combination of weave structures. Here, the very smooth twills, the deeply dimpled waffle weave, and the delicate pattern of the Brighton weave provide an interesting, tactile contrast. On a shaft loom they could be combined in stripes, blocks, or simple patterns depending on the effect desired and the number of shafts available. On an 8-shaft loom, one could work in smaller 4-shaft waffles, twills, and laces to give a similar effect.

*Threading Draft. Small portion of the final drawdown showing the waffle weave, 1/7 twill, 2/2 chevron twill, and shibori pulling threads.*

247

# Pyramid Magic
## Sheila O'Hara

### Wall Hanging in Weft-Backed Weaves (Twills, Satins, etc.)

### Design Process

In 2006 I was invited to go to Cairo to help Michael and Sevinch Deman get their new AVL Jacq2G Jacquard hand loom working for making passementerie. Bill Fredriksson, my husband, was able to go with me. On the first day off, we travelled to the Pyramid Complex in Giza. While inside the Great Pyramid, the lights went out but we continued on to the King's Chamber using Bill's handy "torch." We found ourselves alone in the chamber. We lay down on our backs on the floor in the center of the room and turned out our light. Bill heard an indescribable sound of the universe. I had a vision of a night sky filled with stars and beams of light outlining the edges of the Pyramid. This was followed by still images of artisans from the past - flax harvesters, flax spinners, weavers of linen cloth, stone masons, architects, and papyrus makers. It was an amazing experience!

In 2016, I began vividly remembering my 2006 trip as I listened to a book on CD about fictitious adventures set in Howard Carter's Egypt. I was inspired to capture my vision in a Jacquard tapestry - Pyramid Magic. I enjoyed the challenge of designing with realistic and abstract elements together.

Starting in 2000 with simple 8-shaft satins, twills, and pick and pick weaves, I learned how to turn them into three-shuttle weaves from Nina Jacobs and Cathy Bolding. In 2008, I began using a 16-shaft advancing point twill draft from Bonnie Inouye for the single weft borders on some of my weavings. Then, in ArahWeave, I converted it to the triple-weft weave that you can see in the background in "Pyramid Magic." With three wefts, you can get weft-faced cloth in color a, b or c with the other two wefts showing on the back side. With pick and pick you can have a and b, b and c, or c and a together, with the third weft showing on the back side. The three wefts change colors throughout the three panels. There are 18 blends that shade from blue to orange, plus purples and natural. There is also a very thin gold lurex yarn wound with the shades of orange cotton and a very thin dark blue lurex yarn wound with the shades of blue. There are about twenty weaves used in "Pyramid Magic" (not all shown). To finish, I added about 2" of half-basket weave hems. The piece was woven on an AVL Jacq2G Jacquard hand loom using the loom driver software JacqPoint, with 655 total warp ends.

People seem to have their own interpretation of this piece which is always fun and sometimes surprising. My idea for the future: Have more visions!

248

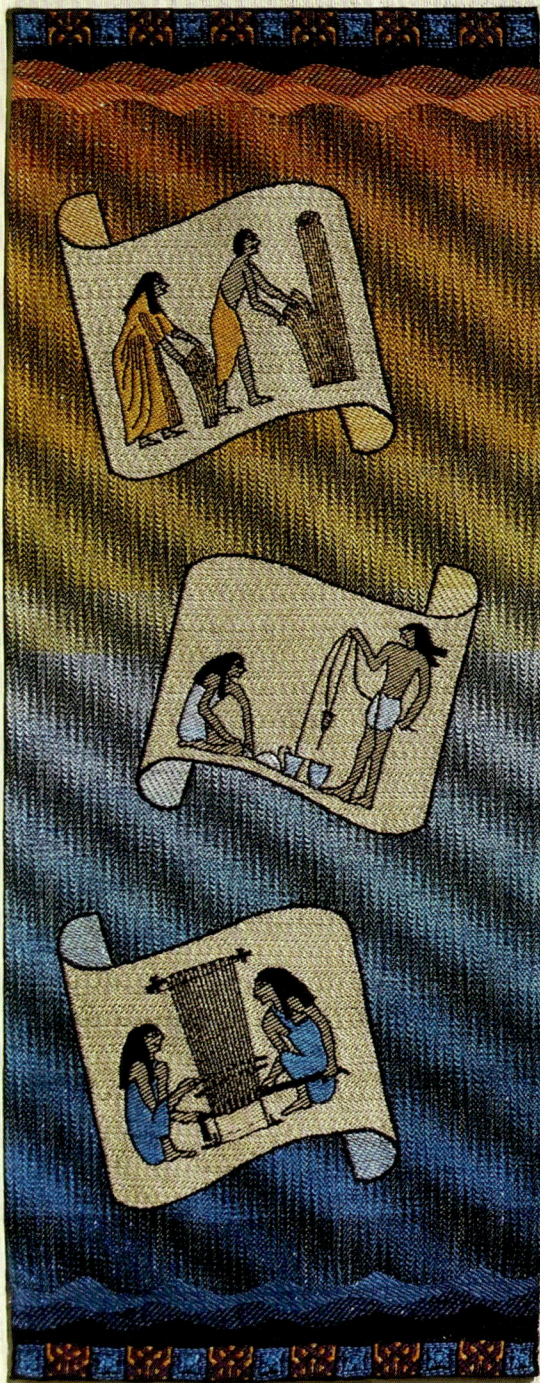

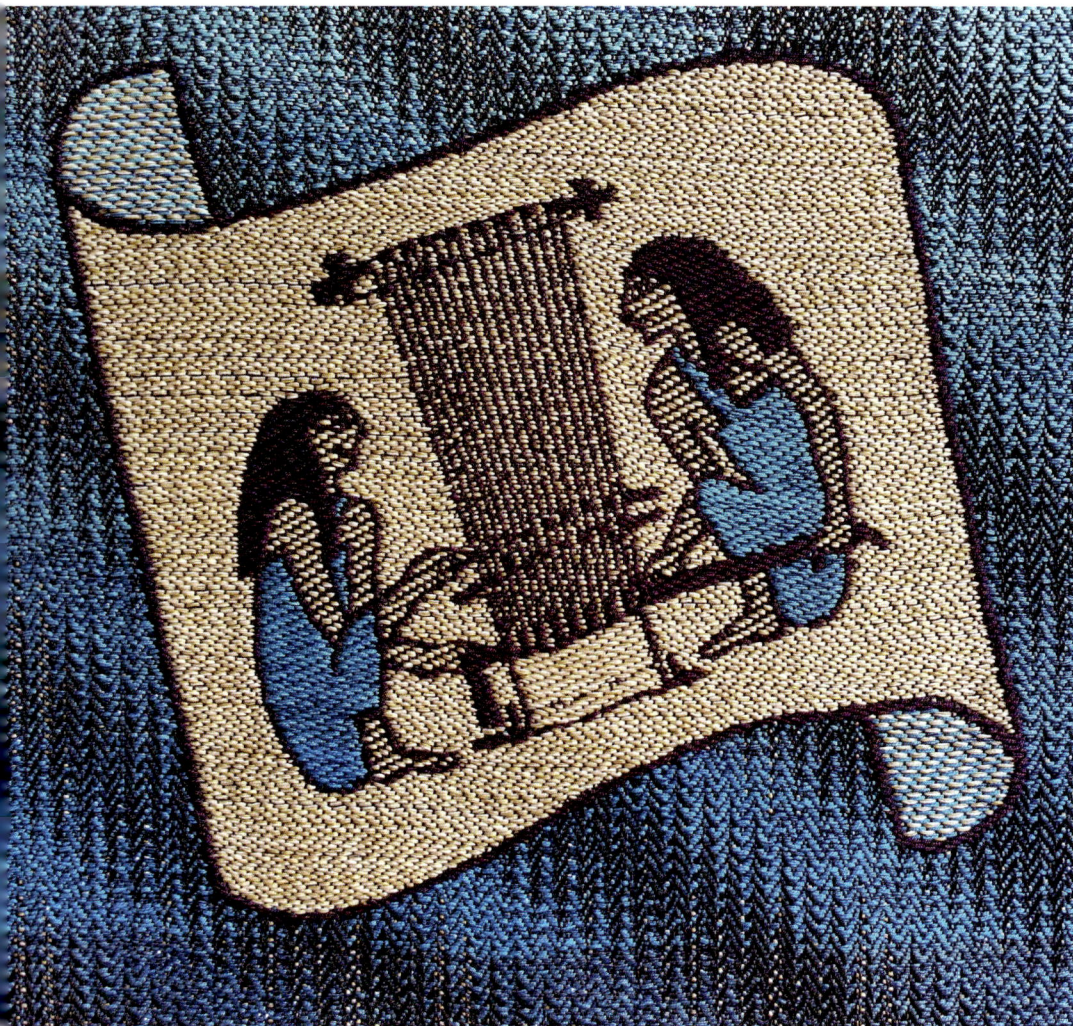

## Weaving Information

Size: Outside panels 51" x 20", center panel 52"x 20"

Warp: 10/2 mercerized cotton, 4200 ypp, black; 30 epi

Weft: 10/2 mercerized cotton, 4200 ypp, two ends wound together on bobbins, 18 blends that shade from blue to orange, purples, and natural; very thin gold lurex yarn wound with the shades of orange cotton and a very thin dark blue lurex yarn wound with the shades of blue; 62 ppi

Source: Original draft

Weave Structures: Weft-backed weaves in twills, satins, etc. (3-weft system); Jacquard

Finishing: Two inches in half-basket weave, using a single 10/2 cotton weft woven at top and bottom of each weaving. Hem is folded twice and stitched to form sleeve for hanging rod.

Draw-in: Weft 8%

## Tips

• To make pieces like these ready for installation, weave a 2" hem in half the weight of the body weft. Machine stitch a ¼" hem. Fold it over a second time and pin it in place. Stitch "in the ditch" of the top and bottom hems on the front of the fabric where the design ends and the border begins. Place a ¼" solid metal rod in the bottom hem that is 1/2" narrower than the width of the weaving, and close the side openings with hand sewing. Then, place a 5/16" aluminum tube in the top hem. Tape a 4-ply rug wool yarn, cut to three times the width of the weaving, to a 1/8" thick metal rod and run the rod through the opening in the tube, centering the yarn. Pull the two ends of the yarn tight and tie an overhand knot, leave a 1" space, and then a second overhand knot. Hang the cord so that the nail goes between the two knots.

• One way to think of Jacquard weaving is like a "weave by number" scenario. Each heddle (or hook) can be lifted individually, so there can be many different interlacements across one continuous weft pick. Create a graphic design with each area of the design having a flat color. Then, assign a weave to each of the colors. The colors in the design do not necessarily match the weft colors, they just enable placement of the chosen structures.

• Shade by grading the weft colors as you weave along. Add sparkle or interest by combining yarns with different reflectivities.

• Make sure you have lots of friends who are weavers so you can ask them questions when needed!

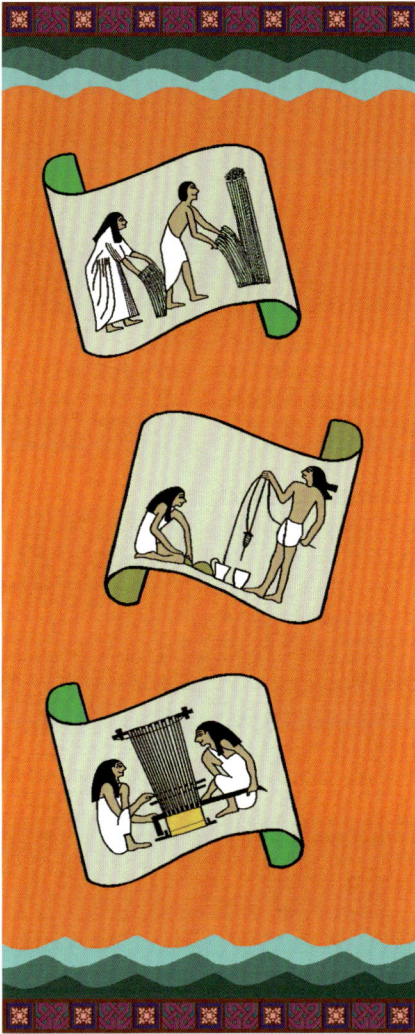

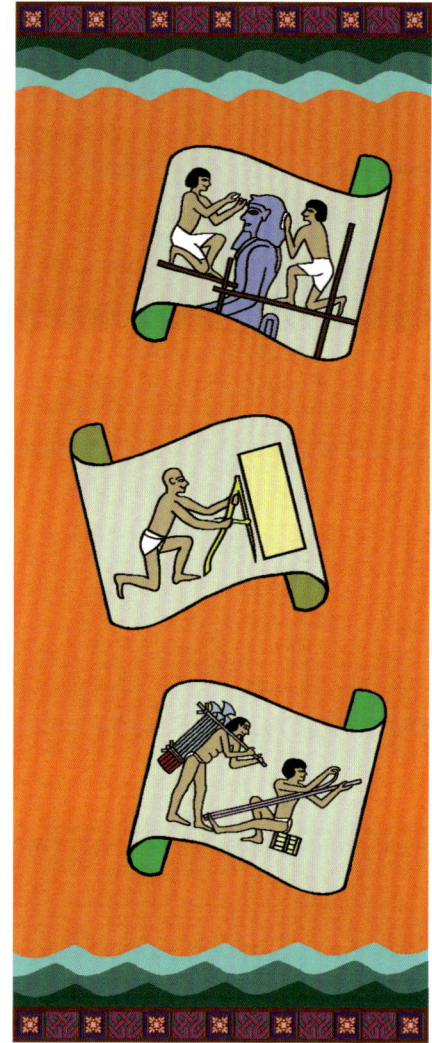

*Three Panel Cartoons. Each color will be assigned its own structure. The colors in the cartoon may or may not match the actual colors in the weaving.*

*Threading Drawdown. Portion of the left panel as a drawdown in ArahWeave Fabric Simulation Mode. Created in ArahWeave by assigning a chosen weave structure to each color in the cartoon, using the designated warp and weft colors, densities, and yarn types.*

251

*Component Threading Drafts. An 8-shaft 1:7 satin was interleaved with a 16-shaft 15:1 satin for a final draft with blue pattern weft and stitchers of purple and orange (compare to top of next page).*

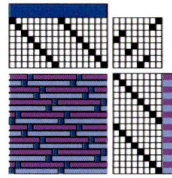

## Draft Development

These three pages demonstrate the development of seven of the twenty drafts used to create the structures in the hangings. Each final draft is created by interleaving two simpler drafts, with all three shown separately as if they were to be woven alone on a shaft loom. The colors have been modified for visibility.

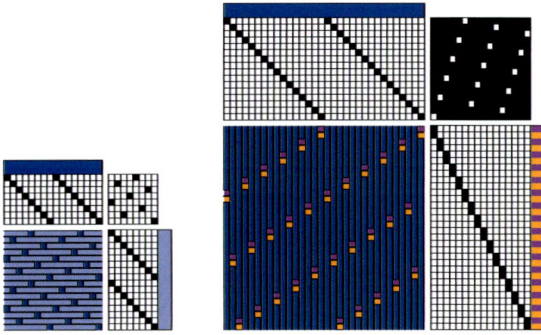

*Component Threading Drafts. An 8-shaft 1:7 satin with paired colors was interleaved with a 16-shaft 15:1 satin for a final draft with blended blue and purple pattern weft and stitchers of purple, orange, and blue.*

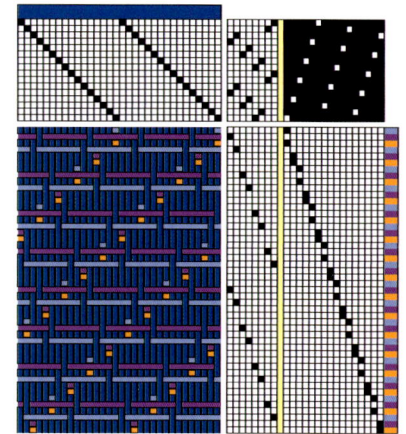

*Component Threading Drafts. An 8-shaft 7:1 satin with blue weft was interleaved with a 32-shaft 31:1 satin for a final draft with no pattern weft and stitchers of purple, orange, and blue.*

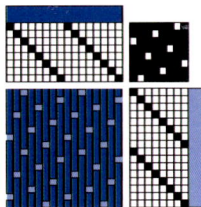

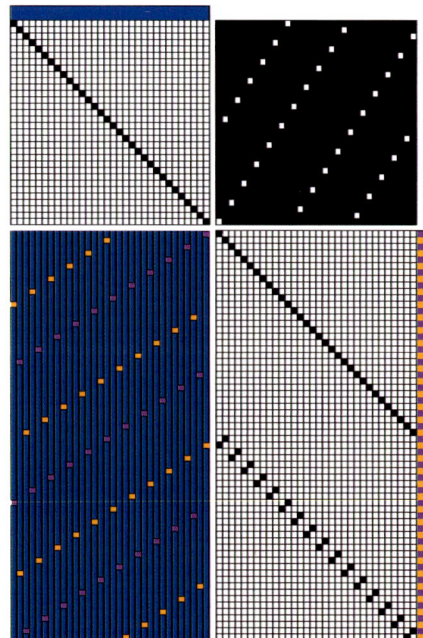

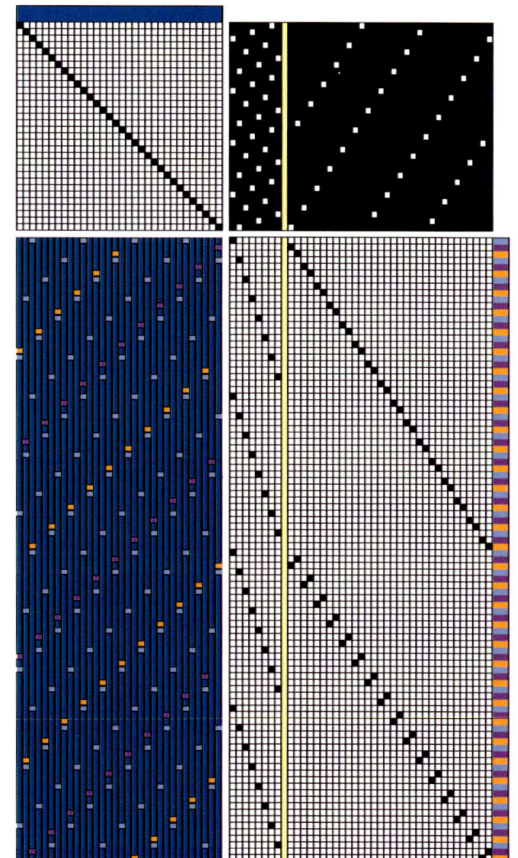

*Right, Component Threading Drafts. An undulating 16-shaft twill was interleaved with an irregular 16-shaft partial 15:1 satin for a final draft with orange pattern weft and stitchers of blue and purple.*

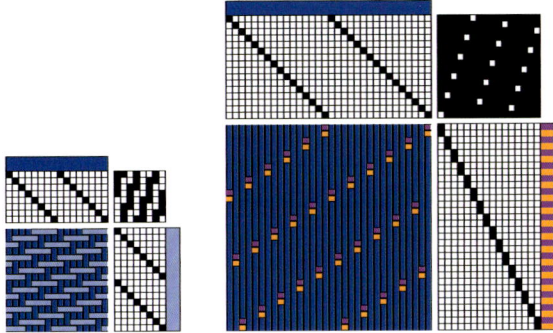

*Component Threading Drafts. An 8-shaft 4:4 satin was interleaved with a 16-shaft 15:1 satin for a final draft with blue pattern weft and stitchers of purple and orange.*

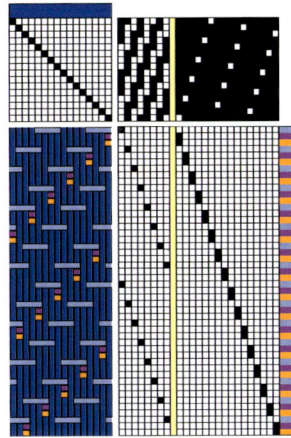

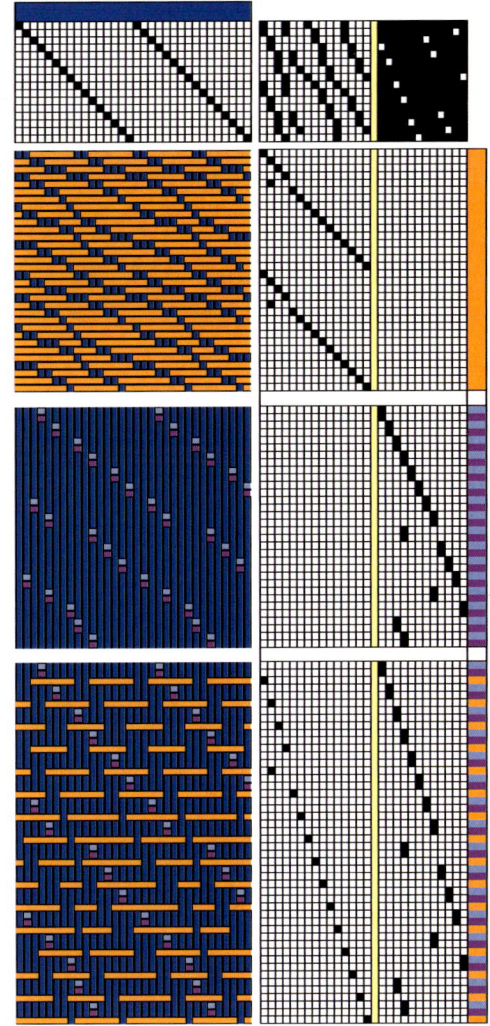

*Component Threading Drafts. An irregular 6-shaft 1:5 satin was inter-leaved with an irregular 12-shaft 11:1 satin (Fressinet, 1905) for a final draft with natural pattern weft and stitchers of purple and blue.*

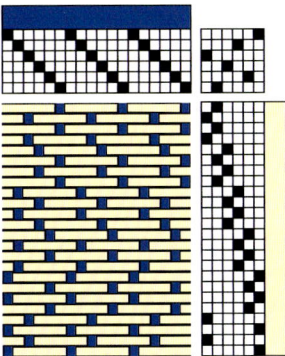

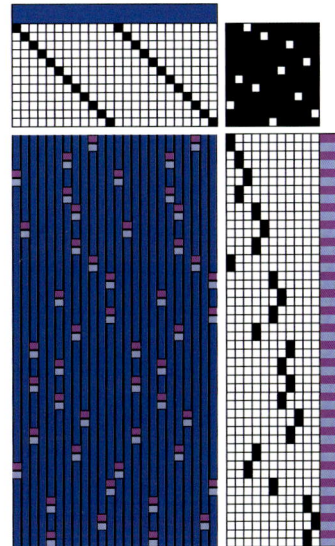

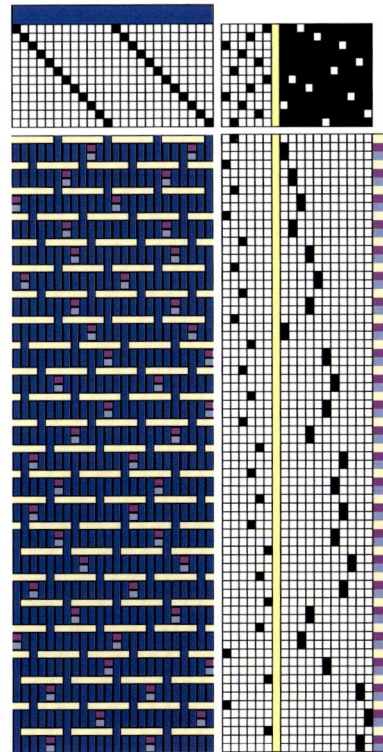

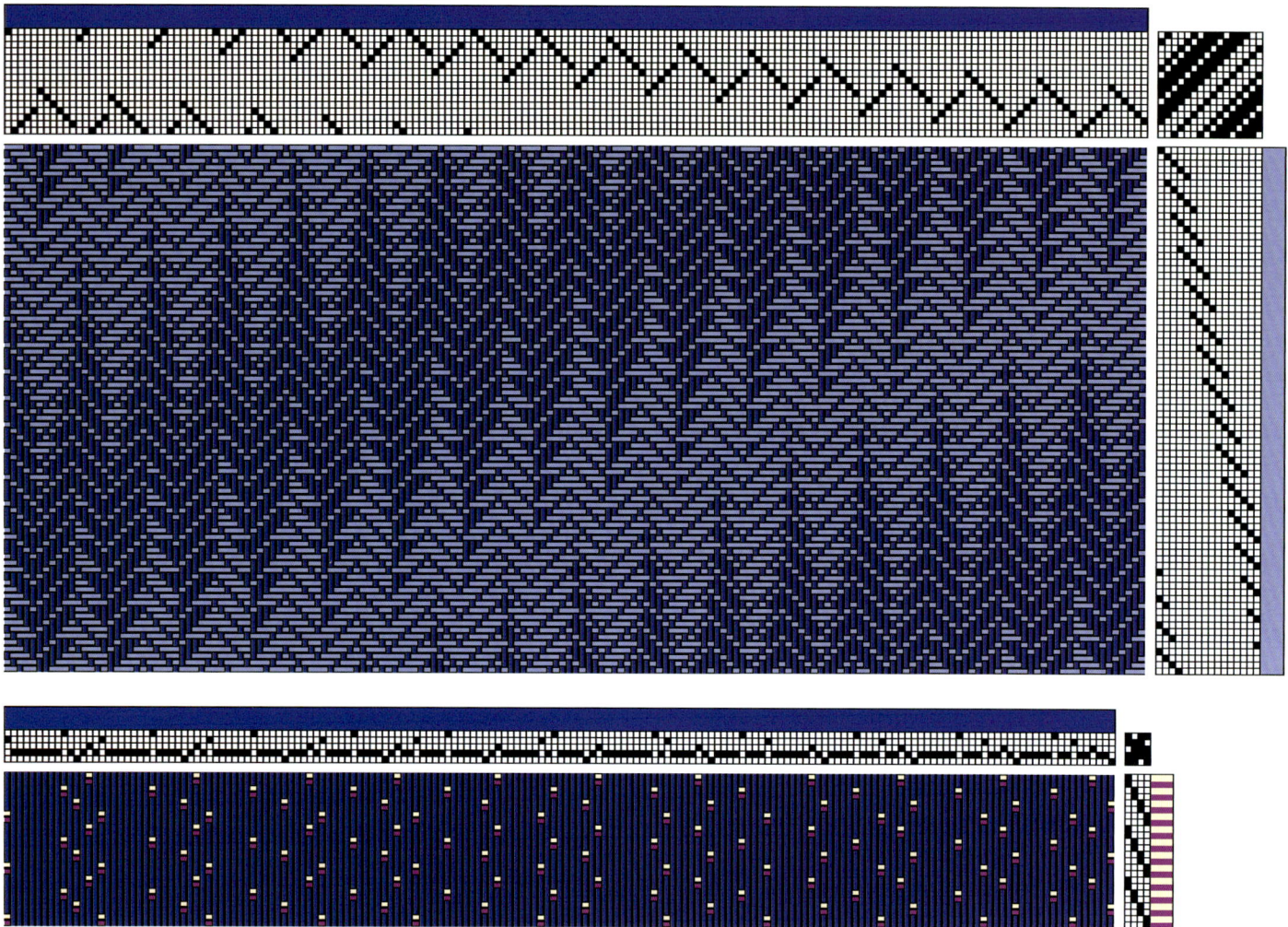

Component Threading Drafts.

Top, 16-shaft advancing twill for the aqua weft with a 3/1/3/1/1/3/1/3 regular twill tie-up. The warp is an 8-shaft herringbone figure which advances by 1 on the repeat. The weft is a straight 5-shaft run which also advances by 1 on each repeat.

Middle, The stitchers in natural and purple wefts form an irregular pattern.

Bottom, A portion of the interleaved drawdown with blue pattern weft and natural and purple stitchers, shown with the actual warp color (black) and aspect ratio. This draft could be woven by itself on 40 shafts.

Note: In all but the last of these drafts, the black warp is shown as dark blue to aid in visualization. Additionally, the weft colors shift along the length of each woven piece.

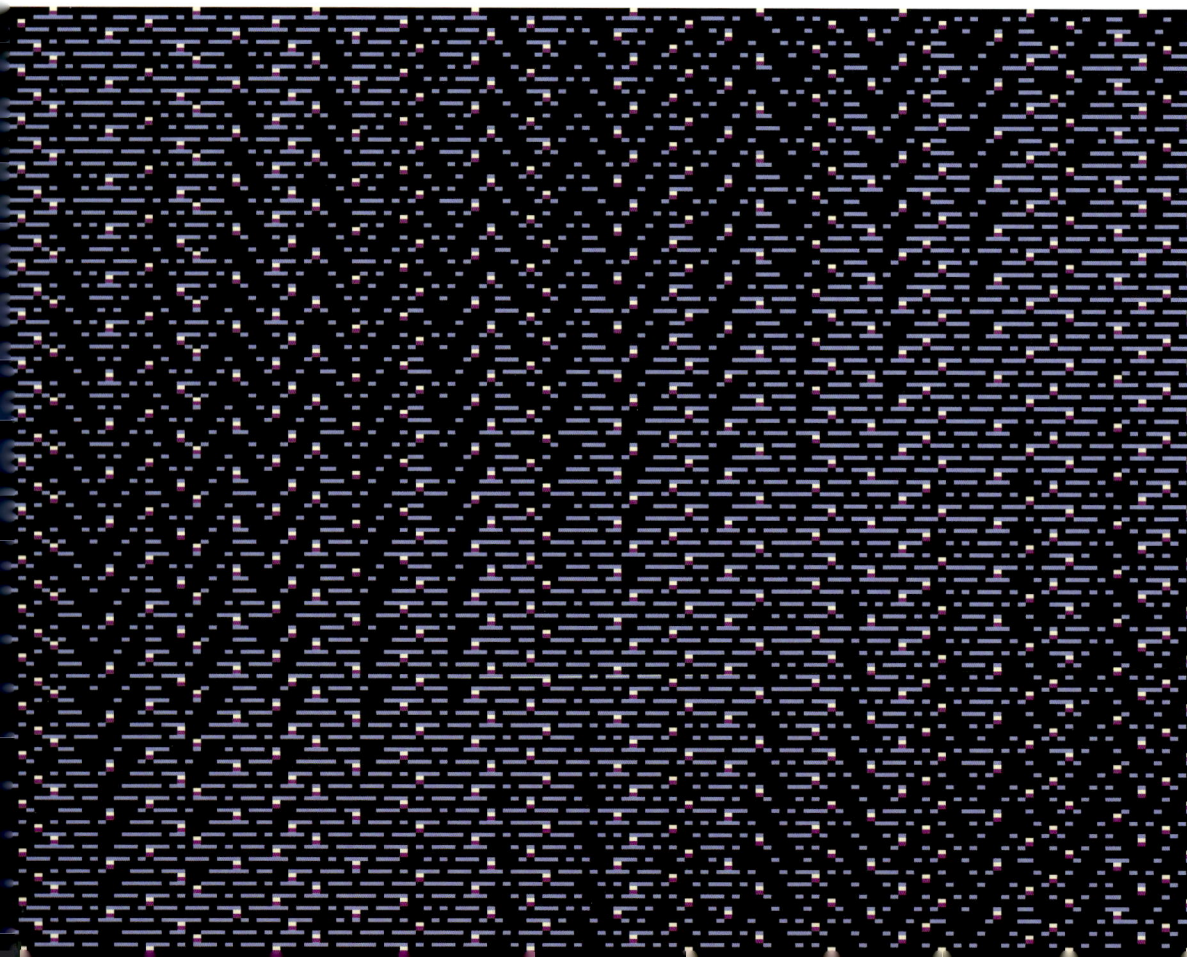

# Glossary

*For more information on individual structures and techniques, see Burnham (1982), Emery (1995), Inouye (2000), Keasbey (1993, 2005), Oelsner (1952), van der Hoogt (1993), and other resources in the References section. Please note that many words are used differently, regionally and over time.*

**Advancing** — A system whereby a sequence of threading or treadling, whether individual threads or blocks, is advanced, or shifted, in a sequential manner on each repeat. Repeating straight lines, as in the first example, are called runs. In the first threading, a threading of 1-2-3-4-5, then 2-3-4-5-6, then 3-4-5-6-7, and so on, has a shift of 1 and run of 5. Much more complex patterns may also be advanced in warp and weft. In the second threading, a curved figure has a shift of 2.

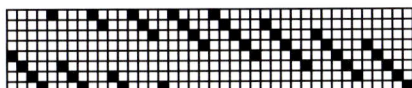

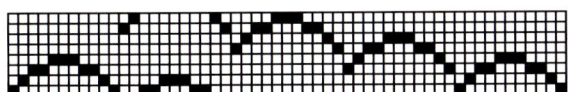

**Asymmetry** — A special case of symmetry without reflections (mirrors), rotations, or glide reflections (half-drops, or mirror and move). It may or may not repeat.

**Balanced Weave** — Having the same epi and ppi.

**Binding** — Generally refers to the interlacement of the warp and weft threads. A binding thread may also be a warp thread that interlaces with a weft pattern thread, such as in lampas, or a set of picks used like tabby to provide additional interlacement and stability to a piece.

**Blended Draft** — A single draft which is composed of two or more threading drafts combined in such a way that each of the original drafts can be woven. For example, a huck threading can be blended with an overshot threading and either the huck lace or the overshot can be woven on the same threading, but not at the same time in the same row of the fabric.

**Block** — A group of threads which act together to weave pattern or background. Common block weaves include summer and winter, twill blocks, and overshot. Simple twills, satins, and plain weave are not block weaves.

**Cartoon** — A simplified drawing showing placement of color, structure, and/or pattern.

**Color-and-Weave** — The use of color in the warp and/or weft to create a pattern different from the pattern caused by the weave structure. Generally, the colors are arranged in some specific order and frequently alternate light and dark hues. One common example is shadow weave.

**Complementary Warp or Weft Ends** — Two or more sets of threads which work together in the warp or weft to complete one function. Neither set can be removed without damaging the integrity of the cloth. Examples include the wefts in boundweave, taqueté, samitum, swivel, and the warps in their turned variants. In some structures and traditions the group working together may be called a passée or pass.

**Design Line** — A line, curve, or other pattern used to produce networked drafts. The term is also sometimes used for a non-networked design that is the basis for further manipulation, such as interleaving. Sometimes called the "pattern line."

**Direct Tie-Up** — A system of connecting one treadle or lever to one shaft. Typically, treadle or lever 1 is tied to shaft 1, treadle or lever 2 to shaft 2, and so on. In order to raise more than one shaft, more than one treadle or lever must be activated simultaneously. For example, to raise shafts 1 and 3, the treadles or levers 1 and 3 would be used. No lamms are used in order to allow the treadles to work independently.

**Double Weave View** — A drawdown showing only one layer (usually the top) of a cloth with two or more layers.

**Draft** — A representation of the threading, tie-up, treadling, and drawdown (or drawup). In a threading draft, it illustrates the interlacement of the warp and weft threads. In a profile draft, it indicates pattern placement.

**Draft Component** — In this book, some drafts are formed by combining two or more drafts or patterns. For example, when two drafts are alternated in an interleaved draft, each has been considered a component of the final draft. Other examples of components include layers in double weave and complex 8-shaft tie arrangements and the pattern groups they tie.

**Drawloom** — A loom having two or more harnesses, each with two or more shafts, other draw pulls, or a combination. The ground harness typically controls the weave structure, such as twill or satin. The pattern harness is used to create the design. There are two common types of draw arrangements. In a shaft-draw system each thread goes through two heddles on two different shafts, one pattern and one ground. In the skillbragd variant, a warp end goes through none, one, or more pattern heddles on pattern shafts plus a ground shaft heddle. In contrast, a figure harness or single-unit draw uses pulls attached to individual pattern heddles or small groups of adjacent heddles. Each thread still goes through two heddles, but the pattern heddles are not grouped onto shafts, allowing greater design freedom.

Echo — Echo threadings and treadlings are a form of interleaving which result from shifting two or more copies of the same design line by a fixed number of shafts or treadles. This is a design technique rather than a structure. The final structure, as always, depends on the interaction of threading, treadling, and tie-up. In the example, an advancing threading curve in aqua is echoed by one in magenta. The magenta curve is shifted four shafts from the aqua curve.

End — One warp thread.

Enlarged Point — A general term for a point which extends past the number of shafts or blocks used before reversing direction. This group includes goose eye and rosepath twills.

EPI — Ends per inch, referring to the number of warp threads in one inch of the reed. If using metric measurements then one would use epc, or ends per centimeter.

To convert from epi to epc, divide the epi number by 2.54 and round accordingly. For example, to convert 24 epi to epc:
24/2.54 = 9.4488 or approximately 9 epc.

To convert from epc to epi, multiply the epc number by 2.54 and round accordingly. For example, to convert 9 epc to epi:
9 x 2.54 = 22.86 or approximately 23 epi.

Expanded Draft — In this book, a draft where colored lines are inserted between tie-downs, binding (tabby), and pattern or sections of pattern in warp, weft, and tie-up, or between blocks or layers, or groups of blocks. The lines do not show in the drawdown. Used to aid understanding of how the draft works. The 8-shaft summer and winter example has been expanded with horizontal blue lines to separate tie-down and pattern shafts in the warp and tie-up, and vertical blue lines to separate tabby, tie-down, and pattern combinations in the tie-up and skeleton treadling.

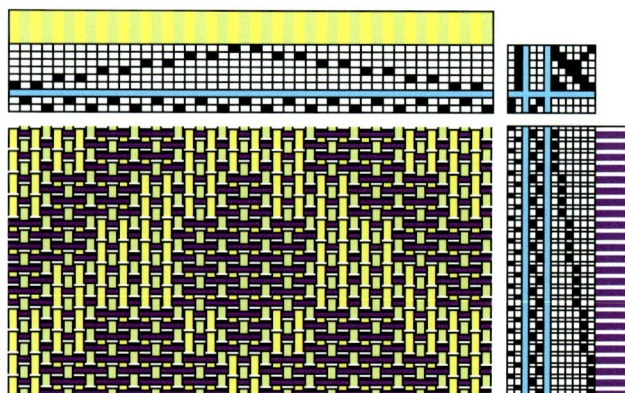

Extended Twill — As used in this book, a twill which repeats pairs of shafts or treadles to extend the twill line. It can give a block effect, or sometimes be used as blocks. Commonly used in overshot threadings. The threading example shows a simple straight line versus an irregularly extended line.

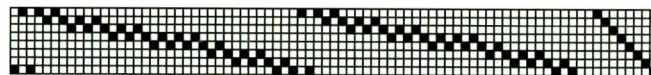

Half Unit, Quarter Unit — When pattern changes before a full unit is completed, one can create half, quarter, and other fractions of a unit. If the pattern change is not always a full unit but is always an even multiple of half of the unit, it is called a half unit. If it is always an even multiple of a quarter of the unit, but not of a full or half unit, it is a quarter unit. Half units are common in summer and winter and other tied unit weaves, 8-shaft satins, etc. In a tied weave, they require an even split of both tie-down and pattern threads and a regularly repeating tie pattern to work neatly. The benefit of fractional units is that they reduce the scale of the design, decrease pixelation, and may allow finer detailing. Not completing the full unit before changing pattern usually causes some irregularities in the appearance of the blocks which should be considered when choosing the fraction to be used.

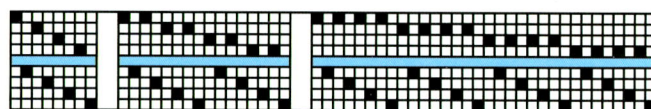

*quarter unit*   *half unit*          *full unit*

Harness — A group of shafts or individual or grouped heddles performing the same task (creating pattern or ground cloth) in a drawloom. Most common looms are single harness and contain two or more shafts within that harness. A standard loom with eight shafts is a single-harness, 8-shaft loom. Sometimes used interchangeably with shaft, as in "8-harness loom," but technically this is incorrect. See Shaft.

Incidental — A warp or weft thread inserted at the end of some but not all blocks to finish the block and allow a smooth, usually odd-even, transition to the next block. Most commonly used in crackle and Swedish lace. It may also refer to a block used similarly in a profile draft.

Initial — The fundamental basis of network drafting. When repeated horizontally and vertically to form a network, it acts as a representation of all possible threading or treadling positions on an underlying structure. Often expressed in terms of the number of shafts required for the base structure ("initial of #"), which does not need to match the number of shafts used in the piece. Thus, an "initial of 8" has a base of eight shafts. While the initial is most often a straight arrangement, point, satin, and other arrangements are also possible.

Interlacement View — A drawdown outlining the edges of the warp and weft threads for easier visualization (*left*).

Interleave — Alternate two or more patterns, or copies of a single pattern, in the warp and/or weft where one (or more) threads or blocks from one draft is followed by one (or more) threads or blocks from the second. Three, four, or more patterns may be interleaved in a similar way. While 1:1 alternations (below) are most common, 1:2, 2:2, and many other arrangements are possible.

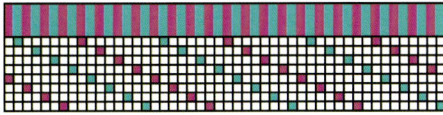

Interval — The distance between the two parallel or echoed lines, sometimes used synonymously with "shift" and occasionally "offset." In determining satin counters, this is the difference between the shaft (or sometimes block) used on adjacent treadles. In the parallel threading above, there is an interval of 4 (1+4=5) between the aqua and magenta lines.

Irregular Block Weave — A block weave which is not consistent in some way, generally requiring an incidental thread between some blocks but not others. Common examples include crackle and Swedish lace.

Irregular Twill Tie-Up — A twill tie-up where the pattern is not the same for each treadle. Irregular twill tie-ups used on a straight twill threading and treadling will form some discontinuous diagonal lines in the fabric even when there are no skips in the twill threading and treadling. In the example, one diagonal warp line is continuous; the other is not. Use of this kind of tie-up does not mean that the resulting fabric is a twill; as always, the final structure depends on the combination of threading, treadling, and tie-up. It is often used in profile drafts as well as threading drafts. Sometimes called an irregular diagonal tie-up.

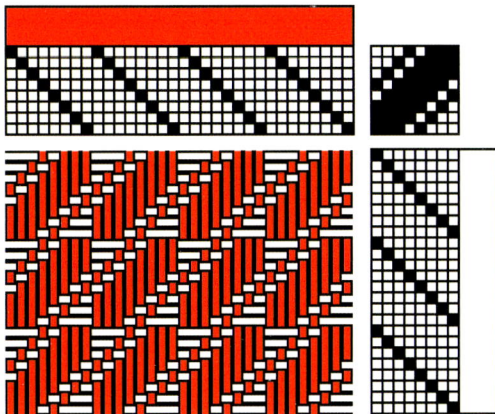

Irregular Unit Weave — A block weave which has some of the characteristics of a unit weave but not all. It may require an incidental to repeat blocks, or the blocks may not be fully independent (that is, something may happen automatically in one block when another is woven as pattern). Common examples include crackle and Swedish lace.

Jacquard Loom — A loom which has the ability to control each thread individually, rather than in groups. Older looms used punch cards to control thread selection; modern looms use a computer to select the threads forming a shed.

Lace Weaves — Weaves based on plain weave with floats in the weft and/or warp. They are generally woven balanced and the finished fabric deflects to accommodate the pattern floats and plain weave background. Examples include huck, Swedish lace, Atwater-Bronson lace (a.k.a. lace Bronson), and spot Bronson. In the canvas variation of these weaves, all pattern threads are doubled.

Liftplan — A representation of the treadling which indicates the shafts (in a threading draft) or blocks (in a profile draft) used in each row of the treadling, rather than through use of a tie-up. For example, in order to activate shafts 1, 4 and 7 to create a shed, a row of the liftplan would have entries in columns 1, 4 and 7. A liftplan is frequently used for computer-aided weaving, pick-up patterns, and for table looms. Compare the 8-shaft summer and winter example (*left*) to the same treadling shown under the entry for skeleton tie-ups.

Long-eyed Heddle — A special heddle with longer than ordinary eye openings used on the pattern harness shafts in a drawloom. The longer eye is necessary to provide adequate traveling room for warp threads to go through both of the heddles on both harnesses.

Mirror — Bilaterally symmetric across a line, e.g., left and right handed. One way to make a mirror in weaving is to create an exact reversal in the threading and/or treadling.

Ms and Vs — A double point of any size which alternates with an inverted single point, looking like an M and a V.

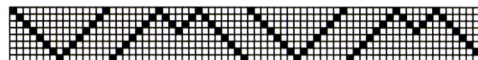

Ms and Ws — A double point of any size which inverts on each repeat, looking like an M and a W.

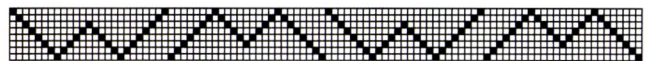

Network Drafting — A draft in which the threading and/or treadling sequences have been developed on a grid of regularly repeating initials (see initial). It is often used to create long, smooth curves which would otherwise extend over more shafts rather than blocky designs. Edges tend to be blurred rather than sharp.

257

**Offset** — A change in the starting point of a pattern which is interleaved with itself. The orange line of the threading example is offset by six threads from the blue line. Sometimes used synonymously with shift.

**On Opposites** — A technique typically used with two pattern shuttles of differing colors. Each weft pick with the first shuttle is followed by its opposite weft pick with the second shuttle. Every pattern shaft raised for the first pick will be lowered for the next pick, and every pattern shaft lowered for the first pick will be raised for the second pick. If it is used with a weave with tie-down shafts, there is a choice of whether to use the same tie-down for both picks or the opposite. A tabby or other binding may or may not be used. The fabric is usually dense and weft-dominant.

**Parallel** — Straight lines that follow a similar path, always the same distance apart from each other. That is, they are always offset by the same number of shafts or treadles, or the equivalent in a profile draft. In the example, three parallel lines in different colors are always the same distance apart.

**Pattern Threads** — Form the main design in warp and weft. There may be a second kind of thread, a tie-down, which forms a base structure (see tie-down and tabby). In this book, the pattern shafts are on higher numbers of the threading draft and the pattern treadles are generally to the right.

**Pick** — One weft thread.

**Polychrome** — Weaving a single pattern line with three or more continuous wefts of different colors. For example, in a pattern with three blocks, in a single group of wefts, the A block might be red, the B, purple, and the C, blue. Simply shifting the color order without changing the treadling changes the color associated with the block. A tabby or other binding may or may not be used. The fabric usually has a dense, weft-dominant pattern. Depending on how the sheds are arranged, the wrong side of the fabric may have long floats.

**PPI** — Picks per inch, refers to the number of weft threads that are in one inch of woven fabric on the loom. If using metric measurements then one would refer to ppc, or picks per centimeter. The conversions for ppi and ppc are similar to those for epi and epc.

To convert from ppi to ppc, divide the ppi number by 2.54 and round accordingly. For example, to convert 24 ppi to ppc:
24/2.54 = 9.4488 or approximately 9 ppc.

To convert from ppc to ppi, multiply the ppc number by 2.54 and round accordingly. For example, to convert 9 ppc to ppi:
9 x 2.54 = 22.86 or approximately 23 ppi.

**Profile Draft** — A special draft for block weaves which indicates the placement of pattern and background (or a second pattern) in the cloth rather than the interlacement of individual threads (see threading draft). That is, each square indicates a group of threads working together rather than a single thread. Typically, the blocks are labelled A, B, C, etc. In this book, a black square in the drawdown indicates pattern occurring in that block unless otherwise indicated. Profile drafts can be converted to threading drafts in any block structure which is compatible with the design constraints.

**Regular Twill Tie-Up** — Sometimes called a plain twill tie-up or a diagonal tie-up, where the ordering of the interlacements is simple and unvaried. That is, each treadle has the same pattern, simply shifted by one shaft up or down relative to its neighbor. Regular twill tie-ups used with twill threadings and treadlings without skips will form continuous diagonal lines in the fabric. The pattern can be abbreviated by a set of numbers, shown in this book in the form Up/Down/Up/Down/etc. For example, a regular 3/3/1/1 tie-up has three shafts up, three down, one up, one down. Use of this kind of tie-up does not mean that the resulting fabric is a twill. As always, the final structure depends on the combination of threading, treadling, and tie-up. These tie-ups are often used in profile drafts as well as threading drafts.

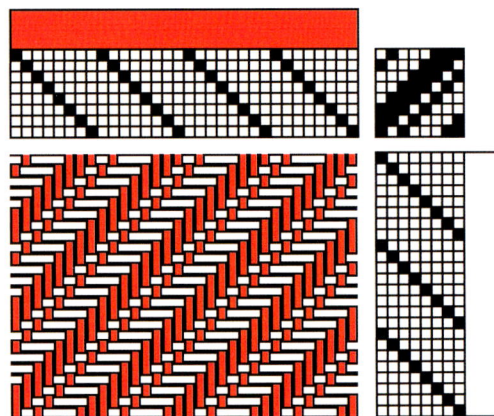

**Satin Tie-Up and Counter** — A systematically rearranged regular twill (or diagonal) tie-up. The counter marks the shift of shafts on adjacent treadles. In the 8-shaft tie-up example, the satin has a counter of 3. Use of this kind of tie-up does not mean that the resulting fabric is a satin. As always, the final structure depends on the combination of threading, treadling, and tie-up. Satin tie-ups are sometimes used in profile drafts as well as threading drafts.

**Shaft** — A frame that is fitted with heddles. When a warp thread is passed through the eye of a heddle it is controlled by that shaft and will be raised or lowered with all the other threads on that shaft. Sometimes the word harness is also used to refer to a shaft, as in "8-harness loom," but technically this is incorrect (see harness).

**Shift** — See interval and offset. A general word for a change between adjacent items or repeating patterns.

**Skeleton Tie-Up** — A tie-up where more than one treadle may be used concurrently, and allowing more than one shaft to be tied to a treadle. Often used when tie-downs are added in different combinations to the pattern treadles in a treadling sequence, as in summer and winter and similar tied weaves. In the summer and winter example (*left*), the tie-downs on shafts 1 and 2 operate independently and are used as needed with a pattern treadle (treadles 5 through 10). This frees up more treadles for pattern sheds. These tie-ups are also used in other structures to increase the number of available pattern sheds on a treadle loom. Compare this example to the same treadling shown under liftplan.

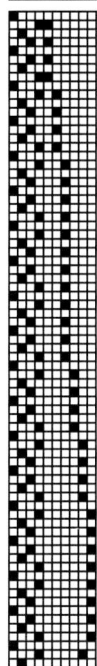

**Supplementary Warp or Weft Ends** (sometimes called supplemental) — A thread which may be removed from the warp or weft without disturbing the integrity of the cloth. Examples include the weft pattern threads in summer and winter and other similar tied unit weaves, overshot, and crackle.

**Symmetry** — The rules governing generation of a consistent pattern. The different symmetries are made by some combination of the four symmetry operations: repetition (translation), reflection (mirroring or reversals), rotation, and/ or glide reflection (a.k.a. half-drop, or mirror and move).

**Tabby** — A weft thread which goes over one then under one warp thread. The tabby weft may alternate or be regularly interspersed with a pattern weft so that an overall background structure of plain weave is formed. Typically used with overshot or other block weaves. Tabby may or may not be shown on a draft. When a draft says, "Use tabby (not shown)" insert alternating picks of tabby between pattern picks. When used alone, without a pattern weft, the correct term is plain weave rather than tabby.

**Threading** — In a threading draft, a visual representation of the sequence of the warp threads through the shafts on the loom. In a profile draft, it represents the order of the blocks in the warp. The number of rows corresponds to the number of shafts or blocks being used; each row corresponds to a particular shaft or block. The number of columns corresponds to the number of warp threads or blocks.

**Threading Draft** — A draft which represents the way individual threads interlace. In this book, if color has not been used, black indicates a warp thread on the surface and white, a weft thread on the surface. Also called simply a draft, or a thread-by-thread draft.

**Tie-Downs** — In tied weaves, threads which always weave the background structure. The tie-down threads function to keep the float length shorter and usually end the block. In this book, they are threaded on the front shafts.

**Tie-Up** — In a threading draft, the shafts tied to each treadle are indicated in the tie-up. Each column is associated with a treadle and each row with a shaft. In a profile draft, the tie-up indicates the blocks weaving pattern together. Each column is associated with a treadling block and each row with a threading block.

**Tied Weaves** — Weaves which have two or more sets of threads with specific functions. One set, the pattern threads, will weave pattern or background as needed. The other set, the tie-downs, always weave the background structure. Usually, the tie-down threads function to keep the float length shorter and end the block. Tied weaves may use a supplementary pattern weft or warp, such as the unit-weaves summer and winter, half satin, and their turned variants. Additionally, laces and other non-supplementary tied weaves may use tie-down threads and may or may not be unit weaves.

**Treadling** — In a threading draft, a visual representation of the sheds and the order in which they are used. In a profile draft, it represents the sequence of block combinations used in the weft. The number of rows corresponds to the number of picks or blocks being used; each row corresponds a particular pick or block. The number of columns corresponds to the number of shafts or different warp blocks.

**Tromp as Writ** — A treadling sequence which specifies that the treadles or block sequence are to be used in the same order as the shafts or blocks are threaded in the threading diagram. The tie-up is independent of the treadling draft. Also called "trompe as writ," "trompt as writ," "treadled as drawn in," and "treadled as written." Often abbreviated "TAW."

**Turned Draft** — Rotating a draft so that the treadling sequence reverses with the threading order. The tie-up is also rotated by 90° so that the shafts become treadles and treadles become shafts.

**Turned Twill Tie-Up** — A tie-up where opposite warp-dominant and weft-dominant twill tie-ups are placed in blocks. Use of this kind of tie-up does not  mean that the resulting fabric is a twill. As always, the final structure depends on the combination of threading, treadling, and tie-up. This type of tie-up is often used in profile drafts as well as threading drafts.

Unblocking — Unblocking the pattern shafts in the warp is an old but less common trick for reducing patterns and making them more graceful (less pixelated). In this sense, unblocking means that the pattern shafts may not change where the tie-down design repeats (as in half and quarter units, first example below). The technique also allows the opportunity to have a varied tie-down design in the warp (*below*, with tie-downs separated from pattern threads), rather than one which simply repeats.

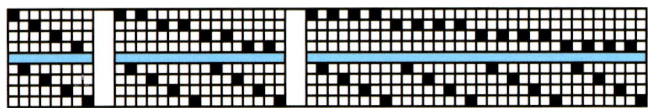

*quarter unit*    *half unit*                    *full unit*

Unit — A block which can be threaded in any order, tied up in any combination, and treadled in any order without introducing long floats. Examples of unit weaves include Atwater-Bronson lace, satin damask blocks, twill blocks, and summer and winter.

Wall of Troy — An asymmetric point arrangement which has a zigzag (∨\ or /∨) shaped repeat that produces a point with one leg longer than the other. Variants may include doubled or irregular points, etc.

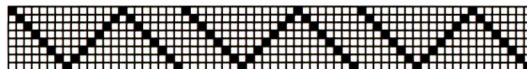

Warp-Faced View — A drawdown for a warp-faced weave, such as rep, showing only the warp colors and pattern on the surface.

Weft-Faced View — A drawdown for a weft-faced weave, such as boundweave, showing only the weft colors and pattern on the surface.

Yarn Counts — The size of a yarn, resulting in the number of yards per pound (yd/lb) or meters per kilogram (m/kg). For example: A yarn count of 8/2 cotton is based on size 8 cotton divided by 2 plies. Size 1 cotton is 840 yd/lb, so size 8 cotton is 840 x 8 yd/lb and size 8/2 cotton is 840 x 8 divided by 2 plies yd/lb or 3360 yd/lb. Yarn count can also be expressed in the Tex or Nm systems, leas for linen, or deniers for silk and synthetics.

*First Complex Weavers Seminars in 1988 (van der Hoogt, 2008).*

# References

Alderman, Sharon D. (2009) Mastering Weave Structures: Transforming Ideas into Great Cloth. Interweave Press.

"ArahWeave." Arahne: CAD/CAM for Weaving, www.arahne.si.

Arn-Grischott, Ursina (1999) Doubleweave on Four to Eight Shafts. Interweave Press.

Autio, Laurie Knapp, Elaine Steward Palmer, Carol Birtwistle, Florence Feldman-Wood, Carmela Ciampa, and Linda Snook, editors (2012) Interlaced: The Weavers' Guild of Boston Celebrates 90 Years of Friendship and Education. Weavers' Guild of Boston, Tiger Press.

Barrett, Clotilde and Eunice Smith (1983) Double Two-Tie Unit Weaves. Weavers' Journal Publications.

Best, Eleanor (1996) The Little Book of Gems. Bestudio.

Best, Eleanor (1996) The Little Crepe Book. Bestudio.

Best, Eleanor (1996) The Little Diamond Book. Bestudio.

Best, Eleanor (1996) The Little Twill Book: Twenty-four Shaft Patterns. Bestudio.

Blair, Amy (2021) Duelling Rabbits Handwovens: Smålandsväv. https://www.youtube.com/watch?v=Phz4sodS9fM

Brown, Amanda "Giraffe Head Wall Decal." www.etsy.com.

Bunke, Kim (2010) "A Family Table" in Summer & Winter Plus, Madelyn van der Hoogt, editor, XRX, Inc. pp. 16-17.

Burnham, Dorothy K. (1981) Warp and Weft: A Dictionary of Textile Terms. Charles Scribner's Sons.

Burnham, Harold B. and Dorothy K. Burnham (1972) Keep Me Warm One Night. University of Toronto Press.

Butterworth, James (1801) A Guide to Universal Manufacture, or, The Webb Analyzed: Containing Rules and Directions, to Enable a Person of the Meanest Capacity, to Draw or Lay Down a Draught on Paper for a Weaver to Begin His Work By. G. Banks.

Collingwood, Peter (1978) The Techniques of Rug Weaving. Watson-Guptill.

Collingwood, Peter (2002) The Techniques of Tablet Weaving. Robin and Russ Handweavers.

Cyrus-Zetterstrom, Ulla (1977) Manual of Swedish Handweaving. Alice Blomquist, translator. Charles T. Bradford Co.

Curran, Georgean (1990) "Sheep!" Handwoven, vol. 11, no. 2, pp. 93-94. Interweave Press.

Dam, Inge (2013) Tablet-Woven Accents for Designer Fabrics: Contemporary Uses for Ancient Technique. Self-published.

Davis, Linda Tilson (2017) Bateman Weaves, The Missing Monograph. Self-published.

Davison, Marguerite Porter (1944) A Handweaver's Pattern Book. Self-published.

Dean, Jenny and Karen Diadick Casselman (2010) Wild Color, Revised and Updated Edition: The Complete Guide to Making and Using Natural Dyes. Potter Craft.

de Ruiter, Erica (1999) Tejido Huave and Beyond. Self-published.

de Ruiter, Erica (2017) Weaving on 3 Shafts /Weven op 3 Schachten. Self-published.

de Ruiter, Erica, with Kati Reeder Meek and Marian Stubenitsky (2016) "Loom-Woven Tubular Selvedges." Complex Weavers Journal no. 111, pp. 26-28.

Dixon, Anne (2007) The Handweaver's Pattern Directory. Interweave Press.

Eatough, Judie and Wanda J. Shelp, editors (2000) Complex Weavers Greatest Hits in Celebration of 21 Years. Complex Weavers.

Ellis, Catharine (2016) Woven Shibori: Revised and Updated. The Weaver's Studio, Interweave Press.

Emery, Irene (1995) The Primary Structures of Fabrics: An Illustrated Classification. Whitney Library of Design.

Eriksson, Mariana, Ulla Getzmann, Gunnel Gustavsson, and Kerstin Lovallius (1995) VÄV: Gamla och glömda tekniker. Fatur & Kultur.

Eyring, Sally (2020) 3-D Hand Loom Weaving: Sculptural Tools and Techniques. Schiffer Publishing.

Falcot, P. (1990) Falcot's Weave Compendium: A Source Book for Textile Designers and Weavers. Ann Sutton, editor. Deirdre McDonald Books, Bellew Publishing.

France, Joseph (1814) See Butterworth, James.

Fressinet, B. (1905) Atlas d'Armures Textiles. Musée des Tissus de la Ville de Saint-Etienne.

Froberg, Kerstin (2012) "Pascal's Triangle as a Basis for Colour Transitions." Complex Weavers Compliation 3, Wanda J. Shelp, editor. Also see Bergdala Spinnhus, www.bergdalaspinnhus.com/artiklar.html.

Fry, Laura (2002) Magic in the Water: Wet Finishing Handwovens. Self-published.

Gehlhaar, Guido (2003) "Diagonal Experiences." TWIST Tablet Weavers International Studies & Techniques, vol. 10, no. 1, p. 1.

Gingras, Marguerite (2001) "A Shawl in Deflected Double Weave." Complex Weavers Journal, no. 66, pp. 52-55.

Gingras, Marguerite (2003) "Swivel." Shuttle Spindle & Dyepot, vol. 34, no. 3, pp. 44-48.

Gordon, Judith (1995) American Star Work Coverlets. Design Books.

Griswold, Ralph (2003) "Designing with Power Sequences." www.handweaving.net/document-detail/234/designing-with-power-sequences-griswold-ralph-e-. University of Arizona.

Harvey, Virginia I., editor (1982) Bateman Blend Weaves. Shuttle Craft Guild Monograph 36, HTH Publishers.

Harvey, Virginia I. (1983) "Bateman Blend Weaves Extended Beyond Eight Harnesses Part I." Complex Weavers Journal, no. 12, p. 6. Also see: Best, Eleanor, et al., editors (1991) A Compilation of Complex Weavers Newsletters 1979-1989.

Harvey, Virginia I. (1983) "Bateman Blend Weaves Extended Beyond Eight Harnesses Part II." Complex Weavers Journal, no. 13, p. 1. Also see: Best, Eleanor, et al., editors (1991) A Compilation of Complex Weavers Newsletters 1979-1989.

Henderson, Linda (2003) Please Weave a Message: Instructions and Graphs for Tablet-woven Calligraphy. Self-published.

Inouye, Bonnie (2000) "Advancing Wall of Troy." Complex Weavers' Greatest Hits: in Celebration of 21 Years, Eatough, Judie and Wanda Shelp, editors. Complex Weavers, p. 45.

Inouye, Bonnie (2000) Exploring Multishaft Design. 1st ed., Weavingdance Press (2nd ed. in progress).

Inouye, Bonnie (2014) "Turned Taqueté: An Introduction." Complex Weavers Journal, no. 105, pp. 36-40.

Johansson, Lillemor (1982) Damask and Opphämta with Weaving Sword or Drawloom. Susan Jones, translator. LTS Förlag.

Keasbey, Doramay (1993) Designing with Blocks for Handweaving. Self-published.

Keasbey, Doramay (2005) Pattern Techniques for Handweavers. Self-published.

Keasbey, Doramay (2006) "Designing Stitched Double Cloth." Best of Weaver's: The Magic of Double Weave, Madelyn van der Hoogt, editor, XRX.

Killeen, Leslie (2014) "Black-and-White Drawdown as a Color Placement Design Tool Used to Create a Taste of Asia." Complex Weavers Journal, no. 106, p. 8.

Lynde, Robyn (2015) "Cozy Throws for Two." Handwoven, vol. 39, no. 4, pp. 48-50. Interweave Press.

Lyon, Nancy (1987) "Crackle Weave." Shuttle Spindle & Dyepot, vol. 19, no. 1, p. 21. Handweavers Guild of America.

Maiwa Handprints, Ltd. "The Maiwa Guide to Natural Dyes". maiwa.com/pages/guide-to-natural-dyes.

McGeary, Gay (1979) Extended Point Twill. Interweave, vol 4, no. 3, pp. 37-39.

McGeary, Gay (2006) A Tale of Two Weavers and a Turtle Shell Pattern. Complex Weavers Journal, no. 82, pp. 50-51.

Meek, Kati Reeder (2000) Reflections from a Flaxen Past: For Love of Lithuanian Weaving. Penannular Press International.

Meek, Kati Reeder (2005) Warp with a Trapeze and Dance with Your Loom. Penannular Press International.

Möller, Andreas. www.weberei-hamburg.com.

Morath, Christian (1784-1810) "Draft number 18048." Christian Morath Pattern Book. Germany. www.handweaving.net/draft-detail/18048/page-15-figure-8-christian-morath-pattern-book-germany-1784-1810.

Nielson, Rosalie (2017) An Exaltation of Blocks. Self-published.

O'Connor, Paul (1996) Loom-Controlled Double Weave from the Notebook of a Double Weaver. Self-published.

Oelsner, G. H. (1915, 1952) "Crepe Weaves." A Handbook of Weaves. Samuel Dale, translator. Dover Publications.

Palmgren, Sigrid (1939) Praktisk Vavbok. Self-published.

Piroch, Sigrid (1990) "Letters and Words in Bronson Lace." Handwoven, vol. 11, no. 2, pp. 68-71.

Polak, Gudrun (2004 a) "TWIST Exchange: Wildly Opposite." TWIST Tablet Weavers International Studies & Techniques, vol. 11, no. 3, p. 11.

Polak, Gudrun (2004 b) "Design Challenge: Patterns on Both Sides." TWIST Tablet Weavers International Studies & Techniques, vol. 11, no. 3, p. 14.

Polak, Gudrun (2006) "Cross Pollination in Fiber Arts." STRANDS, 13, pp. 3-6.

Sandstad, Anne Grete (2002) Aklaer. Forfatteren og Trondersk Forlag.

Schlein, Alice (1994) Network Drafting: An Introduction. Bridgewater Press.

Schlein, Alice (2010) The Liftplan Connection: Designing for Dobby Looms with Photoshop and Photoshop Elements. Bridgewater Press. Also, www.lulu.com.

Schlein, Alice (2012) A Crepe Is Not Just a Pancake. https://weaverly.typepad.com/weaverly/.

Schlein, Alice and Bhakti Ziek (2006) The Woven Pixel. Bridgewater Press. Also, www.lulu.com

Scorgie, Jean (n.d.) "Swivel, Petit Point, & Related Laces." Weaver's Craft, no. 28.

Shelp, Wanda J. and Carolyn Wostenberg (1991) Eight Shafts, A Place to Begin. Ser/Kay Printing.

Shelp, Wanda J., editor (1998) Complex Weavers: A Compilation of Complex Weavers Newsletters May 1990 through September 1997. Complex Weavers.

Shelp, Wanda J., editor (2012a) Complex Weavers Compilation 3. Complex Weavers.

Shelp, Wanda J., editor (2012b) Complex Weavers Compilation 4. Complex Weavers.

Simpson, Janney (2016) "Mix It Up, Layers of Air Scarf." Handwoven, vol. 37, no. 5, pp. 50-52. Interweave Press.

Smayda, Norma, with Gretchen White (2017) Ondulé Textiles: Weaving Contours with a Fan Reed. Schiffer Publishing.

Smayda, Norma, Gretchen White, Jody Brown, and Katharine Schelleng (2009) Weaving Designs by Bertha Gray Hayes: Miniature Overshot Patterns. Schiffer Publishing.

Strickler, Carol (1991) A Weaver's Book of 8-Shaft Patterns. Interweave Press.

Sullivan, Donna (1991) Summer and Winter: A Weave For All Seasons. Interweave Press.

Stubenitsky, Marian (2014) Weaving with Echo and Iris. Margaret Ward, translator. Weefschool de Hoeve, Drukkerij Der Kinderen.

Sutton, Ann, editor (1990) Falcot's Weave Compendium. Bellew Publishing.

van der Hoogt, Madelyn (1993) The Complete Book of Drafting for Handweavers. Shuttle Craft Books.

van der Hoogt, Madelyn (1999) "Deflected Double Weave." Weavers, no. 44, pp. 54-58. XRX, Inc.

van der Hoogt, Madelyn (2007) "School for Weavers: Designing Deflected Doubleweave." Handwoven, vol. 28, no. 1, pp.72-73. Interweave Press.

van der Hoogt, Madelyn (2008) "Madelyn van der Hoogt, CW President 1986-1988." Complex Weavers Journal, no. 87, pp. 14-15.

van der Hoogt, Madelyn, editor (2010) Summer & Winter Plus. XRX, Inc.

van der Venne, Gerda (2011) "Design and Weave: Shawl Borås." VÄV, no. 3, p. 59.

von Tresckow, Sara (2014) When a Single Harness Simply Isn't Enough. Self-published.

Walker, Barbara J. (2012) Ply-Splitting from Drawdowns: Interpreting Weave Structures in Ply-Split Braiding. BJW Publications.

Walker, Barbara J. (2016) Supplementary Warp Patterning. BJW Publications.

Wilson, Susan (2011) Weave Classic Crackle & More. Schiffer Publishing.

Windeknecht, Margaret B. (1976) Creative Monk's Belt. HTH Publishers.

Wolfram, Stephen (2002) A New Kind of Science. Wolfram Media.

Xenakis, David (1982) "Fabrics That Go Bump! An Exploration." The Prairie Wool Companion, no. 3, pp. 18-24. XRX, Inc.

Ziek, Bhakti (2007) "Rant." Complex Weavers Journal, no. 84, pp. 31-33.

Zielinski, S. A. (2015) www.handweaving.net/draft-detail/62725/threading-draft-from-divisional-profile-tieup-master-weaver-draft-61290-fulford-quebec-canada-2005-2015.

# The Weavers

*Each weaver was asked to contribute a brief biography. It meant that they could not always include everything that was important. There are many missing awards, favorite mentors, publication locations, teaching information, and exhibits. Often they belong to study groups or guilds, or had formative educational opportunities which were not mentioned.*

*That said, it is a fascinating and diverse group, with vastly different experience levels, geographical locations, interests, and approaches. However, they are united in their creativity, joy in weaving, and zest for learning in its many forms.*

## Betty Alexander, Montana, USA

Betty weaves for fun, family, and friends. The good times begin in her weaving shed, 250 steps from the back door. Almost any day you may find her weaving dish towels, table linens or scarves for family and friends. Years ago her husband had a few sheep whose job was weed control. They also produced tons of wool, so she learned to spin. This led to tons of yarn, so she learned to weave. It started with a $19 frame loom which hangs on the wall of her weaving shed, but now she weaves on a 16-shaft AVL loom and occasionally on a 4-shaft Harrisville Design loom. She firmly believes in the value of guilds, workshops, seminars, conferences, books, magazines, the internet, and weaving friends. All have had a huge place in teaching her to weave.

## Charlotte Lindsay Allison, Texas, USA

Charlotte began weaving in 1983, taking every workshop available through the years. To be published became a goal and was realized when Interweave Press published several of her works. Charlotte had the privilege of cataloging the Acadian textiles of Audrey Bernard. Through CW, she chaired an Acadian study group which wove all of the Bernard collection. There are many who have influenced her including Madelyn van der Hoogt, Peter Collingwood, Jason Collingwood, Jette Vandermeiden, and Becky Ashenden. What a wonderful world to have been touched by each! Drawloom projects continued to grab her soul. When Charlotte built a small retirement home, her focus turned to weaving for it. Her family and guests sleep under her handwoven blankets and sheets. Bath towels are all woven on the drawloom. Additionally, she has hooked all of the rugs. There are still challenges. She loves the mystery in cloth and loves to learn. Celebrating her 79th birthday, there are so many things Charlotte hopes to create and to share her knowledge.

## Laurie Knapp Autio, Massachusetts, USA

Laurie has always loved patterns - from music to graph paper, geochemical graphs to profile drafts, rock and crystal textures and structures to interlacements and symmetry. She learned to weave in 1985 on a 4-shaft loom bought by her husband with his first paycheck. Her newest loom, a TC-2 Jacquard, was a surprise gift from this same wonderful man. Laces are a passion for their diaphaneity, design possibilities, and ability to break the grid. Japanese textiles and nature influence her work. Daily dog-walking in the woods inspires and relaxes her. Laurie enjoys writing, teaching (especially her advanced weaving group), designing, and figuring out how things relate. She has served as President of CW, Dean of the Weavers' Guild of Boston, Chair of Pioneer Valley Weavers and Weavers of Western Massachusetts, and co-edited *Interlaced* (2012) for the Weavers' Guild of Boston. Her training includes a Ph.D. in geology, a Master Weaver Certificate from Hill Institute, and serving as CW Study Groups Coordinator.

## Andrea Blackmon, Virginia, USA

Andrea became involved with fiber at a very early age. Sewing, crocheting, rug hooking, needlework, beading, and knitting consumed her free time. Weaving began when she was persuaded to take a loom that was taking up precious space at the residential facility where she worked. She reluctantly took the loom home (what did she need with another hobby?) and it sat in her attic for almost two years. When she learned that one of her favorite yarn stores taught weaving, she took a class and has been weaving ever since. That was almost 30 years ago. Currently, she supervises a weaving program for adults with intellectual and developmental disabilities. She is always looking for interesting ways to encourage the participants to develop their fiber skills and to enhance her own. Andrea has added quilting, dyeing, and felting to her list of fiber activities.

## Cally Booker, Dundee, Scotland

Cally reluctantly began weaving when she was dragged to a workshop in 2003. However, as soon as she discovered threading she was captivated. Before long she had filled her home with looms and gone back to college to study handwoven textile design. Cally now weaves full time in her studio in a refurbished jute mill where she also hosts classes and workshops. She still keeps in touch with her former life by teaching undergraduate statistics classes in the evenings. She joined CW in 2010 and is an active member of several study groups, including the Double Weave study group. Although Cally dislikes weaving with more than one shuttle, she can't seem to help herself and keeps coming up with more ideas for double cloth projects. Cally is a former editor of the *Journal for Weavers, Spinners & Dyers* and a Past President of CW.

## Amy Buchan, Montana, USA

Amy started weaving on a 4-shaft table loom in 2000 and quickly moved to a 24-shaft AVL loom. She was encouraged to join Western Weavers, the only multi-shaft guild in the Northern Rockies. There she was mentored by the best weavers in the region, including Wanda Shelp. Guild members encouraged Amy to join CW to participate in the study groups as another outlet for learning how to weave. Amy enjoyed participating in both the Early Weaving Books and Manuscripts and the 24, More or Less study groups for several years and had fun attending CW Seminars. She gained an immense amount of knowledge from other members and cherishes the samples she collected from the groups. Originally from southeastern Pennsylvania where many German weavers settled in the 1800s, Amy loves to weave the old German drafts. She plans to continue focusing on historical weaving and hopes to complete her first coverlet in the near future.

## Ruth Buchman, Massachusetts, USA

Ruth started weaving in high school but couldn't figure out how to move into the next part of her life with a loom. Twenty-five years later, the gift of a chenille scarf inspired her to return to weaving. That was over 20 years ago, and she has been a serious weaver ever since. She studied for four years at the Hill Institute under Jeanetta Jones and is grateful to her for a solid weaving foundation. In 2005, Hill Institute awarded Ruth a Master Weaver Certificate. She has won awards at Complexity, the Blue Ridge Fiber Show, and the New England Weavers Seminar where she is a Weaver of Distinction. Her work has been juried into shows at the Fuller Craft Museum and Artspace in Raleigh, NC. She is a member of the Weavers' Guild of Boston, the Weavers Guild of Springfield, and a study group called the Wednesday Weavers. Ruth enjoys the restrictions imposed by designing for a small number of shafts, and finds it forces her to be creative.

## Su Butler, Illinois, USA

Su began weaving at age three on a pot holder loom. Manipulating the different colored loopers into interesting designs felt natural and pleasing. She studied fiber arts in college, earning a degree in Fine Arts with majors in watercolor painting and weaving. For over 40 years Su has been fascinated with the process of interlacing threads to form cloth. Weave structure, color interaction, surface design, and layering the three continue to keep her spellbound. She views weaving as a tactile dialogue and complexity as a degree of depth, engaging in both on a daily basis as she designs and creates her unique cloth. Su joined CW in 1996 to utilize the study groups and find friendships with like-minded weavers. She has led the Tied Weaves and Beyond study group since 2001. An introvert who likes having quiet time to design and create cloth, the journey fascinates her with pleasing, and often useful, end results.

## Sheila Carey, British Columbia, Canada

Sheila took beginning weaving lessons in 1988 from Noreen Rustad, an early member of CW. Noreen introduced Sheila to CW almost immediately upon seeing her interest in the structure of fabrics. She has only woven on 8- or 16-shaft looms and is still interested in creating complexity on eight shafts. Sheila has been a member of guilds in Prince George, Kelowna, Vernon, Vancouver, Courtenay, and Qualicum, British Columbia. Besides being a CW member continuously since 1989, she has also been active in the Guild of Canadian Weavers and has served as the Association of Northwest Weavers Guilds representative for two guilds. Sheila was briefly a member of the CW Crackle study group, and has been a member of the Double Weave study group for many years, acting as the group administrator since 2008. From 2016 to 2018 she was a member of the Sixteens study group to stretch her interests in other complex structures.

## Inge Dam, Ontario, Canada

Inge was introduced to weaving by a friend in 1982. In 1990 she completed the Ontario Handweavers and Spinners Weaving Certificate course and became an OHS Master Weaver in 1992. Her In-Depth Study was on Iron Age textiles from northern Europe. Tablet-woven borders on several of these pieces piqued Inge's interest in tablet weaving. Research and several years' experience with combining tablet weaving with loom weaving led to publication of a book in 2013, *Tablet-Woven Accents for Designer Fabrics: Contemporary Uses for Ancient Techniques*. Inge has taught workshops in the US, Canada, and England, as well as Convergence and CW Seminars. She has won many awards and her work has appeared in *Weaver's*, *Handwoven*, *Shuttle Spindle & Dyepot*, *Fibre Focus*, and the *Guild of Canadian Weavers Bulletin*. She weaves on a 32-shaft Louët Megado dobby loom, specializing in unique garments which often incorporate tablet weaving and other embellishments.

## Naomie Daslin, Carlow, Ireland

Naomie was fortunate to have the opportunity to study in the Grennan Mill Craft School in Ireland. She gained experience in a broad spectrum of crafts and quickly learned that she belonged in front of the loom. Naomie uses a Glimåkra 8-shaft floor loom and an Ashford 8-shaft table loom and is passionate about double weave and rep weave. She has always had a passion for yarn crafts but there was something about the ancient craft of weaving that fascinated her. She loves the meditative process of weaving and experimenting with different textures and colors. Naomie takes inspiration from everyone and everything: the world around her, nature, memories, and places. Through weaving, everything one imagines can become real! She joined CW to connect with like-minded people and to continue learning and improving as a weaver. Madelyn van der Hoogt and Rosalie Neilson are two of Naomie's favorite weavers.

## Linda Tilson Davis, Oregon, USA

Sewing her own wardrobe beginning in high school, Linda developed an appreciation and interest in fabric. It was logical to leap into weaving in 1974 after she took a job in Boise, Idaho that had a full-service weaving shop, including classes. She never looked back and had numerous looms, belonged to several guilds, and eventually joined CW in 1989. She was a member of the Computer Aided Design Exchange, Beyond Plain Weave Garments, and Tied Weaves study groups. In 2010 she co-founded the Bateman Weaves Study Group and remained coordinator until 2019. As editor of the CW Journal from 2007-2010, she learned more than she ever imagined from fellow CW members who inspired and influenced her work. Linda also taught workshops and seminars, exhibited at CW, national, regional, and local exhibitions, and received numerous awards. In 2017 she published Bateman Weaves, The Missing Monograph. She found relaxation and inspiration from daily walks, hiking, reading, knitting and volunteering in library and community arts activities and events.

## Erica de Ruiter, Malden, Netherlands

As a child Erica was given a box loom made by her father and had an affinity for textiles all her life. Her professional training as an industrial textile designer was in the Bauhaus tradition at Amsterdam School of Fine Arts/Gerrit Rietveld Academy. She designed household textiles until beginning her family. Erica took up handweaving, studying and examining, teaching, traveling, and writing. Erica published her research of a Mexican tribal weave, Tejido Huave and Beyond (1999), in Dutch and English. When she obtained a Louët Magic dobby she joined CW. Erica's genius discovered, devised and developed how to weave on just three shafts, nearly all of structures that modern handweavers believe require four shafts or more. Jan Louët developed a folding loom available with three shafts, christened "Erica" in honor of her and timed the introduction of "Erica" loom to coincide with the 2017 launch of Erica's full-color, 136-page book, Weaving on 3 Shafts (Weven op 3 Schachten), co-produced with Marian Stubenitsky and Selma Sindram.

## Edna Devai, Colorado, USA

Edna came to weaving after a severe car accident in 2000. Weaving provided her with a way to express herself and to use her lifelong experience with textiles. Early in childhood she was introduced to knitting and embroidery and later studied dress making. Mostly self-taught, she enjoys researching textile topics and working out answers to her "What if?" questions. Edna appreciates experienced weavers who are willing to share their knowledge in various forms of publication. To widen her horizon, Edna joined CW in 2008 and became a member of the Fine Threads study group. She is also active in her local guilds and study groups. Historic and folk textiles significantly inspire her work. She weaves on a Louët Megado, likes to use fine linen and silk yarns, and hand finishes all her work. Edna is committed to using materials of exceptional quality to create heirloom textiles for lasting enjoyment.

## Debbie Dickson, Wellington, New Zealand

Debbie learned to weave as a natural progression from knitting and spinning. She started weaving on a rigid heddle loom and currently owns several looms, including an Ashford Knitters loom (a 12" rigid heddle loom), a Mecchia 42" 8-shaft floor loom with manual dobby, and an Ashford 24" 16-shaft table loom. Debbie enjoys all aspects of the weaving process from the initial design and planning through to the final finishing. Most of her recent weaving has been from her own designs. She uses Fiberworks PCW to help the creative process, along with referencing her weaving library for inspiration and ideas. Debbie is a member of Creative Fibre (the New Zealand Spinning, Weaving and Woolcrafts Society, Inc.) She initially joined to expand her spinning knowledge, but after being introduced to weaving this became her primary focus.

## Elaine Dimpelfeld, Connecticut, USA

Elaine started weaving seven years ago after a friend gave her his 4-shaft direct-tie floor loom. She started with a shadow weave scarf and was hooked. Elaine joined CW several years ago at the urging of Laurie Autio as part of an Explorations in Advanced Weaving class. At first she was intimidated but now she is intrigued by every CW Journal article. She would like to thank Janney Simpson and Anne Graham, who taught her to weave, and who encourage exploration. Elaine is still learning but likes to try new weaves, including ones she does not initially like, so that she can find some way to make it her own. She is a member of the Handweavers' Guild of Connecticut and has received awards in their biennial shows. She looks for inspiration for color and design in travels, museums, and walks in nature. She enjoys geometric shapes, combining colors, and designs that flow.

*We are sad to report the passing of Erica de Ruiter (November 24, 1930 - March 11, 2019, left) and Linda Tilson Davis (October 2, 1944 - October 30, 2021) before the completion of this book.*

## Pat Donald, Alabama, USA

Pat started weaving after swearing for at least five years that she would not become a weaver because she was happy as a spinner. She belonged to the Columbia, Missouri Weavers and Spinners' Guild at the time. She started with a rigid heddle loom, decided a multi-shaft loom was in her future, and now owns more than one loom. Pat joined CW in the late 1990s after a weaving friend, Mary Jane Thorne, kept showing her study group sample books. She decided that this was a good way for her to expand her weaving in addition to the varied and wonderful weaving workshops the Columbia Guild offered. Pat is a member of two study groups, Sampling Exchange the Old-Fashioned Way and Early Weaving Books and Manuscripts which she has thoroughly enjoyed. She belongs to several fiber guilds, maintaining her memberships as her profession has led her to different geographic locations. She interacts with Ute Bargmann and others to stimulate weaving interests.

## Karen Donde, North Carolina, USA

Karen was introduced to weaving in 1998 by the South Jersey Guild of Spinners and Handweavers. She began teaching in 2006, and relocated to Asheville, North Carolina, in 2009 to open a weaving studio/classroom with a friend. In 2013, she graduated from Haywood Community College's Professional Crafts Fiber program, in Clyde, North Carolina. Karen weaves one-of-a-kind and commissioned yardage for clothing, accessories, and household textiles. She teaches weaving classes and workshops in Asheville and for guilds and conferences in the US. A journalist in her pre-weaving life, Karen writes for and about weavers, contributing to *Handwoven*, *Weaving Today*, and other craft media. Her fascination with weaving is driven by exploring the infinite ways to create patterned textiles. As a "structure weaver," she is drawn to intricate interlacements, but is thrilled when simple combinations of structure, color, and texture yield a beautiful, complex-looking woven design.

## Jean Down, Ontario, Canada

Jean has been weaving for over 25 years and is a founding partner in Studio Three Fibre Arts which produces uniquely handwoven textiles and fiber art. She focuses on historical weave structures and the development of weaving in eastern Ontario, Canada, using these designs in a modern context. She adapts many weave structures and combines different fibers to create textured cloth. Jean has been a member of the West Carleton Fibre Guild, the Ottawa Valley Weavers and Spinners Guild, and the CW Early Weaving Books and Manuscripts study group for many years. For the past 15 years, Jean has been a member of Weavers Unlimited, a collaboration of weavers who study complex weave structures. Lately, inspired by a workshop with Bonnie Inouye, she has been designing multi-shaft overshot weaves. Since 2003, Jean has exhibited in 15 weaving exhibitions and published articles in *Fibre Focus* and *Handwoven*.

## Eileen Driscoll, New York, USA

Before retirement, Eileen took every class and workshop, attended every conference, and tried to understand every book that she could. Her weaving was sporadic but she held to her goal to create handwoven garments. After retiring and acquiring a 32-shaft loom, Eileen finally began to weave the patterns she envisioned. Participating in the Tied Weaves and Beyond study group was invaluable, especially with Su Butler's mentoring. Having a love for color and ethnic motifs, she incorporates both into her weavings. Many garments, including her current coat project using greca motifs from a temple in Mitla, Mexico, are inspired by her travels in other countries. She finds that the CW seminars and the *CW Journal* fuel her creativity and thanks every member who participates. Recently she has been reviving her statistical skills to analyze data from her local guild's annual sale to help member vendors make smart pricing decisions. Eileen has served on the CW Board as treasurer and Vice President.

## Laurie Duxbury, Virginia, USA

A weaver for over 25 years, Laurie has studied in Sweden and throughout the USA. She weaves in her studio in northern Albemarle County, Virginia where she is active in the Central Virginia Fiberarts Guild. Laurie first became interested in weaving and textile production when, as a child, she visited historic sites in her native Virginia. As she learned the craft of weaving, her interest evolved into a passion for expressing her own creativity through the combination of colorful threads and traditional patterns. She enjoys pushing weave structures to their limits and following the "What if?" questions that pop into her head while she's weaving. She has participated in the local Charlottesville Artisans Studio Tour for several years. Working with fine craftsmen from other media has stretched her as an artist and inspired her to use contemporary colors and textures. In addition to weaving for shows and commissions, she teaches workshops and offers one-on-one instruction.

## Sally Eyring, Massachusetts, USA

Sally has been weaving and building tools since childhood. She earned a BA in Mathematics Education from Arizona State University. After a long career in Information Technology, she earned an MFA from the Art Institute of Boston at Lesley University. Her MFA graduate project described the immigration experience through woven sculptural headdresses. She invented several unique three-dimensional weaving methods after a weaving teacher commented, "When you weave you always get a rectangle." In addition to weaving, Sally renovates and builds looms, teaches, and does glass casting. She has built a tapestry loom from scratch, modified a counterbalance loom into a jack loom, modified multiple horizontal countermarche looms into parallel countermarche looms, and has built both a drawloom and a 32-shaft computer dobby loom. Among other publications, her work has been featured in the *CW Journal*, *Handwoven*, and *Shuttle Spindle & Dyepot*, and her book, *3-D Hand Loom Weaving: Sculptural Tools and Techniques* (2020).

## Kay Faulkner, Queensland, Australia

Kay, a long-time member of CW, was a full-time weaver for over 30 years. The ability to create unique handwoven cloth was the primary focus of her studio practice. She was committed to research and enjoyed pushing the boundaries. The potential of the woven structure was a source of fascination. Recently she had two areas of research: textiles of South East Asia and their application for western-style weaving and multi-shaft ties in tied weaves. Her commitment to research led her to the discovery of woven shibori in parallel with Catharine Ellis 20 years ago. It became a significant component in her work. She published, exhibited extensively, and taught both within Australia and internationally. Since 2015 she operated a weaving school from her studio in Queensland in tandem with her weaving practice. Kay served CW as Second Vice President (2009-2013) and as an Area Representative (2004-2013).

*We are sad to report the passing of Kay Faulkner (February 21, 1955 - May 31, 2019) before the completion of this book.*

## Lucy Ford, Pennsylvania, USA

A long-time knitter, Lucy took a few lessons in weaving over a decade ago, but didn't weave again until 2014. Since that time quite a few looms have cycled through, as she quickly learned four shafts were not enough, and that looms are not one-size-fits-all. She currently has two 8-shaft Schacht looms, both of which she loves. Lucy joined CW in 2016 at the encouragement of a long-time member who is a local weaving friend, and is now a member of the Beyond Plain Weave Garments study group. She is still exploring what she likes to weave best, but knows she does not like weaving rugs. She thoroughly enjoys the intellectual challenge involved in designing, and is working to learn as much as she can about structure. Lucy is a member of the Philadelphia Guild of Handweavers and won the Guild's *Handwoven Magazine* Items for the Home award in 2016, for a double weave windows footstool cover. By day, she is a business school professor.

## Patricia Foster, Berkshire, UK

Pat spent her working life as an engineer, running her own engineering design consultancy for thirty years until 2010. Around 1978 she fell into weaving at the local Technical College and, shortly after, she took a weaving course with Marianne Straub. This was followed by a lengthy weaving course in Finland with exposure to Scandinavian weaving. She acquired a very large 8-shaft Finnish Varpapuu loom on which rugs could be woven. She joined CW about 2004 out of interest in what they were doing. Joining a couple of study groups had an important effect, particularly the Fine Threads study group. Pat is interested in new (to her) drafts and creates her own for her pieces. Complex weaves are a continuing interest and she has learnt a great deal from several US weavers, in particular Bonnie Inouye and Barbara Walker. She has a 32-shaft computer-controlled Megado and a Louët Kombo which she has altered to accommodate a fan reed.

## Brenda Gibson, London, UK

Brenda started weaving on a self-taught basis around the turn of the millennium, with very limited time available whilst pursuing a demanding financial career. After retiring in 2006 she was able to join a regular weaving class for the first time. Weaving took a serious hold on her life, especially as she soon became a class teacher herself. It was almost inevitable that she would join CW soon afterwards, and was a member of the CW Collapse Pleat and Bump study group since she joined CW. A range of workshops with inspirational teachers such as Bonnie Inouye, Marg Coe, and Jette Vandermeiden provided further stimulus and encouragement to teach at CW Seminars in Tacoma, St. Charles, and Reno in 2014, 2016, and 2018 respectively. Her study group memberships are currently The Sixteens (group leader) and Double Weave. Along with her practicing and teaching, Brenda loves ply-split braiding and spinning.

## Marguerite Gingras, Québec, Canada

Marguerite began weaving in 1980 after she inherited her aunt's 4-shaft loom. From her first lesson, she knew that weaving was for her because it combined visual arts and mathematics, her preferred school subjects. She soon became interested in complex structures and joined CW in 1992 after hearing about CW Seminars. There she made good friends. She learned a lot from Bonnie Inouye, including making links between different weave structures. She pursued this weaving approach for many years, teaching and weaving, mostly scarves, greeting cards, and samples for teaching or study groups. Some of her drafts and pieces have appeared in books and magazines, along with articles in French and English. Her recent work includes structures on 32-shaft parallel threadings and textures with different kinds of double weave. She participated in the Computer Aided Design Exchange study group from 1995 to 2014 and has been the Québec CW Area Representative for many years.

## Marlene Golden, California, USA

Marlene learned to weave over 40 years ago in classes at the City College of San Francisco. Kay Sekimachi was a strong influence, providing a sound foundation in weaving. Later, Martha Stanley and Lillian Elliott gave Marlene an invaluable weaving education. During that time, she wove on 4- to 8-shaft looms and managed to weave one or two projects a year along with working outside the home and raising two boys. Retiring in 2001 gave Marlene the opportunity to spend more time weaving as well as expanding her knowledge of more complex weave structures. Working first with a 16-shaft, then a 24-shaft loom, has challenged her to weave cloth of more complexity - cloth that wouldn't be available commercially. She is an active member of Loom & Shuttle Guild, serving as both president and treasurer, is on the Advisory Board of the Textile Arts Council (a support group of the DeYoung Museum), and has served on the Advisory Board of the Conference of Northern California Handweavers.

## Georgia Hadley, Massachusetts, USA

Georgia began her adult life as a painter with an intense interest in making art but family, kids, home, etc. intervened in mid-life. During this time Georgia explored many fiber crafts including knitting, crocheting, needlepoint, rug hooking, and cross stitch. When she began weaving everything came together. Her art background and interest in color, fibers, and pattern fueled her joy in the actual process of weaving and she has never looked back. Georgia graduated from Pratt Institute, taught art history and painting, farmed, and completed the Master Weaver Certificate at Hill Institute (2010). She is a New England Weavers Seminar Weaver of Distinction in the Gallery Show (2015). Her diverse weaving interests include large, colorful uncut flossa wall hangings; intricate, fine, hand-manipulated leno in white to pale yellow; and straight-draw block pattern tablecloths on 24 to 32 shafts in artfully blended middle tones captured from nature.

## Stacey Harvey-Brown, Lot-et-Garonne, France

Stacey has been weaving for over 25 years, and teaching weaving since 2005. The last ten years have been absorbed by explorations into textural surfaces from surface relief fabrics to three-dimensional artworks. She gained an MFA distinction in weaving focusing on geological erosion found in strata and stalactites. Insatiable curiosity leads Stacey down unusual pathways, both technically and artistically, and inspiration is sparked mostly through marine and geological forms. She develops work on her 24-shaft AVL and then distills the essence of the techniques to eight shafts, to be accessible to more weavers through her writing. She has recently moved to southwest France where she has set up The Loom Room France for teaching, workshops, writing books on three-dimensional weaving techniques and further developing her art, exhibiting internationally and locally. She has four hand-Jacquard looms from 1880s. Stacey is a member of the CW Double Weave study group.

## Jan Hayman, Minnesota, USA

Jan learned to weave at the Weavers Guild of Minnesota where she continues to be an active member and frequent volunteer. Her current weaving interests include creating three-dimensional fabrics and exploring the capabilities of the drawloom beyond the joy of creating figures. In season, you will find Jan harvesting and dyeing fiber with plants collected in her family's garden and prairie. This pursuit combines her fiber interests with her former career as a naturalist.

## Lisa Devereux Hill, Massachusetts, USA

Lisa has been weaving for over 25 years, and completed a six-year Master Weaver program at Hill Institute in Florence, MA in 2012. She is former Program Chair for the Weavers of Western Massachusetts and was one of a team of technical editors for *Handwoven* magazine. Lisa finds it funny to harken back many years when she read Madelyn van der Hoogt's article about weavers and their place in the color-structure continuum. She was definitely a "color weaver" and was afraid that even signing up for the Hill Institute program might force her off her determined path to eschew structure (not entirely of course, plain weave, twill, and waffle weave were okay by her). Well, her fears came true, but probably like many people's fears, when confronted they turned out not to be so frightening. Lisa is still enamored with color, but oh, how her lust for structure has grown!

## Susie Hodges, California, USA

Susie joined CW six years ago after she became the proud owner of a 16-shaft Toika computer dobby, a fitting machine for someone descended from generations of Finnish household weavers. She learned to weave from Ed Rossbach at University of California Berkeley and has continued to take weaving and other textile and art classes throughout her life. Susie is also a hand spinner, crocheter, and dyer, and has taught hand knitting nationally. In her younger days, Susie specialized in loom-shaped clothing, but now prefers weaving beautifully patterned rectangles for all uses, domestic and artistic. She is a fan of tied weaves, subtle color effects, and unusual textures. Although new structures are like catnip to her, Susie firmly believes that it is the final use and effect of a woven piece that should be of primary concern, and that four shafts are as good as 16 for achieving that purpose. A retired high school teacher, she lives with her husband, Dave, a retired college professor.

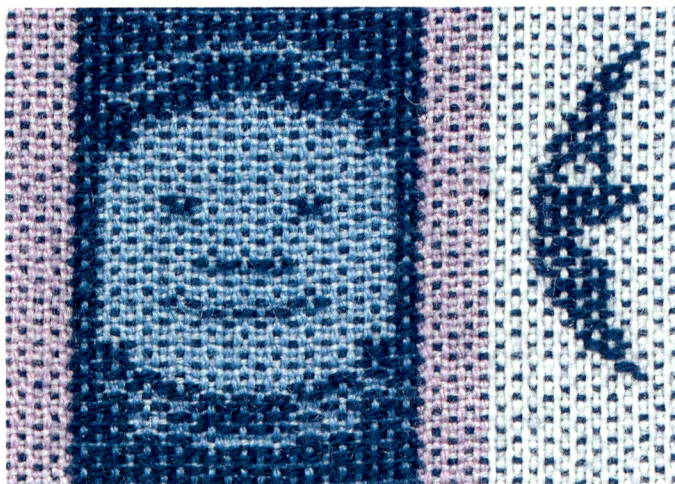

*Detail of scarf by Susie Hodges*

## Sandra Hutton, Colorado, USA

Sandra taught design and marketing of textile items at the university level for approximately 20 years. When her husband exercised his turn for a career move, she became executive director of the International Textile and Apparel Association and moved the office to Colorado. The work was about three-quarter time and allowed her to pursue her love of weaving which started in graduate school. The Front Range of Colorado affords many opportunities for a person interested in textiles to develop a variety of fiber art skills. Sandra is a member of the Boulder, Denver, and Colorado Springs guilds, CW, HGA, Surface Design Association, Textile Society of America, Cross Country Weavers, and participates in several study groups. The study of historic and contemporary textiles helps satisfy her scholarly needs. In addition to her standby Schacht Baby Wolf, Sandra enjoys weaving on a Louët Megado and explorations on her TC-2 Jacquard loom.

## Bonnie Inouye, Colorado, USA

Bonnie has been weaving since 1967, when she built a 4-shaft loom in her dorm room, later buying larger 4-shaft looms. In 1987, she bought a 16-shaft loom and joined CW, attending CW seminars ever since. Presenting seminars for CW has been a special joy and challenge, and she has also presented workshops and seminars in nine countries and many states. She likes using weaving software to create new drafts with flowing lines, unusual textures, intriguing color blends, and woven images that characterize her award-winning textiles. Bonnie travels frequently and loves to meet weavers in other parts of the world. She has written many articles for weaving magazines, especially for *CW Journal*, and is working on the second edition of her book, *Exploring Multishaft Design*, first published in 2000. Verda Elliott was her mentor and friend. Bonnie shares weaving puzzles and new ideas with Marguerite Gingras.

## Bonnie Kay, Michigan, USA

The designs and colors in Bonnie's weaving reflect the influence of 30 years of work and travel. She joined the Peace Corps in 1963 and taught science in Ghana, worked in public health with community organizations, and traveled widely in Africa, South Asia, South America, and the southwestern USA. She developed a great appreciation for the connection between health and economic independence. This led to an interest in local craft projects as a means to generate income and as an expression of community aesthetic traditions. Inspired by the work she saw, Bonnie started to weave in 1988. She uses cotton, Tencel, rayon, and bamboo and loves creating geometric loom-controlled designs. Bonnie has a special interest in double weave patterns and has been experimenting lately with relationships between music, mathematics, and double weave designs. She recently spent six months in Ghana which has renewed her interest in studying Kente cloth designs and adapting them to her own weaving.

## Leslie Killeen, North Carolina, USA

Having a biology/botany education, weaving came to Leslie via a Harrisville Designs kit, a Macomber loom, and an 8-shaft Schacht Baby Wolf Combby. Early on, she decided to focus on eight shafts and facilitated the CW Eight or Less, Make it Complex study group. Even before the Combby, Fiberworks PCW took her to another level. Alice Schlein, Madelyn van der Hoogt, and Randy Darwall each have contributed to her weaving growth as has the Weavers' Guild of Boston, CW, and the Cross Country Weavers. Currently, she is in the CW Designing Fabric study group. With the fewer shafts, Leslie has used a combination of painted warps, uneven block and color rotations, non-traditional fiber choices, and treadling combinations to add complexity to her work. When someone, especially a CW member, thinks that she wove a particular piece on more than eight she just smiles, and was thrilled when her piece in Complexity 2016 exhibit was awarded the CW award. Many of her fabrics end up in her one-of-a-kind vests.

## Peg MacMorris, Colorado, USA

As a child who was fascinated by colonial times, Peg tried a variety of crafts. She finally learned to weave as a young adult at a most inopportune time - in the midst of completing a Ph.D. in Biology. Over the subsequent 20 years or so, a 4-shaft loom resided in her home and she managed to weave a little, but with a busy career and children, she remained a beginner weaver. In 1997 she moved to Colorado, joined Rocky Mountain Weavers Guild, discovered guild workshops, study groups, more shafts, and eventually a 16-shaft Leclerc Weavebird loom. After many opportunities for learning, she has escaped life as a beginner. At the urging of friends, she joined CW and attended her first Seminars in Albuquerque in 2010. Now, in retirement, she has left the lab for multiple study groups, three guilds, and CW. Peg still does experiments, but now they all involve fiber.

## Patricia Martin, California, USA

The recent completion of an MFA-Studio (Fiber), has pushed Patricia's concentrated investigations into how threads act and react as part of her weaving practice. Involvement in CW study groups for several years, such as Beyond Plain Weave and Sixteens, has added valuable intellectual inspiration contributing to her works. Talented, knowledgeable, and experienced weavers have invigorated her to continue to push the material. Her efforts have always revolved around line, color, structure, and how individual threads can construct a textile. Patricia started with fine threads making yardage but has more recently begun to explore a more sculptural format. It is the movement and energy of fiber in motion that has captured her interest. The use of structures and the interactions of threads are the paths currently being pursued. Resources and inspiration are found in old draft books, along with vacations that are planned around textile-related symposia, workshops, and gallery tours. When not traveling, Patricia can be found at her studio teaching a dedicated group of students and exploring the beautiful central coast of California looking for her next inspiration.

## Teresa McFarland, Oregon, USA

Having longed to learn to weave, Teresa started weaving over 11 years ago when she discovered it was taught at a college campus within walking distance of her home in San Francisco. She had been knitting for over 45 years and was beginning to design her own sweaters, mostly in lace. Her only teacher has been the wonderful Janice Sullivan, who inspired her for nine semesters. She joined CW in 2016 after other guild members assured her that the kind of weaving she was drawn to was structurally complex enough. She's now a member of the Portland Handweavers Guild, and has exhibited her work at shows in the San Francisco Bay Area and in Portland. She also makes natural dyes to color her yarns using plant materials such as rabbit brush, oak galls, marigold petals, mushrooms, and lichens. Teresa is a linguist, and what draws her to both weaving and the study of languages is the creation and contemplation of beautiful, complex patterns.

## Gay Orpen McGeary, Pennsylvania, USA

Gay began weaving in 1972, her interest sparked by two antique coverlets she had inherited. Largely self-taught, she started with an old 2-shaft Union rug loom. Now her looms include a Toika 24-shaft computer-assisted loom. These allow her to weave more complex patterns and designs she has derived from early handwritten manuscripts and coverlets, using weaving software to add her own original elements. The fringe on an antique coverlet prompted her to figure out how it was made, beginning a life-long interest in fringes as an important decorative ingredient in the design of her coverlets. She continues to spread her interest in coverlet design and coverlet fringes via workshops and presentations. Gay's articles have appeared in the *CW Journal* and she taught at the 2012 CW Seminar. She considers the CW community an important part of her weaving community. Gay holds an MBA and a CPA. "I guess you could call me a numbers person," she states, explaining her fascination with the complexities of drafting designs and researching weave structures.

## Molly McLaughlin, New Hampshire, USA

Molly started weaving in the early 1990s after wandering into a yarn store and becoming mesmerized by the rows of beautiful colors. Her initial training was as an apprentice to a traditional production weaver. While she found the rigid adherence to tradition frustrating, it also provided a strong foundation that many years later she has grown to appreciate. For quite a while, her weaving was concentrated on rugs and blankets. However, in 2009, her son returned from a trip to India with several pieces of fine silk fabric, and she became obsessed with the idea of weaving very fine silk. She joined the CW Fine Threads study group, and has remained very grateful for the generous encouragement offered by the group's leader, the amazing Lillian Whipple! In addition to CW, Molly is a member of New Hampshire Weavers Guild, Weavers East, and was a humble student in Laurie Autio's Explorations in Advanced Weaving.

## Kati Reeder Meek, Michigan, USA

Kati loves the discipline of weaving, coupled with its creative problem solving. She claims to be an engineer who struggles with the artistic aspect of making cloth. Kati relishes a good challenge and the thrill of success. She likes helping others find the thrill. CW has kept her motivated well beyond what any initially self-taught weaver could dream. She is pleased to call some of the best - and kindest - weavers around the world friends. It was a CW member who told her that her Lithuanian research should be published (*Reflections from a Flaxen Past: For Love of Lithuanian Weaving*, 2001), and another CW member pulled her past 'dead center' on her second book, *Warp with a Trapeze and Dance with Your Loom* (2005), a book requested by many of her linen and tartan students. Her favorite loom is an antique 4-shaft counterbalance with long-eyed heddles. She appreciates the design freedom of the drawloom and loves the great memory help of the computer assist. Kati also spins flax, wool, cotton, and cat hair for the fun of it.

## Beryl Moody, Nevada, USA

Beryl became interested in weaving about 25 years ago after having first learned to spin. She attended a beginning weaving class at San Francisco City College taught by Deborah Corsini and, on occasion, Peggy Osterkamp. From the very beginning multi-shaft weaving was Beryl's main interest. After working on her mother's 8-shaft Gilmore for a few years, she purchased a 24-shaft Louët Magic Dobby loom and joined the brand new CW 24, More or Less study group. In the beginning she used drafts from Falcot's Weave Compendium (Sutton, 1990) and Eleanor Best's tie-up collection books (1996), but over time she learned to design her own drafts using *CW Journal* articles. She also joined the Computer- Aided Design Exchange study group which gave her access to articles from many inventive weavers. Today she is busy weaving household textiles, scarves and shawls, mainly on her 40-shaft AVL, but occasionally on a Schacht Baby Wolf or Wolf Pup loom.

## Wendy Morris, London, UK

Wendy came quite late to weaving but, having been bitten by the bug, quickly embarked on the UK Bradford Certificate in Handwoven Textile Design. Following that, she continued her weaving education informally, joining CW in 2003, becoming First Vice President in 2008 and President in 2010. Having benefited hugely as a beginning weaver from the generosity of weavers worldwide in sharing their knowledge, passing that on to others has always been important to her. In 2009 she and her husband were able to take over The Handweavers Studio in London and develop it into a leading teaching studio with a program of weekly classes, intermediate and specialist workshops, and a two-year Diploma program. They handed the Studio on to another CW member, Dawn Willey, in 2016, giving Wendy more time to pursue her personal weaving interests which lie primarily in exploiting structures and fibers to create collapse, pleat, and other three-dimensional effects.

## Sara Nordling, Indiana, USA

Sara has been involved in fiber art in many forms for most of her life. Weaving, however, didn't enter until Sara was an adult and she was hooked immediately. What began as a hobby turned into a passion and a return to school for a BFA and then an MFA in studio art/textiles. Sara currently teaches at Purdue University, Fort Wayne where she teaches drawing, painting, and design. Teaching these classes keeps her grounded in artistic fundamentals that she uses in her own art. She has been a member of CW for 13 years. Sara has been a member of the Sixteens and Double Weave study groups. Her weaving focuses on various forms of double weave including double weave pleats, pick-up techniques, networking, and blocks. Sara enjoys the technical side of weaving as well as the color, textures, and rhythms weaving provides.

## Sheila O'Hara, California, USA

Sheila began her love for weaving at age 10. Art was part of her surroundings including woodblock prints and kimonos collected by her parents in Japan. Since graduating from California College of the Arts with a BFA in 1976, Sheila has made her living from weaving artworks. In 1984 she bought a 16-shaft AVL Compu-Dobby loom and has recently returned to it. From 2000 to 2006, Sheila took inspiring lessons and rented time on two Jacquard hand looms: Nina Jacobs's TC-1 and Cathy Bolding's AVL-TIS. Thanks to Mim Wynne's generosity, Sheila wove on an AVL Jacq2G from 2008 to 2017. Sheila enjoyed being a member of the CW Jacquard study group from 2003 to 2017. Weaving influences include: Inger Jensen, Kay Sekimachi, Trude Guermonprez, Madelyn van der Hoogt, Jack Lenor Larsen, and Helena Hernmarck. Museums and private clients collect her artworks that have been exhibited and published internationally. She feels very fortunate to have taught workshops worldwide since 1981 and to be teaching weaving in her home studio since 2000.

## Fran Osten, Massachusetts, USA

Fran began weaving in the 1970s on a loom her husband made her. After her first child arrived, she finished the baby blanket then on the loom and returned to weaving 20 years later, when her youngest left for college and she was granted a university sabbatical. Today, Fran works on multi-shaft looms, including her Louët Megado. Using silk, Tencel, or cotton, she begins most of her work with warp yarn she hand dyes, primarily creating wearables. Her work is inspired by the New England landscape and the ever-changing ocean cove outside her studio. Color, drape, and a sense of movement are important to her designs. She likes escaping the orthogonal grid, often using interleaved designs, advancing and network twills, and a variety of tied weaves to do so. Bonnie Inouye's workshops were an important inspiration. Fran is currently exploring structure and design in Laurie Autio's multi-year class. She participates in the Sixteens study group, and is a member of Boston area's Wednesday Weavers and the Weavers' Guild of Boston.

## Elaine Palmer, Massachusetts, USA

Elaine has always been a fiber junkie, sewing her own clothes, quilting, and knitting, so why not weave! She has been weaving for nine years and loves weaving utilitarian items such as kitchen towels on her 16-shaft Toika computerized loom and graphic images on her Glimåkra single unit drawloom. With a BFA in Graphic Design she was an on-figure and product Photo Art Director shooting on location and in studio. Her 30 years of work has included national magazine ads, newspaper advertisements and catalogs for Hang Ten, Eddie Bauer, and Nordstrom. Elaine's professional experience as a Photo Art Director working in the fashion industry was an asset in photographing and styling handwovens and page layout production for the Weavers' Guild of Boston's 90th Anniversary book, *Interlaced* (2012). As a member of three guilds, Elaine enjoys community guild meetings and study groups in such a solitary activity, weaving.

## Penny Peters, California, USA

Penny's father gave her a table loom for Christmas when she was in her twenties. That was the start. Like most, she had a family to raise and a career to follow. Weaving happened in-between, and not much of that. When she semi-retired, Penny borrowed a floor loom and discovered she needed to pursue weaving more seriously. At first the exploration was fairly haphazard, but eventually she joined CW and expanded her horizons. She did her first real study on Bateman's multiple tabby weaves once she graduated to a 16-shaft loom. Inviting Alice Schlein to give a workshop on her latest publication at the time, *The Woven Pixel* (with Bhakti Ziek), really started a whole new weaving life for Penny. She now loves to use Adobe Photoshop to design for her 32-shaft loom. The most important influence on her weaving, though, has been the friends and teachers she met through CW.

## Gudrun Polak, California, USA

Gudrun started out as a handweaver with a 4-shaft loom. Later her husband upgraded her studio and bought an 8-shaft loom. The most significant change was Gudrun's discovery of card weaving. She is fascinated with the technique, flexibility, and even complexity. She joined CW in 2008. The dream was to meet Peter Collingwood at a conference in Tampa, Florida. This did not happen, but she taught two seminars on card weaving. She has been teaching ever since. Gudrun's specialty is pattern development and she is convinced that there is magic in the cards. She finds inspiration in many places, especially weaving books. Since 2000 she has shared many of her patterns and shows her finished weaving, card weaving, and braiding as well as the tools she developed on her website, "The Loomy Bin." Gudrun is a member of Black Sheep Handweavers Guild of Los Altos, California, and the Santa Cruz Textile Arts Guild. She has published articles in *Handwoven*, *TWIST*, *CW Journal*, and *Strands*.

## Susan Porter, New Mexico, USA

Susan began weaving on an inkle loom in college. Simultaneously, she became hooked on photography and quilting. After graduating she focused on quilting and photography, studying black and white photography, and principles of design at the Corcoran School of the Arts and Design in Washington, D.C. Living in small apartments, there wasn't space for the looms she dreamed of, so she promised herself that she would devote her time to weaving when she retired. After moving to New Mexico in 2005 she enrolled in a basic 4-shaft weaving class at the local university. In the years since, she has discovered that while she loves playing with color and texture, her strongest interest is in understanding how threads interlace to form pattern in cloth. Most of her work is done on three 8-shaft looms, although she recently began exploring structures on a 24-shaft Leclerc Weavebird computer-assisted loom.

## Geri Retzlaff, Minnesota, USA

Geri has always loved textiles and fiber. When she was young, her mother taught her to sew. As she grew older she learned to knit and crochet. It wasn't until her retirement from corporate life that she discovered weaving through the Weavers Guild of Minnesota at the State Fair and learned to weave. She was hooked! It is such a great feeling to create something beautiful with her own hands to keep, sell, or give as a gift. This is a joy for her and she has worked hard to improve her skills. She enjoys weaving towels, runners, and shawls, and dyeing and weaving scarves with a few rugs thrown in. She tries to use a new technique or new color combinations with each new project. Geri enjoys her interactions with other weavers and volunteering at her guild. She believes that we all learn so much from each other!

## Belinda Rose, Aberdeenshire, Scotland

Belinda started weaving in 1975, making her own backstrap loom before acquiring table and floor looms. In 2008 a TC-1 digital Jacquard loom, now replaced with a TC-2, joined the collection. Alice Schlein and Bhakti Ziek are weaving inspirations, for their clarity and humor in writing, curiosity and dedication in exploring ideas, and generosity in sharing. Vibeke Vestby also is an inspiration for her determination to produce the TC-2, opening up so much potential for handweavers and designers. As some take comfort in food, Belinda takes comfort in fabric, loving to curl up and stroke soft interesting texture and color. Pieces become shawls or wearable items; sometimes they go on the wall or become cushions. She loves the variety of woven texture, color mixes, and weights. Belinda offers classes, workshops, and one-to-one instruction in tablet weaving, shaft-loom weaving, and Jacquard weaving online and from her rural weaving studio.

## Helen Sellin, Illinois, USA

A handwoven, hand-tailored man's jacket seen on vacation and a weaving demonstration on a small loom at a New Jersey mall during her teens in the 1950s were Helen's initial stimuli. Procurement of a Macomber loom in graduate school started a life-long interest but with limited execution due to life's demands. Madelyn van der Hoogt, her American weaving guru, and Barbro Bengtsson, her Swedish weaving guru, fueled Helen's inherent tendencies toward complexity and ultimately the drawloom. Other memorable landmarks enriching Helen's weaving odyssey include an article by David Xenakis (1982) regarding multiple effects possible on one 8-shaft threading (Roget), *Weaver's* magazine, and long-time CW membership with its seminars. Sample weaving ("Why weave more once you understand how it works? There are so many more things to learn and try!") or large projects, e.g., a stitched doublecloth coverlet, woven genealogy trees, etc., are the output of Helen's intermittent weaving.

## Cheri Shelp, Wyoming, USA

When Cheri was 12 years old, her mother, Wanda, attended a weaving workshop. Upon returning home her mother ordered her first loom and was hooked. She needed another pair of hands for what would become her life-long passion, so she enlisted her daughter. The two used two upside-down chairs in the hallway to make the warp, and when Wanda was done weaving her project, she let Cheri weave off the remaining warp. Cheri's current weaving focus is for historic reenactors, reproducing weave structures and items that were available primarily in the 1840s to 1880s. Her current work includes table linens, breech cloths, sashes, blankets, and coverlets. Cheri plans to expand to nontraditional weaving using nontraditional materials, and more freeform structure work. She currently maintains a role in Western Weavers, a group focused on complex weaves, to which she has belonged for 15 years. Cheri attributes weaving with teaching her that, "Desire and love for a thing make all effort and work insignificant."

## Janney Simpson, Connecticut and Michigan, USA

Janney began weaving in the early 1980s and now teaches weaving at Wesleyan Potters in Middletown, Connecticut and at The Barn in Gaylord, Michigan. She relishes the "ah-ha" moment when new weavers throw a shuttle for the first time. Janney is a past President, Apprentice, and Weaver of Distinction of the Handweavers' Guild of Connecticut. As a member of the Japanese Textiles study group, she enjoys sharing her interest in Sakiori weaving using vintage silk kimono. The harmonious colors in Japanese woodblock prints and simple patterns in kimono often inspire and influence her own color and pattern decisions. She has presented many workshops and lectures on finishing and embellishing handwovens, knitted beaded bags, sakiori, deflected double weave, and weaving with fibers of Micronesia. Privileged to be a student for four years in Laurie Autio's advanced weaving class, Janney strives to create one-of-a-kind pieces using a variety of fibers and weave structures.

## Norma Smayda, Rhode Island, USA

Norma is a master weaver, teacher, and author. In 1974 she established and continues to run the Saunderstown Weaving School. She learned to weave in Norway, and Scandinavian design, colors, and weave structures remain an important focus of her work. She also specializes in 3-shaft weaves and in the contributions of William Henry Harrison Rose and Bertha Gray Hayes. Norma is the co-author of *Weaving Designs by Bertha Gray Hayes: Miniature Overshot Patterns* (2009). More recently, Norma has immersed herself in weaving with fan reeds, and in designing and exhibiting her ondulé textiles which have been featured in two exhibits, the 2017 New England Weavers Seminar and Hera Gallery in Wakefield, RI. She shares this interest in her recently published book, *Ondulé Textiles: Weaving Contours with a Fan Reed* (2017). She has received the New England Weavers Seminar Weaver of Distinction Award, and is a Past President of HGA.

## Lynn Smetko, Texas, USA

Lynn combines a fascination with weaving, technology, and photography when designing for her 40-shaft computer-assisted loom. Photo-editing and weaving software are used to create weave plans that best express the visual characteristics of the chosen subject. She enjoys the design phase as much or more than the actual weaving! Denise Kavanagh was Lynn's weaving mentor. It was at her legacy, the Fine Line Creative Arts Center in St. Charles, Illinois, that Lynn first studied weaving and received exposure to many avenues of expressing woven art. Since then, she has been fortunate to have learned from many experts in the fields of weaving, dyeing and computer design. A longtime member of CW, Lynn feels that it has been invaluable to her development as a weaver and designer. In appreciation, she has given back to the organization by serving as Editor of the *CW Journal*, Secretary, First Vice President, and President.

## Dorothy Solbrig, Massachusetts, USA

Dorothy's great-grandmother was a weaver who lived in Appalachia, in the mountains of North Carolina. One of her aunts inherited her large barn loom, and Dorothy remembers seeing her aunt weave an overshot coverlet. Watching her aunt inspired Dorothy to want to learn to weave. She always liked math, and was fascinated by weaving structures. Later, she realized that what thrilled her about other weavers' work was use of color. Now she loves playing with structures and using them to get different color effects. She has always sewn some of her own clothes, so sewing handwovens followed naturally. Her husband is from Argentina, and some of her weaving inspiration comes from Latin America. Dorothy belongs to two weaving guilds, a group of weavers that meet weekly, and two online study groups of CW. One of the things she loves about weaving is that there is always more to learn.

## Pat Stewart, California, USA

Pat has been weaving in Berkeley, California for 20 years, most of that time on a 24-shaft AVL Compu-Dobby loom. At first she wove mainly yardage for jackets but recently Pat has concentrated on scarves and shawls and has begun an exploration of Jacquard fabric design. Pat particularly enjoys designing and weaving various double weave variations. She creates her designs motivated both by a desire to solve technical aspects of engineering the cloth interlacements and an interest in exploring the effects of color interaction in weaving. For Pat, weaving has become a microcosm for creating order from disparate elements and a way to connect to the cloth-making of other cultures throughout history. She joined CW early on while she was still working as a librarian and has always enjoyed learning from studying articles in the *CW Journal*, indexing it online since 1998.

## Eva Stossel, Pennsylvania, USA

Eva has a BA in studio art from Hunter College. During her last semester in 1976, she learned to weave on a simple frame loom in Gayle Wimmer's fiber arts class and has been weaving ever since. Over the years, Eva's work has evolved to multi-shaft weaving, and she especially enjoys network drafting and experimenting with colors. She weaves on a 16-shaft Macomber treadle loom. Her inspiration to learn multi-shaft weaving came from esteemed weavers like Alice Schlein and Bonnie Inouye, studying their books and articles with great interest. Her weaving experience includes sample weaving for the textile industry, production weaving for scarf designer Fern Devlin, a collaboration with fashion designer Kip Kirkendall, as well as exhibiting and selling her own work. As a member of the Fine Threads study group and the Philadelphia Guild of Handweavers, Eva enjoys learning and sharing with other weavers and writing about her weaving experience on her blog.

## Kay Strike, Wyoming, USA

Kay has loved all aspects of fiber since learning to knit at the age of eight. In 1970, she discovered weaving at a guild in Iowa. She purchased a 4-shaft Kessenich table loom and began happily weaving table runners, place mats, chess boards, and pillow covers. After moving to Cody, Wyoming in 1977, Kay joined the Yellowstone Weavers and Spinners Guild which had been started in 1976 by Vernice Myers and several other weavers who lived in the Big Horn Basin. In 2010 Kay purchased Vernice's 16-shaft AVL mechanical folding dobby loom. With the expert guidance of Vernice and the other weavers of the guild, weaving became a significant part of her life. Joining Western Weavers with Wanda Shelp and Carolyn Wostenberg led to new challenges: joining CW in 2016 and using Fiberworks PCW weaving software. Kay enjoys weaving everything and anything from tapestries and rugs to fine-thread napkins and double weave placemats.

## Anie Toole, Québec, Canada

Anie started weaving in 2012. When an interest in knitting prompted her to sign up for a constructed textile course at the Maison des Métiers d'Art de Québec, she was mostly indifferent her first year weaving. When she figured out how to weave a tube within a tube in her second year complex weaving class, she was hooked into wanting to push the boundaries of what could be done with complex weaving. Anie discovered Complex Weavers while researching a 12-shaft three-dimensional honeycomb project that changed between two, three, four, and six layers. Paul O'Connor's writings led her to attend CW Seminars within two months of joining. Anie particularly enjoys Jacquard looms because of their limitless possibilities when it comes to varying the ratios, layers, and shapes of a surface.

## Alice van Duijnen, Almere, Netherlands

In 2002 this fiberholic realized that "Later, when I am grown up, I will buy a loom" was overdue. Alice started on a small 4-shaft table loom and never looked back. She took classes and the second year she was made aware of CW and immediately joined. Nowadays she weaves on a 32-shaft Louët Megado computer dobby, still discovering the endless possibilities it gives - exploring new structures, variations, and playing with colors and materials. It just never fails to captivate her. After improving her skills in the Fine Threads study group, Alice is currently a member of the Double Weave study group. She likes the experimentation and the endless possibilities of weaving in general and double weave more specifically. Alice enjoys analyzing graphical patterns and images to figure out if they can be translated into weave structures.

## Sara von Tresckow, Wisconsin, USA

Sara began weaving in the late 1970s when living in Schleswig-Holstein, Germany. Soon after beginning, she met Klaus Tidow at the Textile Museum in Neumünster where there was a wonderful drawloom in the vestibule. This meeting led to a strong desire to progress into double-harness techniques in the future. Many yards of fabric and looms later, she now resides in Wisconsin. She owns The Woolgatherers - a brick and mortar shop in Fond du Lac, providing looms, linen and lessons - while finding time to weave. She is an active CW member, has served on the Board, and written several *CW Journal* contributions. Sara is the author of *When a Single Harness Simply Isn't Enough* (2014), a book covering double-harness weaving and how to build and set up a drawloom. She also spins, grows flax, experiments with old techniques from northern Europe, and does Navajo tapestry weaving.

## Barbara J. Walker, Oregon, USA

Barbara's weaving life began at about age nine, when she made a great many of those loopy pot holders. They were indestructible, and her mother used them for decades. Her first experience with a floor loom was in 1984, and she was instantly hooked. Her specialty is weaving with more than one warp. In the late 1980s Barbara joined CW. Her love affair with interlacements has grown to include an addiction to ply-splitting as well as braiding on a marudai and takadai. She is a member of the CW Kumihimo study group. She earned the master level of the HGA Certificate of Excellence in Handweaving in 1990 with a specialty in turned overshot. Barbara exhibits her work widely, has been on the teaching circuit since 1997, and has authored two books and numerous articles in weaving publications. She credits much of her success to her friend and mentor, Norma Smayda.

## Lesley Willcock, Bedfordshire, UK

Lesley has been weaving since 2004 and a member of CW since 2008. As a qualified designer and couture dressmaker, she started weaving to explore different weave structures and create unusual fabrics for use in accessories and garments. Lesley appreciates that, "The more you learn about weaving the more you realize there is to know." Joining CW and various study groups has been a way to expand her knowledge. She takes the opportunity to attend workshops when she can, and considers classes from Alice Schlein and Bonnie Inouye on the design possibilities available for her 32-shaft computer dobby loom as the real eye-openers. Lesley has exhibited her work in the UK and internationally, and has won several exhibition awards including Best in Show at Complexity 2014 and Third Place in 2014 and 2016.

## Marta G. Williams, Michigan, USA

Marta's first exposure to weaving was at eight years old, when she received a 2-shaft loom and a big box of Aunt Lydia's rug yarn in an array of fascinating colors. She did not return to weaving until her mid-thirties, when she took a weaving class at the Kalamazoo Institute of the Arts. She joined the local guild, took every workshop they sponsored, and started weaving baby blankets for all her friends. Her primary interest is in creating fabric for clothing. She remembers the trepidation she felt when cutting into her first handwoven fabric. After retirement, she was able to devote more time and energy to weaving. She joined CW to expand her exposure to weaving experts. Her weavings have been accepted in many juried shows, most recently the 2016 Michigan League of Handweavers' Biennial Show where she was awarded second place in Functional Fiber.

## Susan Wilson, Colorado, USA

Susan learned to weave 50 years ago as an occupational therapy major at the University of New Hampshire. In the early years of her practice she used weaving as a therapeutic medium in the occupational therapy clinic and recalls those patients fondly. However, weaving became her own personal passion immediately. Having studied crackle in college, she found it to be an amazingly versatile structure, and she continued experimenting with it over the years. In 1990 Susan received the HGA Certificate of Excellence in Handweaving, Master Level, with a specialty in crackle. This lead to teaching workshops, writing articles, and joining the CW Crackle study group. In 2011 her book, *Weave Classic Crackle & More*, was published. Susan enjoys pattern weaving, sampling to explore woven structure, and creating household textiles and clothing accessories. And, yes, she does weave structures other than crackle!

## Carolyn Wostenberg, Wyoming, USA

In the early 1980s Carolyn's husband gave her a 4-shaft table loom for Christmas. Wanda Shelp was her first weaving instructor and in that class Carolyn made color and twill structure gamps. Wanda made sure that students used the proper terms for parts of the loom. Later Carolyn learned from Debbie Redding to thread the loom holding the warp-thread cross in her hand. This really made getting a new warp on the loom much faster. A few years later Carolyn got an 8-shaft, 48" floor loom. Wanda thought they should write an 8-shaft book similar to Marguerite Porter Davison's *Handweaver's Pattern Book* (1944). They both wove samples; Wanda did the writing and publishing. In 1991, *Eight Shafts: A Place to Begin* was published. Carolyn thinks Wanda learned more about book publishing than she ever wanted to know! Carolyn has learned many fiber crafts over the years, but weaving has kept her interest for over 35 years. She still finds joy in a piece well planned and woven.

## Roxanne Zahller, Wyoming, USA

Roxanne was a spinner who became a weaver, mostly at the urging - no, shoving - of a wonderful mentor who is no longer with us, Vernice Myers. It was Vernice that convinced her that she wanted to weave, and she was right! Vernice also introduced her to the Western Weavers and CW, where she met other gifted and encouraging mentors: Wanda Shelp, Carolyn Wostenburg, and Betty Alexander, to name just a few. She has had the pleasure of learning from them all for many years and will always appreciate the world of weaving that they have demonstrated so beautifully. Roxanne has enjoyed participating in a CW study group, giving demonstrations, selling her woven goods and winning an HGA award. Passing along the joy of weaving will always be important to her and she will always be grateful to all the weavers before her who did, and continue to do, the same.

# Index

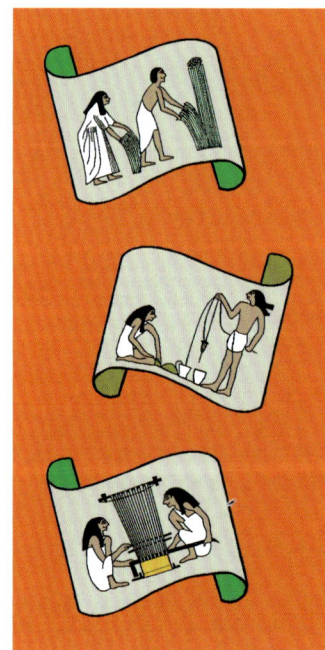

*Cartoon Detail, Sheila O'Hara.*